Martha Gellhorn: the war writer in the field and in the text

Manchester University Press

Martha Gellhorn: the war writer in the field and in the text

Kate McLoughlin

Manchester University Press
Manchester and New York
distributed exclusively in the USA by Palgrave

Published by Manchester University Press
Oxford Road, Manchester M13 9NR, UK
and Room 400, 175 Fifth Avenue, New York, NY 10010, USA
www.manchesteruniversitypress.co.uk

Distributed exclusively in the USA by
Palgrave, 175 Fifth Avenue, New York,
NY 10010, USA

Distributed exclusively in Canada by
UBC Press, University of British Columbia, 2029 West Mall,
Vancouver, BC, Canada V6T 1Z2

British Library Cataloguing-in-Publication Data
A catalogue record for this book is available from the British Library

Library of Congress Cataloging-in-Publication Data applied for

ISBN 978 0 7190 7636 7 *hardback*

First published 2007

16 15 14 13 12 11 10 09 08 07   10 9 8 7 6 5 4 3 2 1

Typeset in 10.5/12.5 Adobe Sabon
by Servis Filmsetting Ltd, Manchester
Printed in Great Britain
by The Cromwell Press Ltd, Trowbridge

For my parents,
Ted and Dorothy McLoughlin

Contents

Figures

Acknowledgements

I should first like to thank Dr Alexander Matthews for his permission to quote from Martha's published and unpublished works and to use photographs of her, and for letting me read his copy of *What Mad Pursuit*. Sandy and Shirlee Matthews have been supportive as well as generous, and, on my two visits to 'Rutherfords', kept me in mind that Martha was a real person and should be respected accordingly. I should also like to thank Martha's brother, Dr Alfred Gellhorn, for so kindly responding to my emails from New York.

My next debt is to Caroline Moorehead, Martha's biographer and editor of her letters, who showed extraordinary generosity in letting me read her papers and work at her kitchen table. I am also most grateful to the other people who knew Martha and were willing to give up their time to talk to me about her: Victoria Glendinning, Elise Becket Smith, the late Graham Watson and Dorothy Watson. Hermione Lee, my D.Phil. supervisor, deserves special thanks for guidance both inspirational and business-like. Sue Jones and Adam Piette, my D.Phil. examiners, gave my thesis painstaking attention and I am grateful to them for their ideas about how to develop it. My thanks are also due to Andrew Hook, who heroically read the book manuscript while on holiday in Florida.

I should also like to thank the following people who have given me support – practical, emotional and intellectual – along the way: Malin Lidström Brock, Katherine Duncan-Jones, Dick Ford, Matthew Frost, Carl Gardner, Paul Giles, Karen Hook, Jeri Johnson, Seamus Perry, Luke Pitcher, Judith Priestman, Fiona Stafford and Kathryn Sutherland. Many other friends and family contributed too: I am grateful to them and to everyone who, unprovoked, sent me cuttings about Martha and told me when her biography was Book of the Week.

I was lucky enough to finish this book with the support of a Junior Research Fellowship at Balliol College, Oxford; a post-doctoral fellowship at the Rothermere American Institute, Oxford; and the

Smith-Reynolds Fellowship awarded by the Ernest Hemingway Foundation. I am grateful to all those institutions and honoured by their faith in me.

Lastly, I would like to thank my parents for their love and support beyond measure. Couldn't have done any of it without you.

Permissions

Quotations from Martha Gellhorn's published and unpublished writings and photographs of her are used by kind permission of Dr Alexander Matthews. The photograph of Martha and the Carpathian Lancers (cover and Figure 10) appears from the Martha Gellhorn Collection in The Howard Gotlieb Archival Research Center at Boston University.

Note on references and abbreviations

The Face of War (cited as *FoW*). The first American edition (New York: Simon and Schuster, 1959) is used for quotations from the 'linking passages' between the collected articles (with the exception of five quotations from the 1998 edition (Cambridge: Granta), which is cited as *FoW 1998*). Unless a particular comparative bibliographical point is being made, however, quotations from the articles are taken from the *Collier's* originals.

The Heart of Another (cited as *HoA*). This was first published by Scribner (New York: 1941). The first British edition (London: Home & Van Thal, 1946) is used.

The Honeyed Peace (cited as *HP*). This was first published by Scribner (New York: 1953). The first British edition (London: André Deutsch, 1954) is used.

The Letters of Martha Gellhorn (selected and edited by Caroline Moorehead (London: Chatto & Windus, 2006)) (cited as *SL*). This volume is used to cite Gellhorn's published letters.

Liana (cited as *L*). This was first published by Scribner (New York: 1944). The only quotation in this book from *Liana* is from Gellhorn's Afterword to the Penguin/Virago edition (London: 1987): this is therefore the edition used.

Love Goes to Press (cited as *LGTP*). This was not published contemporaneously and so the edition used is the University of Nebraska critical edition of 1995, edited by Sandra Spanier (Lincoln, Nebraska, and London: 1995).

The Lowest Trees Have Tops (cited as *LTT*). The first American edition (New York: Dodd, Mead, 1969) is used.

Point of No Return. This was first published by Scribner as *The Wine of Astonishment* (New York: 1948). This is the edition used, cited as *WoA*. However, some quotations are from the Bison Books edition (Lincoln, Nebraska: 1995), and these are cited as *PNR*. *Point of No Return* is always used as the title as it was Gellhorn's original choice.

A Stricken Field (cited as *SF*). The first American edition (New York: Duell, Sloan and Pearce, 1940) is used, except for some quotations from Gellhorn's Afterword to the Virago edition (London: 1986), which is cited as *SF 1986*.

Travels with Myself and Another (cited as *TMA*). This was first published by Dodd, Mead (New York: 1978). There is only one quotation from *Travels with Myself and Another* in this book and it is taken from the British edition of 1979 (London: Allen Lane).

The Trouble I've Seen. This was first published by Morrow (New York: 1936) (and in Britain by Putnam (London: 1937), the edition to which H. G. Wells wrote the Preface). The first American edition of Gellhorn's novellas (New York: Alfred A. Knopf, 1993) is used. This collection first appeared in Britain (London: Sinclair-Stevenson, 1992). The footnote citation is therefore *Novellas*.

Two by Two. Quotations from the short story 'Till Death Us Do Part' in this collection appear in Chapter 5. The collection was first published by Sinclair-Stevenson (London: 1958). The first American collection of Gellhorn's novellas (New York: Alfred A. Knopf, 1993) is used. The footnote citation is therefore *Novellas*.

The View from the Ground (cited as *VfG*). The first American edition (New York: The Atlantic Monthly Press, 1988) is used, with two exceptions. The first is that quotations from *Collier's* articles are from the originals. The second is that quotations from Gellhorn's FERA reports (included in this volume as 'My Dear Mr. Hopkins') are taken from <http://newdeal.feri.org/texts>.

What Mad Pursuit (cited as *WMP*). The first and only American edition (New York: Frederick A. Stokes, 1934) is used.

The Wine of Astonishment. See *Point of No Return*.

Gellhorn's articles are cited with full bibliographical details on first mention in each chapter, and thereafter by title and date. Her unpublished writings are cited by title (sometimes shortened). Her unpublished letters are cited by recipient, date and folio (with recto (r) or verso (v)) (eg. f. 1r). Full details are given in the Bibliography. 'Gellhorn' in a citation always refers to Martha Gellhorn.

Translations in this book are my own, unless otherwise stated.

Introduction

In war, position is vital. Short-term tactics and long-term strategy are about gaining ground. War is located in real terrain and experienced spatially: its terminology is that of fronts and rears, flanks, lines, movements, zones and territory. Conflict is the politicisation of land: as the great Prussian military theorist Carl von Clausewitz wrote, 'it is difficult to distinguish between the abandonment of intentions and the abandonment of the battle-field'.[1] Position is equally vital in writing about war. Should the writer be present on the battle-field, and, if so, where exactly? Should the recording figure be present in the text, and, if so, in what guise?

How war is represented matters crucially to all of us. There is a vast literature on the subject, and war has been treated by many different disciplines – economics, history, philosophy, to name but few. But little attention has so far been paid to the fact that how conflict is written about is radically affected by the stance, and hence the standing, of the recorder.[2] When, for example, a television reporter appears wearing a flak-jacket, tracers in the sky behind her, raising her voice above the noise of explosions, certain messages about war are being transmitted. Outside the battle-field, moreover, such matters have formed an increasingly important part of a theoretical debate questioning the very existence of 'the Author'. Joining that debate, this study of the Second World War writings of the American journalist and fiction writer Martha Gellhorn (1908–98) considers the various standpoints available to the war recorder, identifying the axes (field and text) and plotting the co-ordinates (degree of engagement).

Such standpoints differ, of course, from person to person, from conflict to conflict, and between the sexes. This account of Gellhorn's writings can, therefore, function as a case-study exemplifying an approach. As the subject of such a study, her work is enlightening because she wrote in different genres about war (dispatches, novels, short stories, drama); because she wrote about being a reporter and used the figure in her fiction; because her route to war illustrates the exigencies of access (not least in her rivalry with Ernest Hemingway, to whom she was married from 1940 to 1945); because she had the problematic task of conveying the reality of an overseas war to an isolationist country and, indeed, of persuading that country to take up arms; and because she was particularly conspicuous at the front. Gellhorn shifted along a spectrum of involvement, ranging from dispassionate observation through emphatic presence to proactive participation in the course of conflict. The same can be said about the 'Martha Gellhorn' (and the other fictional women war reporters) constructed in her writings.

What, then, is meant by field and textual 'positionings'?[3] Positioning in the field embraces practical matters such as access to the front; 'getting there' (and where or what 'there' is); status; presence; priority; proximity; perspective; dress and comportment. Textual positioning comprises political, ethical and emotional acts of location which go to the heart of the function of the war recorder and which involve considerations such as tone, voice, 'objectivity' or 'subjectivity' and potential to 'make a difference'. Both derive from the distribution of the incidents of combat in relation to the recording individual (a distribution contingent on personal perception as well as on the current state of communications technology) and from the degree of that individual's emotional engagement with the encounter. From this it should be evident that war representation is treated in this book as an authorial special case. Muddying Foucault's distinction between post-Enlightenment scientific texts received for themselves in the anonymity of established or re-demonstrable truth, in which allusions to the author refer to real persons, and literary texts which are accepted only 'when endowed with the author-function',[4] the textual war reporter is treated here both as a free-floating linguistic construction and as related to a flesh-and-blood recording individual in the field.

The idea that positioning (both in field and text) is constructed, rather than natural, is not new. As the art theorist Erwin Panofsky has suggested, 'perspective' (from the Latin, 'perspectiva' – seeing through) is 'symbolic form' rather than neurological absolute; perspectival construction is a 'systematic abstraction from the structure of [. . .] psychophysiological space'.[5] John Berger has pointed out that (linear) perspective since the Renaissance has centred everything on the eye of the beholder: while this has become the conventional perception of what is 'real', there is 'an inherent contradiction in structuring all images of reality to address a single spectator who could only be in one place at a time'[6] – the so-called 'view from nowhere'. Ernst Gombrich makes the same point: perspective is that which 'enables us to eliminate from our representation anything which could not be seen from one particular vantage point'.[7] If, as Jonathan Crary has it, the observer is 'one who sees within a prescribed set of possibilities'[8] (literal and metaphysical), perspective can be understood as ideological, as the outcome of a range of influences, as *Weltanschauung*.[9]

In the present context, Panofsky's formulation of painterly perspective as the 'transformation of psychophysiological space into mathematical [or artistic or visual] space'[10] becomes, with regard to the orientation of the figure of the war reporter, the transformation of psychophysiological space in the field into textual space. Perspective is constantly being constructed – and not just constructed, but also shifted, zooming in and out like a camera lens. As a result, the siting of the reporter 'produces' the space of war, in a way similar to that suggested by the geographer Henri Lefebvre in his insight that 'the whole of (social) space proceeds from the body':[11] the figure of the recorder becomes the point from which – whether in field or text – the perceived scene radiates or emanates.

Configuring the war recorder in this way means assenting to certain theoretical consequences. This book does not dispute the Lacanian concept of socialised vision[12] as an integral fact of positioning. But it does reject the claim made by Norman Bryson that, since 'there is no viewpoint without vanishing point and no vanishing point without viewing point', the 'annihilation of the subject as center' is therefore 'a condition of the very moment of the look'.[13] Vanishing point produces viewer as much as viewer produces vanishing point: indeed, vanishing point sites the subject in a very specific place. Positing the 'annihilation of the subject' – the so-called 'bodiless eye' – ignores the simple necessity to vision of height and brain. But, as is discussed in Chapter 6, the situation is complicated if another observer enters the scene: Sartre's concept of the looked-at looker[14] calls into question the power of the voyeur – in this case, the war recorder as professional observer – and suggests a more interactive model of watching.

Martha Gellhorn was well aware of the issues. In a long letter to her Bryn Mawr tutor and lifelong friend, Hortense Flexner, written in the early 1970s after her seventh trip to Israel, she discussed the construction of a new novel (never written) about the conflict between the peoples of that land. What she says is so significant, it must be quoted at length:

> What beats me is the tone; I mean the tone of my voice when writing. Personal? Am I there too? Impersonal, the camera eye? I think that would be technically impossible; they were talking to me – to each other too – but I don't see how I can except myself. Yet, can I, would that be best? The narrator who is not there, has no opinion, reports? The new style (vide Mailer, Frady – so good in Harper's on Egypt, Jordan, Israel) is very much to be present: Mailer as egomania, Frady referring to himself as 'he', as a litmus

paper, sounding board, or even as if he were the public. Very odd but successful technique. I don't know, I don't know and this frets me most. In all my war reporting, I said 'We', which was correct for you are never alone in war, and think I hardly used myself, though I can check on that.[15] The first person singular makes me shy: idiotic.

And if I _am_ there, is it possible to be there, in the curious way I was, without ever thinking – until now, weeks afterwards – that I must have seemed very peculiar indeed to them: very old, out of the blue, a foreigner, a woman alone. [. . .] I was Martha; the young live by their first names [. . .]. My last name meant nothing, just a funny name which people find hard to take in.

This all worries me, clearly. The approach: the form or style will depend entirely on whether I am there or not there. It is, I think easier for me not to be there, if I can swing it.

[. . .] Do I write, in my own person, a prologue or epilogue, with my own summing up views?

[. . .] In journalism, I do guide, in the sense that I collect the facts and arrange them as best I can for interest and movement and then somehow tell the reader the meaning of the facts. But here?

[. . .] And yet, how, how, how to write it? What tone? What form? I wonder if it could be varied? I mean, write one chapter as reportage, using 'I', the narrator; write one chapter as a sort of short story, and if the narrator is there at all, have her 'she'. Might that work? I have a feeling that somehow the sound must change – yet I truly do not know how to do it, and also I have no confidence in my writing.[16]

In this remarkable passage, the entire gamut of field and textual positionings is represented and the complex relation between them exposed. A difference between male and female writers is suggested (the 'egomania' of Mailer's first person makes Gellhorn 'shy'), as is the possibility of varying approaches in different genres ('in journalism, I do guide [. . .] but here?'). Self-consciousness ('out of the blue') is admitted. Pronominal anxiety and the problems of belatedly translating field into textual position are registered. Though she nowhere else set out the dilemmas so explicitly, there is every reason to assume that Martha Gellhorn approached each of her writing projects with the same deeply felt concerns about authorial presence, tone and voice.

The project of this book is therefore to identify and offer theoretical explanations for a spectrum of authorial alignments, and illuminate the contradictions and overlaps inherent in it. There are accounts of different versions of 'self' and the relations between them, different stances and different writerly textures. The rest of this Introduction provides an overview of Martha Gellhorn's Second World War career and writings, looking particularly at the conditions in which she produced her dispatches for *Collier's* magazine: a kind of condensed Gellhorn-Guide. Chapter 1, 'Routes to the Second World War', then charts the axes which intersected to form the co-ordinates of her positioning at the outset of the Second World War: her upbringing, her reportorial apprenticeship in Depression America and the Spanish Civil War, and the contemporary climate of ideas, notably the New Reportage and its redefinition of how the writer should orient himself or herself in relation to the reported subject. The four remaining chapters then examine the positionings she occupied during the Second World War.

Chapter 2, 'A walking tape recorder with eyes',[17] begins at one end of the spectrum: the reporter as mechanistic, dispassionate, self-effacing recorder. This includes an analysis of the eye-/I-witness in Gellhorn's writings, concluding with the question of whether it is necessary to be present at a conflict in order to describe it. The demands of presence lead on to Chapter 3, 'Being there: the field'. This opens with the question, 'being where?', and offers an analysis of the charged, 'pastoral' space that is 'the front'. It then investigates the logistics and gendering of 'getting there' and 'getting there first', considering the various options available in the period to women who wished to enter the war zone (e.g. nurse, auxiliary, reporter, troop entertainer, prostitute) and focusing on the specific challenges faced by the woman correspondent. The chapter then examines Gellhorn's own 'getting there', in particular her rivalry with Hemingway, drawing on material held by the Bodleian Library, Oxford. Chapter 4, 'Being there: the text', discusses Gellhorn's writerly construction of reportorial presence both in her dispatches and in her fictional works.

The fifth chapter, 'From presence to participation', moves along the spectrum of positionings to consider the potential for intervention on the part of the war recorder. It begins with an examination of the theoretical background to such possibilities, notably Sartre's concept of *littérature engagée*. It then considers the practical opportunities for, and restrictions on, reportorial participation in the period, such as the Geneva Convention, before analysing Gellhorn's own journalistic theory and practice, finding a trajectory of growing disillusionment on her part in the power of writing to reform. Chapter 6, 'Fatal distraction', finally shows how, in her fiction, Gellhorn went beyond even this disillusionment to suggest the potentially lethal effect of introducing the glamorous woman reporter into the male space of war.

It remains to give an outline of Martha Gellhorn's Second World War career and writings. The bare bones of the former are as follows. Her first dispatch was filed in 1937 from Madrid. In April 1938, she flew to

Czechoslovakia, then under threat from the Nazis, and went on to cover the state of preparedness in Britain and France, going back to Spain for the final winter of the Civil War. She then returned to the United States and Cuba for a year, finding the home outside Havana, La Finca Vigía, that she and Hemingway would share. Her next trip to Europe was in November 1939 to cover the Russo-Finnish conflict, returning to America at Christmas and Cuba in January 1940. There followed almost a year in the United States and Cuba, during which, on 21 November 1940, she married Hemingway. Their 'honeymoon' took them to China, where they witnessed the Sino-Japanese War (January to April 1941). Gellhorn went on alone to Singapore, Hong Kong and the Dutch East Indies, arriving back in the United States in May 1941. She then remained with Hemingway in Cuba, taking a six-week trip to observe the effects of the Second World War in the Caribbean and South America in the autumn of 1942. It was then back to Cuba and Hemingway until October 1943 when Gellhorn flew to Britain. She returned to the Finca in March 1944 to persuade Hemingway to join her in the European Theatre of Operations (ETO): they travelled separately back to Europe in the May. She then remained in Europe for the rest of the war: reporting from England, and following the US armies through Normandy, Italy, liberated France, the Battle of the Bulge, Germany and the opening of the death camps.[18] In 1946, she reported on the Nuremberg Trials and the Paris Peace Conference. Her relationship to the front was, therefore, a curious rhythm of intense engagement and absolute withdrawal.[19]

This, then, was Gellhorn's career in the field. Her Second World War texts are generically various, and careful attention must be paid to their bibliographical positioning. Many of her short stories about the conflict first appeared in the *Atlantic Monthly* and were later collected in *The Heart of Another* (1941) and *The Honeyed Peace* (1953). Another story referred to in this book, 'Till Death Us Do Part', was first published as part of a collection called *Two by Two* in 1958. The rest of her Second World War fiction comprises the novels *A Stricken Field* (1940), *Liana* (1944) (set in the Caribbean, this makes brief reference to the war as a distant event), *Point of No Return* (first published as *The Wine of Astonishment* in 1948), *The Lowest Trees Have Tops* (1969) (again, war features at a distance) and the play *Love Goes to Press* (1946), co-authored with Virginia Cowles. The war journalism with which this book is concerned comprises the articles Gellhorn wrote for *Collier's* magazine, the first published on 17 July 1937 and the last on 14 December 1946. These articles were later collected (along with later pieces) in *The Face of War* (various editions from 1959), *Travels with Myself and Another* (1978) and *The View from the Ground* (1989).

This journalistic output was situated within a specific cultural frame-work. Founded by Peter Collier as *Collier's Once A Week*, in April 1888,[20] the magazine for which Gellhorn corresponded was a pioneer in illustrated and photo-journalism, and one of the 'muck-raking' periodicals of the early years of the twentieth century[21] under the crusading editorship of Norman Hapgood. One of its contributors, the reporter and photographer Frederick Palmer, recalled: 'Robert Collier had made his weekly a valiant organ of the progressive period in the muck-raking era when President Roosevelt sounded his battle-cry against the malefactors of great wealth.'[22] By the late 1930s, *Collier's* was a weekly featuring news, art, photography and serialisation of fiction and non-fiction, designed, according to one of its editors, 'to appeal to a broad cross section of men and women with widely different social, economic and educational backgrounds'.[23] Each issue was of about 74 large-format pages; each cover bore striking artwork by Lawson Wood, Alan Foster, Arthur Crouch and others, reproduced in colour. The cost was 5 cents, until 9 May 1942 when (without explanation or apology) it went up to 10 cents. On the masthead of the issue carrying Gellhorn's first article, William L. Chenery was listed as the Editor, Charles Colebaugh as the Managing Editor and Thomas H. Beck as the Editorial Director. Among the sub-editors were Walter Davenport ('Politics'), Aimee Larkin ('Distaff'), Quentin Reynolds ('Sport') and Kyle Crichton ('Screen and Theater'). Page 4 carried three columns: 'Next Week', trailing future articles; 'This Week', briefly describing the contents; and 'Any Week', a set of brief and humorous topical observations, often referring to readers' letters. By the beginning of 1941, however, the 'Next Week' column – perhaps as a result of political or logistical uncertainties – had been dropped. As for the publication's political leanings, in January 1940, Franklin D. Roosevelt, who was apparently contemplating a career in journalism when his presidential term came to an end, signed a contract with the magazine to become a contributing editor and to supply a minimum of 26 articles a year. Roosevelt died before his name could be added to the masthead, but *Collier's* has been described as his 'mouthpiece'.[24]

Gellhorn's name appeared for the first time in the list of 'sub-editors' on *Collier's* masthead (the names of editors and sub-editors that appeared on page 4 of each issue) on 6 January 1940. She was also frequently billed as a staff-writer, appearing as 'Collier's staff correspondent', for example, in 1940.[25] But this nomenclature is potentially misleading. The *Collier's* archive,[26] which contains Gellhorn's correspondence with the magazine (she dealt mainly with Denver Lindley, another sub-editor), suggests that she worked more in the style of a freelance reporter. 'Dear Gellhorn,

Perhaps I mentioned it before, your piece is very good. What you did to it makes it just right for us,' wrote Lindley about 'Men Without Medals'.[27] In another letter, he told her: 'Sure we'll talk about the piece. Offhand I can't see it at all for *Collier's*. But I don't really know what you have in mind.'[28] While there was some prior discussion, Gellhorn tended to go where she felt drawn and to write what she felt she must. *Collier's* then published her articles after a certain time-lag, in rare cases refusing them. A contract letter of 22 March 1938 extended only to Gellhorn's writing 'three articles on the European situation. As it may be agreed upon subsequently by Collier's Weekly and Miss Gellhorn, she will write additional articles the subjects of which are yet to be decided upon.'[29] Under this decidedly open-ended agreement, Gellhorn received $1,000 for each article accepted and $500 expenses.[30] The title 'sub-editor', then, did not in her case describe any editing role, but rather reflected the fact that the inclusion of her name added a certain lustre to the masthead.

Certain points therefore arise from the publishing circumstances of Gellhorn's pieces in *Collier's*, which demarcate them as a particular kind of journalism (as well as contributing to what might be termed 'institutional' positioning). Firstly, the articles are long. These are not front-page splashes but extended essays of around four thousand words frequently running to three or more pages, usually with the first two pages near the front of the magazine and the rest continued at a later point. This produced a hiatus in the reading experience which might have been filled with perusal of other articles or advertisements. Secondly, although the magazine appeared weekly, her articles have a sporadic distribution.[31] Though coterminous with the chronology of the war, their appearances are too uneven – even with the 'Next Week' trailers – to form an 'inter-narrative': there is no real sense that the reader is being given the 'latest instalment'.[32] Therefore the attributes of other forms of intermittent publication – the Victorian serial novel, say, with its delayed gratification and promise of future return – do not apply.[33]

Thirdly, although Gellhorn filed her copy by cable (and her articles are all headlined, for example, 'Radioed from France', suggesting a degree of urgency), she was not working to tight deadlines. Journalism, unlike (generally speaking) fiction, is associated with newness, speed (Matthew Arnold's 'literature in a hurry'),[34] newsworthiness[35] and ephemerality. Gellhorn herself, interviewed late in life, concurred: 'Fiction is much harder [than journalism] to do, much more rewarding to me and the advantage of it is you have much more time, you have as much time as you want, as much space as you want.'[36] Yet it is important to remember that her own wartime journalism, though, was subject to the exigencies of *magazine*, not newspaper, publication. Time and space were not as tight as in the dailies. '*Collier's*,' noted Nigel Nicolson in an early review, 'gave Miss Gellhorn the licence to go wherever she wanted, and the time and space to be discursive. She was not required to produce hard news. Her business was to get herself to the war, and to say what war felt like.'[37] The magazine was a large enough canvas for her to 'colour',[38] obeying the dictum that her fictional war correspondent Mary Douglas refers to in *A Stricken Field*: 'make it clear, make it colorful, make it lively'.[39] In this illustrated publication, her pieces are trailed, variously, as 'a vivid picture', 'a drama-laden [. . .] picture'.[40]

Fourthly, though journalism is usually 'datable'[41] in that it refers to a specific event in time (most often, the events of a day) and is, consequently, limited to it,[42] in Gellhorn's case there was often a significant interval between a given event and publication of her account of it in *Collier's*.[43] The result was that readers, having already received the facts as 'news', would be looking for a different, perhaps more reflective or analytical, treatment of them. Indeed, in relation to the crisis in the Sudetenland in 1938, Gellhorn telegraphed the magazine on 25 August to tell them to use her articles 'quickly' as they might be 'outdated' by September.[44] (Charles Colebaugh once responded, 'I will tell you some facts about the magazine business and will use, if necessary, forcible means to convince you that having an article on the newsstands four and a half weeks after buying it is not so Goddam slow.')[45]

Fifthly, journalism is *edited*. 'They [the *Collier's* editors] never cut or altered anything I wrote,' Gellhorn later claimed, 'they did, however, invent their own titles for most of my articles.'[46] This is an exaggeration: some blue-pencilling did go on, as is evident in the example given below.[47] Gellhorn's practice was to take notes on what she saw (although battle circumstances obviously sometimes precluded this) and soon after to compose her pieces on a typewriter before cabling them in; they were then subjected to transcription (which brought its own misreadings), editing and placement within specific paratextual contexts. In particular, *Collier's* 6.2 cm column width had a notable stylistic consequence. Gellhorn's pieces arrived over the wire in long strips of all-capitalised prose, separated into 50-word chunks and punctuated in 'cablese' ('stop', 'end bracket' etc.).[48] In the magazine itself, the house-style meant that they had to be re-cast in extremely short – usually two- or three-sentence – paragraphs, which therefore did not coincide with her cabled paragraphing. The 'Night Life in the Sky' cable of 24 January 1945, for example, was taken off the wire as follows:

EYE DECIDED TO TRY VERY HARD TO THINK OF SOMETHING ELSE LIKE FOR INSTANCE A NICE HOT BATH OR NEXT SUMMER

OR GOING TO THE MOVIES OR ANYTHING EXCEPT HOW EYE
WAS ALLEGEDLY GOING TO GET OUT OF THIS PLANE IF NECES-
SARY MEANWHILE A BRISK BUSINESS LIKE CONVERSATION
WENT ON IN THE COCKPIT[49]

This was edited by hand:

I
~~EYE~~ DECIDED TO TRY VERY HARD TO THINK OF SOMETHING
ELSE, LIKE FOR INSTANCE A NICE HOT BATH OR NEXT SUMMER
OR GOING TO THE MOVIES. ~~OR ANYTHING EXCEPT HOW
EYE WAS ALLEGEDLY GOING TO GET OUT OF THIS PLANE IF
NECESSARY~~ MEANWHILE, A BRISK BUSINESS-LIKE CONVERSA-
TION WENT ON IN THE COCKPIT[50]

It appeared in *Collier's* on 17 March 1945 as:

I decided to try very hard to think of something else, like for instance a nice
hot bath or next summer or going to the movies.
Meanwhile, a brisk, businesslike conversation went on in the cockpit[51]

The blue-pencilling removes a thought – how Gellhorn might get out of
the plane in an emergency – which might be seen as an anomalous return
to reality amid her list of pleasant visions, but which might also be seen
as a slight fluctuation in her bravery levels, key to her war correspondent
persona. The new paragraph indentation has the same effect as it moves
the cockpit conversation from its juxtaposition with Gellhorn's attempts
to control her thoughts. The contrast between the pilots' businesslike
attitude and her nervousness is therefore diminished, the point that *they*
have got used to this terror lost. In the later collections of Gellhorn's journalism, *Collier's* mini-paragraphs are changed again, merged into larger
wholes. The version of 'Night Life in the Sky' (now retitled 'The Black
Widow', Gellhorn's original choice)[52] in the 1959 edition of *The Face of
War* returns the 'Meanwhile' sentence to its original place, restoring the
contrast.[53] In this case, the changes in effect brought about by the
Collier's house-style go beyond the stylistic to the semantic.

The example also underlines the sixth point: that the experience of
reading Gellhorn's pieces is not limited to contemporary or later perusals
of *Collier's*. Her journalism can also be 'received' via later collections.
This gives rise to bibliographical points of comparison which will be
made throughout this book. In particular, the paragraph length and
period for reflection which Gellhorn's postwar pieces allowed her produced notable shifts in tone. A certain grandiosity, even sentimentality,
which hovers over her journalistic style becomes, in her collected articles
and fiction, more overt. This is explored in detail in Chapter 2, but here

a brief example can be given. In its original incarnation, in *Collier's* of 28 October 1944, 'Cracking the Gothic Line' contains the line:

And it is awful to die when you know that the war is won anyhow.[54]

In *The Face of War* (1959) this becomes:

And it is awful to die at the end of summer when you are young and have fought a long time and when you remember with all your heart your home and whom you love, and when you know that the war is won anyhow.[55]

The latter version contains more melodious (anapaestic/trochaic) cadences ('ĭt ĭs àwfŭl tŏ dìe ăt thĕ ènd ŏf sùmmĕr'), plus Hemingwayesque polysyndeton (four 'ands') and emotive vocabulary ('heart', 'home', 'love'). The effect is more mawkish, less clear-eyed. Tonal shifts such as this add up to a time-delay effect as Gellhorn 're-issues' her war prose or re-writes her experiences in fiction. The effect is not unlike the practice in seventeenth- and eighteenth-century Royal Society-influenced travel narratives of presenting contemporaneous notes within an explanatory framework added later. 'Let [travellers] therefore always have a Table-Book at hand to set down every thing worth remembering, and then at night more methodically transcribe the Notes they have taken in the day', advise the editors of *A Collection of Voyages and Travels . . .* (1704).[56] Michael McKeon argues that this practice was not intended to engender 'a tension between competing voices',[57] but rather to accumulate layers of historicity. In Gellhorn's case, there *is* something of an antiphonal effect, with attendant consequences in authorial construction and positioning. None the less, the picture is still one of different tonal degrees, rather than of radically different voices sounding in her correspondence and fiction.

The final point to make about Gellhorn's dispatches is that they are *war* journalism, a genre with its own history and exigencies which here can be only briefly sketched (and without reference to the crucial matter of its gendering, which is discussed in depth in Chapter 3). Until the mid nineteenth century, American newspapers obtained accounts of battles from active combatants:[58] from the beginning, therefore, presence and participation had huge epistemic significance for the gathering and dissemination of information about war. The Mexican War (1846–48) was the first to be extensively reported: indeed, newspaper proprietors such as George Wilkins Kendall, founder of the New Orleans *Picayune*, actually agitated for the war in the first place.[59] According to John Hohenberg, 'it was the fashion for correspondents to prove their daring by fighting rather than sit on the side-lines as non-combatants', and, in a manoeuvre that has become a trope of reportorial behaviour, Kendall, one of 40 correspondents in Mexico, captured a Mexican Cavalry flag, was mentioned twice in dispatches and wounded in the knee – behaviour indistinguishable from that of a military combatant.[60]

It has been claimed that the American Civil War (1861–65) 'institutionalised' the role of war correspondent.[61] Certainly, the number of reporters that covered it – over 250 according to some scholars[62] – suggests a growing professionalisation, but the exact nature of the role was still open to definition. Paradoxically perhaps, given the geographical proximity of the hostilities to where the newspapers were published, the fledgling poetics of presence and participation become problematic in both journalistic and fictional Civil War accounts. One of the most famous of the latter, Stephen Crane's *The Red Badge of Courage* (1895), indeed, was written some thirty years after the war had ended. This provoked various critical reactions: here is Harold Frederic in the *New York Times* on 26 January 1896:

> It seems as if the actual sight of a battle has some dynamic quality in it which overwhelms and crushes the literary faculty of the observer. At best he [Crane] gives us a conventional account of what happened, but on analysis you find that this is not what he really saw but what all his reading has taught him that he must have seen.[63]

Crane himself informed a reporter en route to the Graeco-Turkish War of 1897 that 'he was off to Crete because, having written so much about war, he though it high time he should see a little fighting'.[64] Having witnessed the Battle of Velestino, he told Joseph Conrad that *The Red Badge* was 'all right'.[65]

France and Britain refused to accept journalists at the outset of the First World War but reporters rushed to the front anyway. Hohenberg writes of a 'new concept' of foreign correspondents in wartime: 'regulated and censored'.[66] The censor to the American Expeditionary Force (AEF) was one Frederick Palmer, sometime war reporter for *Collier's Magazine* and therefore Martha Gellhorn's predecessor. Before the First World War was over, the value of controlled press coverage had been recognised and some sixty Americans were accredited to the AEF as correspondents, their material subject to Palmer's clearing. Using cable at the 'double urgent' rate – 75 cents per word – it was possible to print news from the battlefields of Europe in New York with the same day's date, a technological advance which, in George Washburn Smalley's words, conferred 'the peremptory brevity which arrested attention'.[67] Now 'being there' took on new ethical and political significance. Richard Harding Davis, another of Gellhorn's predecessors as a *Collier's* correspondent, wrote:

The loss of hundreds of thousands of lives, the wrecking of cities, and the laying waste of half of Europe cannot be brought home to people who learn of it only through newspapers and moving pictures and by sticking pins in a map. Were they nearer to it, near enough to see the women and children fleeing from the shells and to smell the dead on the battle-fields, there would be no talk of neutrality.[68]

For Davis, the task of the reporter had become not only to 'bring home' the war to a distant audience but to bring the audience to the war – in the specific form of encouraging volunteers and lobbying for government intervention: a version of the role explored in detail in Chapter 5.

This briefest of histories of American war reporting reveals influences which delimit Gellhorn's own correspondence. The tradition which informed her practice was at base messy and improvisatory, but it was also increasingly regulated. Within the constraints of Second World War journalism (described in detail in Chapter 3) – particularly the constraints resulting from her sex – Gellhorn, too, had to rely on the makeshift, the unofficial, the imaginative solution. Key to the project were access and stance: the overriding impetus, exceeding even that of peacetime reportage, to be as close as possible to the action. But as well as profiting from the legacy bequeathed by earlier US war correspondents, Gellhorn had to disburden herself of it, to forge her own brand of reporting. War is always the same, but it is also always different, and the poesis of each new conflict demands a new resourcefulness.

The following, then, are what Gellhorn's *Collier's* correspondence is *not*: brief, sensational, regular, written under time pressure, datable, free from editing, limited to its original context, or lacking a generic inheritance. As this book traces the development of her Second World War writings, these points are borne in mind.

Susan Sontag once commented that time eventually positions most photographs at the level of art: the image that mobilises conscience is always linked to a given historical moment.[69] But Nadine Gordimer took a different view. 'The imagination has a longer reach,' she wrote, referring to the difference between 'testimony' and 'imaginative writing' in post-apartheid South Africa: 'when testimony has been filed, out of date, poetry continues to carry the experience from which the narrative has fallen away'.[70] Planes of alignment in relation to historical subject matter like wars fall through various dimensions: time, space, politics, ethics, personal feeling. This book tries to discover Martha Gellhorn, war reporter, and 'Martha Gellhorn', 'war reporter', at the intersections, which lie both in the field and in the text.

Notes

1 Clausewitz, Carl von, *On War*, trans. Howard, Michael and Paret, Peter (Princeton, New Jersey: Princeton University Press, 1976) 234.

2 The term 'recorder' is used to cover all those who represent war (journalists, fiction-writers, photographers etc.).

3 'Position' can be logical or philosophical or military (*OED* I 1, 7c), as well as physical. It can be relative or absolute and can signify 'appropriate place' (*OED* II 7a), so that it is possible to be in a position that is out of position. 'To position' can mean 'to situate' or 'to determine the situation of' (*OED* 1a, b). 'Positioning', a verbal noun, is the act of putting into position. It is used in this book in preference to 'position' because it connotes a deliberate, constructed placement.

4 Foucault, Michel, 'What Is an Author?', *Modern Criticism and Theory: A Reader*, ed. Lodge, David and Wood, Nigel (Harlow and New York: Longman, 2000) 174–87: 179–80, 181, 182.

5 Panofsky, Erwin, *Perspective as Symbolic Form* (New York: Zone Books, 1991) 27, 30.

6 Berger, John, *Ways of Seeing* (London and Harmondsworth: BBC and Penguin, 1972) 16.

7 Gombrich, E. H., 'Standards of Truth: The Arrested Image and the Moving Eye', *The Language of Images*, ed. Mitchell, W. T. J. (Chicago and London: University of Chicago, 1980) 181–217: 193.

8 Crary, Jonathan, *Techniques of the Observer* (Cambridge, Mass., and London: MIT Press, 1990) 6.

9 Mitchell, W. T. J., *Picture Theory. Essays on Verbal and Visual Representation* (Chicago: University of Chicago, 1994) 19.

10 Panofsky, *Perspective as Symbolic Form*, 66.

11 Lefebvre, Henri, *The Production of Space* (Oxford and Cambridge, Mass.: Blackwell, 1991) 405.

12 Lacan, Jacques, *The Four Fundamental Concepts of Psycho-Analysis*, ed. Miller, Jacques-Alain, trans. Sheridan, Alan (New York and London: W. W. Norton, 1978) 67–119.

13 Bryson, Norman, 'The Gaze in the Extended Field', *Vision and Visuality (Dia Art Foundation Discussions in Contemporary Culture 2)*, ed. Foster, Hal (Seattle: Bay Press, 1988) 87–108: 91.

14 Sartre, Jean-Paul, *Being and Nothingness*, trans. Barnes, Hazel E., and with an introduction by Warnock, Mary (London: Routledge, 1969) 252–302.

15 She did, as this book will show.

16 Gellhorn, letter to Hortense Flexner, early 1970s, ff. 14r–16r.

17 The title is taken from Gellhorn's reflections on the 1939–40 Russo-Finnish conflict (*FoW*, 44).

18 Orsagh, Jacqueline, 'A Critical Biography of Martha Gellhorn' (unpublished doctoral thesis, Michigan State University, 1977) *passim*.

19 This rhythm is made to seem deliberate in a *Vogue* article on Gellhorn: 'Mrs Ernest Hemingway [. . .] divides her life into two halves: one year spent quietly, novel writing; one year, dangerously, as staff correspondent for *Collier's*' ('News Makers and News Breakers', *Vogue* (London) (March 1944) 42–3).

20 In the period in which Gellhorn was corresponding for it, the magazine's name was *Collier's. The National Weekly* but in this book it is referred to, for simplicity's sake, as *Collier's*.

21 Inglis, Fred, *People's Witness. The Journalist in Modern Politics* (New Haven and London: Yale University Press, 2002) 41.

22 Palmer, Frederick, *With My Own Eyes. A Personal History of Battle Years* (London: Jarrolds, 1934) 235.

23 Burger, Knox, ed., *Collier's Best. A Selection of Short Stories from the Magazine* (New York: Harper & Brothers, 1951) vii.

24 Winfield, Betty Houchin, *FDR and the News Media* (New York: Columbia University Press, 1994) 63, 172.

25 'Next Week', *Collier's* (27 January 1940) 4.

26 The Crowell-Collier Publishing Company Records, Manuscripts and Archives Division, The New York Public Library: Astor, Lenox and Tilden Foundations.

27 Letter of 20 January 1938, f. 1r.

28 Lindley, Denver, letter of 27 January 1938, f. 1r. It is not known which article is being referred to.

29 Contract of 22 March 1938, f. 1r.

30 Worth about $14,000 and $7,000 today.

31 They appear fairly regularly, though not every week, from July 1937 until December 1938 (covering the Spanish Civil War, prewar France and Britain and the annexation of the Sudetenland); they next appear in January and February 1940 (the Russo-Finnish war); next from May to August 1941 (the Sino-Japanese war); then in November and December 1942 (Puerto Rico and Surinam); then the bulk almost weekly from March 1944 to September 1945 (the Normandy invasions, the Eighth Army's progress up Italy; the Allies' advancement across Fortress Europe; the Battle of the Bulge; the entry into Germany; the liberation of the death camps; the return home of the troops). The last two articles, in 1946, concern the Nuremburg Trials and the Paris Peace Conference.

32 None the less, there is some relation: Gellhorn asked *Collier's* to publish 'Come Ahead, Adolf!', 'The Lord Will Provide for England' and 'Guns Against France' 'more or less close together' because 'they help each other out and people will understand them better if they're all together' (Gellhorn, letter to Denver Lindley of 7 July 1938, f. 1r). They appeared on 6 August, 17 September and 8 October 1938, respectively.

33 Hughes, Linda K. and Lund, Michael, *The Victorian Serial* (Charlottesville and London: University of Virginia, 1991) 4.

34 Quoted in Frus, Phyllis, *The Politics and Poetics of Journalistic Narrative* (Cambridge: Cambridge University Press, 1994) 17, but otherwise unsourced.

With modern technology, news is now capable of being 'real-time' – that is, instantaneous (McNair, Brian, *News and Journalism in the UK* (London: Routledge, 1999) 62).

35 Stuart Hall's 'criterion of the significant' (Hall, Stuart, 'A World at One with Itself', *The Manufacture of News: Social Problems, Deviance and the Mass Media*, ed. Cohen, Stanley and Young, Jock (London: Constable, 1973) 85–94: 86).

36 Shakespeare, Nicholas (dir. and interviewer), 'Omnibus', BBC1, 1991.

37 Nicolson, Nigel, 'A Woman at the Wars', *New Statesman* LVIII 1492 (17 October 1959), 517–18: 517.

38 Although sometimes not large enough: when Gellhorn proposed a series of articles on industrial problems in America to Charles Colebaugh (letter of 31 March 1940), he replied that there was 'little space [. . .] in which to be leisurely and thoughtful' (letter to Martha Gellhorn of 12 April 1940, f. 1r).

39 *SF* 82.

40 'Next Week', *Collier's* (30 July 1938) 4, 'Next Week', *Collier's* (10 September 1938) 4 and 'Next Week', *Collier's* (13 January 1940) 4.

41 Carey, John, ed., *The Faber Book of Reportage* (London and Boston: Faber and Faber, 1987) xxix.

42 Cf. Ezra Pound's 'literature is news that STAYS news' (Pound, Ezra, *Abc of Reading* (London: Routledge, 1934) 13).

43 To give one example, Gellhorn's account of D-Day+1 (7 June 1944), 'Hangdog Herrenvolk', appeared in *Collier's* only on 29 July 1944.

44 Gellhorn, telegraph to Denver Lindley, 25 August 1938, f. 1r.

45 Letter of 5 September 1941, f. 1r.

46 (*FoW* 13). In a letter to Charles Colebaugh of 22 October 1938, she wrote, 'I am calling my article "Mr. Chamberlain's Peace". That seems to me a perfect description. But if you don't like that, I suggest as an alternative, "Obituary of a Democracy". Both are accurate' (*SL* 69). *Collier's* opted for the latter. In the same letter, Gellhorn remarked, 'I am not writing these things [the British betrayal of Czechoslovakia at Munich] in my article. Perhaps I am wrong, but I have always tried to be as non-political and pictorial as possible for you, believing that was the way you wanted things done' (*SL* 68).

47 'Night Life in the Sky' draft cable, 24 January 1945.

48 See 'Night Life in the Sky' draft cable, 24 January 1945.

49 'Night Life in the Sky' draft cable, 24 January 1945.

50 'Night Life in the Sky' draft cable, 24 January 1945.

51 Gellhorn, 'Night Life in the Sky', *Collier's* (17 March 1945) 18–19, 31: 19.

52 'Night Life in the Sky' draft cable, 24 January 1945.

53 *FoW* 206.

54 57.

55 167.

56 Churchill, Awnsham and Churchill, John, eds, *A Collection of Voyages and Travels. . .* (London: 1704) I lxxv; quoted in McKeon, Michael, *The Origins of the English Novel 1600–1740* (London: Radius, 1988) 103.

57 McKeon, *The Origins of the English Novel*, 103.
58 Robertson, Michael, *Stephen Crane, Journalism, and the Making of Modern American Literature* (New York and Chichester: Columbia University Press, 1997) 141.
59 Hohenberg, John, *Foreign Correspondence: The Great Reporters and Their Times* (New York and London: Columbia University Press, 1967) 39.
60 Hohenberg, *Foreign Correspondence* 25, 39, 42.
61 Robertson, *Stephen Crane*, 141.
62 Downs, Robert B. and Downs, Jane B., *Journalists of the United States* (Jefferson, North Carolina and London: McFarland, 1991) 14.
63 Quoted in Aaron, Daniel, *The Unwritten War. American Writers and the Civil War* (New York: Alfred A. Knopf, 1973) 219. Martha Gellhorn herself commented on *The Red Badge*: 'I've read a fine book called "The History of Rose Hanks" [by Joseph Stanley Pennell (1944)] [. . .] the wonder of the book is the way that boy writes about the Civil War as if he had fought in it. I don't think Crane is as good' (*SL* 163). Pennell taught Gellhorn English at John Burroughs School.
64 Quoted in Robertson, *Stephen Crane*, 141.
65 Quoted in Colvert, James B., 'Introduction', *The University of Virginia Edition of the Works of Stephen Crane. Volume IX. Reports of War. War Dispatches. Great Battles of the World*, ed. Bowers, Fredson (Charlottesville: University Press of Virginia, 1971) xix–xxix: xix. Notably, Crane's *The Open Boat* (1897) has the subtitle, *A Tale Intended to Be After the Fact*.
66 Hohenberg, *Foreign Correspondence*, 217.
67 Smalley, George Washburn, *Anglo-American Memories* (London: Duckworth, 1911) 125.
68 Davis, Richard Harding, *With the Allies* (London: Duckworth, 1915) 8.
69 Sontag, Susan, *On Photography* (Harmondsworth: Penguin, 1979) 21, 17.
70 Gordimer, Nadine, *Writing and Being* (Cambridge, Mass., and London: Harvard University Press, 1995) 41, 42.

1

Routes to the Second World War

How did Martha Gellhorn 'get' to the Second World War? The logistics and politics of access are discussed in Chapter 3: here the question refers rather to *why* she became a war reporter and the intellectual climate that informed that early reporting. This chapter plots Gellhorn's co-ordinates at the brink of the Second World War by charting the axes of influence that intersected to produce them: her upbringing and early career to the end of the Spanish Civil War and the New Reportage of the 1930s.

'A hurry to get started'[1]

Gellhorn's family tradition was one of liberalism and reform.[2] Her maternal grandparents, the Fischels, settled in St Louis, Missouri. Dr Washington Fischel was an 'eminent physician' while Martha Ellis Fischel helped found the Society for Ethical Culture, agitated for an eight-hour working day for servants and developed the idea of domestic work as a 'science' with acknowledged skills. Their daughter, Edna, Gellhorn's mother, was an active social reformer. According to a local history, she served on the St Louis' Mayor's Race Relations Commission, the Homer G. Phillips Advisory Committee, the boards of the Urban League and the People's Art Center, the committee to mediate the Funsten Nut Company strike, the Social Security Commission, the Slum Clearance Commission, the Mayor's Committee to resolve the International Ladies' Garment Workers Union reorganising strike, the Governor's Committee on the Status of Women, the Committee to Revive the Missouri Constitution, the League of Women Voters and the Citizens' Committee on Nuclear Information.[3] She established a progressive school; founded the American Association for the United Nations; helped found the American League of Women Voters; was an active suffragist; and campaigned for 'wrapped bread, free clinics, smoke abatement, tuberculosis-screened milk, improved divorce laws and stricter child-labour laws'.[4] The *St Louis Daily Globe-Democrat* said

that 'her unselfish devotion has figured for years in many civic enterprises'.[5] The *Greater St Louis Magazine*, in a piece entitled 'Dame Edna
of Saint Louis,' said:

> It would be impossible to list all the projects she backed. [. . .] She was not
> a feminist, but a citizen who happened to be a woman. [. . .] If a secular
> age such as ours can be said to produce saints, she like her friend, Eleanor
> Roosevelt, is one.[6]

Martha's second husband, T. S. Matthews, noted that his mother-in-law's
'civic firepower has been estimated as "the rough equivalent of six
marine battalions" '.[7] Edna Gellhorn herself said of her own activities,
'I was inspired by the message that women had something to contribute.'[8] For Martha, she was 'miraculous' – 'beautiful, brave, selfless
[. . .] always ready to laugh and admire and love and see'.[9]

Gellhorn's father, George, 'a brilliant physician-surgeon',[10] born and
educated in Germany, like Edna half-Jewish,[11] was Professor of
Gynaecology and Obstetrics at the St Louis University School of
Medicine and consultant at four city hospitals.[12] In 1923 he published a
monograph, *Non-Operative Treatment in Gynecology*, dedicated 'To
My Wife',[13] in which he made his own contribution to the amelioration
of the female condition: 'The realization has slowly gained ground that
certain gynecologic complaints are not due to lesion of the genital organs
but have their roots in some other organ, or else are caused by purely
psychic factors.'[14] He was an exacting father. In a letter of summer 1935
to Martha, he wrote exasperatedly: 'Show the world, show your mother
and your father that you can do more than merely *talk* about the things
you can do.'[15] The Gellhorn home at 4366 McPherson Street, St Louis,[16]
welcomed visitors. Critical argument was encouraged. Gellhorn attended
the progressive John Burroughs School founded by her mother[17] and in
1926 went, as had Edna herself, to the women's college, Bryn Mawr.
Liberalism, making a contribution, active reform, open-mindedness and
thinking for oneself were therefore the familial heritage that Gellhorn
carried firstly into the field of social reportage and then into the war zone.

'The Thirties' is a section in *The View from the Ground* written by
Gellhorn in 1989 and intended to function as an introductory afterword
to her pieces collected from that decade. As such, it demands a cautious
critical approach: 'the Martha Gellhorn of the 1930s' is not necessarily
coincident with 'the Martha Gellhorn of the 1930s as recollected by
the Martha Gellhorn of 1989'. None the less, with that caveat, it is
instructive to see how Gellhorn (re)constructs her 1930s persona and
preoccupations.

An exuberant sense of new freedom and possibilities emerges: 'my life began in February 1930'.[18] In this spirit of impatience, to 'get things done', she left Bryn Mawr at the end of her junior year and by February 1930 was aged 21 and in Paris, already the veteran of a cub reporter job on the Hearst-owned *Albany Times Union* and with articles published in the Pulitzer-owned, liberal-leaning *St Louis Post-Dispatch* and the progressive *New Republic*.

This sense of impatience, 'a hurry to get started'[19] on things, to reveal, reform, redress, never leaves Gellhorn's writing. Her account of her time in Paris, conforming to one of the principal traits of the New Reportage, emphasises the value of personal experience and empathy. The years 1930 to 1934 were, for her, 'an education at last'.[20] She is careful to dissociate her existence in Paris from that of 'the cozy literary world' inhabited by the 'gifted Americans and British' who settled in the city in the 1920s.[21] Such a world was not 'real life':

> Real life was the terrible English mill towns, the terrible mining towns in northern France, slums, strikes, protest marches broken up by the mounted Garde Republicaine, frantic underpaid workers and frantic half-starved unemployed. Real life was the Have-nots.[22]

Stating her priorities, Gellhorn is also here revealing that she travelled and saw these things for herself. But her knowledge goes beyond that of mere external observation: she has experienced personally the conditions that she will write about:

> Because of my own poverty, fretting over centimes, make-do or do-without, keeping up my appearance on half a shoe string, I absorbed a sense of what true poverty means, the kind you never chose and cannot escape, the prison of it.[23]

This is, as noted, a retrospectively constructed existence. To see her '30s' thematic and stylistic tendencies in their original inchoate form, attention must be turned to one of Gellhorn's earliest articles, 'Toronto Express', published in the *New Republic* on 30 April 1930. The piece takes the form of the recounted journey (a classic New Reportage mise-en-scène), opening with a statement of personal observation: 'I have been looking at these people [the other passengers] [. . .]. There was not one face that said anything: that had any apparent interest in living or going on a trip.'[24] This might be taken as the normal boredom caused by a long train ride, but Gellhorn metaphorises the journey so that what she sees on the North Americans' faces is political apathy. She compares the 'deadness' of the Toronto-bound passengers with the attitudes of those she has met on European train journeys. On a Paris to Grenoble trip, for example, there was 'a feeling that the train and the compartment were a world apart, new and full of brief possibilities'.[25] Even more significantly, on the train from Breslau to Berlin:

> [a] man remarked that there would be another war [. . .]. I said, No, I didn't believe him [. . .] all I could say was, No, we won't have it. Then he stood up and bowed and smiled at me and my insistence and said: *Le flambeau est à vous tous. Portez-le*.[26]

Again, on a trip from Aix-les-Bains to Geneva, Gellhorn recognised that journeys, for Europeans, 'hold the elements of the impossible: new people, new places, the uncertainty and fascination of traveling'.[27] The open-endedness of journey is, in Europe at least, aligned with political unease and uncertainty regarding imminent war. By contrast, in 'all the trains across this country [America]' people are 'taking things so for granted'. In this sense, 'Toronto Express' may be read as a dramatisation of, and the earliest instance of Gellhorn warning against, political complacency.

In France, Gellhorn wrote her first novel. *What Mad Pursuit* was published in 1934, though Gellhorn later suppressed it on the grounds of it being juvenilia. Certain passages do smack of undergraduate humour though there are also instances of writing as striking as anything Gellhorn produced: a villa 'simper[s] on a hill'; someone's arms hang 'like cut branches at his side'; the sky resembles 'a blue plate glass from Woolworth's'; the beach lies like 'a blond eyelash' between the pine-trees and the sea.[28] As a whole, the work presents many of the themes which Gellhorn treated throughout her career, as well as her first fictional woman reporter, Charis Day (a surname which resonates with the etymology of 'journalism'). Charis is hailed as 'a latter-day, perverse, and female Galahad'[29] and a 'Joan of Arc':[30] heroic martial referents which reflect Gellhorn's early views about the power of journalism to achieve reforming change. Charis protests no fewer than five causes in the novel: seven blacks wrongly accused of rape; a friend's expulsion from college; the state's treatment of an old war veteran ('you've got to do something');[31] the Woollen Mill workers' strike and the false imprisonment of a 'dangerous Red' framed for a labour bombing.[32] The sense is, however, that these instances are vehicles for studies in indignation rather than, as in 'Toronto Express' or in Gellhorn's later work, attempts to invoke similar anger in the reader. Though this is a novel about conscience written in France in the early 1930s, there is no allusion to fascism or the rise of Hitler.

Where the novel does anticipate Gellhorn's later writings is in its characterisation of the woman journalist. One of the epigraphs is taken from

Thomas Wolfe's *Look Homeward, Angel* (1929): 'the hunger that haunts and hurts Americans and makes them exiles at home and strangers wherever they go'.[33] Charis, too, is positioned as a solitary itinerant ('I don't do anything [. . .] I move'),[34] the transient and roving reporter who must remain essentially separate from those she observes:

> She felt herself apart from all this [*sic*] people, and without means of understanding them or sharing in their lives. And gradually she wondered if she belonged anywhere, if there was any purpose to her goings and comings.[35]

'I'm always alone', she says more than once,[36] and the syphilis she has contracted by the end isolates her still further as she avoids human contact. Within the male culture of the newsroom, Charis feels her pariah status particularly acutely. The reporters of the Philadelphia *Clarion Trumpet* – 'a miserable blatt'[37] – regard her 'as a lady and pointedly didn't invite her on their parties'.[38] When asked to join in their roulette game, 'no one ever received the Legion of Honor with more respectful gratitude than that with which she accepted this invitation to be one of the boys'.[39] Attempting to win acceptance in this masculine milieu, she gambles heavily, 'hoping that they would think her a good sport, hoping that they would include her in their parties' and drinks whisky, 'which she abhorred', to earn their good favour.[40] Even so, she is told that she is 'much too fiery for straight reporting'[41] and transferred to 'the Woman's Page', which is therefore demarcated as a venue for excessive emotion.

Charis's experiences in the journalistic arena prefigure Gellhorn's in the war zone: gender identity becomes cause for anxiety. It occurs to Charis 'as a happy shock' on her nineteenth birthday 'that her appearance [is] useful'.[42] Her court appearance in defence of the Woollen Mill strikers causes the prosecutor to feel he has lost, 'all because this girl was pretty'.[43] The result is that the charismatic Charis herself becomes the story – 'COLLEGE GIRL REPORTER DEFENDS STRIKES' is the Drayton *Herald's* headline[44] – another instance of the reporter as 'distinctive'. She broods, 'didn't anyone realise that the strikers had been brutally beaten up and arrested on a false charge and that she wasn't a cute little girl looking for publicity?'[45] Gellhorn herself was to become increasingly concerned about the potentially harmful distraction caused by the glamorous woman war reporter: a concern which had implications for field and textual positioning.

The overriding sense of the novel is one of powerlessness. 'I am nothing and I've done nothing. I don't fit in anywhere; I'm not needed; I don't matter,' thinks Gellhorn's 19-year-old heroine.[46] Principled stands

and bold gestures achieve nothing: 'why did one always fail to do whatever it was that made an ending a success?'[47] She tells herself:

> Not heroes, not heroes, not heroes; only polliwogs,[48] embryos that won't
> grow into anything; not heroes and never will be [. . .]. We'd better take
> Turkish baths and keep our looks, it's all we've got. Just our faces and there
> are better faces.[49]

Three times the role of hero is explicitly disowned. The sense of the
ephemerality of good looks (another diurnal implication of 'Day') and
the image of abortion ('embryos that won't grow into anything'), hinting
at Charis's own implied but unmentioned termination, look towards the
end of Gellhorn's war writing and its disillusionment in the power to
effect enduring, helpful change.

In the same *New Republic* issue as 'Toronto Express' there is (to make a
'co-textual' point) an article by E. G. Nourse entitled 'Hard Times for
Farmers' which takes as its subject 'America's most pressing domestic
problem, the long-continued depression in agriculture'.[50] Gellhorn had
thought 'trouble [. . .] a European speciality', but in 1934, she writes, 'it
dawned on me that my own country was in trouble [. . .] I decided to
return and offer my services to the nation'.[51] The tone is typically self-
mocking but adds unmistakably to the carefully (and retrospectively)
constructed persona: that of the writer, who, like the soldier, will 'serve'.
Gellhorn's 'service to the nation' in the Depression took the form of
acting as a field reporter (note here the faint, premonitory hint of 'battle-
field reporter') for the Federal Emergency Relief Administration (FERA),
an institution of Franklin D. Roosevelt's New Deal.
   The FERA had been established by the Federal Emergency Relief Act of
12 May 1933 to dispense relief ($500 million appropriated by Congress)
to the unemployed. As Gellhorn recounts it, Harry Hopkins, its director,
was hiring a few people to travel around the country and report back to
him on how it worked in practice. At least at the outset, then, Gellhorn's
reportorial remit was within the aegis of the Rooseveltian regime. For two
years, she travelled the country, receiving $75 a week, train vouchers and
a $5-a-day travel allowance for food and hotels. At the time, she found
these 'untold riches' and they made her much better off than the objects
of her scrutiny: while she was 'rich enough to buy ordinary clothes', they
were 'barefoot and in rags'.[52] She recollected writing 'innumerable reports'
of which she kept no copies. What does remain of her FERA fieldwork are
six early reports (from Gaston County, North Carolina (11 and 19
November 1934); Massachusetts (25 November 1934); Providence,
Rhode Island (25 November 1934); and Camden, New Jersey (25 April

1935)),[53] three of which are reproduced as 'My Dear Mr Hopkins' in *The View from the Ground*, and *The Trouble I've Seen*. But before discussing them further, an account must be given of the theoretical and practical movement which informs them: the 1930s New Reportage.

The New Reportage

In its 22 January 1935 issue, *The New Masses*, 'unofficial cultural organ' of the Communist Party USA (CPUSA), published a Call for an inaugural American Writers' Congress. The Congress took place at Mecca Temple, New York City, from 26 to 28 April 1935. (Gellhorn was to give a paper at the second in 1937.) Speaker after speaker gave the 'American Writer' a very precise positioning: part of an international, reforming movement against the threats of capitalism and fascism. Specifically, the American Writer was expected to take an active role, both textually and extra-textually, in 'building a new world',[54] a process which the conference, as the Call to Congress promised, would facilitate: 'This Congress will be devoted to the exposition of all phases of a writer's participation against war, the preservation of civil liberties and the destruction of fascist tendencies everywhere.'[55] This language marks a precise geopolitical situation. 1935 saw the end of the hard-left, revolutionary Third Period in communism and the beginning of a broader anti-fascist Popular Front, adopted that year as official policy at the Seventh World Congress of the Comintern. In America, the 'People's Front', a loose conglomeration of organisations, was co-ordinated by the CPUSA.[56] But traces of Third Period politics remained in the language of some of the delegates, for example in the paper by *New Masses* editor Joseph North.[57] North's paper, 'Reportage', introduced the term, if not the genre, to the United States. The form, he proclaimed, had 'evolved into one of the most important [. . .] of the revolutionary movement'.[58] Not confined to works of non-fiction, reportage's aim was 'to present the fact, the occurrence, in all its open and hidden aspects'.[59]

In theoretical terms, Keith Williams positions the New Reportage as a reaction against modernism's experimentalism: it would not, however, regress to the unproblematised realism of the nineteenth-century novel, with its dangerous tendencies to conceal both its own fictiveness and the subjective status of reality.[60] The genre would, instead, evince a *reasoned* objectivity, which did not simply present a fact but showed how it came into existence and its consequences: what the Soviet documentarist Sergei Tretyakov termed 'the biography of things'.[61] 'To the writer of reportage, the fact he is describing is no corpse,' wrote North, 'it is alive, it has a place on earth'.[62] The anthropomorphic metaphor recurs in two key essays of the 1930s by the Hungarian Marxist theorist Georg Lukács: 'Reportage or Portrayal?' (1932) and 'Narrate or Describe?' (1936). Lukács distinguished between 'narration', the mode of lived-through experience, and 'description' or external observation.[63] The latter would result in 'still lives', 'corpses': inhuman, unimaginative presentations of objects which ignored their modes of production.[64] Lukács termed this superficial objectivity, 'reportage',[65] its writers in the main petit-bourgeois opponents of capitalism. Yet he also identified a 'genuine reportage', which would 'always present a connection, disclose causes and propose consequences'.[66] Grounded in Marxist materialist theory, the New Reportage resembled what the anthropologist Clifford Geertz later termed 'thick description': the excavation of the 'stratified hierarchy of meaningful structures' invisible to surface observation.[67] And self-reflexivity gave New Reportage works another kind of 'thickness': that of textual and typographical 'collage'. An example is John Dos Passos's *U.S.A.* trilogy, in which 'Newsreel' sections (comprising fragments from newspapers, headlines, billboards) alternate, in a variety of fonts, sizes and effects (italics, small capitals), with 'Camera Eye' sections (authorial experience rendered in stream-of-consciousness), narratives of various characters and brief biographies of figures as diverse as J. P. Morgan, Theodore Roosevelt and John Reed. This fragmentary-yet-exhaustive aesthetic is described by Williams as a new 'objectivity', in the literal sense of 'objects' placed in the text.[68]

As its theoretical premises suggest, the New Reportage was a politicised genre. This was made clear in the inaugural editorial of the journal, *FACT*, launched by Storm Jameson, Stephen Spender and others in April 1937:

> Encyclopaedists led by Diderot were responsible for the French Revolution. Their essential work was the spreading of *information*. This knowledge produced action. FACT's editors are endeavouring to be the modern encyclopaedists.[69]

As this indicates, in 1930s Europe, the presentation of fact ('fact', that is, understood in North's Marxist sense 'with all its open and hidden aspects') was a key means of educating and, crucially, mobilising public opinion. At the first International Writers' Congress for the Defence of Culture, held in June 1935 in Paris,[70] the French delegation also argued for a return to humanist encyclopaedism. In the Soviet Union, 'socialist realism' was adopted as the official artistic doctrine at the Congress of Soviet Writers in 1934.[71] Reporting to the inaugural American Writers' Congress in 1935, his language reflecting the still-extant Third Period politics, Matthew Josephson noted that Soviet authors 'participated by turning their craft into an instrument of the revolution', the social novel being seen as 'an instrument of political education'.[72]

What, then, were the recourses available to the bourgeois writer of New Reportage hoping to avoid Lukács's descriptive deadness? 'The middle-class writer,' noted Storm Jameson, 'does not even know what the wife of a man earning two pounds a week wears'.[73] There was only one way to find out: the writer (like Geertz's anthropologist) 'should be willing to go and *live* for a long enough time at one of the points of departure of the new society'.[74] Invoking the early usage of 'documentary',[75] the journey became both the practical and literary means of 'finding out'. In Britain, in a line of descent from Cobbett's *Rural Rides* (1821–), appeared J. B. Priestley's *English Journey* (1934); Orwell's *Down and Out in Paris and London* (1933) and *The Road to Wigan Pier* (1937); and Jack Hilton's *English Ways* (1940). In America, many works of the 1930s and 1940s took the form of a words-and-pictures journey through the country's underside. Gellhorn's 'Toronto Express' and *The Trouble I've Seen* are not illustrated, but none the less take their place alongside Erskine Caldwell and Margaret Bourke-White's *You Have See Their Faces* (1937) and *Say, Is This the USA?* (1941), Dorothea Lange and Paul Taylor's *American Exodus* (1939), James Agee and Walker Evans's *Let Us Now Praise Famous Men* (1939), Oliver La Farge and Helen Post's *As Long as the Grass Shall Grow* (1940), Eleanor Roosevelt (Martha Gellhorn's mentor) and Frances Macgregor's *This Is America* (1942), Eudora Welty's *One Time, One Place. A Mississippi Album* (1971, but featuring photographs taken in 1929).

At the American Writers' Congress, Joseph North explicitly acknowledged a distinguished seam of documentarist work by United States writers: travelling eye-witness reporters Agnes Smedley, John Spivak and John Reed, and before them, Stephen Crane and Richard Harding Davis.[76] 'This book is a slice of intensified history – history as I saw it,' wrote Reed in the preface to his account of the November Revolution, *Ten Days that Shook the World* (1919).[77] He continued:

> I must confine myself to a chronicle of those events which I myself observed and experienced, and those supported by reliable evidence. [. . .] In the struggle my sympathies were not neutral. But in telling the story of those great days I have tried to see events with the eye of a conscientious reporter, interested in setting down the truth.[78]

Reed places himself within the field, observing and experiencing; in the text, by means of the first person singular; and simultaneously in both by reproducing facsimiles of passes issued to him by the Military Revolutionary Committee of Petrograd, a bibliographical tactic which reappears in the memoirs of war reporters.[79] But, as Storm Jameson reiterated, the fact of the writer's presence must not obscure his or her true reason for being there:

> The first thing a socialist writer has to realise is that there is no value in the emotions, the spiritual writhings, started in him by the sight, smell, and touch of poverty. The emotions are no doubt unavoidable. There is no need to record them. Let him go and pour them down the drain.[80]

'[The writer's] mind must remain cool,' Jameson insisted in *FACT*, 'coldly and industriously presenting, arranging, selecting, discarding.'[81] In the same journal, and on the same grounds, she criticised Orwell's *The Road to Wigan Pier*: 'it is time we middle-class socialists shut down on our personal problems'.[82] The qualities she valued she found instead in the diary of Anne Frank: 'detached understanding and serenity', 'coolness'.[83] But if this was a theoretical requirement of the New Reportage, in practice it was flouted. Instances will be given from Martha Gellhorn's own work, but the most striking examples are James Agee's extraordinary responses to his subjects in *Let Us Now Praise Famous Men*. 'I lie down inside each one,' wrote Agee. 'I become not my own shape and weight and self, but that of each of them [. . .]. I know almost the dreams they will not remember.'[84] This, then, is a paradox within New Reportage theoretical demands: the indispensability of both the writer's presence in the field and his or her absence from the text.

If lived experience of Depression conditions could not be gained by the writer herself, the other obvious source was the people who did have first-hand knowledge of them. Arthur Calder-Marshall pointed out the 'command of language and vividness of description' of the depositions in the Report of the Gresford Colliery disaster reprinted in *FACT*. The same applied, Calder-Marshall continued, to the verbal statements made to the police and in the 'everyday conversation of workers'. This was because 'the worker takes his imagery from experience, the semi-articulate bourgeois from the phrase book'.[85] In 1937, the Mass Observation Archive was launched by Charles Madge and Thomas Harrisson to record conditions of life in Britain in the words of those living it. The approach was mirrored in other spheres: the use of the case-study and 'participant-observer' method pioneered at the sociology department at the University of Chicago in the 1920s; the 'worcorrs' (worker correspondents) of *The New Masses*; pulp 'confession literature'.[86] When Martha Gellhorn reports, verbatim, the views of those affected by the Depression and, later, by war, it is part of the same impetus.

The New Reportage was politicised, then, but did it have a precise partisan alignment? As noted, in the 1930s, hard-left revolutionary

Third Period politics were replaced by anti-fascist coalitions. Complicating this, as Judy Kutulas has shown, was the continuing opposition between the progressives of the People's Front and the anti-Stalinist liberals of the generation born post-1900.[87] The New Reportage was the exclusive possession of none of these groups: indeed, its practitioners also included those with no political affiliation. It was, moreover, susceptible to recruitment by the Roosevelt regime itself. William Stott argues that what began as oppositional under Herbert Hoover became institutionalised under Roosevelt. Hoover minimised the effects of the 1929 Crash in order (to give Stott's charitable explanation) to restore consumer confidence: as a result, his successor inherited a situation about which the basic socio-economic data were unavailable.[88] From Stott emerges a picture of government-sponsored fact-finding driven by the President's personal inquisitiveness. Key to this project was the work of the FERA field reporters, Martha Gellhorn among them, in observing conditions. The information they accumulated was then re-delivered to the nation by FDR via his radio 'Fireside Chats'[89] in an ironical state appropriation of encyclopaedism. Another New Deal agency, the Works Progress Administration (WPA), promoted documentarist art projects. Gellhorn herself wrote an article for *The Spectator* praising these enterprises:

> There are more murals in America now than anyone dreamed existed before; there is a vast geographic, historic, economic guide book of America in progress, employing thousands of jobless writers and journalists; there are orchestras everywhere you turn [. . .]. Someone deserves congratulations.[90]

The image of a kindly, fireside President is undermined by Stott's separate suggestion that the real motive for uncovering the bleak data of the Depression was to gain sympathy for the administration's New Deal reforms. Crucially, the facts related were remediable by government initiatives.[91] Daniel Aaron's assessment seems accurately to encapsulate the mood of uneasy acceptance in those on the left: 'The New Deal was at least beginning to grapple with the problems of the Depression; undoubtedly the Roosevelt administration won over a good many incipient radicals.'[92] In particular, the passing of the Wagner Act (the National Labor Relations Act 1933), giving trade union rights, and the Social Security Act 1935, providing for unemployment benefits, old-age pensions, aid to the disabled, maternity care, public health work and vocational rehabilitation, won progressive favour.[93] The forms of the New Reportage, if not its radical premises, were, therefore, despoiled by the Roosevelt administration. Even so, as Williams suggests, although documentarism entered the mainstream, the radical agenda of the journals of the 1910s and 1920s (*The Masses, The Comrade, The Liberator, The New Masses*) endured in aesthetic form: the piecemeal, object-loaded, textually self-reflexive nature of the New Reportage subtly disrupted the representational complacencies of the New Deal.[94]

'My Dear Mr Hopkins' and *The Trouble I've Seen*

The New Reportage laid special emphasis on the relation between writer and subject matter and Gellhorn's FERA reports contain classic statements of its methodology. 'I'm giving you this picture as I have been able to see it and through the eyes of the people (supposedly informed) with whom I talked,' she states,[95] noting that she has visited homes and workplaces, and spoken to owners and employees, the unemployed, union presidents, social workers, teachers and doctors in order to present a balanced picture. These people are quoted directly, voice after voice:

'It's a terrible thing when decent people have to beg . . .' 'We always tried to be as honest and decent as we could and we've worked all our lives; and what has it come to . . .' 'What's the use of looking for work any more; there isn't any. And look at the children. How would you feel if you saw your own kids like that: half naked and sick . . .'[96]

Certain constructions convey a sense of scrupulous fairness, of reasoned objectivity. The arrangement of facts is methodical: in the New Jersey report, 'housing' is followed by 'household equipment', 'health' and 'prostitution'.[97] Representative 'cases' are labelled as such. Statistics, particularly the amount of relief a family is receiving, are stated meticulously. The style is simple, laconic, economic; the tone scientific; paragraphs are short. Causes and consequences are given:

I have seen a village where the latrines drain nicely down a gully to a well from which they get their drinking water. Nobody thinks anything about this; but half the population is both syphilitic and moronic; and why they aren't all dead of typhoid I don't know. (It would probably be a blessing if they were.)[98]

But the last quotation also illustrates a contrasting feature of the accounts – the presence, both textual and actual, of the (well-paid) reporter: self-identifying as a witness ('I have seen'), sarcastic ('nicely'), angry ('why they aren't all dead [. . .] I don't know'), concerned ('nobody thinks anything about this'). Alongside the carefully constructed objectivity, there is – facilitated by the epistolary form – a personal, emotional response which strikes a more spontaneous note. This

response is recreated in the reader by the writer's eye for the telling individual detail. Particularly memorable is the draw where the prizes are 'a
chicken, a duck, four cans of something, and a bushel of potatoes' and
the people wait 'with passionate eagerness' to see if they are going to be
able to take some food home.[99] As noted, such moments are by no means
unique in New Reportage texts: indeed, in comparison with, for
example, James Agee's complex feelings of love and sexual desire for his
subjects, they are highly controlled. But they mitigate the governing tone
of clinical rectitude and prefigure Gellhorn's responses to the war zone.

The principal themes of Gellhorn's FERA reports are the eroding faith in
the President; the fact that it is formerly respectable people who are being
brought to destitution and the human consequences of this; the corrup-
tion of factory owners and some Relief administrators; and the importance of home, property and the ability to plan for the future. Having
conveyed her views in letters to Harry Hopkins, Gellhorn was next to
treat these themes in different literary form.

Like many New Reportage texts which straddle the ontological divide
between fiction and journalism, *The Trouble I've Seen* defies easy generic
categorisation. In the section 'The Thirties' of *The View from the
Ground*, Gellhorn refers to it as 'my book on the unemployed'.[100]
Graham Greene reviewed it in *The Spectator* under 'Short Stories'.[101] The
New York Times reported that 'after turning in her report [to Hopkins]',
Gellhorn 'rewrote four sections of it as short stories that formed a novel
on a central theme'.[102] The *New York World Telegram* found the pieces
'so true they that they hurt'.[103] The *Times Literary Supplement* review
stated:

> These pieces are presented as fiction, and doubtless are intended as such
> with all the usual 'no reference to any living person' implication; but the
> author, Mr. H. G. Wells and the publisher both inform us, has actually been
> a FERA worker, and knows beyond a doubt what she is writing about.[104]

Trouble is included in *The Novellas of Martha Gellhorn* (1992) where it
is described as 'a collection'.[105] Perhaps this is the most apt term for the
work, which consists of four accounts or case-studies: 'Mrs Maddison',
'Joe and Pete', 'Jim' and 'Ruby'. But there is a further generic ambiguity.
While 'My Dear Mr Hopkins' is pure fact, the cases which make up *The
Trouble I've Seen* are not descriptions of real individuals but composite
portraits based on what the writer has observed. They are, therefore, in
the mode of what Lukács termed 'reportage novels'.[106]

Grouping together four unconnected cases achieves a montage effect,
reinforced by the scenic intra-structure. The New Reportage aesthetic is

also evident in the 'thick description' of Depression existence. In her FERA reports, Gellhorn coins a term: 'the demoralisation point'.[107] *The Trouble I've Seen* does not merely present this point but reveals the slow path to reaching it. Whatever may have been envisaged for the American people by her Founding Father near-namesake,[108] the protagonist of the first story, Mrs Maddison, is now living in a riverside shack, the walls papered, ironically enough, with advertisements for consumer luxuries.[109] The opening scene presents her dressing up in pitiful patched and second-hand clothes in order to go up-town to the Relief office. Assessing herself in the cracked mirror, she is satisfied that she looks like 'a woman who had clothes and a place to put them on nicely' for 'she didn't want the relief people to put her in the same class with the negroes, who unconcernedly paraded their want'.[110] Later, the reader is told about her attempts to cover the walls of the shack:

> It had taken her several weeks, and finally she'd gone to the public library and been eager about wanting old magazines to read. 'I wouldn't tell them I used them on my walls,' she said to Maybelle. 'They'd think I was poor and begging for something. But just wanting to read; well, that's something even rich folks can do.'[111]

This verges on snobbery on Mrs Maddison's part. There are two possible thematic justifications for it. The first is to show exactly where the Depression had its impact: on the lives of the lower middle classes, the American heartlands. The second is to allow the portrayal of the devastating human consequences when self-respect is finally lost.

Richard Sennett, writing on the sociology of respect, remarks that 'the hard counsel of equality comes home to people within the welfare system when they feel their own claims to the attention of others lie solely in their problems',[112] an observation that might be the theme of *The Trouble I've Seen*. Federal relief produces a troubled response in both those who dispense and receive it. As Gellhorn notes in 'My Dear Mr Hopkins', home visits by means-assessing relief workers hurt and offended the unemployed.[113] In a May 1935 article in *Survey Graphic*, a magazine dedicated to social problems (and the publication in which Gellhorn's article, 'Returning Prosperity' was published on 26 February 1937), Russell H. Kurtz wrote:

> The American temperament does not welcome the thought that relief, on a large scale, is to be with us for a long time to come. The prospect is depressing to a people who are tired of the whole 'un-American' experience of doling out public aid to men whose only request is that they be allowed to earn their own way. Relief is defeatist: it chafes our national spirit and humbles our pride.[114]

The point is dramatised in 'Joe and Pete':

> 'I won't have strangers coming in my house poking around. I can work,'
> Pete said. And then, suddenly, he shouted it, waving his arms crazily over
> his head. 'I can work! I can work!'[115]

This captures the frustration and bewilderment earlier reported by
Gellhorn to Hopkins: 'they are, for no reason they can understand,
forced to be beggars asking for charity'.[116] As a consequence, the characters insist that relief is a right rather than a favour. 'I'll get what's my
right but I'll not have anyone thinking I'm charity,' vows Mrs Maddison,
insisting, 'a self-respecting woman's gotta right to [ask for work]'.[117]
Having made this point, Gellhorn can convey the anguish of a character
who, having faced extreme deprivation, is given a 'treat' by the relief
system and yet cannot enjoy it in the knowledge of its source. ' "Charity
food, that's what I'm eating," ' storms Bill suddenly, having been eating
in silence his mother-in-law's lavish dinner of tinned salmon and toma-
toes, ' "just old canned stuff they give to paupers and niggers. Can't git
our own stuff; has to be give to us. I don't take any of that Relief; by God,
I'd rather starve." '[118]

The 'demoralisation point' is the loss of such self-respect. Two things
are key to preventing it, summed up in Mrs Maddison's musings to
herself: 'We were real folks once; we had places to live, and we had fam-
ilies, and we knew what we'd be doing the next year and the next one.'[119]
Pride in property ('we had places to live') and the ability to look to the
future ('we knew what we'd be doing') are essential, Gellhorn suggests,
to the maintenance of human dignity (Sennett configures them as the possibility for self-development, self-sufficiency and the ability to give back
to others).[120] Maybelle looks at her houseboat 'with love and anxiety',[121]
while Mrs Maddison tends her shack 'with passionate care':[122] 'now,' she
feels, it is 'a place any woman might be proud to live in'.[123] This makes
her 'feel like a woman of property'[124] and, crucially, she is even able to
begin to make plans for a parlour. The section titled 'Mrs Maddison
Returns to the Land' exposes the failure of the New Deal 'rural rehabilitation' project.[125] Intended to be a means of providing work and subsistence for the unemployed, the enterprise instead consigned people to
inadequate housing and back-breaking work on unpromising soil. None
the less, Mrs Maddison views 'their land, the acres which were theirs' as
something that will make them 'respectable, steady, rooted people with
a future'.[126]

The obvious expression of the link between owning land and having
a future is planting: putting seeds in the ground signifies belief both in
some degree of permanence and in gratification to come. The ability to

plan, to aspire, even to dream, Gellhorn shows, is sustaining and slow to die. Having been made unemployed, Pete is excited to earn a dollar raking gravel and immediately begins to imagine the possibilities of selling gum and shoestrings: 'Active, and hopeful, his mind plotted the new luminous future. He could probably get a store before he was through.'[127] Jim has dreamt of becoming a surgeon; when he buys an accordion, he sees himself as a talented musician: 'He knew he would be able to play the accordion at once, because he wanted to [. . .]. It was reason enough to live until spring.'[128] Jim and Lou indulge in pure fantasising, describing to each other their 'days' spent riding, driving, eating at the Country Club and planning which colleges to send their imaginary future offspring to. These 'alternative realities' – daydreams, plans, the adverts on Mrs Madison's walls, Ruby's coasting – function as psychological oases in these Depression narratives (such devices are also used in war narratives). The inability to construct them is a symptom of the 'demoralisation point'. In 'Joe and Pete', Mabel's reaching of this point seems the natural outcome of a number of overwhelming setbacks:

> She was too tired now to argue this thing. What did it matter, anyhow? There were only a certain number of reasons for living, and then you didn't have them any more. 'What's the difference,' she said slowly [. . .]. 'We haven't got the baby, so it don't matter. We don't have to do all this. We don't have to.'[129]

The reader is inclined to agree with Mabel because the narrative has led inexorably to this point: the experiences, in Lukács's terms, have been 'lived through'. A similar effect is achieved in Gellhorn's accounts of those seeking employment. In 'My Dear Mr Hopkins', she reports that it takes 'from three to six months for a man to stop going around looking for work', after which he gives up in 'disgust'.[130] The reader gets vicarious understanding of this gradual, insidious process through Pete, whose day of trudging after jobs in the rain leaves him 'soaked' and 'breathless'[131] – less obviously employable than when he started out – and Jim, who after a week of walking starts to 'look like a tramp'.[132]

The Trouble I've Seen shares with 'My Dear Mr Hopkins' typical characteristics of the New Reportage: reasoned objectivity; dramatised facts that have been personally witnessed or experienced;[133] self-reflexivity. Unlike the FERA reports (and Gellhorn's later novels), the collection is not marked by the construction of any authorial presence within the text and would therefore satisfy Storm Jameson's requirements of the socialist writer. In this sense, *The Trouble I've Seen* might be seen to be situated on the far end of the participatory spectrum where the self-effacement of the author is complete. But to what extent does it – and Gellhorn's FERA reports – share what, after J. L. Austin, might be termed the New Reportage's 'perlocutionary' element: the intention and effect of bringing about change in the extra-textual world?[134] To answer this, it is necessary to consider their – and their author's – precise relation to the Roosevelt New Deal.

'It was the only time that I have fully trusted and respected the American Presidency,' writes Gellhorn in 'The Thirties': 'the New Deal, the Roosevelt regime, was truly geared to concern for the majority of the citizens'.[135] Gellhorn enjoyed a personal relationship with the Roosevelts. Edna Gellhorn and Eleanor Roosevelt had been friends since college days.[136] After a few months as a FERA field reporter, 'so outraged by the wretched treatment of the unemployed',[137] Gellhorn sent in her resignation to Harry Hopkins but he persuaded her instead to talk to Mrs Roosevelt, who invited her to dinner, giving her the chance to speak directly to the President. Later, having been 'fired'[138] from the FERA after an incident discussed more fully below, Gellhorn accepted the Roosevelts' invitation to live for a while with them at the White House. In her 'My Day' column, Eleanor Roosevelt herself describes reading 'Mrs Maddison' to an audience at the Colony Club, New York City:

> I cannot tell you how Martha Gellhorn, young, pretty, college graduate, good home, more or less Junior League background, with a touch of exquisite Paris clothes and 'esprit' thrown in, can write as she does. She has an understanding of many people and many situations and she can make them live for us.[139]

The admiration was mutual. Gellhorn corresponded with Eleanor Roosevelt for years, describing her after her death as 'a cherished friend'.[140] There seems to have been real affection between the two, as their letters reveal. Gellhorn opens one letter to the First Lady, 'what a schemozzle!', and concludes it:

> I love you enormously as you know, and think you are an absolute blooming wonder, as you also know. Always,
>
> Marty[141]

Elsewhere, she confessed:

> I realize that I write to you just as if you were you, or H. G. Wells, or someone I know very well. And not at all as if you were the most important woman in America (as you are). It isn't disrespectful, is it? I'd hate to seem that, for one second.[142]

Much later in life, to the art historian, Bernard Berenson, she said frankly:

> Roosevelt was a charmer and a superbly gifted politician; but she was all the nobility, all the conscience, all the soul; and she was it alone – a shy woman, hungry for tenderness and warmth [. . .] one of the very few really great of the world.[143]

Mrs. Roosevelt gave Gellhorn advice on her writing ('Mr. Hemingway is right. I think you lose the flow of thought by too much rewriting'),[144] concluding her letter, 'of course, you may come here [the White House] at any time you feel like it. Much love.'[145] In her introduction to the collected 'My Day' columns, Gellhorn wrote:

> *Empathy* is not my favourite word, I use it as shorthand for wisdom of heart and imagination. With Mrs. Roosevelt, empathy reached the rank of genius; nothing in the human condition [. . .] was beyond her understanding.[146]

If the First Lady's influence did not extend to prose style – 'as these columns prove, she was [. . .] not a writer; they are artless,' commented Gellhorn[147] – it none the less appears to have been a benign, and lasting, source of inspiration. It would not be going too far to suggest that Gellhorn saw Mrs Roosevelt as a second mother.

From these brief biographical details, it is tempting to site Gellhorn's accounts of 1930s America within the auspices of the New Deal, literally inside the Roosevelt White House. The title, *The Trouble I've Seen*, comes from the black spiritual, one version of which goes 'Nobody know de trouble I see / Nobody knows but Jesus'. In addition to adverting, once again, to the author's personal witnessing of the 'trouble', it hints, that, apart from this, it is known only to a higher authority. In Gellhorn's accounts, that authority isn't so much Jesus as FDR: she writes of the people having 'an almost mystic belief in Mr. Roosevelt': 'he is at once God and their intimate friend'.[148] The President's picture is up in every household, holding 'the place of honor over the mantel' like 'the Italian peasant's Madonna'.[149] Mrs Maddison comments that, 'Mr. Roosevelt's a fine man. He's got a good kind face and he's doing what he can for us'; she has 'an entirely personal conception of Government' – relief means that 'Mr. Roosevelt [was] not forgetting her'. Dismayed that Alec and Sabine have given up on rural rehabilitation, her final act on the farm is to write a letter to the President, explaining their problems and excusing her son.[150]

Yet, at the same time that Gellhorn records this faith in the President, she describes the inadequacies of New Deal reforms. The rural rehabilitation project is a disaster. The FERA subsidises private industry 'by the giving of supplementary relief to people employed in private industry but not making a subsistence living':[151] 'One might also note that the ERA [*sic*] preserves a fine labor market for these seasonal industries, which casually lay people off knowing they can always get them back when they need them.'[152] The Administration pays doctors who are positively dangerous, fails to ensure that union members are re-employed after strikes (Pete's fate), takes sides, has administrators who are 'criminally incompetent'. 'The similarity in relationships between relief administrators and dissatisfied relief clients and industrial magnets [*sic*] and dissatisfied labor would be laughable, if it weren't sad and revolting,' Gellhorn says candidly.[153] Disease, malnutrition, overcrowding, lack of sanitation, unemployment, inadequate education and child prostitution (the subject of 'Ruby') continue. Shoe factories are closing while the poor have nothing to put on their feet. A 'serf class' is being created. In these circumstances, it makes Gellhorn 'raging mad to hear talk of "red revolution" '.[154]

Ultimately, text cannot contain her rage. In Coeur D'Alene, Idaho, as Gellhorn recalls it, she found the unemployed 'victimized as often before by a crooked contractor'. She continues the anecdote:

> I convinced a few hesitant men to break the windows of the FERA office at night. Afterwards someone would surely come and look into their grievances. Then I moved on to the next stop, Seattle, while the FBI showed up at speed in Coeur D'Alene, alarmed by that first puny act of violence. Naturally the men told the FBI that the Relief lady had suggested this good idea; the contractor was arrested for fraud [. . .] and I was recalled to Washington.[155]

The moment is an important one as it reveals the fine line Gellhorn trod between direct action and writing with directness. At this point, it would be possible to locate her stance outside the auspices of the New Deal and in critical opposition to it – but it was now that she accepted the Roosevelts' invitation to live at the White House.

Her stay was short but symbolic: there is something in the manner of 'returning to the fold' about it which complicates her positioning in relation to the Roosevelt administration. Despite her strong views, Gellhorn was not politically committed in the sense of being affiliated to any particular group. She was not a member of any Popular Front organisation (the closest she came was her associations in the Spanish Civil War), nor yet was she explicitly anti-Stalinist, though she shared the critical detachment of the anti-Stalinist liberals.[156] What she hated was human suffering: firstly that caused by economic deprivation, then that caused by war. If Coeur d'Alene may be aligned with the underclass, with progressive or revolutionary intention, culminating in direct action, the return to the White House places her alongside the more mainstream liberal New Deal believers like Eleanor Roosevelt herself, for whom propaganda and persuasion took the place of violent protest. But Gellhorn soon found that she 'needed the complete mole existence for writing and departed from the White House [. . .] as soon as a friend offered me his empty remote house in Connecticut'.[157] There she completed *The Trouble I've Seen*, described by Graham Greene as 'explicitly political'.[158] Gellhorn's trajectory from Coeur d'Alene to Pennsylvania Avenue to writerly seclusion in Connecticut can be seen as metaphor for her political alignment. She was insider and outsider with regard to both radical politics and the New Deal, but her natural movement was from action in the field to uncompromising criticism within the text.

The Spanish Civil War

In 1936, there was a new phenomenon to analyse and participate in. The Call to Congress issued to American Writers in January 1935 was premonitory: 'this Congress will be devoted to the exposition of all phases of a writer's *participation against war* [. . .] and *the destruction of fascist tendencies* everywhere'.[159] The Second American Writers' Congress took place from 4 to 6 June 1937 at Carnegie Hall, New York City (both Gellhorn and Hemingway gave addresses at it – 'a wonderful show', according to Gellhorn).[160] In his introduction to the conference's collected papers, Joseph Freeman notes that, at the time, 'the front pages [of the newspapers] were carrying reports of the civil war in Spain, and, a month later, added reports of Japan's assault upon China'.[161] As at the inaugural congress, Freeman reveals, the present emphasis was upon experience, participation and the remediable power of writing. But the Moscow Trials had caused a shift in political feeling. The progressives wanted the 1937 conference to be non-partisan and moderate; the communists, accepting that their presence might hamper success, bowed out.[162] This was a People's Front event, with Spain at the centre – and, given the multiplicity of anti-Franco positions (liberals were worried that joining the war might curtail New Deal reforms; dissident Marxists felt the republican Spanish government was not radical enough; others said the anarchist and separatist groups like the Partido Obrero de Unificación Marxista (POUM) and the Confederación Nacional de Trabajo threatened the anti-fascist fight) – the battle was cast as a simple struggle between fascism and democracy.[163]

Titles of the papers given at the conference reveal the prevailing preoccupation: 'The Writer and Politics' (Earl Browder), 'The Dialectics of Culture Under Nazism' (Henry Slochower), 'A Writer's Social

Obligations' (Eugene Holmes), 'The American Writer Faces the Future' (Granville Hicks). Delegates, Freeman notes, felt themselves to be 'prewar' rather than 'postwar' and were 'passionately interested in [. . .] how they could assist the world struggle against fascism'. Having temporarily turned, in the disillusionment caused by the Treaty of Versailles and the New Economic Policy in Russia, to 'naturalistic descriptions of the American scene, aesthetic experiments in the capitals of Europe [. . .] and the exploration of the unconscious', American progressive writing had now, with 'the advent of the Nazis' and the 'economic crises', gained a 'second wind'.[164] In 'The Democratic Tradition in American Letters', Newton Arvin argues that individual action on the part of writers represents a 'necessary breach' with American literary tradition but none the less petitions a canon which can be made use of in 'our own struggles'.[165] Other speakers, like Arvin, use bellicose language in calling for direct participation. World events have personally affected writers, claims Malcolm Cowley, citing Hitler's rise to power (the exiling of German writers, the book-burnings); the New Deal (the devaluation of the dollar bringing expatriate writers home, the Federal Writers' Projects); the CIO (the rise of trade unionism in the arts) and the Moscow Trials. Writers now 'ought to stay home and fight'.[166] Browder, leader of the CPUSA, who attended only the opening session, reiterates the theme in a key statement about writerly positioning:

> Writers can stand aside from the struggles that are now rending the world [. . .] only at the cost of removing themselves from the life of the people, which is to say, from the source of all strength in art. [. . .] The Ivory Tower has been irretrievably shattered by the bombs of Hitler and Mussolini. [. . .] We must always remember [. . .] that the struggle in which we are enlisted is a war.[167]

Similarly, in the course of demanding assistance for the Soviet Union, Holmes claims that 'in the wake of the social obligation to fight fascism there is the imperative obligation to help to change the world. Interpreting it is no longer enough.'[168] Finally, there are the words of Granville Hicks:

> What of the author who tells us politics is none of his – or her – business? [. . .] The only problem with this program of aloofness is that it will not work [. . .]. Try to be aloof while the storm-troopers' clubs are beating upon your skull![169]

While the belligerent language of the conference speakers is directed against the 'twin evils'[170] of war and fascism, the Call to Congress is explicit about the present threat: 'Spain is the first real battlefield'.[171]

Papers on 'The Writer Fighting in Spain' and 'The Writer and War' were given by Martha Gellhorn and Ernest Hemingway respectively.

Gellhorn gave her paper on the afternoon of 5 June to a closed session of the congress at the New School for Social Research. 'Writers Fighting in Spain' could as easily be re-titled 'Fighters Writing in Spain': Gellhorn describes those on the Republic's side who learn play-lines, compose poetry and produce newspapers during stints in the trenches. These are the ultimate exemplars of the participant-writer but the journalists in Spain also work 'under great danger', dodging shells to get to the Telefónica in order to wire home their pieces.[172] Gellhorn concludes:

> A writer must also be a man of action now. Action takes time, and time is what we all need most. But a man who has given a year of his life, without heroics or boastfulness, to the war in Spain, or who, in the same way, has given a year of his life to steel strikes, or to the unemployed, or to the problems of racial prejudice, has not lost or wasted time [. . .]. If you should survive such action, what you have to say about it afterwards is the truth, is necessary and real, and it will last.[173]

Stanley Weintraub describes Gellhorn's performance as 'Hemingway-ish'[174] but this is more than a fine-sounding peroration. It contains three key points. Firstly, the writer is defined as a man of action[175] (the gender implications are explored in subsequent chapters). Secondly, direct personal experience – the veteran's perspective – is linked to truth. Thirdly, the economic problems of the Depression (to which Gellhorn herself had given a year of her life as a FERA reporter) are aligned with the Spanish Civil War. Gellhorn here positions herself with anti-Franco politics, though, again (unlike, say, the progressive Josephine Herbst), she did not affiliate herself with any narrower faction. The broad, non-partisan nature of the 1937 Congress was her natural stage.

The distinct 'writerliness' of the Spanish Civil War has been extensively noted: Valentine Cunningham describes the urge to 'go over' and produce some kind of eye-witness (or 'I-witness') testimony as a 'compulsion'.[176] The challenge issued by Nancy Cunard, W. H. Auden and others (published in 1937 by *The Left Review* as *Authors Take Sides on the Spanish War*)[177] was uncompromising: 'the equivocal attitude, the Ivory Tower, the paradoxical, the ironic detachment, will no longer do'.[178] While a minority of writers who answered maintained, textually and actually, their 'ironic detachment' – T. S. Eliot's famous response was that, 'while I am naturally sympathetic, I still feel convinced that it is best that at least a few men of letters should remain isolated, and take no part in these collective activities'[179] – the overwhelming majority replied with passionate support for the Republican side.[180] The policy of non-intervention regarding Spain adopted by the United States, Britain and France utterly dismayed many, provoking in writers a contrary impulse that was as aesthetic as it was political. From 1936, the 'worcorrs' would give way to the 'warcorrs', but to what extent was writing developed to convey Depression conditions apt to convey the conditions of conflict?

It was particularly apt, having been honed in similar circumstances. Industrial plant was suggestive of matériel: here is Theodore Dreiser on the Carnegie steel works: 'There is such popping and spluttering here as might justly be classified as explosions. The blast and roar with which some parts of the metal are reduced remind one vividly of artillery practice at close quarters.'[181] Instances of industrial unrest were themselves warlike: large firms like Goodyear Tyres bought army-type machine-guns, gas guns and grenades: munitions 'entirely unsuited for use except in carrying out offensive action of a military character against large crowds of people'.[182] John Hevener describes the industrial dispute between the coal miners and operators of Harlan County, Kentucky, as a 'prolonged and violent conflict':[183] in such encounters as 'the Battle of Evarts' (5 May 1931), 'machine gun, rifle and pistol bullets flew for half an hour' and there were 'between four and 11 deaths'.[184]

Consonant with this, the language used to characterise such disputes is bellicose, divisive. Florence Reece's song makes the point:

If you go to Harlan County
There is no neutral there.
[. . .]
Which side are you on?
Which side are you on?[185]

Dreiser's *Harlan Miners Speak* (1932), a collection of essays and witness statements taken by Dreiser and his colleagues, opens with a statement of purpose of the 'National Committee for the Defense of Political Prisoners', formed 'to aid workers organize and defend themselves against terror and suppression'[186] and part of the progressive Popular Front. The Committee (which included, alongside Dreiser, John Dos Passos, Sherwood Anderson and Bruce Crawford, publisher of *Crawford's Weekly*) is described as an 'invading body', whose mission is to enter the Kentucky coal-fields, 'inform the American public of what [is] going on' and 'persuade officials [. . .] to a more equitable course of action'.[187] Dreiser writes of a 'besieged community'; of requiring 'military protection'; the owners are 'making war' on the miners.[188] In another essay in the collection, Lester Cohen comments: 'Today Kentucky is again a "dark and bloody ground". Harlan and Bell counties have heard the rattle of machine guns, the roar of dynamite, the curses of thugs, and the multitudinous voices of industrial warfare.'[189] This deploys typical war writing tropes: ordnance onomatopoeia, accumulation of short phrases to mimic the bustle of battle, concentration of values in the 'ground'. The last contains ironic resonances: as Melvin P. Levy points out in another essay in the volume, mining had destroyed the superior geological strata of the region, while the coal produced went straight 'to the war-accelerated factories of the Great Lakes'.[190] The Committee members themselves are regarded 'pretty much as a spy is regarded in wartime':[191] both Crawford and Boris Israel were shot in the legs. This illustrates a key point: while a bourgeois writer could perhaps never hope truly to understand the experience of the very poorest in the Depression from within, war could be the experience of anybody. This fact contributed, in the Spanish Civil War (another class conflict) and the Second World War, to the overwhelming impetus to reach the front.

Martha Gellhorn's own status in Spain was initially ambiguous. In the summer of 1936, as she recalls it in *The Face of War*, she had been doing research for a novel (never published) in the Weltkriegsbibliothek in Stuttgart:

> The Nazi newspapers began to speak of fighting in Spain. They did not talk of war; the impression I got was of a bloodthirsty rabble, attacking the forces of decency and order. This Spanish rabble, which was the duly elected Republic of Spain, was always referred to as 'Red Swine-dogs.' The Nazi papers had one solid value: Whatever they were against, you could be for.[192]

As a result, there occurred a shift in Gellhorn's political leanings – 'I had stopped being a pacifist and become an anti-fascist'[193] – a discernible move towards (Popular Front) activism. She returned briefly to America, and, in December 1936, in Key West, Florida, she met Ernest Hemingway. In New York, an editor[194] of *Collier's* gave her a letter which 'said, to whom it might concern, that the bearer, Martha Gellhorn, was a special correspondent for *Collier's* in Spain'[195] (it was *Collier's* standard practice to issue such letters to foreign correspondents). Armed with this, Gellhorn arrived in Barcelona in early March 1937 and made her way via Valencia to Madrid, where Hemingway was already established as a reporter for the North American Newspaper Alliance (NANA).[196] Other journalists in the city included Herbert Matthews of the *New York Times*, Jay Allen (*Chicago Tribune*), Sefton Delmer (*Daily Express*), Arthur Koestler (*News Chronicle*), Antoine de St-Exupéry (*Paris Soir*), Mikhail Koltsov (*Pravda*) and Ilya Ehrenberg (*Izvestia*); George Orwell, too, had come to Spain, 'with some notion of writing newspaper articles'.[197]

In Madrid, Gellhorn 'tagged along behind the war correspondents [. . .] did nothing except learn a little Spanish and a little about war, and visit the wounded'[198] until 'either Hemingway or [Herbert] Matthews, but she thinks, probably Hemingway'[199] suggested that she should write, as the only way in which she could serve the *Causa*. Gellhorn continues the story:

> I mailed my first Madrid article to *Collier's*, not expecting them to publish it; but I did have that letter, so I knew *Collier's* address. *Collier's* accepted the piece and after my next article put my name on the masthead. I learned this by accident. Once on the masthead, I was evidently a war correspondent. It began like that.[200]

Hemingway put the circulation of *Collier's* at the time as 'a million':[201] in fact, in 1936 it was 2.4 million.[202] Gellhorn wrote three articles about Spain for *Collier's*, one for *Story Magazine* and one for *The New Yorker*;[203] she also transmuted her experiences into several fictionalised accounts: 'Zoo in Madrid', 'About Shorty' and 'A Sense of Direction'.

Gellhorn's Spanish Civil War writings build on her New Reportage Depression writings, with a growing emphasis on authorial textual presence. 'Only the Shells Whine', published in *Collier's* on 17 July 1937 and trailed with the information that she had 'for six weeks [. . .] lived in [the] city [Madrid]',[204] provides examples. At the outset, the correspondent-persona is, via the second person singular, sited in field and text:

> At first the shells went over: you could hear the thud as they left the Fascists' guns, a sort of groaning cough, then you heard them fluttering toward you. As they came closer the sound went faster and straighter and sharper and then, very fast, you heard the great booming noise when they hit.[205]

Having established 'presence' – and precise spatial location within the war scene – Gellhorn uses a zoom-lens technique to home in on particular incidents. Structurally, rather than typographically, her methodology resembles collage or even cubism: her own experiences in the city at war are interspersed with vignettes of the economic and social existence of the *Madrileños*.[206] A little boy is killed in the square when a 'small piece of twisted steel, hot and very sharp' takes him in the throat; the writer visits a shoe shop, a family in their roofless apartment, the Palace hotel which has been turned into a makeshift hospital, the theatre; speaks with a concierge, a Spaniard waiting for the shells to stop, a soldier.[207] The bombing described at the beginning is subtly shown to have effects on real lives. Here, as Lukács demanded, are facts made vivid because they are dramatised with their causes and consequences.

Consonant with this is the verbatim reproduction of the words of those who have personally experienced the war's effects. Here, from 'City at War', are two Spanish women whose apartment has been bombed:

> They were chatty and glad to be alive and they said everything was quite all right – look, the whole back of the apartment could still be lived in, three rooms, not as bright or as nice as the rooms that had been destroyed, but still they were not without a home. If only the front part didn't fall into the street and hurt someone.[208]

This is 'letting the people speak', but the apparent objectivity of the passage demands closer scrutiny. It is significant *how* the women's words are conveyed: the use of free indirect discourse means that, grammatically speaking, the writer could not be more closely allied with their point of view. This grammatical proximity recapitulates a political proximity. The quiet, courageous stoicism of those on the side of the *Causa* is constantly registered. 'It is very regrettable,' Gellhorn quotes her hotel concierge saying about the bombed-out rooms.[209] The shoe salesman tells his customers politely, 'I think we had better move farther back into the shop. The window might break and cut you.' A Hungarian lying in hospital refuses politely 'to talk about his wound because it was of no importance [. . .] at any rate he would be able to limp'.[210] At times, this heroism becomes almost self-parodying – the salesman pointedly unconcerned about his own safety, the Hungarian limping manfully on – but the key point here is the partisan nature of Gellhorn's own political sympathies, expressed implicitly in these examples in her admiring depiction of the Republicans and elsewhere more overtly. (Nowhere does she report anti-Franco atrocities.)[211] Phillip Knightley claims that personal engagement in a cause renders war correspondents 'unable to fulfil their duty', a weakness he finds 'unforgivable', and Mick Hume takes the point even further, describing the 'journalism of attachment' as 'a twisted sort of therapy'.[212] New Reportage theorists, of course, did not regard partisanship as unethical – theirs was, after all, a leftist agenda – but it should be registered that, in Gellhorn's work, 'letting the people speak' has a tendency to become 'accepting unquestioned what the people say'.

How, in this her first conflict, does Gellhorn construct and position the correspondent-persona? One element of this has already been suggested: in 'Only the Shells Whine', the journalist enters the Spanish family's ruined apartment and – by means of the first person singular this time – is also present in the text. Sounds and sensations place the reporter's actual presence beyond doubt:

I went downstairs into the lobby, practicing on the way how to breathe. You couldn't help breathing strangely, just taking the air into your throat and not being able to inhale it. [. . .] suddenly a shell landed, and there was a fountain of granite cobbles flying up into the air, and the silver lyddite smoke floated off softly.[213]

The vocabulary here ('fountain', 'silver', 'floated', 'softly') bespeaks a poetic sensibility, while the use of the second person singular reaches out to draw the reader into the scene. Equally important is Gellhorn's textual persona who is already being constructed as a fearless, feeling, independent woman (rather like her construction of the Republican Spaniards), with a self-deprecating attitude. To the concierge who apologises for the bombing, Gellhorn reports, 'I said yes, indeed, it was not very nice, was it?'[214] This sounds like Hemingway-esque understatement (a stylistic influence discussed further in the next chapter), but there is a curious difference. Here is a typical example, from Hemingway's first dispatch from Spain, dated 18 March 1937:

Only by a half-hour had we missed flying into the dog-fight in which the Insurgent planes were driven off by Government pursuit ships. Personally I didn't mind. We were a trimotor job ourselves, and there might have been confusion.[215]

'There might have been confusion' is airily brave but Hemingway's litotic humour, unlike Gellhorn's, tends to be an expression of (understandable) fear, rather than bravery. While the textual Hemingway is saying, 'I didn't want to be in an aerial dog-fight', the textual Gellhorn is saying 'I didn't mind the bombs'.

But presence alone is not enough. Gellhorn's accounts of Spain contain instances of what might be termed the 'normality trope' (even as it destabilises normality): a device with which, she firstly suggests war's closeness through familiar comparisons and, secondly, reveals Americans' involvement in the conflict. An instance of the former comes from 'Only the Shells Whine': 'It seemed a little crazy to be living in a hotel, like a hotel in Des Moines or New Orleans, with a lobby and wicker chairs [. . .] and meantime it was like a trench where they lay down an artillery barrage.'[216] As suggested earlier in relation to 'Toronto Express', there is an ideological element to the simile: if being in the Spanish Civil War is like being in a hotel in Iowa, it is also true that the war *is* close to Iowa because of its political significance. The same point is made by the second version of the 'normality trope'. This is from 'Men Without Medals':

It was a strange thing, walking through that olive grove, bending your head against the dusty wind, and seeing the faces from Mississippi and Ohio and New York and California, and hearing the voices that you'd heard at a baseball game, in the subway, on any campus, in any hamburger joint, any-where in America. [. . .] The plain [outside Madrid] lay below us, as quiet and beautiful as wheat fields in Idaho.[217]

Again, the point for Gellhorn's readers is not just that Americans have voluntarily participated in the war but that America – like it or not – is in it (in the sense of being affected by it), too, and hence the official policy of non-interventionism cannot quarantine the country from European events.

These instances, then, are attempts to pique and mobilise public (and Presidential) opinion. In this sense, writing, with a specific real change in mind, becomes perlocutionary. Gellhorn made other practical contri-butions. She undertook a 22-lecture tour of the US to gain support and money for Spain (her speaking skills were singled out for praise in a *New York Times* article).[218] She arranged for a White House showing of Joris Ivens's film, *The Spanish Earth*.[219] She wrote to Mrs. Roosevelt of the importance of the United States repealing the Neutrality Act:

> We sit here and hope to heaven that a sense of justice and a sense of self-protection will guide the House and the Senate. [. . .] All along it has made me proud to know that you were always understanding this [. . .]. But words are going to do nothing [. . .]. Around now, the people of Spain need airplanes.[220]

Interviewed by her home paper, the *St Louis Daily Globe-Democrat*, she insisted:

> There has been complete indifference to the war in Spain because of the misinformation given out about the situation. [. . .] I don't believe people have realized that their own democracies will surely be threatened if the Spanish democracy is defeated.[221]

The anonymous interviewer commented:

> Just let this adventurous young woman get a whiff of some social crisis, and before you can say 'Jack Robinson', she's 'in' on the ground floor champi-oning the under dog with all the courage and enthusiasm of which she's capable. [. . .] When the flood broke out last Spring in Southern Missouri, Miss Gellhorn arrived with the Red Cross and the relief nurses, assisting in the actual work of repair and, at the same time, gathering material for her prolific articles. She has poked her decorative little nose into the labor con-ditions in the English textile factories, the home life of the share-croppers of the South and the workings of the boom towns of the Texas oil fields.[222]

Later that year, Gellhorn was to use the flood referred to here to render intelligible to *Collier's* readers the practical and political plight of the Sudetens under threat from Nazi Germany: 'I have seen the way refugees live in America when the Mississippi rises and drives them from their homes. These people were fleeing too, from something they had not made, as innocent as the people who escape the danger of the rising river'.[223] Locating the refugee experience in America, she 'brings home' the European crisis: a textual tactic she honed in Spain.

The defeat of the Spanish Republic, closely followed by the Nazi–Soviet Pact, caused deep disillusionment in writers on the Left. Critics have defined the moment as the point 'at which writers [. . .] gave up politics completely'; 'the end of [. . .] socialist realism'; 'the decay of liberalism'; the forcing back of writers to 'absolute doubt'.[224] 'The journey [. . .] which was supposed to accelerate the doubting leftist author into commitment and action [. . .] ended by returning him sooner or later to the personal, the inactive, the uncommitted,' writes Cunningham.[225] These assessments, while true, deserve qualification in the present case: Gellhorn carried her participatory idealism into her Second World War writings, to which this book now turns. But of Spain, she did write later: 'nothing in my life has so affected my thinking as the losing of that war. It is, very banally, like the death of all loved things.'[226]

The year 1939 was the end of Gellhorn's 'apprenticeship'. Writing in and about the Depression had provided her with a learning experience which brought issues of 'being there' – both practical and theoretical – to the fore. New Reportage writers all faced, and variously responded to, the problems of how precisely the recording individual should relate to, and be placed regarding, his or her human subjects: an ongoing problem during war. Their work showed that 'objectivity' was not necessarily the same as 'impartiality', while the experiences of Dreiser and others proved that industrial unrest itself was warlike – not only in terms of its violence but also in its demand for participation. To reprise the mathematical conceit, the axes of influence described in this chapter have both been in the minus, bringing Martha Gellhorn to the zero point at the outset of the Second World War. As she set forth from that point into the war, she had a blank field to fill in.

Notes

1 *L* 1.
2 Where used on its own, the surname 'Gellhorn' refers to Martha Gellhorn, unless otherwise indicated.
3 Corbett, Katharine T., *In Her Place. A Guide to St. Louis Women's History* (St Louis, Missouri: Missouri Historical Society Press, undated) 234.
4 Moorehead, Caroline, *Martha Gellhorn: A Life* (London: Chatto & Windus, 2003) 20.

5 'Martha Gellhorn Sees Spain as Breeding Place for World War', *St Louis Daily Globe-Democrat* (28 January 1938) 2C.

6 'Dame Edna of Saint Louis', *Greater St Louis Magazine* (November 1968) 21–2: 21, 22.

7 Matthews, T. S., *O My America! Notes on a Trip* (New York: Simon & Schuster, 1962) 12–13.

8 Corbett, *In Her Place* 235.

9 Gellhorn, letter to Bernard Berenson, 17 August 1959, f. 2r.

10 'Martha Gellhorn Sees Spain as Breeding Place for World War', 28 January 1938, 2C.

11 Moorehead, *Martha Gellhorn*, 18.

12 Gellhorn, George, *Non-Operative Treatment in Gynecology* (New York and London: D. Appleton, 1923) iii.

13 Gellhorn, George, *Non-Operative Treatment*, v.

14 Gellhorn, George, *Non-Operative Treatment*, vii.

15 Gellhorn, George, letter of Summer 1935, f. 4r.

16 *What Mad Pursuit* is dedicated to it.

17 The original John Burroughs, a teacher and naturalist from New York state, became a friend of Walt Whitman during the Civil War (Morris Jr, Roy, *The Better Angel: Walt Whitman in the Civil War* (Oxford: Oxford University Press, 2000) 150f).

18 *VfG* 66.

19 *L* 1.

20 *VfG* 67.

21 *VfG* 67. Hemingway is obviously included in this implied criticism. *What Mad Pursuit* refers to 'that deadly group who fought in the war and calls itself "The Lost Generation" ' (*WMP* 75).

22 *VfG* 68.

23 *VfG* 68.

24 'Toronto Express', *New Republic* LXII 804 (30 April 1930) 297–8: 297.

25 'Toronto Express', 30 April 1930, 297.

26 'The torch now belongs to all of you. Carry it.' 'Toronto Express', 30 April 1930, 297.

27 'Toronto Express', 30 April 1930, 298.

28 *WMP* 91, 127, 196, 200.

29 *WMP* 23.

30 *WMP* 80. Note that Mary Douglas in *A Stricken Field* remarks, 'I'm not Joan of Arc, I'm only a journalist' (*SF* 177).

31 *WMP* 29.

32 *WMP* 107–8.

33 *WMP* preliminary pages. The other epigraph is from Hemingway's *A Farewell to Arms* (1929): 'nothing ever happens to the brave'.

34 *WMP* 154.

35 *WMP* 148.

36 *WMP* 74, 273.

37 *WMP* 26.
38 *WMP* 41.
39 *WMP* 42.
40 *WMP* 42.
41 *WMP* 65.
42 *WMP* 46.
43 *WMP* 63.
44 *WMP* 60.
45 *WMP* 65.
46 *WMP* 150.
47 *WMP* 65.
48 Tadpoles.
49 *WMP* 74.
50 Nourse, E. G., 'Hard Times for Farmers', *New Republic* LXII 804 (30 April 1930) 288–91: 288.
51 *VfG* 69.
52 *VfG* 70. $75 is worth about $1,000 and $5 about $73 today. None the less, Gellhorn later commented that Hopkins was not 'delving deep' into the public purse (*VfG* 69).
53 These are reproduced at <http://newdeal.feri.org/texts>. The letter from Camden, New Jersey, appears in *SL* at 33–5.
54 Frank, Waldo, 'Foreword', *American Writers' Congress*, ed. Hart, Henry (London: Martin Lawrence, 1936) 5.
55 Hart, Henry, 'Introduction', *American Writers' Congress*, ed. Hart, 9–17: 10–11.
56 Kutulas, Judy, *The Long War. The Intellectual People's Front and Anti-Stalinism* (Durham and London: Duke University Press, 1995) 1.
57 Martha Gellhorn had lunch on her 29th birthday with Joe North in Spain, during the Civil War: at the end of the day, he was 'still there but drunker and very nice' ('Diary', for 8 November 1937, unfoliated).
58 North, Joseph, 'Reportage', *American Writers' Congress*, ed. Hart, 120–3: 120.
59 North, 'Reportage' 120.
60 Williams, Keith, 'Reportage in the Thirties' (unpublished doctoral thesis, University of Oxford, 1991) 13; 'Post/Modern Documentary: Orwell, Agee and the New Reportage', *Rewriting the Thirties. Modernism and After*, ed. Williams, Keith and Matthews, Steven (London and New York: Longman, 1997) 163–81: 164–5.
61 Quoted in Williams, 'Reportage in the Thirties', 138. Williams perceptively points out that this approach fills the gap identified by Roland Barthes in his analysis of myth (Williams, Keith, 'The Will to Objectivity: Egon Erwin Kisch's "Der Rasende Reporter" ', *Modern Language Review*, 85 (1990) 92–106: 105). 'In passing from history to nature, myth [. . .] abolishes the complexity of human acts' (Barthes, Roland, *Mythologies* (London: Vintage, 1993) 145).

62 North, 'Reportage', 121.

63 The distinction corresponds to Plato's mimetic and diegetic modes as set out in *The Republic* (393–394): the former a kind of ventriloquism or dramatisation, the latter overt authorial explication (Plato, *The Republic*, trans. Lee, Desmond (Harmondsworth: Penguin, 1985) 149–57). More simply, these modes might be stated as 'show' and 'tell'.

64 'Narrate or Describe?', *Writer and Critic and Other Essays*, ed. Kahn, Arthur (London: Merlin Press, 1970) 110–48: 130, 133; Lukács, Georg, 'Reportage or Portrayal?', *Essays on Realism*, ed. Livingstone, Rodney (London: Lawrence and Wishart, 1980) 45–75: 54.

65 Lukács, 'Narrate or Describe?', 134; Lukács, 'Reportage or Portrayal?', 48.

66 Lukács, 'Reportage or Portrayal?', 49.

67 Geertz, Clifford, *The Interpretation of Cultures* (London: Fontana, 1993) 6, 7.

68 Williams, Keith, "History as I Saw It': Inter-War New Reportage', *Literature & History* (Autumn 1992) 39–54: 47.

69 'Ourselves', 'Editorial', *FACT* (1 April 1937) 6–8. They might have mentioned other forebears: Adam Smith and *The Theory of Moral Sentiments* (1759); David Hume; Ludwig Feuerbach's *The Essence of Christianity* (1841) (translated by George Eliot and influence on her 'religion of humanity'); Eliot's own 'The Natural History of German Life' (1856), to cite but few. In this 1856 essay, Eliot called for 'a real knowledge of the People, with a thorough study of their habits, their study, their motives' (Eliot, George, *Essays of George Eliot*, ed. Pinney, Thomas (New York: Columbia University Press, 1963) 272). Such knowledge was to be acquired in the manner of Wilhelm Heinrich von Riehl, whose volumes of *Naturgeschichte des Volks* she was reviewing: 'wanderings over the hills and plains' and 'immediate intercourse with the people' (Eliot, *Essays*, 286).

70 Monteath, Peter, *Writing the Good Fight. Political Commitment in the International Literature of the Spanish Civil War* (Westport, Conn., and London: Greenwood Press, 1994) 68.

71 Piper, Don, 'Soviet Union', *The Second World War in Fiction*, ed. Klein, Holger Michael (London and Basingstoke: Macmillan, 1984) 131–72: 134.

72 Josephson, Matthew, 'The Role of the Writer in the Soviet Union', *American Writers' Congress*, ed. Hart, 38–45: 43, 44.

73 Jameson, Storm, 'Documents', *FACT* (15 July 1937) 9–18: 10–11.

74 Jameson, 'Documents', 13, original emphasis. Accordingly, the genre has obvious affinities with the 'New Journalism' of the 1880s and again of the 1960s. The former has been described as 'the journalistic art of structuring reality, rather than recording it' (Smith, Anthony, 'The Long Road to Objectivity and Back Again: The Kinds of Truth We Get in Journalism', *Newspaper History from the Seventeenth Century to the Present Day*, ed. Bryce, George, Curran, James and Wright, Pauline (London: Constable, 1978) 153–71: 168). The four key devices of the latter, according to Tom Wolfe, were 'scene by scene construction; the recording of dialogue in full;

the presentation of each scene through the eyes of a participating character and the recording of everyday details' (Wolfe, Tom, *The New Journalism* (New York: Harper and Row, 1973) 31).

75 From the Latin, *documentum* – proof, lesson (*docere*, to teach) (*OED*). The French term for travel films was '*documentaires*'. In a February 1926 *New York Sun* review, the British film producer, John Grierson, described Robert Flaherty's *Moana*, a film about South Sea Islanders, as a 'documentary' (Hardy, Forsyth, ed., *Grierson on Documentary* (London: Collins, 1946) 11): this was the first instance of its use to describe factual works. But Grierson defined 'documentary' as 'the creative treatment of actuality': the informative 'shorts' that did 'not dramatise or reveal in an aesthetic sense' were not what he intended by the term (Grierson, John, 'The First Principles of Documentary', *Grierson on Documentary*, ed. Hardy, Forsyth (London: Collins, 1946) 78–89: 79). Similarly, the film-maker Joris Ivens opined, 'the distinction between *document* and *documentary* is quite clear. Do we demand objectivity in the evidence presented at a trial? No, the only demand is that each piece of evidence be [a] full [. . .] subjective, truthful, honest presentation of the witness' attitude' (Ivens, Joris, *The Camera and I* (Berlin: Seven Seas Books, 1969) 137).

76 North, 'Reportage', 120. He might also have mentioned the reforming journalism of 1902–12 (for which Theodore Roosevelt coined the term 'muckraking') in *Everybody's*, *McClure's*, *The Independent*, the *Cosmopolitan* and *Collier's*, which included articles by writers such as Ida M. Tarbell and Lincoln Steffens, whose series for *McClure's* were collected as *History of the Standard Oil Company* (1904) and *Shame of the Cities* (1904), respectively.

77 Reed, John, *Ten Days that Shook the World* (London: Lawrence & Wishart, 1961) ix.

78 Reed, *Ten Days*, ix, xiii.

79 Reed, *Ten Days*, 136, 137. The Imperial War Museum's *Women and War* (13 October 2003 to 18 April 2004) exhibited Martha Gellhorn's passport (issued by the United States Immigration Service, Florida, dated 26 December 1942, signed 'Martha G. Hemingway'). Passports, bearing photographs and visas, are evidence of presence and itinerary.

80 Jameson, 'Documents', 11.

81 Jameson, 'Documents', 12, 15–16.

82 Jameson, Storm, 'Socialists Born and Made', *FACT* (May 1937) 87.

83 Jameson, Storm, 'Foreword', *The Diary of Anne Frank* (London: Pan Books, 1954) 5–11: 9. This requirement marks a difference between the New Reportage and the New Journalism of the 1960s. The latter placed emphasis on the reporter doing his or her own 'leg-work' (Mills, Nicolaus, ed., *The New Journalism. A Historical Anthology* (New York: McGraw-Hill, 1974) xiv), although this seems to have been for reasons of surface vividness rather than for ontological validity. John Hollowell, referring to the 1960s New Journalism, notes that 'a tendency to self-display' – in

particular attention to how the story is obtained – has itself become 'part of the action' (Hollowell, John, *Fact & Fiction. The New Journalism and the Nonfiction Novel* (Chapel Hill: University of North Carolina, 1977) 52, 49). The result is a 'blur between public and private worlds', between the news-subject and the reporter's personality. Mick Hume even argues that this kind of journalism exists 'to give a sense of purpose and self-importance to the journalists themselves' (Hume, Mick, *Whose War Is It Anyway? The Dangers of the Journalism of Attachment* (London: InformInc, 1997) 4).

84 Agee, James and Evans, Walker, *Let Us Now Praise Famous Men* (Boston: Houghton Mifflin, 1960) 58.
85 Calder-Marshall, Arthur *et al.*, 'Fiction', *FACT* 4 (1937) 38–44: 39–40.
86 Stott, William, *Documentary Expression and Thirties America* (London, Oxford, New York: Oxford University Press, 1973) 156, 164, 192.
87 Kutulas, *The Long War*, 15 and *passim*.
88 Stott, *Documentary Expression*, 68, 71, 92.
89 Stott, *Documentary Expression*, 96.
90 Gellhorn, 'The Federal Theatre', *Spectator* (10 July 1936) 51–2: 52.
91 Stott, *Documentary Expression*, 18, 21.
92 Aaron, Daniel, *Writers on the Left* (Oxford and New York: Oxford University Press, 1977) 156.
93 Kutulas, *The Long War*, 88.
94 Williams, 'Post/Modern Documentary', 173. Williams detects the influence of the Russian Formalists in these practices (Williams, 'Reportage in the Thirties', 30), in particular Victor Shklovsky's concept of *ostranenie* (defamiliarisation): 'art [as] a way of experiencing the artfulness of an object' (Shklovsky, Viktor, 'Art as Technique', *Modern Literary Theory: A Reader*, ed. Rice, Philip and Waugh, Patricia (London and New York: Hodder Headline, 1996) 17–21: 18).
95 <http://newdeal.feri.org/texts/hopkins/hop22.htm>.
96 <http://newdeal.feri.org/texts/hopkins/hop22.htm>.
97 <http://newdeal.feri.org/texts/hopkins/hop01/htm>.
98 <http://newdeal.feri.org/texts/hopkins/hop08.htm>.
99 <http://newdeal.feri.org/texts/hopkins/hop01/htm>.
100 *VfG* 68.
101 Greene, Graham, 'Short Stories', *Spectator* (22 May 1937) 950.
102 'Hemingway Weds Magazine Writer', *New York Times* (22 November 1940) 25.
103 'Girl Investigator Writes of Experiences in FERA', *New York World Telegram* (19 September 1936).
104 'The New Novels – American Tragedies', *Times Literary Supplement* (6 June 1936) 477. Wells wrote the preface to the Putnam edition.
105 *Novellas*, x.
106 Complicating Lukács's 'narrate/describe' dichotomy was a separate, tripartite, generic division. Here the distinction is between reportage, the

novel and the reportage novel – i.e. 'fact' (the actual), 'fiction' (the invented) and 'faction' (the composite or representative). Although Lukács warned that the reportage novel might only provide an unsatisfactory version of the truth, the narrative mode (that of revealing causes and consequences) would redeem it (Lukács, 'Reportage or Portrayal' 51–2).

107 <http://newdeal.feri.org/texts/hopkins/hop01/htm>.

108 James Madison (1751–1836).

109 The same phenomenon appears in Agee and Evans's *Let Us Now Praise Famous Men*, in which both text and photographs reveal a mantelpiece decorated with calendars and adverts – in this case, however, of digestive remedies, silently testifying to the inadequacies of Depression diets (163–4). The Farm Security Administration photographers, Walker Evans among them, were instructed to capture 'the wall decorations in homes as an index to the different income groups and their reactions' (quoted in Tagg, John, 'The Currency of the Photograph', *Thinking Photography*, ed. Burgin, Victor (Basingstoke: Macmillan, 1982) 110–41: 126).

110 *Novellas*, 4.

111 *Novellas*, 11.

112 Sennett, Richard, *Respect: The Formation of Character in a World of Inequality* (London: Allen Lane, 2003) xv.

113 <http://newdeal.feri.org/texts/hopkins/hop22.htm>.

114 Kurtz, Russell H., 'Relief and the American Temperament', *Survey Graphic* (May 1935), reproduced on <http://xroads.virginia.edu/~1930s>.

115 *Novellas*, 73.

116 <http://newdeal.feri.org/texts/hopkins/hop22.htm>.

117 *Novellas*, 4, 8.

118 *Novellas*, 14.

119 *Novellas*, 8.

120 Sennett, *Respect*, 63–4.

121 *Novellas*, 4.

122 *Novellas*, 10.

123 *Novellas*, 11.

124 *Novellas*, 11.

125 Of which the subjects in *Famous Men* are also clients. One family is given a 'sick steer to do their plowing with; [. . .] no seed or fertilizer [. . .] until the end of May' (Agee and Evans, *Let Us Now Praise Famous Men* 35).

126 *Novellas*, 30.

127 *Novellas*, 76.

128 *Novellas*, 103.

129 *Novellas*, 73.

130 <http://newdeal.feri.org/texts/hopkins/hop01/htm>.

131 *Novellas*, 63.

132 *Novellas*, 97.

133 The French translation of *The Troubles I've Seen*, *Détresse Américaine*, was praised, *Globe-Democrat* readers were told, by Léon Daudet as

follows: 'the simplicity and exactitude of her picture of these sufferers shows that she feels their troubles profoundly' (Clark, Olga, 'Martha Gellhorn's Book Translated for Paris Readers', *St Louis Daily Globe-Democrat* (2 February 1939) 1C).

134 Austin coined the term 'perlocutionary [speech] act' to signify 'what we bring about or achieve *by* saying something' (Austin, J. L., *How to Do Things with Words* (Oxford: The Clarendon Press, 1962) 108). It is adopted here to refer to the effect of bringing about or achieving something *by* writing.

135 *VfG* 72.

136 Moorehead, *Martha Gellhorn*, 96.

137 *VfG* 70.

138 *VfG* 72.

139 Roosevelt, Eleanor, *Eleanor Roosevelt's 'My Day': Her Acclaimed Columns 1936–1945* (New York: Pharos Books, 1989) 29.

140 *Novellas* xiii.

141 Gellhorn, letter to Eleanor Roosevelt, 16 May 1948, f. 1r.

142 Gellhorn, letter to Eleanor Roosevelt, 2 December 1936, f. 4r.

143 Gellhorn, 10 August 1953, f. 1r.

144 Eleanor Roosevelt, letter to Martha Gellhorn, 16 January 1937, f. 1r. Gellhorn had written that 'the book [*The Trouble I've Seen*] is horribly bad [. . .] Hemingway says the thing to do is simply write it and be brave enough to cancel it out if it's no good' (Gellhorn, letter to Eleanor Roosevelt, 16 January 1937, f. 1r).

145 Eleanor Roosevelt, letter of 16 January 1937, f. 1r.

146 Gellhorn, 'Introduction', *Eleanor Roosevelt's 'My Day': Her Acclaimed Columns 1936–1945* (New York: Pharos Books, 1989) ix–xiii: ix–x.

147 Gellhorn, 'Introduction to *My Day* Columns', 1989, xi.

148 <http://newdeal.feri.org/texts/hopkins/hop08.htm>. In a letter of 3 December 1938 to Mrs. Roosevelt, Gellhorn commented on Spain: 'there is some confusion as to who is God, whether it is the Quakers, or the Red Cross, or the White House, or the Roosevelts' (Gellhorn, 3 December 1938, f. 1r).

149 <http://newdeal.feri.org/texts/hopkins/hop08.htm>.

150 *Novellas*, 26, 30, 34.

151 <http://newdeal.feri.org/texts/hopkins/hop01/htm>.

152 <http://newdeal.feri.org/texts/hopkins/hop01/htm>.

153 <http://newdeal.feri.org/texts/hopkins/hop01/htm>.

154 <http://newdeal.feri.org/texts/hopkins/hop08.htm>.

155 *VfG* 71. The incident echoes Charis Day's experiences in *What Mad Pursuit*: her editor tells her, 'a reporter is supposed to collect news [. . .] not to be a labor agitator' (*WMP* 59).

156 Kutulas, *The Long War*, 3.

157 *VfG* 72. It is likely the friend was George Campbell Becket, Martha's lawyer, who owned a property in Lakeville, Connecticut.

158 Greene, 'Short Stories', 950.
159 Hart, 'Introduction', 10–11, my emphasis
160 Gellhorn, letter of ? June 1937 to Eleanor Roosevelt (*SL* 53).
161 Freeman, Joseph, 'Towards the Forties', *The Writer in a Changing World*, ed. Hart, Henry (London: Lawrence and Wishart, 1937) 9–33: 9.
162 Kutulas, *The Long War*, 101.
163 Kutulas, *The Long War*, 98. This multiplicity of positions emerged again in the reception of Hemingway's Spanish Civil War texts, *The Fifth Column* (1938) and *For Whom the Bell Tolls* (1940). He was criticised variously for not being political enough (Alfred Kazin in the *New York Herald Tribune Books*), for being a Communist dupe (Edmund Wilson in the *Atlantic*), for being vindictive to the anarchists (Dwight MacDonald in the *Partisan Review*), for not being anti-Stalinist enough (Edmund Wilson in the *Nation*), for being too anti-Stalinist (Lionel Trilling in the *Partisan Review*, winter 1939), for prizing experience over intellect (Trilling in the *Partisan Review*, January 1941) and for having too little experience (Arturo Barea in *Horizon*). *Life* magazine of 12 July 1937 suggested a politically anodyne position: 'Since *The Sun Also Rises* Mr. Hemingway's delight in splendid Spanish poseurs has given way to a humanitarian sympathy for the rising Spanish masses' (Hemingway, Ernest, 'The War in Spain Makes a Movie with Captions by Ernest Hemingway', *LIFE* 3/2 (12 July 1937) 20–5: 20).
164 Freeman, 'Towards the Forties', 9, 24, 27, 33.
165 Arvin, Newton, 'The Democratic Tradition in American Letters', *The Writer in a Changing World*, ed. Hart, 34–43: 35, 43 and *passim*.
166 Cowley, Malcolm, 'The Seven Years of Crisis', *The Writer in a Changing World*, ed. Hart, 44–7: 44, 45.
167 Browder, Earl, 'The Writer and Politics', *The Writer in a Changing World*, ed. Hart, 48–55: 48, 49.
168 Holmes, Eugene, 'A Writer's Social Obligations', *The Writer in a Changing World*, ed. Hart, 172–9: 175.
169 Hicks, Granville, 'The American Writer Faces the Future', *The Writer in a Changing World*, ed. Hart, 180–94: 187.
170 Hicks, 'The American Writer', 188.
171 Hart, ed., *The Writer in a Changing World*, 196.
172 Gellhorn, 'Writers Fighting in Spain', *The Writer in a Changing World*, ed. Hart, 63–8: 66–7. In his paper, Hemingway noted that American correspondents in Spain work for an average of $65 per week 'uninsured' (Hemingway, Ernest, 'The Writer and War', *The Writer in a Changing World*, ed. Hart, 69–73: 70).
173 Gellhorn, 'Writers Fighting in Spain', 1937, 67–8.
174 Weintraub, Stanley, *The Last Great Cause. The Intellectuals and the Spanish Civil War* (London: W. H. Allen, 1968) 283.
175 Cf. Falstaff: 'The undeserver may sleep, when the man of action is called on' (*II Henry IV*, II.iv.406).

176 Cunningham, Valentine, 'Introduction', *Spanish Front: Writers on the Civil War*, ed. Cunningham, Valentine (Oxford and New York: Oxford University Press, 1986) xix–xxxiii: xxiv.

177 This was published in the United States by the League of American Writers, offspring of the American Writers' Congress (Kutulas, *The Long War* 101, 90).

178 *Authors Take Sides on the Spanish War* (London: The Left Review, 1937) unpaginated.

179 *Authors Take Sides on the Spanish War*, 1937, unpaginated.

180 Even if, as Valentine Cunningham points out, the compilers 'fiddle[d] their results a little' (Cunningham, Valentine, *British Writers of the Thirties* (Oxford and New York: Oxford University Press, 1988) 438).

181 Dreiser, Theodore, *The Carnegie Works at Pittsburgh* (Chelsea, New York: Private Printing, 1927) 21. Gellhorn wrote to Bertrand de Jouvenel in 1930 that she 'love[d] that old goofer Dreiser for all his cheap journalese style: he's angry and alive' (*SL* 7–8; see also Gellhorn, letter to Bernard Berenson, 30 March 1954, f. 1r).

182 Craig, David and Egan, Michael, *Extreme Situations. Literature and Crisis from the Great War to the Atom Bomb* (London and Basingstoke: Macmillan, 1979) 150–1.

183 Hevener, John W., *Which Side Are You On? The Harlan County Coal Miners, 1931–39* (Urbana, Chicago, London: University of Illinois, 1978) ix.

184 Levy, Melvin P., 'Class War in Kentucky', *Harlan Miners Speak*, ed. Dreiser, Theodore (New York: Scribner, 1970) 20–37: 33.

185 Quoted in Hevener, *Which Side Are You On?*, x. Boris Israel, in *Harlan Miners Speak*, commented, 'in a war you're either on one side or the other' (Israel, Boris, 'Representing the Press', *Harlan Miners Speak*, ed. Dreiser, 80–2: 81).

186 Dreiser, Theodore *et al.*, ed., *Harlan Miners Speak*, ix.

187 Dreiser, Theodore, 'Introduction', *Harlan Miners Speak*, ed. Dreiser, 3–16: 4–5.

188 Dreiser, 'Introduction' 5, 7, 8.

189 Cohen, Lester, 'Bloody Ground', *Harlan Miners Speak*, ed. Dreiser, 17–19: 18–19.

190 Levy, 'Class War', 24, 23.

191 Crawford, Bruce, 'Harlan County and the Press', *Harlan Miners Speak*, ed. Dreiser, 75–80: 75.

192 *FoW* 9.

193 *FoW* 10.

194 Carlos Baker and Caroline Moorehead name the provider of the letter as Kyle Crichton (Baker, Carlos, *Ernest Hemingway. A Life Story* (Harmondsworth: Penguin, 1972) 462; Moorehead, *Martha Gellhorn* 129), who was 'screen and theater' editor for *Collier's*.

195 *FoW* 11.

196 Baker, Carlos, *Ernest Hemingway* 451f.

197 Orwell, George, *Homage to Catalonia* (London: Penguin, 2000) 2.

198 *FoW* 12.

199 Orsagh, Jacqueline, 'A Critical Biography of Martha Gellhorn' (unpublished doctoral thesis, Michigan State University, 1977) 68.

200 *FoW* 12. In fact, Gellhorn's first article published in *Collier's* was 'Only the Shells Whine' (17 July 1937): the issue has her name on the front cover (rather than on the 'masthead', which the present author takes to be the list of editors and sub-editors that appears on page 4 of each issue). Her next piece to appear was 'Men Without Medals' (15 January 1938) when her name is again on the cover. Her name first appeared on the masthead on 6 January 1940, when she was billed as 'Scandinavia'. She remained as 'Martha Gellhorn – Scandinavia' until 12 October 1940, and was then 'Martha Gellhorn – Articles' from 19 October 1940 to 22 March 1941; 'Martha Gellhorn – The Orient' from 29 March 1941 to 6 September 1941; 'Martha Gellhorn – Articles' again from 13 September 1941 to 26 December 1942; 'Martha Gellhorn – Invasions' from 24 June 1944 to 7 October 1944; and 'Martha Gellhorn – France' from 14 October 1944 to 29 September 1944.

201 Orsagh, 'A Critical Biography', 68.

202 Ayer, N. W., *Directory of Newspapers and Periodicals* (Philadelphia: N. W. Ayer and Sons, 1936) 1188.

203 Gellhorn described another article on Spain in a letter of 6 December 1938 to Charles Colebaugh (*SL* 70–1) and mentioned it again in a letter of 3 February 1939 to Denver Lindley, saying 'I hope you can run it' (f. 1r). Lindley replied to her on 6 or 8 February 1939, 'we're not using your article. I'm sorry' (f. 1r). The piece never did appear in *Collier's* but it can be found as 'The Third Winter' in *The Face of War* (1959 and later editions), dated November 1938. In a letter of 17 July 1941, Gellhorn told Charles Colebaugh, 'I sold you an article once about Barcelona, and events made it outdated before it could be published: it was my responsibility' (f. 3r). (The letter appears in *SL* at pp. 112–13, but this remark is omitted.)

204 'Next Week', *Collier's* (10 July 1937) 4.

205 Gellhorn, 'Only the Shells Whine', *Collier's* (17 July 1937) 12–13, 64–5: 12.

206 Gellhorn described this narrative technique as 'like a novel' (letter to Charles Colebaugh of 6 December 1938: *SL* 71).

207 Gellhorn, 'Only the Shells Whine', 17 July 1937, 64, 13, 65.

208 Gellhorn, 'City at War', *Collier's* (2 April 1938) 18–19, 59–60: 19.

209 Gellhorn, 'Only the Shells Whine', 17 July 1937, 13.

210 Gellhorn, 'Only the Shells Whine', 17 July 1937, 13, 65.

211 A point also made by Caroline Moorehead in *Martha Gellhorn* (150).

212 Knightley, Phillip, *The First Casualty. The War Correspondent as Hero and Myth-Maker from the Crimea to Kosovo* (London: Prion Books, 2000) 234, 232; Hume, Mick, *Whose War Is It Anyway? The Dangers of the Journalism of Attachment* (London: InformInc, 1997) 18. Conversely, Fred

Inglis argues that no journalist should be required to 'extinguish human emotion and judgments' (Inglis, Fred, *People's Witness. The Journalist in Modern Politics* (New Haven and London: Yale University Press, 2002) 21).

213 Gellhorn, 'Only the Shells Whine', 17 July 1937, 12.

214 Gellhorn, 'Only the Shells Whine', 17 July 1937, 12.

215 Hemingway, Ernest, *By-Line: Ernest Hemingway*, ed. White, William (New York: Simon & Schuster, 1998) 257.

216 Gellhorn, 'Only the Shells Whine', 17 July 1937, 18.

217 Gellhorn, 'Men without Medals', *Collier's* (15 January 1938) 9–10, 49: 10.

218 'Women Lecturers Found Unpopular', *New York Times* (28 November 1937) 1–2.

219 The film, which Hemingway helped make and narrated, was funded by the 'Contemporary Historians' group (to which Hemingway, Lillian Hellman and Dorothy Parker belonged), part of the progressive Popular Front (Kutulas, *The Long War*, 100). It was criticised by anti-Stalinists for omitting mention of Stalin's purges of the POUM (Kutulas, *The Long War*, 123). See also *SL* 52 (letter to Eleanor Roosevelt of ? June 1937), 55–6 (letter to Eleanor Roosevelt of 8 July 1937).

220 Gellhorn, letter to Eleanor Roosevelt, 24/25 April 1938, ff. 2r, 4r. Part of this quotation appears in *SL* at 61.

221 'Martha Gellhorn Sees Spain as Breeding Place for World War', 28 January 1938, 2C.

222 'Martha Gellhorn Sees Spain as Breeding Place for World War', 28 January 1938, 2C.

223 Gellhorn, 'Obituary of a Democracy', *Collier's* (10 December 1938) 12–13, 28, 32–3, 36: 28.

224 Benson, Frederick R., *Writers in Arms. The Literary Impact of the Spanish Civil War* (London: University of London, 1968) 276; Cunningham, Valentine, ed., *The Penguin Book of Spanish Civil War Verse* (Harmondsworth: Penguin, 1980) 86; Homberger, Eric, 'The American War Novel and the Defeated Liberal', *The Second World War in Literature: Eight Essays*, ed. Higgins, Ian (Edinburgh and London: Scottish Academic Press, 1986) 32–44: 39; Piette, Adam, *Imagination at War: British Fiction and Poetry 1939–1945* (London: Papermac, 1995) 82.

225 Cunningham, *British Writers of the Thirties* 460.

226 Letter to Hortense Flexner and Wyncie King of 8 June 1940: *SL* 93.

2

'A walking tape recorder with eyes'[1]

On 26 January 1918, a two-page photographic spread was published in *Collier's* magazine. Under a photograph of a medium-sized dust-cloud is the caption, 'The man who took this snapshot of an exploding shell was under fire for hours – hours with sudden death'. Under a photograph of a blurred dirigible on the facing page are the words, 'The man who made this picture of a Zeppelin also spent hours on the job – hours with an airbrush'. The text on the first page explains:

> Nine out of ten real war photographs are as unexciting as [that] reproduced above – [. . .] taken from cover because the photographer would have been instantly shot if he had exposed himself. To the uninitiated eye the photographs on the opposite page – all [. . .] of them fakes – are more like war. It is only when you look closely at the picture of the Zeppelin that you realise how the photographer cut a photograph of a Zeppelin in two, joined the parts at an angle, and painted in the smoke.[2]

The piece invokes two expectations brought to war recording: authenticity and 'excitement'. It also hints at another, crucial to the first two: proximity ('taken from cover because the photographer would have been instantly shot if he had exposed himself'). The positioning to be explored in this chapter corresponds to *Collier's* first photo: that of the candid 'camera eye',[3] a shorthand (potentially misleading) for 'objectivity'.

As an authorial stance, 'objectivity' is, in field and text, at the opposite end of the spectrum from 'engagement': in this configuration, the reportorial figure is, at least at first sight, effaced, non-intervening, dispassionate, 'under cover'.[4] Martha Gellhorn, who occupies the position at various junctures in her prose, likened it to being 'a walking tape recorder with eyes',[5] an image which encapsulates the idea of mechanical, emotionless, unmediated transcription. Yet, as will be explored in this chapter, Gellhorn had a problematic relationship with 'objectivity', and 'a walking tape recorder with eyes' becomes not so much a figure for genuineness as for a certain tonal control (albeit a control which on occasion 'slips' or 'blinks') appropriate to the solemn task of bearing witness. Consequently, the alignment begins to bleed into the next positioning on the spectrum, for to witness, in however self-effacing a way, is contingent on being there to see.

Objectivity and war

'Objectivity', as Anthony Smith points out, is the term used to describe the most enduring quality exacted of journalism. Readers expect the events a newspaper reports to have happened; that those to which it gives greatest importance are worthy of priority; that a process of checking will have been carried out; that information placed in various categories (sport etc.) will belong in them; and that information concerning goods for sale will be presented differently from other information.[6] Above all, the expectation is that reports will not be unreasonably biased, selective or otherwise distorted. Such expectations underlay the anguish which greeted revelations in 2003 that a *New York Times* reporter, Jayson Blair, had forged details to authenticate his 'date-lines' (the dates-plus-location which attest to a journalist's 'being there'). These principles also underlie certain requirements made by some of war writing, whether journalism or fiction. 'The ideal of truth inherent in entirely unpretentious objectivity,' writes W. G. Sebald, 'proves itself the only legitimate reason for continuing to produce literature in the face of total destruction.'[7] The purpose of this section is to investigate the ontogeny of such assumptions and requirements; to answer the questions, 'to what extent, and why, was objectivity important when Martha Gellhorn was reporting the Second World War, and what at that time was meant by "objectivity"?'

Like any idea, (journalistic) objectivity has a history. The traditional source of news in the early modern period was the sermon,[8] which came with its own unimpeachable authority. In the seventeenth century, when news came to be defined ideologically, there arose a 'pressing need' to establish legally the nature of 'factual' information.[9] Licensing of the press in this period was not so much a form of censorship as an attempt on the part of the authorities to prevent people being deceived: the argument against it was that truth and lies should be allowed to engage in open encounter.[10] In the eighteenth century, the licensing system failed. The preoccupation of journalism was not so much the accurate reporting of facts as the fate of the various political factions: indeed, there were no techniques for providing an 'unblemished version of events'.[11] The only guarantee of accuracy was provenance. As the *Daily Courant*, the first daily in English, promised in its debut edition of 21 April 1702:

The Author has taken care to be duly furnished with all that comes from Abroad in any language [. . .] at the beginning of each Article he will quote the Foreign Paper whence 'tis taken [. . .]. Nor will he take it upon him to give any comments or conjectures of his own, but will relate only the Matter of Fact.[12]

This is objectivity as impartiality (or, rather, impersonality): as titles from the period – *The Mercury*, *The Post Boy*, *The Courant* – indicate, papers regarded themselves simply as passive 'carriers' of news. Consonant with this was the development of shorthand in the 1750s: a person could now specialise in observing an event and recording it with precision. In Smith's words, the reporter acquired an 'aura of neutrality' as an impersonal transmitter of event to reader.[13]

In the United States, papers were originally party organs, and therefore unashamedly partisan. Two developments changed this situation: the rise, in the 1830s, of the penny press and the advent of the telegraph.[14] The penny papers were 'impartial and independent' while the telegraph enabled the emergence of wire agencies such as the Associated Press (founded 1848),[15] which, supplying information to many clients simultaneously, had to be ideologically neutral to be acceptable to them all.[16] Reduced to a link in this wire circuit, the correspondent took on the qualities of the cyborg, the part-human/part-machine posited by Donna Haraway,[17] not least because the technology meant that one observer was interchangeable with another, generating a standardised, impersonal prose style unattributable to any particular writer.[18] This replicated the effect of shorthand, suggesting a directly proportional correlation between speed of communications technology and impartiality of prose. Concurrent with telegraphic developments was the emergence of the role of editor and the ensuing development of the newspaper-as-organisation, with professional codes and ethics, such as the guarantee of authenticity.

The sensationalistic circulation wars of the 1880s and 1890s caused a sea-change. With the so-called 'Yellow Journalism' of papers such as Pulitzer's *New York World* and Hearst's *New York Journal*, writers and correspondents became 'big names', spelling the end of objectivity-as-impersonality. Instead, there was a growth in 'new genres of subjective reporting', such as the political column.[19] The signed news story or 'by-line' began to appear. By the twentieth century, a professionalised journalism with its own ethics and etiquette had developed. In the United States, Joseph Pulitzer helped found the first university school of journalism, at Columbia, in 1913, and, of course, established the prizes for 'serious journalism', especially 'that which has helped social reform', which still bear his name.[20] This professionalisation of journalism provoked in *belletrists* a reaction which has been termed a 'sacralisation' of the art of fiction.[21] In a 1893 essay, 'The Man of Letters as a Man of Business', William Dean Howells, while remaining friendly to the press, remarked that to write 'to pay [. . .] provisions bills' was 'ridiculous', 'repulsive' and 'shabby': literature was, and should remain, 'the most intimate [. . .] of the arts'.[22] This hierarchical division between 'private' fiction, the preserve of the gentleman-amateur, and 'public', commercialised journalism provides the dramatic tension in Henry James's *The Bostonians* (1886), ironically since James himself was a shrewd negotiator in the literary marketplace and even wrote for the New York *Sun*.[23] The opposition between *belles lettres* and commercialised journalism assumes further significance in the novel as another set of values are loaded onto the scales. Basil Ransom, an opponent of women's rights and of Verena Tarrant's public speaking, bursts out: 'The whole generation is womanized; the masculine tone is passing out of the world; it's a feminine, a nervous, hysterical, chattering, canting age.'[24] To translate the private sphere into the public – to make 'the person food for newsboys' – is gendered as feminine, 'mediocre'.[25] There is some irony in this, given that, in the period, newspapers were owned, edited, written and read almost exclusively by men, and given, in particular, the enormous difficulties Martha Gellhorn and other aspiring women journalists would face in the profession.

During and after the First World War, the burgeoning public relations industry spawned a distrust of official 'facts', consonant with contemporary modernist scepticism and the collapse of the belief that transcendent 'truth' existed and could be accessed. A resolution passed by the American Society of Newspaper Editors in 1933 stated that 'editors should devote a larger amount of attention and space to explanatory and interpretative news'.[26] Practitioners of journalism had arrived, albeit from a different direction, at the same conclusion as New Reportage theorists: the facts must be explained.

'Objectivity', then, is historically specific. As Martha Gellhorn began her career in the 1930s, the term no longer meant – could no longer mean – unadorned 'truth' neutrally mediated.[27] Yet if the metaphysic foundered, the ideal did not. As methodology, it persisted as eye-witness journalism and a continuing reluctance to accept official versions of 'the facts'. As style, it continued in three ways. The first was by means of devices that might be termed 'truth tropes':[28] verbatim reporting, the use of statistics, the citing of sources, the incorporation of original documents and the use of corroborative evidence. The second was in the practice of providing interpretation of, or contextualising, the facts. The third was in the tendency to reveal, rather than conceal, partiality and textual constructedness. (Such methodology and style were, of course, hallmarks of the New Reportage.) Gaye Tuchman has described this version of objectivity as a 'strategic ritual', performed by journalists as a defensive measure against forms of attack from criticism to libel suits.[29] But things are different in war, and objectivity is no exception: the next task is to examine the influence on the concept of wartime conditions.

If, by the late 1930s, objectivity was understood and deployed principally as a set of truth tropes, it was due, in part, to the decline in the reputation of transcendent verities – the so-called 'grand narratives' rejected by modernism. In war, access even to lowly narratives is under threat. During the Second World War, according to Phillip Knightley, 'correspondents argued that even if they wanted to challenge the official version of events, they could not because they were totally dependent on the military to be able to see the war at all.'[30] Daniel Boorstin's concept of the 'pseudo-event' – a planned 'synthetic novelty' such as an interview or press conference[31] – is particularly prevalent in war due to the relative 'eventlessness' of the phenomenon: this produces natural distortion.[32] The psychological effect of conflict, moreover has, according to W. G. Sebald, a deleterious effect on accurate recall:

> People who have escaped with nothing but their lives do generally have something discontinuous about them, a curiously erratic quality, one so much at variance with authentic recollection that it easily suggests rumour-mongering and invention [. . .] the apparently unimpaired ability – shown in most of the eye-witness reports – of everyday language to go on functioning as usual raises doubts of the authenticity of the experiences they record.[33]

Yet, at the same time as it gives rise to censorship and propaganda and impairs personal recollection, war, as noted at the outset of this chapter, demands authentic recording. Reasons for this are not difficult to proffer. Gellhorn's novel *Point of No Return* suggests one as it presents a character considering the gap between the understanding of war of the combatant and of the civilian on whose behalf he is fighting:

> His parents lived beyond time and measurable space in a world that seemed grotesque to him, a scurrying loud patriotic antheap where everyone babbled his stupid head off about the war as if any of them knew what they were talking about.[34]

The gap is potentially a matter not merely of wrong impressions but of actual alienation between those who fight in a war and those who do not. As Paul Fussell notes, public innocence about the Second World War drove troops to 'fury':[35] for them, having 'the truth told' about combat constituted a vital opportunity to re-connect with their former lives.

Narrating war is, crucially, also a political act: the 'so that it will never happen again' argument may be hopelessly idealistic – war shows no sign of letting up – but records can be kept straight and the link between violence and government policy kept in public view.[36] Narratives of conflict can be important, too, as means of psychic re-integration, of the putting-back-together of self. Jonathan Shay, a psychiatrist who works with Vietnam veterans suffering from what is now called post-traumatic stress disorder (PTSD), argues that psychological recovery from such trauma is dependent upon its 'communalization': specifically, the construction of a personal narrative of events which receives sympathetic hearing.[37] Lawrence Tritle concurs with this, citing research which has shown that the re-experiencing of traumatic situations stimulates the production of neuro-hormones with psycho-active tranquillising properties.[38] Truly telling and re-telling war may be, then, at some psychic level, curative, as an early literary instance of a veteran hearing recounts of the combat he has participated in suggests: 'Odysseus broke down as the famous minstrel sang this lay [of Troy], and his cheeks were wet with the tears that ran down from his eyes.'[39] To replay, to represent a battle, is to achieve some form of psychological 'closure'. For all these reasons, therefore, authenticity is at a premium in conflict. When Sebald calls for imperfect reminiscences to be supplemented with 'artificial and synoptic' views,[40] it is an instance of war intensifying the demand for traditional objectivity.

The notion of objectivity as a set of 'truth tropes' therefore demands careful scrutiny when it appears in wartime. Rather than forming a defensive strategy or 'strategic ritual', it seems to be a complex engagement with the notion of trust, falling within the class of 'communication-as-ritual', in the sense of a shared rite purporting to promote and enable participation, fellowship, communion and community.[41] In particular, 'proofs of honesty' enlist readers' and audiences' support: an example is Hollywood's two-pronged tactics in the Second World War of exposing the tricks of enemy propaganda and revealing its own constructedness with behind-the-scenes shots and explanations of film-making technology.[42] Of course, trust can be manufactured cynically: journalistic allusions to the process of covering a story may be no more than double-bluff to mask the fact of collusion.[43] Overall, though, it seems right to conclude of the Second World War period that objectivity continued to be a construct, though it was also haunted by more traditional epistemics and seems to have been a key part of communication made in good faith.

'Exactly as it was'[44]

'I wasn't objective about Dachau,' said Martha Gellhorn in a television interview with John Pilger in 1983, 'what was there to be objective about?' She continued:

> I did not invent anything. I did neither suppress nor invent, I reported it exactly as it was. If you report what you see, unless your eyes are bad, I don't see how you can be other than objective. You don't conceal anything, you don't add anything, it's there in front of you. That's what you see, that's what you report.[45]

'I wasn't objective' and 'I reported it exactly as it was' appear to be used here as antonyms. Gellhorn's remarks therefore reveal the complexity of her attitude towards 'objectivity', and also suggest that a re-definition is in order. If she thought she wasn't being objective, 'objective' must have meant something other than faithful reporting, for this latter was of supreme importance to her. She had 'an almost pathological reverence for the truth,' noted Rosie Boycott, '[. . .] no fiction could be as important as the need to bear witness to the atrocities'.[46] What Gellhorn meant by 'all this objectivity shit'[47] seems to have been a combination of a stylistic construction, or textual positioning, and a species of reportorial ethics: the representation of a balanced range of opinion, or even a pointed lack of stated opinion. Her own ethics worked differently. 'The core of Martha really was: [. . .] who are the baddies? Who are the goodies?' said Victoria Glendinning.[48] When it came to a subject like Dachau, how could anyone *not* say what they thought? What could possibly be the balancing view?

The point, therefore, is not to search for impartiality in Gellhorn's writings. 'You go into a hospital, and it's full of wounded kids,' she once said: 'So you write what you see and how it is. You don't say there's 37 wounded children in this hospital, but maybe there's 38 wounded children on the other side. You write what you see.'[49] 'Objectivity' in her work must therefore be understood in other terms: above all as a matter of stylistic restraint. Evident even in her remarks to Pilger, this comprises emphatic, briskly structured sentences; hard, clear images; a deliberate suppression of emotion and a determinedly unflinching gaze ('she did not flicker an eye-lid,' commented Nigel Nicolson in a review of *The Face of War*).[50] The steady gaze invokes the figure of the eye-witness reporter, a construction returned to in the last section of this chapter after Gellhorn's searchlight stylistics have been analysed. In the discussion which follows, special attention is paid to Gellhorn's (and others') accounts of the Nazi death camps, for it is in relation to this subject in particular that the tension between an indispensable tonal control and an equally visceral emotional response is in starkest relief.

'A second way of telling'

A passage from Gellhorn's article 'Obituary of a Democracy' (first published in *Collier's* on 10 December 1938) – an instance of a war reporter reporting on a report of war – acknowledges two modes of relating traumatic events. A Czech executive is describing the Nazis' annexation of the Sudetenland:

> He began to talk in a gray, matter-of-fact voice. He spoke like a professor, making his points on the map. There were only two ways that people spoke in Czechoslovakia, and this was the second way. When they talked they all spoke with terrible and violent control; but later, as the story went on, the control snapped and people – these serious, quiet, inarticulate people – wept as they talked, with fury and helplessness. Or else they talked coldly, stating facts, trying to keep their voices and their minds dead.[51]

The 'second way of telling', that of 'terrible and violent control', of speaking 'coldly, stating facts' in 'gray, matter-of-fact' voices, is presented as an admired ideal in Gellhorn's work, an operational poesis that, for her, appears to have been self-authenticating. Her early conception of journalism was as 'a guiding light': 'If people were told the truth, if dishonor and injustice were clearly shown to them, they would at once demand the saving action, punishment of wrong-doers, and care for the innocent.'[52] Later, more disillusioned with the power of writing to change things ('the guiding light of journalism was no stronger than a glow-worm'),[53] she none the less kept faith in its ability at least to record: 'I now think the act of keeping the record straight it valuable in itself. Serious, honest, journalism is essential, not because it is a guiding light but because it is a form of honorable behavior.'[54] The 'second way of telling' is therefore not solely a stylistic matter: aligned with a certain set of 'honorable' values, it actually becomes the means of defending them. In Gellhorn's writing, the mode is synonymous with authorial effacement and explicit repudiations of personal feeling, the implication being that the presence of such feeling might, or might be perceived to, compromise 'truth'.[55] 'In my opinion,' she told a friend thirty years after the war, 'the reporter should be there [in the text] as little as possible: nothing about the reporter matters [. . .]. I was always cutting and deleting from my articles, to eliminate as much as possible the sound of me screaming.'[56] Frequently, she described her role in relation to war as that of a 'witness',[57] a word which evokes the solemn forensic standards of the law court.

'Forensic' seems an apt word to describe a tone and methodology the necessity of which, with regard to war crimes, seems to have been, from the beginning, universally appreciated. A party of 18 American newspaper and magazine editors, among them William L. Chenery of *Collier's*, who visited Buchenwald and Dachau at Eisenhower's invitation, felt able to report only when they had

> visited and spent considerable time investigating the prison camps [. . .] interviewed recently freed political prisoners, slave laborers and civilians of many nationalities [. . .] studied a great mass of documents covering the German occupation of France which contained photographic evidence and testimony taken in many places and painstakingly authenticated with the sworn statements of witnesses and victims.[58]

The Second World War correspondent Iris Carpenter said in her 1946 memoirs, of Buchenwald and Oświęcim (Auschwitz):

> It is hard to write of it all without yielding to the temptation to color-sweep and word-picture one's own emotion and reaction. Accordingly, correspondents agreed to document what they saw in the baldest statement of plain fact. We chronicled the fantastic, dreadful narrative of what Nazidom was [. . .] in the simplest language and with the most carefully authenticated evidence we could find.[59]

The *New York Times* noted the judicial air with which Senator Aben W. Barkley and Congressman R. Ewing Thomason read an account of the camps to a Congressional Committee considering the unprecedented charge of 'crimes against humanity':

> Both Messrs. Barkley and Thomason put the extraordinary indictment in level, passionless tones, like prosecutors opening the trial of a case of high crime. There was no demonstration in either House; members sat with faces sick with horror. The proceeding took a judicial tone. [. . .] The report said emphatically that all conclusions were reached only on three classes of evidence: visual inspection of camps by members, testimony of eye-witnesses to atrocities and common and universally agreeing knowledge of each camp. Not even the evidence of the Allied military authorities was included.[60]

The same standard of evidence was praised by Gellhorn in one of her last pieces of the period for *Collier's*, 'The Paths of Glory' (published on 9 November 1946), on the Nuremberg Trials: 'It was a quiet court and a cold one. There was no anger here and no hate and no question of vengeance.'[61] The president of the tribunal, the British Attorney-General, Geoffrey Lawrence, speaks in the 'second way': a 'slow, careful and immensely quiet voice reading without haste or passion'.[62] It is a voice that, for Gellhorn, stands as 'a symbol of what all civilised people want and mean by justice',[63] a value also conferred by the quality of the admitted testimony: 'all proved, all sworn to by witnesses, the witnesses checked and counterchecked, the documents verified'.[64]

Numerous examples in which Gellhorn states and deploys the 'second way of telling' can be given. The Polish doctor who shows her round the clinic in Dachau speaks 'with great detachment'.[65] The point is expanded as Jacob Levy steps into her shoes in *Point of No Return*. Like the Czech executive, the doctor has learned to present the dead in a 'dead', or deadpan, way:

> The doctor watched with that polite smile; his cold eyes watched to see how an outsider would receive news from this world of darkness where they all lived. [. . .] He could do nothing except keep a record for the future, if there was a future. [. . .] He had learned to observe everything, dispassionate as the dead.[66]

In *A Stricken Field*, the American reporter Mary Douglas muses when she gets to Prague:

> There were the flat basic facts that you had to assemble: how many coal mines had the Nazis taken; how much of the textile industry, the glass, the porcelain, the sugar was lost; how many hectares of timber, hops, flax, tobacco had been seized; what had happened to the railroads; [. . .]. Statistics were only black marks to her, and if she learned that an unpronounceable Czech manufacturing town had become German it meant nothing, until she thought of the people who worked in the factories, and where would they go now.[67]

Mary thinks of the 'dreary interviews' she must do 'to get the facts about the break-up of their economy'[68] and the implication is that the practices of objective journalism are at best wearisome. Yet, the Sudetens' account of what has happened which she agrees to smuggle out at the end of the novel impresses her by being 'a simply worded statement' that 'read[s] flatly, being written with no emotion'.[69] For the refugee who entrusts her with it, 'to tell the truth, so that it shall not disappear and be forgotten, is our fighting'.[70] Phyllis Lassner rightly contends that *A Stricken Field* is an argument 'against modernist privileging of suggestion over verisimilitude' for the reason that Gellhorn 'refuses to endanger victims by risking the possibility that readers may fail to understand'.[71] Tonal control is also a form of 'fighting' – evidence of the author's absolute determination that the status of what she says will be impervious to challenge – a determination shared by all those who testify in the face of deniers of the Holocaust. In this sense, the 'second way of telling' is, for Gellhorn, its own validation and an indication of political standing.

What, then, are the stylistic elements of this textual stance? In a letter to the art historian Bernard Berenson, Gellhorn reveals some of her technical preoccupations, having been asked by him for her views on his 'Sketch for a Self Portrait'. 'Why do you invert so many sentences?' she asks, suggesting that 'This turmoil has never quite subsided, not even now.' is better than 'Quite subsided this turmoil never has, not even now.'[72] She explains:

> I don't see what you gain by that inversion; I think it is an awkward usage; no one talks like that, the sound is not better, nor the sense clearer. [. . .] I am also touched by an occasional archaic slang, 'frosh and sopher,' for instance. That has a curious quaintness like a Norfolk jacket; do you do it on purpose?[73]

Here, then, are the foundations of Gellhorn's own style: aimed at reproducing the rhythms and sounds of current speech; clear; felicitous.[74] 'I think I ought to learn to leave more out,' she writes elsewhere, 'gaps of portentous silence should appear, and words should not be so accursed explicit.'[75] In a letter of 30 October 1969 to George Paoloczi-Horvath, she recommends reading 'the real vocabulary of communication, the words that are short and have solid meaning and color'.[76] She laboured intensively over her own prose (whether it *becomes* laboured is discussed in 'Blinks' below), in letter after letter agonising about what she has produced. From Finland, she wrote to Hortense Flexner:

> I reread my first article, the one about the crossing,[77] and found it unspeakably lousy as I find all the others. I am ashamed of such writing but it goes too fast and I do not have time, or perhaps will or talent, to do it really well.[78]

To Denver Lindley, a *Collier's* editor, she wrote on 1 June 1938, 'I want to know what you think about this':

> I am just about gaga. Before I started to write this out, I threw out at least half my notes. Then I wrote it and cut it 3 times. Then I couldn't read it anymore and had it copied. Then I cut it again, as you will see. And it is still too long and I can't make sense about it anymore, having worked on it too long.[79]

As this reveals, for Gellhorn, writing prose was a crafted, managed, above all a *controlled*, practice.

To name specific influences on this prose is difficult as the record of Gellhorn's reading is patchy, though, apparently, 'a book a day' was her 'average consumption'.[80] Probably the best source of information is her correspondence with Berenson through the 1950s. In these letters, she mentions approvingly the Bible;[81] Walter Pater;[82] Dostoevsky;[83] Dreiser;[84] Edmund Wilson;[85] Flaubert;[86] Bertrand Russell;[87] Ivy

Compton-Burnett;[88] Isaiah Berlin;[89] L. P. Hartley's *The Go-Between*;[90] 'that cautionary and tormenting diary of Virginia Woolf' ('I learned something of spiritual usefulness from one entry' – the value of gentle exercise and reading good writing);[91] T. S. Eliot's *The Confidential Agent*;[92] E. M. Forster's *The Hill of Devi* (an 'absolute delight');[93] Claud Cockburn's *In Time of Trouble*;[94] Meyer Levin's *Compulsion*;[95] John Cheever's *The Wapshott Chronicle*;[96] Madame Yourcenar's *Memoirs d'Hadrien* ('wonderful');[97] Chekhov;[98] and Henry James.[99] In other correspondence, she writes of finding D. H. Lawrence 'dreadful and undisciplined'.[100] Elizabeth Bowen, Kay Boyle and Katherine Anne Porter made her 'excited and eager and alert' but 'finally there was nothing to see'.[101] 'Normal' Mailer was 'very childish' though she was 'deeply impressed by his vitality'.[102] Arthur Koestler, Nelson Algren, Nicolas Aldanov and Ira Wolfert she found 'full of juice, with good sharp new cyes'.[103] She wrote a 'dear sir' letter praising Hans Habe's *A Thousand Shall Fall* ('at last, IN FACT, not in the large dreary dim words, someone has told what any army must have in order to fight') which Harcourt, Brace used as an advert in the *New York Times*.[104] As a child, she 'adored' Robert Browning.[105] She knew Colette, H. G. Wells, Graham Greene, Dorothy Parker, Somerset Maugham and Rosamond Lehmann personally. It is difficult to generalise about this eclectic reading matter, but Gellhorn seems to have concentrated on contemporary fiction and non-fiction, war writing and, to a lesser extent, philosophy. The experimental writers on the list are outnumbered by those writing solid social realism. The books she noted were those that made her angry and that she felt would similarly move others: George Steer's *The Tree of Gernika* (1938) ('beautifully written and true') and Nelson Algren's *Never Come Morning* (1942) ('wonderful quick and sort of desperate ways of saying things') are mentioned in her correspondence.[106] Alfred Gellhorn confirms that his sister was 'semi-addicted' to thrillers.[107]

One Second World War correspondent whose prose style Gellhorn is definitely known to have admired was Alan Moorehead,[108] like Mary Welsh Hemingway a reporter for Beaverbrook's *Daily Express*. Here is Moorehead on the fighting at Salerno:

> Slowly the time passed. We were all keyed up. Towards midnight we were disturbed by a sound overhead. These weren't British planes. German bombers! Flying out to sea. The moon shone as a weak crescent, very low on the horizon. We recognised nothing at sea. Suddenly on the horizon terrific AA fire opened up: 'A Convoy'.[109]

This is laconic to the point of being elliptical and Gellhorn rarely reaches this level of terseness. Her prose is built up of short, simple sentences, simple vocabulary, co-ordinating conjunctions and few descriptive words: the aim is ever 'sharper and tighter'.[110] The style it most resembles is, as others have noted, Ernest Hemingway's. With regard to this, Victoria Glendinning makes the intriguing suggestion that the 'Hemingway style was really the Martha Gellhorn style'.[111] Gellhorn herself early said that she wanted to avoid 'parodying' Hemingway's prose[112] and comparisons with him made her angry: 'I am accused of writing, thinking, talking like Mr. Hemingway and as yet people have only not told me that I had a black moustache, but that will come.'[113] Yet she conceded (in a sentence that itself reveals the affinity) that he had 'magic': 'He doesn't know how it comes or how to make it, but when I read his book[114] I see it, clear as water and carrying like the music of a flute and it is not separate from what he writes, but running all through it.'[115]

Debate in fact still rages over where Hemingway's style itself 'came from'. Most recently, Ronald Weber has disputed Charles Fenton's 1954 thesis that it was forged in the newsrooms of the *Kansas City Star* (the paper's style-sheet ran, 'Use short first paragraphs. Use vigorous English. Be positive, not negative') and the *Toronto Daily Star*.[116] Certainly, in a 21 July 1918 piece for the *Kansas City Star*, 'At the End of the Ambulance Run', the young reporter was still writing like this:

> It was merely one of the many cases that came to the city dispensary from night to night – and from day to day for that matter; but the night shift, perhaps, has a wider range of the life and death tragedy – and even comedy, of the city.[117]

The 'mature' Hemingway would not include redundancies such as 'and from day to day for that matter' or 'perhaps', nor the abstractions of 'tragedy' and 'comedy'. But the piece also contains such laconic histories as 'At another time (it happens quite often) a young girl took poison'.[118] This stylistically foreshadows the documentary vignettes of *in our time* (1924), included as inter-chapters in *In Our Time* (1925), where Hemingway himself claimed the style to have originated:[119] 'There was a woman having a kid with a young girl holding a blanket over her and crying. Scared sick looking at it. It rained all through the evacuation.'[120] Already, then, 'At the End of the Ambulance Run' has the direct force of Hemingway's developed style. It is a style also evident in a 4 March 1922 piece for the *Toronto Daily Star*, 'Try Bobsledding If You Want Thrills', now leavened with self-deprecatory humour:

> If you want a thrill of the sort that starts at the base of your spine in a shiver and ends with your nearly swallowing your heart, as it leaps with a jump into your mouth, try bobsledding on a mountain road at 50 miles an hour.

[. . .] There is a steering wheel about twice as big as a doughnut for the victim in front to hang on to.[121]

This is very similar to Gellhorn's 'Night Life in the Sky' (*Collier's*, 17 March 1945): 'I thought that (a) my stomach was going to be flattened against my backbone, and (b) that I was going to strangle.'[122] But Gellhorn was writing drily, acerbically, directly, at the age of 21, as one of her earliest articles, on the matinée idol Rudy Vallée, shows:

> It is a respectable voice, and it is a relief to have a man sing like a human being and not like a hydraulic drill. Perhaps the secret lies in the Vallée type of beauty, which reminds one of the Lifebuoy Soap advertisements, or the Sloan's Liniment pictures in their better moments.[123]

The point here is not to try to 'prove' whether the style originated with Hemingway or Gellhorn – the matter is probably insoluble and 'plain speaking' was anyway in the air – but to identify and characterise it.

At base it is a mode of discourse which elicits, rather than expresses, emotion: if not overdone, it comes across as hard and true. Here, for example, is Hemingway opening 'The G.I. and the General' (*Collier's*, 4 November 1944):

> The wheat was ripe but there was no one there to cut it now, and tank tracks led through it to where the tanks lay pushed into the hedge that topped the ridge that looked across the wooded country to the hill we would have to take tomorrow.[124]

And here is Gellhorn opening 'Cracking the Gothic Line' (*Collier's*, 28 October 1944):

> The Gothic Line, from where we stood, was a smashed village, an asphalt road and a pinkish brown hill. On this dusty mined lane leading up to the village, the road and the hill, the infantry was waiting to attack. They stood single file, spaced well apart and did not speak.[125]

And here is the same passage in its 1959 version in *The Face of War*, 'The Gothic Line':

> The Gothic Line, from where we stood, was a smashed village, an asphalt road, and a pinkish-brown hill. On a dusty mined lane leading up to the village, the road and the hill, the Canadian infantry was waiting to attack. They stood single file, spaced well apart, and did not speak and their faces said nothing either.[126]

Hemingway's is the sparest of the three (only two adjectives), though Gellhorn's first version is very similar. Her second version is an example of the effect produced when the control slips. Adding clarifying details

('*a* dusty mined lane', '*Canadian* infantry') and punctuation (the hyphen-
ated 'pinkish-brown') may help the sense (the piece is now being
presented, to a later generation, as an argument against nuclear proliferation),[127] but seems fussy. 'And their faces said nothing either' actually
detracts from the original impact of a silent, waiting army. Gellhorn's
lapses of control are important and are discussed in detail later in the
chapter, but for the moment it can be observed that the original opening
of 'Cracking the Gothic Line' shows her restrained tone at its truest and
most authoritative: sombre, sonorous, relentless.[128]

The unflinching gaze

Gellhorn closes her 1940 novel, *A Stricken Field*, with the woman war
correspondent protagonist, Mary Douglas, flying out of Czechoslovakia
to the west and safety. 'Not one' of her fellow passengers 'looked out the
windows behind them at the wand-like steeples of Prague growing
smaller and finer in the distance.'[129] Her *Collier's* article 'Dachau:
Experimental Murder' opens with the same perspectival motif: the
reporter up in an aeroplane. Again, none of the passengers in the C-47
out of Germany looks out of the windows, all turn away from the
country 'with hatred and sickness'[130] until a soldier says suddenly: 'We
got to talk about it, see? We got to talk about it if anyone believes us or
not.'[131] In *Point of No Return*, Jacob Levy, being taken, like Gellhorn,
round the newly liberated Dachau, keeps coming up against the same
truth. Immediately inside the camp, 'he started to turn and go back' but
is deterred by the risk of 'calling attention to himself and probably being
asked for his pass',[132] a formality which would reveal that his presence
is unauthorised and which would thrust into the spotlight his identity,
already a sensitive subject in the book. Led by a former inmate, Heinrich,
who speaks in an 'amiable dead voice',[133] with 'grey unexcited con-
tempt',[134] through the 'still or swaying bodies' of the prisoners, Jacob
keeps his eyes on his feet.[135] Finally, as Heinrich leads him the long way
round to the gate, they come upon the pile of corpses: 'Jacob Levy could
not turn back. He could not, in front of this man who had lived here for
twelve years, break and run.'[136] A crucial element of the 'second way of
telling' for Gellhorn is the imperative not to 'break and run': the necessity of the unflinching gaze.

Clear-sightedness, both literal and figurative, is at a premium in
conflict. Here is the art critic Robert Hughes on Francesco de Goya:

> The words he wrote on one plate of his great series of etchings, *Los
> Desastres de la Guerra* (The Disasters of War) are still the declaration of

every documentarian, every realist, every artist who would be thought unflinching: *Yo lo vi*, 'I saw it'. And these are balanced by their contrary, the title of another 'Disaster': *No se puede mirar*, 'One cannot look at this'.[137]

In the late war period, the point is at its starkest in the context of the news beginning to filter through about the liberated Nazi death camps. Alan Moorehead, visiting Belsen, found that, in the women's barracks, 'having no stomach for this sort of thing I was only able to look for a second or two':[138]

'I've had enough of this,' I said to the captain.
'Come on,' he said, 'you've got to go through one of the men's huts yet. That's what you're here for.'[139]

But, as though Moorehead has closed his eyes, there is a lacuna in the text: the next thing that is mentioned is the party emerging from the men's barracks 'into the light again'.[140] The gaze has, momentarily, been averted. The issue was a live one. The *New York Times* reported on 2 May 1945 that newsreels taken by the Army Signal Corps of the recently opened-up Nordhausen, Buchenwald, Ohrdruf and Hadamar and shown in theatres in the city had been 'generally received by audiences in silence or with muttered expressions of outrage'.[141] The article continued:

Although some of the reels were prefaced with warnings to the audience not to look 'if you are susceptible to gruesome sights', there were no indications that many persons took refuge in shutting their eyes, and the response apparent in theaters indicated that the patrons were determined to see.

Only the manager of the Radio City Music Hall declined to show the reels as the venue was 'patronized by a large proportion of women and children' and he 'felt it a protection to them to keep the films from their eyes'. Overall, coverage of the death camps by the paper was itself relatively low-key. The liberation of Dachau, for instance, merited a small column at the bottom of the front page on 1 May 1945 and continued on page 5[142] where it was surrounded by ads for Bergdorf Goodman and other Fifth Avenue boutiques.[143] Only a small photograph was published on 11 May, taken by the US Signal Corps of 'Wedding Rings of Buchenwald Victims',[144] and on 8 May an article entitled 'Oswiecim Killings Placed as 4,000,000' appeared on page 12.[145]

For Gellhorn, looking was a moral imperative from the beginning. The cub reporter heroine of her 1934 novel, *What Mad Pursuit*, confronted with her first corpse in the city morgue, forces herself to steel her nerves: 'You are a reporter, she told herself. You were sent here to get a story.

Get the story. You can't faint, you coward; you can't faint; this is your job.'[146] Gellhorn frequently linked sight and objective truth. 'The point of these articles is that they are true,' she remarked of her collection of Second World War journalism, 'they tell what I saw.'[147] She promised to act as the 'eyes for [people's] conscience', occupant of 'a ringside seat at the spectacle of history in the making'.[148] In the epigraph to *A Stricken Field*, 'from a Medieval Chronicle', the importance of the steadfast, unaverted gaze is asserted (and gendered):

> There were young knights among them who had never been present at a stricken field. Some could not look upon it [. . .]. Then Jean de Rye, an aged knight [. . .] who had been sore wounded in the battle, rode up to the group of young knights and said, 'Are ye maidens with your downcast eyes? Look well upon it. See all of it. Close your eyes to nothing.'[149]

In Gellhorn's work, the unflinching gaze is a matter both of a refusal to overlook and a refusal to spare the reader (though, again, the point must be made, as with her Spanish Civil War pieces, that, even if she witnessed them, there is no record of atrocities on the Allied side). This makes for uncompromising description, as in the following:

> The Germans thought it would be a good idea to put human beings into these boxes and literally burn them alive. It would take quite a while to die in those closed metal-lined boxes. First your feet burned, and when in agony you tried to raise yourself, you reached for red-hot hooks. As you could not stand, you were forced to lean against the side walls of the box, also red hot.[150]

Here the mundanity of tone ('thought it would be a good idea', 'quite a while') seems to act as an instrument of detachment, in a way similar to that in which the photographer Margaret Bourke-White, writing of Buchenwald, regarded her camera:

> I kept telling myself that I would believe the indescribably horrible sight [. . .] before me only when I had a chance to look at my own photographs. Using the camera [. . .] interposed a slight barrier between myself and the white horror in front of me.[151]

Gellhorn's tonal equivalent of the cold camera-eye serves to hold the faces of her readers towards the horror, a practice explained elsewhere in her impatience with those who are not there in person to see: 'you wonder what happens to a magnificent division of brave men after the war. And you wonder who is going to thank them and how, and will it be enough?'[152]

But on 3 February 1945, a letter Martha Gellhorn never intended the public to see was published in *Collier's*. 'I shall never forgive *Collier's* for their lapse in taste and honour in publishing pieces of a letter I wrote them very late at night when I was too tired and too disgusted not to tell the truth,' she complained bitterly to Allen Grover.[153] The editorial decision to go against her wishes was taken because the piece was 'so revealing of the war-weary state of mind'.[154] It conveyed what Gellhorn had elsewhere called her 'journalistic saturation point':[155]

> Today I saw pictures of two bodies, dug up from some boneyard in Toulouse. They were the bodies of what had once been two Frenchmen aged 32 and 29, but they had been tortured by the Gestapo until they died. I look at anything, you see, because I do not admit that one can turn away; one has no right to spare oneself. But I never saw faces (decayed in death, of course, anyhow) with gouged-out eyes. I thought I'd seen it all but evidently not.[156]

It is the language of limits reached: 'I must have a rest,' she told her editors.[157] But she did not, and what lay ahead was Dachau, where, she said, she could look and listen to no more.[158]

The truth is that for Gellhorn, as for other journalists, 'looking' was a matter of emotional self-discipline, something she had to force herself to do. Frequently, the consequences were traumatic. The same is true of her tonal control. As her letter to Grover reveals – 'I was too tired and too disgusted not to tell the truth' – the fastidious restraint of her prose was, to some degree, a front, constructed by a strenuous act of will. Years later, she confirmed this: 'I [. . .] *turned myself* into a walking tape recorder with eyes'.[159] To give an example: while admiring the 'slow, careful and immensely quiet voice' of the British Attorney-General at Nuremberg,[160] Gellhorn was also feeling, as she watched the defendants, 'such outrage that it choked you':[161]

> Because of this unimposing gang [. . .] ten million soldiers, sailors and airmen and civilians are dead as victims of war, and twelve million men, women and children are dead in gas chambers and furnaces. In great common graves where they were shot, in the stockyards that were concentration camps, dead of hunger and disease and exhaustion, dead all over Europe. And all these deaths were horrible. What these men and their half-dozen deceased partners were able to do, no famines, no plagues, no acts of God ever did: They produced destruction as the world has never seen destruction.[162]

This is not (to say the least) the language of the impersonal, unfeeling observer, the journalist as mechanistic recorder. There is prejudice in the very fact that Gellhorn is, in assuming the defendants' guilt, prejudging (albeit with good reason) the outcome of the trial. 'Paths of Glory' therefore suggests a latent fact about the controlled tone: that it must be deliberately assumed or learnt – a matter of conscious suppression of an instinctive response, rather in the manner of a doctor acquiring emotional distance. On this point, the Second World War correspondent Iris Carpenter is enlightening:

> The trait that anyone living in a front-line hospital would choose to borrow from the nurses, could he choose any he wanted to make the living easier, would be the way nurses can seemingly leave hospital in the hospital. [. . .] A blind drops in the mind over all they have left behind – or so it seems. It does not take many weeks of living in a hospital to find, however, that the blind does not shut the harrowing from a nurse's mind any more than it would from anyone else's however often she drops it. The strain tells – tells heavily and variously.[163]

Few of the hospital personnel, in fact, 'succeeded in quite sealing themselves inside the chrysalis of complete detachment'.[164]

Control (emotional as well as tonal) is, then, self-protective, a defence mechanism: Gellhorn wrote that she suspended thought and judgement 'for the purposes of mental hygiene'.[165] The sterile style therefore actually reproduces the process of traumatic experience as well as being an apt way of reporting it. Again, here is Gellhorn's account of the gas chambers in 'Death of a Dutch Town':

> These twelve hundred Jews, old and young, men, women and children, were taken to a rather nice-looking building and told they could have showers. As they had lived in misery and filth for months, they were very happy. They were ordered to undress and leave their clothes outside; notably they were to leave their shoes. From vents which looked like air vents, the Germans pumped what they call 'blue gas' into the clean white-tiled bathrooms. It appears that this gas works faster on slightly humid naked bodies. In some few minutes, twelve hundred people were dead, but not before the SS man had heard them scream and had watched them die in what agony we cannot know. Then the shoes were all carefully sorted and sent back to Germany, and before the mass cremations, all gold fillings and gold teeth were removed from the corpses.[166]

This is rhetorically a highly complex piece, not least because its restrained matter-of-factness suggests – and thereby invokes outrage at – the matter-of-factness (as well as the fact) of the killings. None the less, emotive words are very few. In the light of this, it is useful to compare with it another account Gellhorn gave of her reaction to the gas chambers, through the fictionalised figure of the journalist Mary Hallett ('Marushka') in her short story 'Till Death Us Do Part':

> They found her [Marushka] in bed in the dingy Hotel du Pré on the Left Bank. She was frightening to see, and babbled about the number of sacks of human ash to be used as fertilizer which you could hope to get in a good day's work at the crematorium, and the month's quota of female hair for mattresses which kept very steady, year after year, and how it was

surprising the amount of gold you could collect from teeth, which of course
had to be removed before the crematorium but would that be after the gas
chamber or before?[167]

That Gellhorn could envisage a response bed-ridden and 'babbling' indicates that the calmness of the previous account was a deliberate textual
strategy which took no little personal effort to achieve.[168] The point is
that, just as the gaze falters, the tonal control slips: indeed, paradoxically,
it seems to be the very practice of tonal restraint which catalyses the emotional response. The following section looks at the points at which the
'walking tape recorder with eyes' blinks, and is replaced by a very human
presence: angry, emotional, sentimental.

At the outset, it is worth quoting remarks Gellhorn made at a 1996
round-table discussion organised by the Freedom Forum European Centre:

> The thing about objectivity absolutely fascinates me. The assumption being
> that the reporter is made of plastic or something of the sort, and has no
> reaction to anything.
>
> You know, you're supposed to see death and destruction and just regard
> that as if you have no opinion about it. I find that absolutely mad. I don't
> see how any human being, male or female, cannot react to what it sees, and
> we react emotionally, not only intellectually, both.
>
> I mean obviously sentimentality has to be avoided, but the idea that there
> is such a thing as total objectivity assumes that the human being has no feel-
> ings, has no reaction to anything and is totally cold to anything it sees,
> which I find impossible, I mean subhuman, not normal, so all they're trying
> I suppose to have you do is not be totally on one side or the other, maybe
> that's what they mean by objectivity.
>
> But of course emotional reactions are valid. They're valid in the reporter,
> they're valid in the writing and they're valid in the reader or the viewer, and
> it would seem to be very useful in fact to use them, to work on them in order
> to evoke in people sympathy, and sympathy is I suppose a subjective feeling.[169]

These comments make the link between sympathy and spectacle.[170] For
the reporter, this is direct observation; for the reader, an imaginative pro-
jection dependent upon vivid evocation (the *hypotyposis* trope).
Sympathy was crucial to Gellhorn's practice and poesis: another 'blink'
of the walking tape-recorder's eye.

'Blinks'

Gellhorn was 'pessimistic that her reports would change policies,'
according to her brother, Alfred, 'but she was passionate that "the
record" be kept. [. . .] She also wanted her distress and disgust with
the power crazed heads of government who instigated or sanctioned

organized murder to be loudly heard.'[171] But in the course of maintaining the level tone necessary for the proper 'keeping of the record', Gellhorn's 'distress and disgust', as well as her partisanship, on occasion show through. The word 'disgust' is significant. These angry explosions through the surface of textual equanimity are akin to the reactions to confrontation with the abject (in particular the corpse) described by Julia Kristeva: 'spasmes et vomissements qui me protègent'.[172] The spastic response is, then, another defence mechanism.

Such spasms, or 'blinks', have at times been regarded as peculiarly feminine,[173] even by women journalists themselves. At the 1996 discussion mentioned above, a female BBC editor argued that male journalists have a resistance to emotional subjects which female journalists lack;[174] another woman reporter suggested that women have greater 'genetic compassion'.[175] But it was also noted that such perceptions might be gender assumptions. Kate Adie observed 'an automatic suspicion that if women are working on a story, that you are going for the soft underbelly of the story and you have somehow come back in a ragged emotional state, unable to cope with the rigours of professional journalistic standards'.[176] A further speaker noted that the 'humanisation' of war reporting is called the 'feminisation' of war reporting.[177] The gendering of war reportage is discussed more fully in the next chapter but here it can be registered that tone itself has gender connotations.

Anger is the principal emotion governing Gellhorn's war prose. For the most part, she conveys her wrath through cold irony, but 'Obituary of a Democracy' is a good example of a piece where volcanic rage erupts through this tonal crust. The Munich Pact, she told Eleanor Roosevelt, made her 'so angry and so disgusted that I feel a little dazed'.[178] The article on Czechoslovakia's betrayal is uncompromising. Gellhorn makes her usual attempt to present the facts in a controlled way. But her anger mounts: 'it cost four million dollars a day to mobilize the army, and now it is going home'.[179] At the frontier, she says simply, 'You couldn't believe it: it didn't make any sense.'[180] The outburst finally comes:

> I can tell you stories about beatings and brandings and executions with names and addresses attached to them. [. . .] I've seen an old man with his front teeth knocked out and his ribs almost showing through a mess of red meat on his side and his arms black and swollen from the beatings, and I can't bear to hear any more.[181]

Even as her rage breaks out, Gellhorn works to control it, turning to look over a fence to a calming, rural view. But the 'blink' registers, its impact increased by the tension engendered by its suppression.

These spasms of rage are not the only 'blinks'. Gellhorn's belief that it was her 'duty', even 'mission',[182] to record meant that she agonised about what she produced, going over her work again and again.[183] This practice of intense re-writing was possible, however, not for her original *Collier's* pieces, which had to be finished in a relatively short space of time, but only for her collected pieces, the linking sections in the collections and her fiction.[184] It is in these latter incarnations that, the immediate context past, the impression is strongest that Gellhorn felt she was writing 'history',[185] for 'the record' – specifically against the Bomb – and there are two tonal results. The first is a tendency to sentimentalise, the second to moralise.

The Face of War provides examples. On 18 February 1959, Gellhorn wrote to Bernard Berenson that she had finished the first draft: 'now the rewriting will start'.[186] Six months previously, she had told him:

> I have been doing a book [. . .] obsessed, sweating, haunted, and bowed daily over one's typewriter. [. . .] I selected some 20 articles from all my war reporting (from four different wars), tidied up the worst grammar, cut out the worst long-windedness, and wrote introductions to each war [. . .]. I am calling this book 'The Face of War'.[187]

'Hacking away' at this task had taken her 'the last five or more months, but steadily and fiercely in the last six weeks'.[188] In her Introduction to the published (1959) edition, she stated that the collected articles were:

> Reprinted as originally published except: where the grammar was so snarled as to be meaningless, I tidied it a bit; where hasty repetition of words became too irritating, I found some variations; where extraneous material or the long-windedness of those who write too fast was a real interference, I cut. As any reader will see, this was the lightest, quickest first-aid job.[189]

'The lightest, quickest first-aid job' is a something of an understatement: the variants between the original and collected articles run, in each case, into the hundreds. The 'rewriting', as Gellhorn's letters to Berenson suggest, was intense. The account of Dachau is a good example to focus on in detail as it occurs in original *Collier's* form (as 'Dachau: Experimental Murder'),[190] in *The Face of War* (as the more resonant synecdoche, 'Dachau') and in *Point of No Return*. Gellhorn herself stated that, in the collected piece, she 'inserted ten sentences'.[191] In fact, there are some 165 variants between this version and the original. Many of these are accidentals but there are also significant substantives.[192] Here, for example, is 'Dachau: Experimental Murder' on the crematoria:

> We have all seen the dead like bundles lying on all the roads of half the earth, but nowhere was there anything like this.[193]

Refuting Gellhorn's claim that she 'cut' long-windedness, in 'Dachau', this becomes:

> We have all seen a great deal now; we have seen too many wars and too much violent dying; we have seen hospitals, bloody and messy as butcher shops; we have seen the dead like bundles lying on all the roads of half the earth. But nowhere was there anything like this.[194]

In *Point of No Return*, the same piles of bodies are described thus:

> On the right was the pile of prisoners, naked, putrefying, yellow skeletons. There was just enough flesh to melt and make this smell, in the sun. The pile was as high as a small house. On the left was a mound of S.S. troopers, dressed in their black uniforms, and looking like giants compared to the faggots of the Dachau dead.[195]

And here is Jacob Levy's considered reaction to them:

> He thought the war was a good thing and he would write and tell Poppa so. They did not make the war because of Dachau; if they had, he would certainly have heard about Dachau long ago. But in the end, they reached it. And the S.S. guards were there, piled up dead in a mound; and their dogs were dead. So the war was a good thing.[196]

The simple declarative sentence of the original version becomes, in the collected piece, something more ornate: the anaphoric accumulation (the repeated 'we have seen . . .') creates, even in a few clauses, an emotional crescendo effect. Reserve and rectitude turn into their opposites: more 'writerly', the impact is paradoxically less sure. Notably, both versions are 'ekphrastic' in that they connote an absent image: the reader is told what the bodies are *not* like. In the novel, by contrast, the scene is given concrete particulars: colours, smells, dimensions. But the last-quoted passage, Jacob's definitive comment on Dachau, has, again, the strength of Gellhorn's most direct prose. 'So the war was a good thing' captures a certain crazed simplicity redolent of a traumatised mind.

The linking passages in *The Face of War* also contain writing of which the following is typical:

> Before any city was cleaned of its rubble and made whole, before the remnants of a tortured people found their home in Israel, before the last already forgotten burned pilot had suffered the last stitching skin graft, the human race was busy hating and fearing again, and growing new cancers. [. . .] If we will not learn, is there any hope for us? The answer is that we cannot help hoping; we do not control it. We are given a supply which only runs out in death, perhaps because each one of us knows love, the source of hope.[197]

Gellhorn seems here to have adopted the role of public conscience, even seer: in this persona, a certain pomposity begins to creep into her statements. She acknowledged as much herself, writing to Bernard Berenson that *The Face of War* would not 'please anyone', that the links were 'heavy, angry, moralizing introductions, which will bore, irritate and embarrass everyone'.[198] 'It is hard,' she confessed in the general introduction, 'not to sound like a harangue, not to boom or squeak.'[199] This public voice, moreover – monitory, counselling – has the effect of cancelling out authorial effacement. In place of the dispassionate, unflinching, all-seeing 'walking tape recorder with eyes' is the human reporter, disgusted and enraged by what she has seen. The next section provides a brief introduction to the figure of the eye-witness, crucial to war literature and to Gellhorn's work in particular.

The eye-witness

The implied contract between eye-witness reporter and reader ('you can believe it because I saw it happen') is one of enormous potency. In English law, it underpins the type of evidence known as 'direct testimony' (as opposed to hearsay): 'a witness's statement that he perceived a fact in issue [. . .] with one of his five senses, [i]n other words, [. . .] testimony relating to facts of which the witness has or claims to have personal or first-hand knowledge.'[200] Trials are one kind of staging of 'crises of truth': in historical contexts, the eye-witness bears an awesome responsibility not only to, but on behalf of, others.[201]

The term 'witness' itself is fruitfully polysemic. The *OED* gives various definitions: 'attestation'; 'the action or condition of being an observer of an event'; 'testimony'; 'evidential mark or sign, a token'; 'a manuscript or early version which is regarded as evidence of authority for the text' (a kind of copy-text – Martha Gellhorn's on-the-spot scribblings, perhaps, as opposed to the versions of her articles which appear in her collections?); 'one who testifies for Christ [. . .] esp[ecially] by death, a martyr'; 'to be present as an observer at; to see with one's own eyes'.[202] The multiplying connotations are of authenticity, presence, truth, proof, verification. In religious terms, 'to witness' signifies, *inter alia*, to bear faith, particularly by martyrdom, but the earliest biblical 'witnesses' were stones or pillars used to demarcate territory[203] – a nice instance of a witness creating, as well as observing, the subject space. The religious connotations of witnessing also underline the fact that the *ethos*[204] of the speaker or writer (named by Aristotle in 'The Art of Rhetoric' as the first 'proof' by which speech may be guaranteed)[205] assumes tremendous importance. Whether the witness can be an actor-in-events is debatable, but in every sense, the presence of the figure as onlooker is assumed.

The image and aesthetic were present in Depression literature: in wartime, they became more vital than ever. Gellhorn's *Collier's* predecessor, Frederick Palmer, chose as the epigraph to his war memoirs, *With My Own Eyes* (1934), Plautus's 'one eyewitness is worth ten hearsays',[206] while in *his* memoirs, *More Than Meets the Eye* (1961), *Collier's* photographer Carl Mydans noted, 'the camera must always be there'.[207] In *Eyewitness in Abyssinia* (1937), the *New York Times* reporter Herbert Matthews stated: 'I know that the accounts of the battles which I sent my paper were correct, for the simple reason that I saw [. . .] them with my own eyes.'[208] This was corroborated by Joris Ivens in *The Camera and I* (1969): 'Matthews never believed anything he had not seen with his own eyes.'[209] Indeed, such was the accepted importance of the eyewitness account that it even gained satirical treatment in Evelyn Waugh's *Scoop* (1948). When reluctant reporter-to-be William Boot asks his editor if going to war-torn Ishmaelia 'mightn't be rather dangerous?', he is told:

> 'You'll be surprised to find how far the war correspondents keep from the fighting. Why Hitchcock reported the whole Abyssinian campaign from Asmara and gave us some of the most colourful, eye-witness stuff we ever printed.'[210]

This comic example makes a serious point: eye-witness testimony is a construct, or set of stylistic conventions, as much as an epistemology, even when not assembled with such blatant artificiality as this. As Michel de Certeau puts it:

> The modern age, which first arose out of a methodic effort of observation and accuracy that struggled against credulity and based itself on a contract between the seen and the real, now transforms this relation and offers to *sight* precisely what must be *believed*.[211]

In other words, citing the fact that someone has seen something produces an overwhelming obligation to believe.

Undermining this obligation is scientific research into the psychology of eye-witnessing: 'interventions' such as the provision of misinformation can affect the mental process of retrieval.[212] More significantly, the research shows that a witness's confidence in his or her recall has only a weak correlation with its actual accuracy. None the less, such confidence greatly increases others' belief in the witness (another legitimation for the second way of telling).[213] But despite the psychological evidence, 'seeing is believing', the mother of all truth tropes, retains great force in war literature. Moving on from self-effacing objectivity, the next chapter considers the significance, in field and text, of 'being there' to see.

Notes

1 *FoW* 44.
2 'Real War Pictures and the Other Kind', *Collier's* (26 January 1918) 12–13.
3 Most famous, of course, in Christopher Isherwood's formulation in *Goodbye to Berlin* (1939): 'I am a camera with its shutter open, quite passive, recording, not thinking' (Isherwood, Christopher, *The Berlin Novels* (London: Vintage, 1999) 243).
4 Storm Jameson wrote in *FACT* in 1937: 'As the photographer does, so must the writer keep himself out of the picture [. . .]. The emotion [. . .] must not be squeezed from it by the writer, running forward with a, "When I saw this, I felt, I suffered, I rejoiced" ' (Jameson, Storm, 'Documents', *FACT* (15 July 1937) 9–18: 15–16).
5 *FoW* 44.
6 Smith, Anthony, 'The Long Road to Objectivity and Back Again: The Kinds of Truth We Get in Journalism', *Newspaper History from the Seventeenth Century to the Present Day*, ed. Bryce, George, Curran, James and Wright, Pauline (London: Constable, 1978) 153–71: 152.
7 Sebald, W. G., *On the Natural History of Destruction*, trans. Bell, Anthea (London: Hamish Hamilton, 2003) 53.
8 McKeon, Michael, *The Origins of the English Novel 1600–1740* (London: Radius, 1988) 46.
9 Davis, Lennard J., *Factual Fictions: The Origins of the English Novel* (New York: Columbia University Press, 1983) 71.
10 Davis, *Factual Fictions*, 71.
11 Smith, 'The Long Road to Objectivity', 158.
12 Quoted in Smith, 'The Long Road to Objectivity', 159.
13 Smith, 'The Long Road to Objectivity', 162.
14 The telegraph was invented by Samuel Morse in 1844 and the Atlantic cable was laid in 1866 (Hohenberg, John, *Foreign Correspondence. The Great Reporters and Their Times* (New York and London: Columbia University Press, 1967) 14, 16).
15 Schudson, Michael, *Discovering the News: A Social History of American Newspapers* (New York: Basic Books, 1978) 4.
16 McNair, Brian, *News and Journalism in the UK* (London: Routledge, 1999) 31.
17 Haraway, Donna, 'A Manifesto for Cyborgs: Science, Technology, and Socialist Feminism in the 1980s', *The Haraway Reader* (New York and London: Routledge, 2004) 7–45: 25.
18 Frus, Phyllis, *The Politics and Poetics of Journalistic Narrative* (Cambridge: Cambridge University Press, 1994) 67.
19 Schudson, *Discovering the News* 7.

20 Inglis, Fred, *People's Witness. The Journalist in Modern Politics* (New Haven and London: Yale University Press, 2002) 46.

21 Levine, Lawrence W., *Highbrow/Lowbrow. The Emergence of Cultural Hierarchy in America* (Cambridge, Mass., and London: Harvard University Press, 1988) 83–168. Gellhorn herself revealed something of this attitude when she told Eleanor Roosevelt that reviews describing *The Trouble I've Seen* as journalism 'nearly broke my heart' (letter of 1/2 November 1941, f. 1r). A decade later, receiving the same criticism for *The Honeyed Peace*, she confided to Bernard Berenson, 'having considered myself a story teller all my life, I am beginning to wonder' (Gellhorn, letter of 11 September 1953, f. 1v); 'I begin [. . .] to wonder whether I am a teller of stories at all?' (*SL* 244).

22 Howells, William Dean, *Literature and Life* (New York: Harper, 1902) 3, 2.

23 Robertson, Michael, *Stephen Crane, Journalism, and the Making of Modern American Literature* (New York and Chichester: Columbia University Press, 1997) 21, 39, 40.

24 James, Henry, *The Bostonians* (London: The Bodley Head, 1967) 334.

25 James, *The Bostonians* 334.

26 Schudson, *Discovering the News* 148.

27 The word was in 'common parlance' by that decade (Schudson, *Discovering the News* 156).

28 Otherwise known as the *amplificatio* topos of classical rhetoric; Henry James's 'solidity of specification' (James, Henry, *The Art of Fiction and Other Essays* (New York: Oxford University Press, 1948) 11); and Roland Barthes's '*notations*', structurally superfluous details, which add up to the 'reality effect' (Barthes, Roland, 'The Reality Effect', *French Literary Theory Today*, ed. Todorov, Tzvetan, trans. Carter, R. (New York: Cambridge University Press, 1982) 11–17: 11, 15).

29 Tuchman, Gaye, 'Objectivity as Strategic Ritual: An Examination of Newsmen's Notions of Objectivity', *American Journal of Sociology*, 77/4 (1972) 660–79: 663, 676.

30 Knightley, Phillip, *The First Casualty. The War Correspondent as Hero and Myth-Maker from the Crimea to Kosovo* (London: Prion Books, 2000) 352.

31 Boorstin, Daniel J., *The Image* (London: Weidenfeld and Nicolson, 1961) 9.

32 According to Frus, news management in war goes even beyond the 'pseudo-event' (Frus, *The Politics and Poetics of Journalistic Narrative*, xv).

33 Sebald, *On the Natural History of Destruction*, 25–6.

34 *PNR* 23.

35 Fussell, Paul, *Wartime. Understanding and Behaviour in the Second World War* (Oxford: Oxford University Press, 1989) 270.

36 See Rawlinson, Mark, *British Writing of the Second World War* (Oxford: The Clarendon Press, 2000) 12.

37 Shay, Jonathan, *Achilles in Vietnam: Combat Trauma and the Undoing of Character* (New York and London: Simon & Schuster Touchstone, 1995) 4, 55, 188–92. It should simultaneously be noted that some combatants would reject a 'talking cure', preferring the option of *not* relating their experiences.
38 Tritle, Lawrence A., *From Melos to My Lai: War and Survival* (London, New York: Routledge, 2000) 69.
39 Homer, *The Iliad* Bk VIII, ll. 521–2.
40 Sebald, *On the Natural History of Destruction*, 26.
41 Carey, James W., *Communication as Culture: Essays on Media and Society* (Winchester, Mass., and London: Unwin Hyman, 1989) 5, 18.
42 Doherty, Thomas, *Projections of War. Hollywood, American Culture, and World War II* (New York: Columbia University Press, 1993) 34.
43 Frus, *The Politics and Poetics of Journalistic Narrative*, vi.
44 Gellhorn in Pilger, 'The Outsiders', broadcast interview, 1983.
45 Gellhorn in Pilger, 'The Outsiders', broadcast interview, 1983.
46 Boycott, Rosie, 'We Drank and Smoked, I Was One of Her Chaps', *The Times* (20 September 2003) 10–11: 10.
47 Quoted in Moorehead, Caroline, *Martha Gellhorn: A Life* (London: Chatto & Windus, 2003) 6.
48 Quoted in Ferrari, Michelle, compiler, *Reporting America at War. An Oral History*, commentary by Tobin, James (New York: Hyperion, 2003) 40.
49 Quoted in Lyman, Rick, 'Obituary', *New York Times* (17 February 1998) B11, and 'Obituaries – Martha Gellhorn', 17 February 1998, 23.
50 Nicolson, Nigel, 'A Woman at the Wars', *New Statesman* LVIII 1492 (17 October 1959) 517–18: 517.
51 Gellhorn, 'Obituary of a Democracy', *Collier's* (10 December 1938) 12–13, 28, 32–3, 36: 33.
52 *FoW* 1.
53 *FoW* 2.
54 *FoW* 2.
55 As Storm Jameson had recommended: 'there is no need to record them [the writer's emotions]. Let him go and pour them down the drain' (Jameson, 'Documents' 12, 15–16).
56 Letter to Betsy Drake of 15 January 1972: *SL* 378.
57 *FoW* 1998 381, 382.
58 'Editors Condemn Nazis' Brutality', *New York Times* (6 May 1945) 8.
59 Carpenter, Iris, *No Woman's World* (Boston: Houghton Mifflin, 1946) 303.
60 White, William S., 'War Crimes Report Horrifies Capital', *New York Times* (16 May 1945) 10.
61 Gellhorn, 'The Paths of Glory', *Collier's* (9 November 1946) 21, 74–6: 21.
62 Gellhorn, 'The Paths of Glory', 9 November 1946, 74.
63 Gellhorn, 'The Paths of Glory', 9 November 1946, 74.
64 Gellhorn, 'The Paths of Glory', 9 November 1946, 76.
65 Gellhorn, 'Dachau: Experimental Murder', *Collier's* (23 June 1945) 16, 28, 30: 16.

66 WoA 277–8.
67 SF 21.
68 SF 210.
69 SF 280.
70 SF 284.
71 Lassner, Phyllis, 'Camp follower of Catastrophe': Martha Gellhorn's World War II Challenge to the Modernist War', *Modern Fiction Studies*, 44/3 (Fall 1998), 799.
72 Gellhorn, 17 July 1953, f. 1v.
73 Gellhorn, 17 July 1953, f. 1v. 'Frosh' is North American slang for a college freshman (*OED* 2); 'sopher' is most likely slang for 'sophomore'.
74 That these might also be the defining characteristics of Hemingway's style is explored further below.
75 Gellhorn, letter to Bernard Berenson, 8 August 195?, f. 1r.
76 Gellhorn, letter of 30 October 1969, f. 3r. This appears in *SL* at 357–8 but the quoted remark is omitted.
77 This refers to Gellhorn's 'Slow Boat to War' (*Collier's* (6 January 1940) 10–12, 45).
78 Gellhorn, 20 December 1940, f. 1r.
79 *SL* 63. She is most probably referring to 'Guns Against France' (*Collier's* (8 October 1938) 14–15, 34, 36–7).
80 Gellhorn, letter to Sandy Gellhorn, 13 November 1969, f. 34r.
81 Gellhorn, letter of 13 May 1950, f. 1v.
82 Gellhorn, letter of 25 April 1953, f. 1v.
83 Gellhorn, letter of 15 March 1954, f. 2r.
84 Gellhorn, letter of 30 March 1954, f. 1r.
85 Gellhorn, letter of 14 December 1955, f. 1r.
86 Gellhorn, letter of 14 March 1956, f. 1v.
87 Gellhorn, letter of 8 January 1959, f. 1r.
88 Gellhorn, letter of 12 December ?1959, f. 1v.
89 Gellhorn, letter of 12 December ?1959, f. 3r.
90 Gellhorn, letter of 12 December ?1959, f. 3r.
91 Gellhorn, letter of 14 November ?1959, f. 2r.
92 Gellhorn, letter of 12 December ?1959, f. 3r.
93 Gellhorn, letter of 27 December 1953, f. 1v.
94 Gellhorn, letter of 23 March 1956, f. 1v.
95 Gellhorn, letter of 4 October 1957, f. 2r.
96 Gellhorn, letter of 4 October 1957, f. 2r.
97 Gellhorn, undated letter, f. 2v.
98 Gellhorn, letter of 6 September 1956, f. 2v.
99 Gellhorn, letter of 10 March 195?, f. 2v.
100 Gellhorn, letter of 17 May 1944 to Hortense Flexner: *SL* 163.
101 Gellhorn, letter of 17 October 1941 to Max Perkins: *SL* 118–19.
102 Gellhorn, letter to Sandy Gellhorn, 13 November 1969, f. 34r.
103 Gellhorn, letter to Allen Grover, 14 July 1943, f. 2r.

104 Gellhorn, advertisement for Hans Habe's *A Thousand Shall Fall*, *New York Times* (27 August 1941) 17. This was a memoir of Habe's experiences in the 21st Foreign Volunteers Regiment, The Twelfth Army (Habe, Hans, *A Thousand Shall Fall* (London: George Harrap, 1942) 7).
105 Gellhorn, 'Saturday at Creve Coeur', undated, 2.
106 Gellhorn, letters to Eleanor Roosevelt of 24/25 April 1938 and Nelson Algren of 24 June 1942: *SL* 60, 129.
107 Email to author, 1 December 2003.
108 Interview with Caroline Moorehead, Alan Moorehead's daughter, by the author, 4 December 2003. The two met in Italy during the war.
109 Moorehead, Alan, *Eclipse* (London: Granta, 2000) 38. Moorehead had, according to his compatriot, Phillip Knightley, 'the detachment of being Australian'. He also, like Gellhorn, 'went vertually [*sic*] where he liked, following what he considered to be the story, forging his own fame, seeking his own destiny' (Knightley, Phillip, 'Introduction', *Eclipse* by Moorehead, Alan (London: Granta, 2000) xiii–xvii: xv).
110 Gellhorn, letter of 17 October 1941 to Max Perkins: *SL* 118.
111 Quoted in Ferrari, *Reporting America at War*, 37–8.
112 Moorehead, *Martha Gellhorn*, 126.
113 Letter to Hortense Flexner, 'Saturday' (no month or year given), f. 2r. Gellhorn first mentions Hemingway's style in a letter to Bertrand de Jouvenel in 1930 (*SL* 7–8).
114 The draft *For Whom the Bell Tolls*.
115 Gellhorn, letter to Hortense Flexner, 8 June 1940 (*SL* 93). She went on to call *Green Hills of Africa* 'lamentable' (Gellhorn, letter to Bernard Berenson, 14 April 1954, f. 1v): 'not funny only mean, not straight only pompous and the boasts come out in the sneering tone' (f. 1r). Hemingway himself intimated that Gellhorn had learned from him (Hemingway, letter to Bernard Berenson, 27 May 1953, f. 2r; exact words cannot be quoted for copyright reasons). In another letter to Berenson (9 July 1955), he enclosed a cutting of Gellhorn's short story 'The Smell of Lilies' from the *Atlantic Monthly* (August 1956), which he had extensively annotated, criticising and mocking her style – again, it is not legally possible to quote from it.
116 Weber, Ronald, *Hemingway's Art of Non-Fiction* (Basingstoke: Macmillan, 1990) 6. Another thesis is that it was *radio* broadcasting, developed in the 1920s, which honed the style of short sentences and simple vocabulary (Stephens, Mitchell, *A History of News* (Fort Worth: Harcourt Brace, 1997) 271).
117 Hemingway, Ernest, *Ernest Hemingway, Cub Reporter*, ed. Bruccoli, Matthew J. (Pittsburgh: University of Pittsburgh, 1970) 28.
118 Hemingway, *Ernest Hemingway, Cub Reporter*, 31.
119 Robertson, *Stephen Crane*, 202.
120 Hemingway, Ernest, *In Our Time* (London: Jonathan Cape, 1926) 27.
121 Hemingway, Ernest, *Dateline: Toronto. The Complete 'Toronto Star' Dispatches, 1920–1924*, ed. White, William (New York: Scribner, 1985) 101.

122 Gellhorn, 'Night Life in the Sky', *Collier's* (17 March 1945) 18–19, 31: 31.

123 Gellhorn, 'Rudy Vallée: God's Gift to Us Girls', *New Republic* LIX 766 (7 August 1929) 310–11: 311.

124 Hemingway, Ernest, 'The G.I. and the General', *Collier's* (4 November 1944) 11, 46–7: 11. With its co-ordinating conjunctions and accumulated clauses, this could be the opening of *A Farewell to Arms* (1929): 'In the late summer of that year we lived in a house in a village that looked across the river and the plain to the mountains' (Hemingway, Ernest, *A Farewell to Arms* (London: Vintage, 1999) 1).

125 Gellhorn, 'Cracking the Gothic Line', *Collier's* (28 October 1944) 24, 57–8: 24.

126 *FoW* 166.

127 *FoW* 5.

128 This was, incidentally, the general tonal atmosphere of contemporary publications. The *New York Times* of the late war period is remarkable for the number of advertisements it carried for black clothing: 'Abraham & Straus. Everlasting Lure of Black', *New York Times* (6 May 1945) 16; 'B. Altman & Co. Summer Black', *New York Times* (6 May 1945) 9; and 'Russel's. Your Coat in Black Persian', *New York Times* (6 May 1945) 6 in a single issue.

129 *SF* 300.

130 Gellhorn, 'Dachau: Experimental Murder', 23 June 1945, 16.

131 Gellhorn, 'Dachau: Experimental Murder', 23 June 1945, 16.

132 *WoA* 272.

133 *WoA* 276.

134 *WoA* 278.

135 *WoA* 273.

136 *WoA* 284.

137 Hughes, Robert, 'The Unflinching Eye', *Guardian* (4 October 2003) 4–6: 4. Gellhorn herself said of Goya's etchings, 'what wonders they are' (Gellhorn, letter to Eleanor Roosevelt, 3 December 1938, f. 2r).

138 Moorehead, *Eclipse* 254.

139 Moorehead, *Eclipse* 255.

140 Moorehead, *Eclipse* 255.

141 'Camp Horror Films Are Exhibited Here', *New York Times* (2 May 1945) 3.

142 'Dachau Captured by Americans Who Kill Guards, Liberate 32,000', *New York Times* (1 May 1945) 1, 5.

143 The article reappeared, in condensed form, in the review of the week's news on Sunday, 6 May 1945 ('Story of Dachau', *New York Times* (6 May 1945) E2). There were also short pieces on the camps on 6, 14 and 16 May ('Editors Condemn Nazis' Brutality', *New York Times* (6 May 1945) 8; 'Nazi Horrors Told by Saltonstall', *New York Times* (14 May 1945) 3; White, William S., 'War Crimes Report Horrifies Capital').

144 'Wedding Rings of Buchenwald Victims', *New York Times* (11 May 1945) 6.

145 Sulzberger, C. L., 'Oswiecim Killings Placed at 4,000,000', *New York Times* (8 May 1945) 12.

146 *WMP* 36.

147 *FoW* 8.

148 *FoW* 1, 2.

149 *SF* preliminary pages. The epigraph was written by Ernest Hemingway because Gellhorn could not find the passage she was looking for in Thucydides' *History of the Peloponnesian War* (Hemingway, Ernest, *The Only Thing That Counts. The Ernest Hemingway - Maxwell Perkins Correspondence*, ed. Bruccoli, Matthew J. (New York: Scribner, 1996) 327). The present author would take issue with Jean Gallagher's account of the disrupted female gaze in *SF* (Gallagher, Jean, *The World Wars Through the Female Gaze* (Carbondale and Edwardsville: Southern Illinois University Press, 1998)): the novel is peculiarly clear-sighted.

150 Gellhorn, 'The Wounds of Paris', *Collier's* (4 November 1944) 72, 74: 74.

151 Quoted in Moeller, Susan D., *Shooting War: Photography and the American Experience of Combat* (New York: Basic Books, 1989) 209.

152 Gellhorn, 'Rough and Tumble', *Collier's* (2 December 1944) 12, 70: 70.

153 Gellhorn, letter of 12 March 1945, f. 1r

154 Porter, Amy, 'The Week's Work', *Collier's* (3 February 1945) 73.

155 Gellhorn, letter to Hortense Flexner, 20 December 1940, f. 1r. In a letter to her mother of 14 November 1944, she expressed the same sentiment: 'my horror about the war has gotten beyond the place where I can control it [. . .] every dead (*sic*) seems to be part of me, and I have a feeling of such absolute and terrible despair that I can scarcely handle it' (*SL* 172).

156 Porter, Amy, 'The Week's Work', 3 February 1945, 73.

157 Porter, Amy, 'The Week's Work', 3 February 1945, 73.

158 Gellhorn, 'Dachau: Experimental Murder', 23 June 1945, 28.

159 *FoW* 44, my emphasis.

160 Gellhorn, 'The Paths of Glory', 9 November 1946, 74.

161 Gellhorn, 'The Paths of Glory', 9 November 1946, 21.

162 Gellhorn, 'The Paths of Glory', 9 November 1946, 21.

163 Carpenter, *No Woman's World*, 50–1.

164 Carpenter, *No Woman's World*, 147.

165 *FoW* 44. *Point of No Return* was, Gellhorn later said, an (unsuccessful) attempt to 'exorcise' Dachau (letter of 15 January 1972 to Betsy Drake (*SL* 378)).

166 'Death of a Dutch Town', *Collier's* (23 December 1944) 21, 58–9: 59.

167 *Novellas* 298.

168 Gellhorn was not alone in this. Alan Moorehead's account of Belsen contains the dispassionate sentence, 'There were many forms lying on the earth partly covered in rags, but it was not possible to say whether they were alive or dead or simply in the process of dying' (Moorehead, *Eclipse* 251). But later comes this: 'it seems a pity to give way to the downright childishness of saying that all Germans are natural black-hearted fiends capable of

murdering and torturing and starving people at the drop of a hat'
(Moorehead, *Eclipse*, 258) – of course, in the act of *not* giving way to the
sentiment, Moorehead nevertheless expresses it (the *paralipsis* topos). Iris
Carpenter, despite vowing only to document 'in the baldest statement of
plainest fact', none the less found herself giving a German hausfrau 'a very
full and brutal word-picture before I could regain my self-control'
(Carpenter, *No Woman's World*, 303, 308).

169 Freedom Forum European Centre, 'Freedom Forum Europe Pays Tribute
to Martha Gellhorn' (London: Freedom Forum European Centre,
1996) 4–5.

170 See Jaffe, Audrey, *Scenes of Sympathy: Identity and Representation in
Victorian Fiction* (Ithaca and London: Cornell University Press, 2000) and
Marshall, David, *The Surprising Effects of Sympathy: Marivaux, Diderot,
Rousseau, and Mary Shelley* (Chicago and London: University of Chicago,
1988).

171 Alfred Gellhorn, email to the author, 4 December 2003.

172 'Spasms and vomitings that protect me'. Kristeva, Julia, *Pouvoirs de l'horreur. Essais sur l'abjection* (Paris: Éditions du Seuil, 1980) 10.

173 Cf. Hemingway's 'Are ye maidens with your downcast eyes?' (*SF* preliminary pages), quoted above.

174 Freedom Forum European Centre, 3.

175 Freedom Forum European Centre, 7.

176 Freedom Forum European Centre, 4.

177 Freedom Forum European Centre, 6.

178 Gellhorn, letter to Eleanor Roosevelt, 19 October 1938, f. 1r.

179 Gellhorn, 'Obituary of a Democracy', 10 December 1938, 13.

180 Gellhorn, 'Obituary of a Democracy', 10 December 1938, 32.

181 Gellhorn, 'Obituary of a Democracy', 10 December 1938, 32.

182 Caroline Moorehead, interview, 4 December 2003.

183 Caroline Moorehead, interview, 4 December 2003.

184 'Everything I have ever written has come through journalism first [. . .]
since I have to see before I can imagine,' Gellhorn told Hemingway in a
letter of 13 December 1943 (*SL* 158).

185 *SF* 9.

186 Gellhorn, letter of 18 February 1959, f. 1r.

187 Gellhorn, letter of 17 August 1958, f. 1v.

188 Gellhorn, letter of 17 August 1958, f. 1v.

189 *FoW* 245.

190 Gellhorn, 'Dachau: Experimental Murder', 30.

191 *FoW* 245.

192 The following are some of the additions in 'Dachau': 'The Polish surgeon had
only his four front upper teeth left, the others on both sides having been
knocked out by a guard one day, because the guard felt like breaking teeth.
This act did not seem a matter of surprise to the doctor or to anyone else.
No brutality could surprise them any more. They were used to a systematic

cruelty that had gone on, in this concentration camp, for twelve years.';
'Now in the clean empty building a woman, alone in a cell, screamed for a
long time on one terrible note, was silent for a moment, and screamed again.
She had gone mad in the last few days; we came too late for her.'; 'What had
killed most of these people was hunger; starvation was simply routine. A
man worked those incredible hours on that diet and lived in such overcrowding as cannot be imagined, the bodies packed into airless barracks, and
woke each morning weaker, waiting for his death.'; 'The same half-naked
skeleton who had been dug out of the death train shuffled back into the
doctor's office. He said something in Polish; his voice was no stronger than
a whisper. The Polish doctor clapped his hands gently and said, "Bravo." I
asked what they were talking about.' (*FoW* 237, 238–9, 239, 241–2).

193 Gellhorn, 'Dachau: Experimental Murder', 23 June 1945, 30.
194 *FoW* 240.
195 *WoA* 284.
196 *WoA* 304–5.
197 *FoW* 243–4.
198 Gellhorn, 17 August 1958, f. 1r.
199 *FoW* 5.
200 Keane, Adrian, *The Modern Law of Evidence* 2nd edition (London:
     Butterworths, 1989) 8.
201 Felman, Shoshana, and Laub, Dori, *Testimony: Crises of Witnessing in
     Literature, Psychoanalysis, and History* (New York and London:
     Routledge, 1992) 6, 3.
202 As noun: 2a, 2b, 2d, 7, 7c, 8a; as verb: 4.
203 Genesis 31: 45–52. Similar boundary markers, quadrangular pillars topped
     with a bust (frequently of Hermes), were known in Greek as *hermae* (props
     or supports), completing the link with communication via the messenger
     god (see Crapanzano, Vincent, 'Hermes' Dilemma: The Making of
     Subversion in Ethnographic Description', *Writing Culture: The Poetics
     and Politics of Ethnography*, ed. Clifford, James and Marcus, George E.
     (Berkeley, Los Angeles and London: University of California, 1986)).
204 From the Greek *ethos* (character, a person's (moral) nature or disposition).
205 I.ii.3. Aristotle, 'The Art of Rhetoric', trans. Freese, John Henry (Loeb
     Classical Library) (London and Cambridge, Mass.: William Heinemann,
     1957) 16–17.
206 Palmer, Frederick, *With My Own Eyes. A Personal History of Battle Years*
     (London: Jarrolds, 1934) v. In *What Mad Pursuit*, Charis Day's fellow stu-
     dents are 'cribbing Plautus' (*WMP*, p. 7).
207 Mydans, Carl, *More Than Meets the Eye* (London: Hutchinson, 1961) 8.
208 Matthews, Herbert, *Eyewitness in Abyssinia. With Marshal Badoglio's
     Forces to Addis Ababa* (London: Martin Secker & Warburg, 1937) 15.
209 Ivens, Joris, *The Camera and I* (Berlin: Seven Seas Books, 1969) 112.
210 Waugh, Evelyn, *Scoop: A Novel About Journalists* (London: Chapman and
     Hall, 1948) 32.

211 De Certeau, Michel, *The Practice of Everyday Life* (Berkeley, Los Angeles and London: University of California, 1984) 186–7.

212 Hall, David F., Loftus, Elizabeth F. and Tousignant, James P., 'Postevent Information and Changes in Recollection for a Natural Event', *Eyewitness Testimony: Psychological Perspectives*, ed. Wells, Gary L. and Loftus, Elizabeth F. (Cambridge: Cambridge University Press, 1984) 124–41: 126.

213 Wells, Gary L. and Murray, Donna M., 'Eyewitness Confidence', *Eyewitness Testimony: Psychological Perspectives*, ed. Wells and Loftus (Cambridge: Cambridge University Press, 1984) 155–70: 165.

Being there: the field

'Perhaps,' mused Martha Gellhorn, 'it is impossible to understand any-thing truly unless it happened to you, yourself'.[1] American war report-ing up to the brink of the Second World War was a history of developments in communications technology aimed at getting the cor-respondent (and hence the reader) ever closer to the action. The ethics and aesthetics of the New Reportage demanded that the reporter gain personal experience of the subject matter. Philip Rahv, in a 1940 article, 'The Cult of Experience in American Writing', found the difference between European and American 'left-wing' writing of the 1930s, to be that the former comprised the expression of 'political ideas and beliefs', an intellectual project, while the latter comprised 'class war as an experience'.[2] 'Being There' was firmly established as the *sine qua non*. At the same time, it also raised the paradox with which the previ-ous chapter concluded: the subjectivity of presence undermines the 'objectivity' of empirical verification. Might it not, indeed, be possible to get *too* close?

The question helps to introduce the themes to be treated in this chapter and the next. 'Being there' is not just a matter of presence. It is also a question of *where*, precisely, to be, and how to get there, when to get there, and how close or distant (geographically, physically, polit-ically, emotionally) to place oneself in relation to the subject when one has arrived. The granting and gaining of access to conflict tends to disadvantage women war recorders, a phenomenon Martha Gellhorn experienced personally, particularly in her efforts, in rivalry with Hemingway, to gain entry – physically and discursively – to the D-Day beaches. Discussion of these complex theoretical points is, of necessity, lengthy, and Gellhorn's own positioning in the field and her competition with Hemingway are reserved for the chapter's final section.

Presence

A history of being there is coterminous with war recording. Given that this stretches over several millennia, only the briefest of examples can be given here, with the caveat that, while presence has always been a priority, the actual experience of access remains specific to each conflict. Writers with combatant experience range from Thucydides, Xenophon, Polybius, Arrian and Aeschylus to Stendhal at Waterloo and Tolstoy at Sevastopol to the First World War trench poets to the countless unknown soldiers who put their experiences into words. In his *History of the Peleponnesian War*, Thucydides gives an account of his methodology:

> With regard to my factual reporting of the events of the war I have made it a principle not to write down the first story that came my way, and not even to be guided by my own general impressions; either I was present myself at the events which I have described or else I heard of them from eye-witnesses whose reports I have checked with as much thoroughness as possible.[3]

This, of course, introduces a different position: here the war writer is not necessarily coincident with the combatant. 'Being there', it should be remembered, can connote not necessarily immersion in battle but close observation of it.

For non-combatant war writers, the premium is then on proximity. Shakespeare's war reporters – those figures who bring news of the trend of fortunes on the battle-field – enhance the status of their accounts by vouching for their presence at the scene which they describe.[4] In *II Henry IV*, for instance, Northumberland, hearing the (erroneous) information from Bardolph that the rebels' side is winning, asks anxiously: 'How is this deriv'd? Saw you the field?'[5] A 'certain lord, neat, and trimly dress'd', 'perfumed like a milliner' and holding his snuff-box to his nose to protect himself from the smell of the corpses,[6] is, when he attempts to interview Hotspur, given short shrift:

> He questioned me: amongst the rest, demanded
> My prisoners in your Majesty's behalf.
> I then, all smarting with my wounds being cold,
> To be so pest'red with a popinjay,
> Out of my grief and my impatience
> Answer'd neglectingly I know not what –
> He should, or he should not – for he made me mad
> To see him shine so brisk, and smell so sweet,
> And talk so like a waiting-gentlewoman
> Of guns, and drums, and wounds.[7]

This is also significant in terms of the gendering of war reporting. Here, the figure who reports on, but does not participate in, combat is effeminate, a 'waiting-gentlewoman', specifically contrasted with 'many a good tall fellow'.[8]

In the twentieth century, titles of journalists' memoirs from the First and Second World Wars continue to underline the great premium attached to being there: Richard Harding Davis, *With the Allies* (1915), *With the French in France & Salonika* (1916); Frank Palmer Sibley, *With the Yankee Division in France* (1919); Arthur Ruhl, *Antwerp to Gallipoli. A Year of War on Many Fronts – and Behind Them* (1916); Granville Fortescue, *At the Front with Three Armies. My Adventures in the Great War* (1914); Harold Ashton, *First from the Front* (1914); Charles H. Grasty, *Flashes from the Front* (1914); Frederick Palmer, *With My Own Eyes. A Personal History of Battle Years* (1934); M. N. Jeffries, *Front Everywhere* (1935); Herbert Matthews, *Eyewitness in Abyssinia. With Marshal Badoglio's Forces to Addis Ababa* (1937); and Ed Murrow, *This Is London* (1941). Statements and hard evidence of presence pepper these accounts (like those of the New Reportage) and are invariably used as advertising material by publishers. Frederick Palmer's *With My Own Eyes* features reproductions of a letter from Theodore Roosevelt by way of a 'passport' and of Palmer's 'credentials with the British Army'.[9] The end-pages of the book contain further authenticating detail:

> America's most famous War Correspondent [. . .] saw many wars before the World War [i.e. the First World War] – the Greco-Turkish in 1895, he was with the American troops throughout the Philippine conflict; saw the Spanish-American War; accompanied the Allied contingents [. . .] during the Boxer rebellion; endured the hardships and dangers of the unwelcome observer during the Russo-Japanese war; and watched, understood and described that usually insoluble mystery – warfare in the Balkans.[10]

The message is clear: experiencing war confers the authority to describe war (in Palmer's case, it also conferred the authority to censor war). Sixty years later, the blurb on BBC reporter John Simpson's memoirs, *Strange Places, Questionable People* (1998), was making similar claims: 'from being punched in the stomach by Harold Wilson [. . .], to escaping summary execution in Beirut, flying into Teheran with the returning Ayatollah Khomeini, and narrowly avoiding entrapment by a beautiful Czech secret agent, John Simpson has had an astonishingly eventful career'.[11]

Presence continues to be significant: indeed 'being there' has recently itself become the subject of intense reporting (or 'meta-reporting'?) and a heavily politicised issue. The Second Gulf War inaugurated the term, if not the concept, 'embedded' journalism, with the US Armed Forces announcing on 3 March 2003:

> About 800 members of the press – including 20 percent from non-U.S. media – will be assigned slots in specific ground units, aviation units, ships and headquarters throughout the combat zone. They will remain 'embedded' with those units as long as they wish and are supposed to have what these Pentagon ground rules described as 'minimally restrictive' access to U.S. forces throughout their day.[12]

Eventually, out of the thousand journalists covering the war, around 660 were embedded with the American military and 150 with the British.[13] For some commentators, the result was that 'the coverage of certain aspects of the war was more detailed, because of the privileged access that these journalists were granted'[14] but this is disputed by, among others, John Simpson. Simpson preferred not to be an 'embed', noting that those embedded 'were beholden to those they had to report on'.[15] But *not* being embedded had other consequences. Nelson and Rose report:

> The Pentagon, in several meetings with editors, warned of the safety risks in covering a war. 'The battlefield's a dangerous place, and it's going to be a dangerous place even embedded with our forces. It will be even a more dangerous place, though, for reporters that are out there not in an embedded status,' said deputy Pentagon spokesman Bryan Whitman at a late February briefing.[16]

The implication is that non-embeds might actually be targeted by *coalition* forces. Many saw embedding as a means for the military to control the media, hence its institution and encouragement by the Pentagon.

Similar credentials have been demanded of the writer of war fiction. Ernest Hemingway wrote to Edmund Wilson on 25 November 1923, criticising Willa Cather's *One of Ours* (1922) for its lack of first-hand knowledge of combat. According to Hemingway, Cather had derived her final scene in the trenches from D. W. Griffiths's *Birth of a Nation*: 'I identified episode after episode. Catherized. Poor woman she had to get her experience from somewhere.'[17] Later, in the notorious *New Yorker* profile by Lillian Ross:

> He mentioned a war writer who, he said was apparently thinking of himself as a Tolstoy who'd be able to play Tolstoy only on the Bryn Mawr field-hockey team. 'He never hears a shot fired in anger, and he sets out to beat who? Tolstoy, an artillery officer who fought at Sevastopol, who knew his stuff, who was a hell of a man anywhere.'[18]

Presence combined with 'invention', Hemingway explained in *Men at War* (1942), produced the highest form of truth: 'A writer's job is to tell the truth. His statement of fidelity to the truth should be so high that his invention, out of his experience, should produce a truer account than anything factual can be.'[19] Later, in *Across the River and into the Trees* (1950), Colonel Cantwell comments, 'almost any liar writes more convincingly than a man who was there'.[20] Though convincingness is here associated with absence, the remark does again align presence with truth (as well as with maleness – 'a *man* who was there').

The link between presence and evocation confronted Hemingway directly in the critical reception of his Spanish Civil War texts *The Fifth Column* (1938) and *For Whom the Bell Tolls* (1940). Several reviewers found the former politically and experientially inauthentic.[21] *For Whom the Bell Tolls* drew an open letter, dated 20 November 1940 and forwarded to the *Daily Worker*, from Alvah Bessie, Milton Wolff and other Lincoln Brigade luminaries, containing charges of distortion and slander.[22] In the communist *Partisan Review*, Lionel Trilling invoked Rahv's 'Cult of Experience' essay to condemn Robert Jordan's death as 'devastatingly meaningless'. Hemingway, he wrote, had described the cynicism, intrigue and shabby vice of the Russian politicos, pointedly questioned the political virtue of La Pasionaria, painted André Marty as a homicidal psychopath under the protection of the Comintern, spoken out about the sins of the Loyalist leaders and shown only small and uncertain inclination to extenuate the special sins of the communists. Had Jordan been *intellectually* aware that all these things had contributed to his death, instead of merely 'experiencing' the badness, the novel should have 'truly represented the whole tragedy of the Spanish war'.[23] A diametrically opposed view was taken by Arturo Barea in *Horizon*. Listing the novel's 'grave linguistic-psychological mistakes', Barea concluded that its failure was due to the fact that: 'He [Hemingway] was always a spectator who wanted to be an actor, and who wanted to write as if he had been an actor. Yet it is not enough to look on: to write truthfully you must live and you must feel what you are living.'[24] Unsurprisingly, Hemingway reacted to such criticism by citing his extensive experience: 'I was in wars, commanded troops, was wounded etc. before you were dry behind the ears,' he told Milt Wolff.[25] As this chapter goes on to show, the 'veteran's perspective' was crucial not only to the poesis of his writings but also to his very self-construction.

'Being there' has been applied as a litmus-test not only to journalism and fiction about war but to *criticism* of those genres, as an exchange between Paul Fussell, Michael Walzer and Ian Clark makes clear. In his essay, 'Thank God for the Atom Bomb', Fussell, himself a Second World War veteran, argues that the bombing of Hiroshima and Nagasaki was a necessary and welcome end to the appalling experiences of hundreds of thousands of combatants. In 'An Exchange of Views', printed in the same collection, Walzer disagrees: 'with Fussell, seemingly there are no limits at all [. . .] the bombing was an act of terrorism'.[26] But it is Fussell's contention that the views of those who did not fight themselves are of an inferior order of validity. '*Pace* Fussell,' says Clark, entering the argument, 'moral judgement is not tied to direct experience. The gulf can be bridged by imagination and empathy.'[27] In his introduction to E. B. Sledge's *With the Old Breed at Peleliu and Okinawa* (1990), Fussell reprises his theme. Sledge's account is worthy because, as a combatant, he knows that bullets 'snap' whereas 'authors and screenwriters think they whine'. 'It is artillery shells that whine,' adds Fussell, 'while mortar shells whisper faintly'.[28] These additional details, not to be found in Sledge's description, make the point: not so much that Sledge knows war but that *Fussell*, a veteran like Sledge, does, and, by implication, is qualified to judge accounts of it. It is in this context that a distinguished writer on war like John Keegan feels obliged to open his *The Face of War* (1976): 'I have not been in a battle; nor near one, nor heard one from afar, nor seen the aftermath [. . .]. And I grow increasingly convinced that I have very little idea of what a battle can be like.'[29]

If 'being there' is important, it is even more important to be there *first*. The many legendary instances of priority trumping presence (or newsworthiness trumping epistemics) include Marguerite Duras reaching Dachau for the *Herald Tribune* before the American troops arrived; Doon Campbell getting first to the Normandy beaches for Reuters; Max Hastings of the *Evening Standard* walking first into Port Stanley in 1982; Bob McKeown making the first live broadcast (for CBS) from Kuwait City in 1991; Tim Marshall (Sky News) welcoming British forces into Pristina in 1999; and, in the Afghan War of 2002, John Simpson 'liberating' Kabul.[30] Journalists' memoirs frequently boast of scoops (a combination of getting there first and getting the news back first): Sefton Delmer, for instance, records his triumph in sending 'the first uncensored dispatch from a London staff reporter to cover the [Spanish] revolutionary scene' and notes that 'my report splashed on the front page was the first dispatch to be published by any British paper from the armies advancing on Madrid'.[31] To anticipate later discussion on the role of female war reporters, it is worth noting that 'women's firsts' form a subgenre of this phenomenon: Iris Carpenter remarks that she was 'one of the first women to land' on the first air-strip established by the Allies in

France.[32] Such 'firsts' themselves become the 'peg' or 'frame'[33] for the news material, transforming the reporter into the story.

Why is it so important to 'be there' at war? One suggestion is that battle is 'learned' through physical immersion: knowledge of war is, like sexual knowledge (or, more mundanely, the ability to ride a bicycle), 'acquired in the body'.[34] To write about war, therefore, becomes a right to be earned: as Jonathan Shay puts it, if a person is willing to experience 'some of the rage, terror, grief etc.', 'the combatant is less likely to shout, "You weren't there, so shut up!" '[35] To describe conflict without having earned this right can be perceived as a form of exploitation of others' suffering ('I do not know what category of sin that comes under,' remarks Hemingway's Colonel Cantwell)[36] or an affront to the principle met in Chapter 2 that war, because of its horrors, must be described as accurately as possible. The right may also be experienced as an obligation: John Simpson claims that journalists 'wanted to be there [in Iraq] as they felt it was their duty – this mattered more than their personal safety'.[37] According to Lawrence Tritle, there is a gulf of 'embarrassment' between those with combat experience and those without, accounting for the 'cryptic and elusive language' of relations of war which tells the listener that 'since you didn't participate [. . .] you must remain outside'.[38] This attitude, of course, serves to exclude women (traditionally non-combatants) from the art of true war representation. 'Being there' therefore becomes mystic knowledge, even myth.

The myth, however, can be challenged: the opposing argument is that the experiential gulf is fertile for creative exploitation. André Malraux learned of the fighting in Barcelona and Toledo from a distance, Victor Serge was never in Spain after 1917, Arturo Barea saw no combat, Picasso painted *Guernica* in Paris.[39] Stephen Spender commented on the last:

> *Guernica* is in no sense reportage; it is not a picture of some horror which Picasso has seen and has been through himself. It is the picture of a horror reported in the newspapers, of which he has read accounts and perhaps seen photographs.
> This kind of second-hand experience, from the newspapers, the news-reel, the wireless, is one of the dominating realities of our time. The many people who are not in direct contact with the disasters falling on civilization live in a waking nightmare of second-hand experience because the person overtaken by a disaster has at least a more limited vision than the camera's wide, cold, recording eye, and at least has no opportunity to imagine horrors worse than what he is seeing and experiencing.[40]

Imagining, or anticipating, 'horrors' is a property of Gothic, which exploits threat and the uncanniness of uncertainty, a prime example being Dickens's Newgate sketch of condemned men awaiting their execution.[41] The art of *not* being there, so conceived, might actually bring the viewer or reader closer to the essence of the experience.

Supporting this argument are the various (still faint) questionings of the authenticity of the survivor's viewpoint. To survive is itself an atypical combat experience: 'war is war only if it generates non-survivors'.[42] Moreover, as Robert Graves observed (perhaps defensively) in a letter to the *Times Literary Supplement* on 26 June 1930:

> But what is meant by the *truthfulness* of war books? [. . .] I would even paradoxically say that the memoirs of a man who went through some of the worst experiences of trench warfare are not truthful if they do not contain a high proportion of falsities. High explosive barrages will make a temporary liar or visionary of anyone.[43]

Examples can be given of combatants feeling obliged to revisit the field of battle, as though understanding can only be retrospective, when others have defined 'what happened', raising the possibility that war is in fact 'post war'. Stendhal's diffident Fabrizio del Dongo in *The Charterhouse of Parma* (1839) is comically unsure whether or not he has participated in the Battle of Waterloo:

> His chief sorrow was that he had not asked [. . .] 'Have I really taken part in a battle?' It seemed to him that he had, and he would have been supremely happy if he could have been certain of this. [. . .] Was what he had seen a real battle? And, if so, was that battle Waterloo? [. . .] He was always trying to find in the newspapers, or in published accounts of the battle, some description or other which would enable him to identify the ground he had covered.[44]

In *The Red Badge of Courage*, Stephen Crane's Henry Fleming has similar doubt about the status of his own combat experience: 'It suddenly occurred to the youth that the fight in which he had been, was, after all, but perfunctory popping. In the hearing of this present din he was doubtful if he had seen real battle scenes.'[45] Martha Gellhorn herself noted the phenomenon. 'It is remarkable how quickly soldiers start sight-seeing where they have fought,' she wrote, 'perhaps trying now to discover what really happened'.[46] Evelyn Hinz notes that Ovid's biological theory of genesis 'locates the agonistic principle within the human psyche', giving this as the explanation of why those who have never been in war can write about it 'so well'.[47] Psychologists working on trauma recall agree that it is not necessary to *possess* or *own* the truth in order effectively to bear witness to it.[48] The point here is not to undermine – or underestimate – the importance of 'being there' but to stress that 'presence' covers a continuum of engagement, including the imaginative.

Being where?

So, if the war recorder must 'be there', where (or what) exactly is 'there'? The answer seems to be 'the front', a word in itself suggestive of priority and precedence. The *OED* gives the definition 'the foremost line or part of an army or battalion',[49] but this is problematic. A line, conventionally figured, is without depth. It is possible to be in front of it (though this would involve the paradox of being in front of the front) or behind it but, unless a member of it, not 'within' it. Fortunately, the *OED* provides another, more helpful definition, a 'wider [in two senses] sense': 'the foremost part of the ground occupied, or in wider sense, of the field of operations; the part next the enemy'.[50] Thus re-configured (or widened), the front becomes not a line but a space – a space, indeed, with strategic and political significance ('next the enemy'), capable of being demarcated. Neatly enough, this must be a front with a back.

'The front', the locus of 'being there', is indeed a highly charged space, at once shifting and exclusive, delimited and self-regulating. In the light of these properties, an appropriate term for its construction and tendencies is 'pastoral'. The term, obviously, is intended here in a radical sense: the front is no Arcadia. None the less, it is 'a space apart' (a literal enclosure – battle, for the most part, takes place outdoors), a place where things are different, uncanny. As such, it resembles the type of Renaissance pastoral setting (often a wood) which is set against 'official' society (often the court) and which functions as a critique of it.[51] This is pastoral as ideology, the 'natural expression', in William Empson's words, 'for a sense of social injustice'.[52] In Empsonian terms, the front is educative space and elegy, proletarian (the ranks) and childlike (the language of the 'grunts'). Given that this version of the 'field' is as much political and experiential as physical, Helen Cooper's formulation of pastoral as 'a mode of thought'[53] well describes it. As the modernist geographer J. Nicholas Entrikin further explains, 'the geographical concept of place refers to an areal context of events, objects and actions, including natural elements and human constructions, both material and ideal [. . .] both a centre of meaning and the external context of our actions'.[54] In this configuration, place is kinetic rather than static. Mary Borden, a First World War nurse and writer of war sketches, used the apt term 'forbidden zone' for her writings because:

> The strip of land immediately behind the zone of fire where I was stationed went by that name in the French Army. We were moved up and down inside it; our hospital unit was shifted from Flanders to the Somme, then to Champagne, and then back again to Belgium, but we never left 'La Zone Interdite'.[55]

As this suggests, the 'front' is a shifting rather than a sta[ble]
experience. Furthermore, as each war's relation to its pre[decessor is]
an 'anxiety of influence' (like works in the literary canon)[, it is]
already imprinted with texts: the front is the locus of memo[ry and rep-]
resentation of past conflicts.[56] It is in, and in relation to, th[e]
front, that the war reporter sites himself or herself. Conse[quentl]y, it is
possible to see the reportorial figure as, like the shepherd,[57] both itinerant and liminal.

Crucially, the 'front' is also a gendered space. Daphne Spain expands
the concept: for her, 'women and men are spatially segregated in ways
that reduce women's access to knowledge and therefore reinforce their
lower status'.[58] Spain is here discussing the layout of American colleges
but the idea applies to war in general and the Second World War in particular: excluded from the combat zone, women lack knowledge of it –
to their obvious detriment as journalists. The next section considers the
various means by which women did gain access to this space.

The gendering of getting there

The gendering of war is ancient but not absolute. The idea that men are
from Mars, women are from Venus (or that fighting is a natural male
activity, domesticity a female) is paradigmatic[59] but, as Cooper, Munich
and Squier point out, obscures the real complexity of the issue, overlook-
ing both female aggressiveness and male tendencies to non-aggression.[60]
There are recorded instances since the seventeenth century of individual
women becoming soldiers, most often disguising their sex in masculine
attire.[61] Over 250 women fought in the American Civil War, though it is
thought that their service did not affect the outcome of battles or alter the
course of the conflict.[62] What changed the situation was the increasing
regimentation both of the military and of battle: once the field had been
'colourful and confusing',[63] but by the nineteenth century there were uniforms and hence uniformity.[64] Disguising one's sex was accordingly more
difficult. Women were edged off the field.

Margaret and Patrice Higonnet propose the model of the 'double
helix' to illustrate the 'persistent system of gender relations' which, in
modern warfare, remains a 'structure of subordination'.[65] The conceit
is that, with women occupying one 'strip' of the helix and men the
other, however high women ascend, their standing will always be considered inferior to men's. If women move into the factories when male
factory workers move into the battle zones, this thesis therefore runs,
factory work is re-configured as ancillary. The double helix effect may
account for the connection made by the time of the First World War

between anti-militarism and feminism: writing in 1915, C. K. Ogden and Mary Sargant Florence considered that 'war [. . .] has kept women in perpetual subjection' as it 'creates a nucleus of exclusively male professions'.[66] For some feminists, the question was therefore whether women should accept male-defined support roles (the 'nurturers of warriors'), given that this was a species of subjection.[67] It was in this vein that Virginia Woolf was to express admiration, in *Three Guineas* (1938), for a woman who declared that she would not even 'so much as darn a sock' to help the war effort.[68] Other feminists, including Emmeline Pankhurst, took the line that the opportunity to serve formed part of women's rights.[69] No one, however, went so far as to claim that such rights included that of taking up arms.[70]

The capacities in which women could get to see the front (or, at least, get near it) in the First and Second World Wars – as opposed to performing 'war work' outside the front – were, therefore, limited: the various branches of the auxiliary services, nursing, 'troop entertaining', prostitution.[71] Arthur Ruhl, reporter for *Collier's*, met a 'pale, Broadway tomboy sort of girl' on the ship on his way over to Europe on the outbreak of the First World War:

> 'Listen here! [. . .] I'm going to see this thing – d'you know what I mean? – for what it'll do to me – *you* know – for its effect on my *mind*! [. . .] I don't mind things – I mean blood – *you* know – they don't affect me, and I've read about nursing – I've *prepared* for this! Now, I don't know how to go about it, but it seems to me that a woman who can – *you* know – go right with 'em – jolly 'em along – might be just what they'd want – d'you know what I mean?'[72]

The Scottish doctor Caroline Matthews volunteered to serve at her own expense with the Serbian Field Army Unit. As her ship set sail, Matthews saw 'a fine manly group' of 'dockers and Tommies' on the quay,[73] and reflected:

> Their fellow-countrywomen were sailing to a foreign land, midst the perils of War, for Britain's greater glory [. . .]. We women could not give our lives for Britain in the same manner which is open to our brothers, but war brings more in its train than the carnage of battlefields [. . .]. Thank God, we women can 'do our bit' – beneath the Red Cross – for the Crosses of St. George, St. Andrew, St. Patrick and St. David![74]

Later, Matthews makes a further observation regarding women's roles in war: 'for once I was glad to be a woman. Had I been a man my life would have been of value to the Empire'.[75] There are various positionings here, creating a somewhat confusing picture of the woman in war: both valuable and devalued (able to do something men cannot but only because their lives are unimportant); at once freelance (self-financing), partisan (working for the glory of Britain) and neutral (under the Red Cross).

It is significant that the unknown girl on Arthur Ruhl's ship and Caroline Matthews are healthcare workers. Sandra M. Gilbert's thesis with regard to the First World War is that women's roles, limited though they were, could actually be empowering. While the violence of conflict dehumanised and emasculated men (transforming them into the denizens of 'No Man's Land'), the women who tended them remained (for the most part) whole, healthy and strong.[76] Seen in this light, women's wartime occupations, far from 'support roles', were positions of dominance, rendering the war a 'festival of female misrule'.[77] This view is to some extent corroborated by Caroline Matthews: the women setting forth to war are clearly elevated in some way above the 'dockers and Tommies' who must remain on the quay. Yet it remains the case that these occupations were ancillary – and women who took men's jobs for the duration were paid less than the men they replaced had been.[78] Women were still not fighting at the front.

Furthermore, if, on the one hand, hospital work signifies direct participation in the war experience, on the other, what is being experienced is not battle itself but the physical signs of battle's effects: the injuries of those recuperating or dying. In the Peircean sense, these signs are iconic.[79] In terms of war writing, hospital accounts are therefore representative of a particular sub-genre: concentration on the 'outskirts' of war (at least when combat is located as the central experience) – such phenomena as eve-of-battle scenes, preparation, waiting and recovery. An apt term for this sub-genre is *parapolemics*: the temporal and spatial borders of war. Martha Gellhorn herself filed many reports about hospitals[80] and, of course, the point has gender implications. Ward visits were part of what, even in the nineteenth century, was already known as 'the woman's angle'. Walt Whitman's engagement with the American Civil War famously took the form of visiting tens of thousands of wounded and dying young soldiers in the hospitals serving the conflict. In 'Three Years Summ'd Up', he estimated that he had made over six hundred hospital tours and gone among eighty to a hundred thousand of the wounded and sick, 'as sustainer of spirit and body in some degree, in time of need'. The visits varied from an hour or two to all day or night, for 'with dear or critical cases, I generally watch'd all night'.[81] Ambrose Bierce called such palliative instincts 'womanish',[82] and in a February 1882 piece for the *Women's Journal* entitled 'Unmanly Manhood', a reviewer commented: 'Whitman is an author who for all his physique and his freedom from home-ties, never personally followed the drum, but only heard it from the comparatively remote distance of the hospital'.[83]

In this instance, it is not strictly Whitman's role of tending to patients that is being gendered as 'unmanly'. During the Civil War, male hospital attendants outnumbered female by about five or six to one, and the legendary Clara Barton, nurse at Lacy Mansion and 'dead shot with a pistol', was held to be 'more boy than girl'.[84] Whitman himself wrote in 'Female Nurses for Soldiers': 'it remains to be distinctly said that few or no young ladies, under the irresistible conventions of society, answer the practical requirements of nurses for soldiers'.[85] Caring for the sick was not automatically considered a female occupation. What is being configured as feminine, then, is *distance* – Whitman's 'comparative remoteness' from the action (albeit a 'remoteness' enabling greater intimacy). In 1996, Martha Gellhorn recalled:

> I never knew any men reporters who ever went near a hospital and I was a great frequenter of hospitals because that's where you really see the price of war. But I didn't have deadlines, most of the men did. Also they were much more interested in temporary military gains and losses, which I wasn't.[86]

By the time Gellhorn was reporting, military nursing was virtually exclusively a female occupation. But, again, the gender divide is not so much between aggression and gentleness as between proximity and distance (as well as between deadline-types). Whether healthcare roles (including hospital visiting) are aligned with vitality and dominance (as Gilbert has it) or with tenderness and quietude, they none the less remain parapolemical, located in the rear echelons and perceived as subjacent to the central experience of combat.

Having made the case that the First World War conferred dominant, life-saving roles on women, Gilbert goes on to propose that this was reversed in the Second when 'the front became indistinguishable from the home front',[87] returning women to passive, supportive, domestic occupations.[88] Women's status in the Second World War was as complex as the myriad individual experiences it embraced but, overall, seems to have conformed to the 'double helix' model. In May 1941, a bill to establish the Women's Army Auxiliary Corps was introduced to Congress by Representative Edith Nourse Rogers.[89] A House Resolution of May 1942 created the WAAC (later the Women's Army Corps, or WAC) with an authorised strength of 150,000.[90] For the first time, this gave American women partial military status. Women were accepted on the same basis in the Navy in July 1942 as WAVES (Women Accepted for Volunteer Emergency Service), the Coast Guard in November 1942 as SPARS (Semper PARatus) and the Marines in February 1943.[91] By the end of the Second World War, 350,000 had served but women never

comprised more than 2 per cent of the American military during the conflict.[92] The United States' explicit policy, moreover, was that they were
not to hold any combat positions nor any positions in units with a
combat mission: this kept the WAVES off the ships and prevented WACs
from drilling with real weapons.[93] As D'Ann Campbell notes, 'releasing
men to fight was the most important objective'.[94] But the fighting men
needed to know that the women they fought to protect back home stayed
back home.[95] Recruitment propaganda was re-orientated to accommodate these fears. An Army Air Force pamphlet, 'How You Can Enlist
More WACS', recommended the following line: 'He wants the same
sweet girl waiting for him when the war is over. What he doesn't know
is that you will not only stay just as feminine, but that your charm and
appreciation of his problems will increase'.[96] Hostility to American
women joining the services remained high throughout the war,[97] and
similar unease was felt towards women working in the munitions, aircraft and ship-building industries supplying the Allied armies. The only
occupation unanimously felt fitting for women was, again, nursing.[98] By
now, the nurse was a 'well-trained, efficient specialist, conversant with
the latest technology and devoted to a cooperative health care endeav-
our'[99] – a position of dominance in Gilbert's terms – though still deliberately removed from the war's most dangerous areas.[100] The roles
available to women in the Second World War, compared to men's,
remained parapolemical.[101] As a British song, recorded by Arthur Askey
and Gracie Fields, put it:

> It's the girl that makes the thing that holds the oil that oils the ring
> That works the thingummybob THAT'S GOING TO WIN THE WAR.[102]

In the early 21st century, women, though full members of the American
and British armed forces, still do not fight as ground troops in the front
line: the debate as to whether they should be allowed to do so continues
to rage.

In Martha Gellhorn's article 'Postcards from Italy', published in *Collier's*
on 1 July 1944, three roles for women can be discerned. There is, of
course, Gellhorn's own: that of journalist providing information about a
particular theatre of combat (or, at least, about the conditions for its male
players). The others are depicted in two photographs accompanying the
piece. The first of these is captioned, 'USO shows in Italy are glory for
the soldiers and as tough for the troupers as anything they've done. Here
Janet Evans and Sgt. James Hearne do a turn' (Figure 1).[103] In the photo,
Sgt. Hearne and the unranked Janet Evans are dancing (the 'Hands,
Knees and Boomps-a-Daisy'?): specifically, they are bumping their

Figure 1 Entertaining the troops, *Collier's*, 1 July 1944

bottoms together. Hearne is in uniform while Evans is wearing what might be described as 'semi-uniform': a military-style cap and jacket twinned with an extremely short flared skirt which she is twitching up with one hand to reveal her knickers.

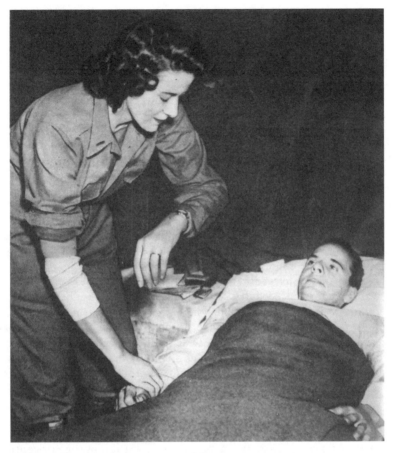

Figure 2 Tending the wounded, *Collier's*, 1 July 1944

The second photo is captioned, 'In the tent hospitals the injured cheer one another up. True to the tradition, Lieut. Cordelia Cooks, first Army nurse to be wounded in Italy, tends an artilleryman' (Figure 2).[104] The artilleryman is lying in bed while Lieut. Cooks takes his pulse. Though she has sustained a war injury herself, she is re-assigned to the para-polemical. Her expression and the way her hand touches his wrist are soothing, sensual even, the antithesis of belligerent: holding an arm as opposed to bearing arms.

These images would have been supplied by *Collier's* editors and are not mentioned in Gellhorn's text. What they silently reinforce are, of course, the stereotypes of women in combat: the text might be that of the woman as information-giver but the images are of the woman as angelic nurturer and as provider of titillation.

'That most horrific of all the horrific developments of modern war'[105]

In her pointedly titled memoirs, *No Woman's World* (1946), Iris Carpenter, correspondent for the North Atlantic Newspaper Alliance (NANA) and others, gives a clear idea of the restrictions faced by women reporters in the Second World War:

> The British and American War Departments differed officially in their attitude toward that most horrific of all the horrific developments of modern war – the woman war correspondent. The British War Office, voicing the dictates of Monty, who regarded women in the field as bad luck, bad business, and something to be scotched vigorously [*sic*] as an enemy advance,[106] said flatly, 'We will not tolerate them'.
>
> [. . .] The Americans, on the other hand, admitted that 'certain phases of war should be covered by women'. They issued them with uniforms, inoculations, the simulated rank of Captain, the handicap of military discipline, and the alleged status of a fully accredited correspondent. [. . .] It was generally conceded that sex could be a handicap, but had better not be, since 'womanhood' as such had no place on a battlefield.
>
> [. . .] Most American commanders would concede, if forced to, that there were angles of the war picture which could better be written about by women. Some would even go so far as admitting that since a man's viewpoint and a woman's differed so widely, no picture could be complete unless it carried both. Invariably, however, they preferred to have it done on somebody else's territory.[107]

The double helix effect is once again in play. The role of war correspondent is a special case: not a support occupation in the conventional sense, it is still distinct from the actual fighting and, within it, women tend to be subordinated, literally, in terms of where they are allowed to go, and professionally, in terms of the kind of stories they are allowed to write.[108] Daphne Spain's concept of the gendered space as an exclusive and excluding locus of knowledge is particularly apt in a discussion of the access issues confronting women war journalists. The theme is one of a hierarchy of information, with women reporters for the most part restricted to the home and factories – those 'left behind'. In the 1930s, Gellhorn's mentor Eleanor Roosevelt decreed that only women could cover her press conferences,[109] a notable fillip, but otherwise women correspondents were barred from press briefings until late in the Second World War[110] and not officially allowed to go to the front. The consensus seems to be that they won overseas assignments only by agreeing to cover the parapolemical 'women's angle' for a growing female readership.[111] Judging from the adverts *Collier's* carried in the period (Du Pont No. 7 Car Polish (23 June 1941), Fortune Shoes for Men, Long's Hats (14 November 1942), Johnnie Walker whisky (26 December 1942), Jockey Underwear ('mild, masculine comfort', 1 April 1944), 'Jones' Haps' ('men find comfort never known before, thanks to HAPS, the ONE-piece Shirt 'n' Shorts! [. . .] Guaranteed the most convenient underwear you ever wore, or money back', 6 May 1944), Gem Razors and Blades (20 May 1944), Yello-Bole pipe tobacco (20 May 1944), Seaforth Grooming Aids for men (23 December 1944), Sol Hepatica laxative ('Gloom in Dad's Room', 23 June 1945)), Gellhorn was writing for an audience of which the majority were men. None the less, Aimee Larkin was listed on the masthead as the 'Distaff' editor and there was a small number of advertisements apparently aimed at women (Mojud hosiery, Woolfoam washing liquid, Dromedary Gingerbread Mix (18 November 1944)). As 'Uncle Ned's Home Repair Hints' (23 June 1945) with its division of tasks between husband and wife suggested, although the 'woman's angle' was an 'innocuous' means to 'get there',[112] a mixed audience could be assumed once access had been attained.

'Getting there' has both 'macro' and 'micro' aspects:[113] in the Second World War it embraced crossing the Atlantic as well as gaining entry to messes and riding in fighter planes. Once in France, women reporters were confined to field hospitals which were, paradoxically, nearer to the enemy lines than the press camps occupied by the male journalists and therefore more dangerous.[114] 'Why none of us ever got killed, hurt or taken prisoner,' writes Carpenter, 'no one will ever know'.[115] The women could not leave the hospitals without the Commanding Officer's permission and only then with officer escort (the officers were unwilling to leave the hospitals); they had to beg for transport and 'risk their necks' by jeeping in forward zones without briefing.[116] Their copy had to be sent through the ordinary field-message service, arriving four to seven days after it was written and making no sense anyway as it was censored in London rather than in the field.[117] 'Under such circumstances,' Carpenter reflects, 'it seemed obvious that the women correspondent nuisance would be short-lived. Hospital stories were no longer automatic column fillers. Trying to get anything else meant breaking the rules.'[118]

None the less, despite these limitations, American and British women did attain the war zone – and often attained it first. In addition to Carpenter and Gellhorn, Margaret Bourke-White (photographer for *Life*), Mary Marvin Breckenridge (of CBS), Lee Carson (International News Service), Ruth Cowan (Associated Press), Virginia Cowles (*Sunday Times*), Mary Welsh Hemingway (*Daily Express*), Marguerite Higgins

(*New York Herald Tribune*), Helen Kirkpatrick (*Chicago Daily News*), Lee Miller (photographer for *Vogue*), Anne O'Hare McCormick (*New York Times*), Inez Robb (International News Service), Sigrid Schultz[119] (*Chicago Tribune*), Ann Stringer (University Press), Dorothy Thompson (*New York Herald Tribune*) and Sonia Tomara (*New York Herald Tribune*) all reported from the European Theatre of Operations during the Second World War.[120]

To characterise the range of stratagems, disguises, hitched lifts, concealments, improvisation and sheer chutzpah by which women correspondents penetrated and circulated within the war zone, it is helpful to turn to the thinking of Michel de Certeau. De Certeau terms 'strategy' the 'calculus of force-relationships which becomes possible when a subject of will and power (a proprietor, an enterprise, a city, a scientific institution) can be isolated from an "environment"'.[121] The 'tactic', on the other hand, is 'a calculus which cannot count on a "proper" (a spatial or institutional localization)' and belongs to the 'other': clever tricks, knowing how to get away with things, 'hunter's cunning', manoeuvres, polymorphic simulations, joyful discoveries. De Certeau explains:

> A tactic insinuates itself into the other's place, fragmentarily, without taking it over in its entirety [. . .]. Because it does not have a place, a tactic depends on time – it is always on the watch for opportunities that must be seized 'on the wing'. [. . .] It must constantly manipulate events in order to turn them into 'opportunities'.[122]

De Certeau is writing of 'the practice of everyday life', specifically consumerism, but his model is peculiarly apt to describe the woman correspondent's relation to the war zone. The 'subject of will and power' matches the military authorities, the 'spatial or institutional localization' the war zone in which the tactic is exercised by the woman reporter. Like the consumer in a high capitalist economy, the woman war correspondent must trace 'wandering lines' (*lignes d'erre*): trajectories which describe the 'interests and desires that are neither determined nor captured by the systems in which they develop'.[123] The tactic, therefore, has a subversive topographical element to it: a means of temporarily occupying, even appropriating, forbidden space. Martha Gellhorn, like other women correspondents, proved remarkably inventive and resourceful as such a tactician. 'I am simply a born visitor,' she wrote, 'meant to go, as a stranger, into someone else's territory'.[124]

Encapsulating this figure is the notion of kinesis. The reporter is the opposite of what Gaston Bachelard, in his analysis of 'topophilia', terms the 'sheltered being':[125] inhabitant of hotels, camps and foxholes, the war journalist's existence is one of danger, contingency, shallowness, impermanence, itinerancy. On not a few occasions, reporters have been mistaken for spies,[126] a phenomenon suggestive of borderline status – the journalist and the spy must both be part of, but essentially separate from, the subject of their observation. Other avatars might be the ethnographer[127] or the scientist on a field trip: figures who are both outsiders and insiders, observers and participants. There is a flâneur-like aspect to the war recorder, as well as a sense in which he or she, in sending back accounts of battle, accumulates the spoils of war.

Arthur Ruhl referred to 'excursions' arranged by the authorities in the First World War,[128] reinforcing the idea that visits to the front by non-combatants (whether journalists or politicians) were a form of tourism, carefully managed – mapped and gridded – by the military. His vocabulary of 'strolling' and 'motoring' conjures up an image of the war reporter as day tripper out in a charabanc.[129] Gellhorn, whose dispatches frequently take the form of journeys, exploiting different modes of transport (jeep, ship, fighter plane, bomber, train), was, in John Simpson's words, 'one of the great travellers of the 20th century'[130] and herself called travelling 'the final joy of living [. . .] the delight of surprise, the delight of glimpses into lives, the lightness and freedom'.[131] But on occasion, she expressed scepticism about the figure of the travelling correspondent. In *What Mad Pursuit*, Charis Day feels herself to be 'a chronic tourist, with all the uselessness of the breed'.[132] 'Portrait of a Lady' refers to war reporting as 'tourism',[133] and in 'About Shorty', the woman journalist narrator disparagingly refers to herself and her colleagues as 'Press tourists'.[134] Stressing again the comparative safety of the visitor, Gellhorn deprecatingly described herself as 'an unscathed tourist of wars'.[135] The motility and agility of 'Martha Gellhorn' in the journalistic text is a far cry from the day tripper but 'tourist' does encapsulate some important features of the construction: the circularity of engagement and withdrawal; the faint echo of the military 'tour' of duty; and the discernable 'turning' or inflection of the reportorial figure.

Martha Gellhorn in the field

Having outlined in general the challenges faced by women correspondents in the Second World War, this chapter now homes in on one particular issue of access: the rivalry between Gellhorn and Hemingway over witnessing D-Day. Before addressing this, however, it is worth noting the pattern of Gellhorn's relationship with the front, as it reveals the vocational quality of her impulse to attend battle. Her two main periods of intense engagement with the conflict in the ETO came at either end of the war: first Czechoslovakia and Finland, then the push from D-Day. Her description of her feelings during the period of withdrawal demands quoting at length:

> We were drinking daiquiris in a mingy little bar on the Mexican border and talking about cattle-raising in Arizona. A tattered Indian child came in, with some clutched newspapers and said, 'Con la guerra, la guerra' mildly. No one noticed him the first time round. Then the word caught, we called to the boy, he sold us a Mexican paper, damp with his own sweat. Smeary type announced Pearl Harbor and America's declaration of war. It seemed a dreadful way for a great nation to get into a war – blown in, with its fleet down.
>
> Between that time and November 1943, when I finally reached England (filled with joy to be there, to be home in the world again), I was para-lyzed by conflicting emotions: private duty, public disgust and a longing to forget both and join those who were suffering the war. It is too hard to sit on the outside and watch what you can neither help not change; it is far easier to close your eyes and your mind and jump into the general misery, where you have almost no choices left, but a lot of splendid company.[136]

Gellhorn here uses the word 'caught' to express the claims of war, a choice which suggests a certain inescapability about her attraction. The word 'paralyzed' is also significant. What she is describing is a personal 'lull', analogous to 'lulls' at large. The 'lull' is an interlude in the midst of conflict (or between conflicts), a temporary cessation of hostilities, characterised both by quiescence and by anxiegenic suspense ('when will things start up again?'). As such, it is a charged temporal space in the way that 'the front' is a charged physical space: this time, a space of tensely suspended animation. Indeed, Henry Green, in his short story 'The Lull' (1943), which concerns London firemen waiting for the Blitz to resume, uses this very word: the men 'are passing through a period which may be compared with the experience of changing fast trains' as an unseen approach 'keeps them *suspended*'.[137] The experience is well summed up in Gellhorn's word 'caught' – incidentally, the title of a 1943 novel by Green, again concerning the London Auxiliary Fire Service and explor-ing different states of capture.[138]

The lull, the 'meantime', is a space aside from war. It is reconfigured (albeit in relation to a different conflict – the Korean War) in Gellhorn's novel *The Lowest Trees Have Tops* (1967), a work explicitly preoccupied with temporal space (and described by its author as 'escape literature').[139] The narrator, Susanna, is a journalist who has withdrawn (or retired) to the paradisical Mexican village of San Ignacio del Tule, where 'the chief commodity [. . .] is time and the people [. . .] enjoy wasting it'.[140] Susanna muses:

> In the afternoons, I lay on a mat on the lawn, watched the clouds and day-dreamed [. . .]. Somewhere beyond our plateau, in the real world, people suffered and contended [. . .]. Here in this glowing air, time seemed to be standing still, which was my favourite way for time to act.[141]

This, then, is suspended time, or 'no time'. Though Susanna describes it as her 'favourite way for time to act', there is a greater sense in the novel that suspended time is oppressive. On hearing that there has been an armistice in Korea, Susanna 'bursts into tears'.[142] Given that she does not know anyone fighting there, her emotion puzzles her neighbour, who assumes that she is weeping 'from joy'.[143] Another interpretation is that the tears derive from a sense of being excluded from 'suffering and con-tention', from missing out on action of historical significance, albeit wil-fully.[144] Unsurprisingly, at the end of the novel, Susanna is planning to leave Tule for Paris.

Martha Gellhorn's attitude to war was much the same. Though she withdrew from it, the 'lulls' were difficult periods for her. Conflict drew her, however much she hated it: to remain away from the war zone was 'like being blind'.[145] In a sense, 'being there' defined her: in a letter to Hortense Flexner, she wrote despairingly of life at the Finca, 'I saw myself forever tied down to telling the servants to scrub the bathroom floors'.[146] By contrast, when setting off for China in 1940, she felt 'husky as a well-pastured horse and definitely rarin' to go'.[147]

As much as other women, Gellhorn faced practical limitations on her ability to access the front. On 26 January 1942, Charles Colebaugh wrote to tell her that the Public Relations department of the War Department had sent a letter, 'with Mrs. Martha Ellis G. Hemingway as its subject', saying that 'it is against [. . .] policy to accredit women cor-respondents "for attachment to the headquarters of any United States Army forces actually operating in the field"'.[148] So much was standard practice and Colebaugh was pessimistic about the chances of getting a personal exception to it. Gellhorn's immediate reaction was to query the parameters of her limitations:

> What is that War Department thing about female journalists, exactly? Does it mean that no female journalist can be attached to US forces (the way the guys cover on naval task forces, or link up with aviation or army abroad.) Is that all? Or is it a blanket refusal to allow women correspondents to travel into war zones? That can't be, because of Eve Curie and Clair Luce. Does it

then just mean that if a woman correspondent wants to go on, covering war, she has to attach herself to foreign armies? For instance, could I get to the Free French in Africa? It's only a hypothetical question, but please answer. I want to know how that works. Is it a flat no-transport-anywhere order, or a flat no-reporting-on-US-forces order?[149]

In a subsequent letter, she questioned whether the policy meant that, even if she succeeded in accessing the field, the fact of her sex would preclude certain subjects, recognising that the war zone was as much a physiological space as a physical one:

> Say one was a woman (horrid thought) and was [. . .] in Egypt covering the English. And say one saw a US bomber squadron, attached to the British for instance. Would one be forbidden to speak to the boys or write one line about them, being as one was a woman. It do [*sic*] seem odd.[150]

Later in the war, having escaped from the internment imposed on her after she stowed away on a hospital ship to reach Omaha beach, she wrote a haughty-toned letter to a Colonel Lawrence of the American Expeditionary Force's Public Relations Office (PRO):

> As you know, General Eisenhower stated that men and women correspondents would be treated alike, and would be afforded equal opportunities to fulfill their assignments. This was later qualified to mean that, when American women military personnel (in this case Army nurses) went to France, women correspondents would also be allowed to cross. As far as I know, nurses were working in France towards the end of the first week of the invasion, but though eighteen days have now elapsed since the landing, women correspondents are still unable to cover the war.
> [. . .]
> I have tried to be allowed to do the work I was sent to England to do and I have been unable to do it. I have reported war in Spain, Finland, China and Italy, and now I find myself plainly unable to continue my work in this theatre, for no reason that I can discover than that I am a woman. Being a professional journalist, I do not find this an adequate reason for being barred.
> [. . .]
> I have, too frequently, received the impression that women war correspondents were an irritating nuisance, who, very tiresomely, kept asking to be allowed to do their job. I wish to point out that none of us would have our jobs unless we knew how to do them, and this curious condescending treatment is as ridiculous as it is undignified.[151]

This was, then, an ongoing battle with the authorities, a constant testing of limits, but accessing the front was never a more prickly issue than in Gellhorn's rivalry with Ernest Hemingway. Their 'honeymoon' in

China, during the Sino-Japanese War, provided a taste of things to come. In a telegram of 18 June 1941, *Collier's* editor William Chenery told Gellhorn:

MISTER HEM PM JUNE EIGHTEENTH SCOOPS MISS G COLLIER'S JUNE 28 STOP CAN'T YOU WRITERS PROTECT YOUR STORIES BETTER STOP PLEASE REASSURE RELATIVE EAST INDIES.[152]

Hemingway defended himself in a reply of 18 June (dated 1942 but in fact 1941)[153] and Gellhorn herself confessed to Chenery:

I never went to Cheng-tu: Ernest did [. . .]. When he came back, I picked his brains and stole from him. He was very decent about it; and in his article he goes into all the technical detail on Chengtu [*sic*]; but I used the best color. He, on the other hand, was offered six thousand plunks to write a piece about the China front and would not, for fear of stealing my story. So we both thought the front was the story [. . .]. And what you liked was Chengtu.[154]

The competitiveness between the two came to a head in their efforts to 'be there' on D-Day, 6 June 1944 (otherwise known as the Normandy Invasions or 'Operation Overlord'), and it is this to which the rest of this chapter is devoted.

D-Day

Material held in the Bodleian Library, Oxford – a cache of letters between Gellhorn, Hemingway and Gellhorn's mother, released into the public domain on Gellhorn's death in 1998 – sheds important light on the matter. This material is discussed below, but at the outset a preliminary ethical point needs to be addressed. In correspondence with Sandra Spanier over *Love Goes to Press*, Gellhorn pressed her view that reference to the 'D-Day saga' between Hemingway and herself was 'needless', 'irrelevant' and 'distasteful'.[155] In the light of this, can an extended analysis of the matter be justified? The decision to offer one in the present case has been made in the knowledge of Gellhorn's dislike of being paired with her former husband: ultimately, the choice was made on the grounds that her comments related only to the D-Day rivalry in the context of the plot of *Love Goes to Press*; that her record (as will be seen) speaks for itself; that it is important to establish the exact sequence of events (the precise dating of Gellhorn's landing has not been attempted elsewhere) and that it is a unique opportunity to observe the differing fortunes of men and women in the field.

The relevant letter from the cache in question is from Ernest Hemingway to his mother-in-law, Edna Gellhorn,[156] dated 18 February 1945.[157] This letter, written when Hemingway was staying at the Paris Ritz, is self-exculpatory in tone (by this time the couple were estranged) and much of its antagonism towards Gellhorn centres on his perception of her treatment of him when he was in hospital in London with concussion after a car accident in May 1944. In the March of that year, Gellhorn, who had been reporting from England and Holland, returned to Cuba for another attempt to persuade her husband to go to the ETO: the assistant British Air Attaché, Roald Dahl, would allocate him a seat on a plane across the Atlantic if he would report on the RAF in any American publication. The result was, Gellhorn told Bernice Kert in an interview on 15 February 1982, that

> Ernest began at once to rave at me, the word is not too strong [. . .] my crime really was to have been at war when he had not, but that was not how he put it. I was supposedly insane, I only wanted excitement and danger, I had no responsibility to anyone, I was selfish beyond belief.[158]

The memory sums up a personal relationship whose very dynamic centred on the issue of 'being there'.

Hemingway did, in the end, choose a magazine to write for. That the publication he selected was *Collier's* – Gellhorn's magazine – has, as with so much about their lives, been variously interpreted. Each publication could only have one accredited correspondent to cover the European theatre: by choosing *Collier's*, it could be said that Hemingway did Gellhorn out of a job. She told Bernice Kert in the interview on 15 February 1982: 'I was totally blocked [. . .] having taken *Collier's* he automatically destroyed my chances of covering the fighting war.'[159] The term 'fighting war' is revealing: another war – that is, the parapolemical war of hospitals and the home front – would be all that was left for Gellhorn. She expanded on the point in the Afterword to the 1995 edition of *Point of No Return*:

> These [PRO] officers permitted only one correspondent from a magazine to report in combat zones. As I had taken second place on my magazine, I was forbidden to work where the war was being fought. This was absurd and intolerable. I went AWOL.[160]

Yet there is another angle. As Iris Carpenter noted, the US War Department's ruling was that female correspondents could 'go no farther forward than women's services go [. . .] Women were accredited to the war zones. They did not have accreditation to military units, as required for admission to press camps at the front.'[161] If it wanted front-line coverage, therefore, *Collier's* would have had to find someone other than Gellhorn anyway. But Gellhorn's sense of injustice at Hemingway's choice remained for the rest of her life. His decision had a further consequence which illustrates gender difference in access to war: while he was flown to London, Gellhorn crossed the Atlantic as the only passenger aboard a ship with a cargo of dynamite, arriving to find him in hospital after an accident following a party.

In his letter to Edna Gellhorn, Hemingway complains that when Martha visited him in the hospital she told him that they would not share a room in the hotel. She would no longer take his surname or remain faithful.[162] The rights and wrongs of the matter are tricky to judge. Accusing Gellhorn of competitiveness, Hemingway only reveals his own frustration or resentment at her independence, particularly as expressed in her mobility as a war journalist. In a coda to the letter,[163] in which he morbidly writes that he expects his children to die, he praises his new partner, Mary Welsh, in terms that suggest his true assessment of Gellhorn's 'place': he has always needed to be looked after; that is what wives are for. Quite what Edna Gellhorn – Bryn Mawr graduate, founder member of the National League of Women Voters, Civil Service Commissioner and activist in the United Nations – must have made of this sentiment is only to be imagined.

Hemingway gives a specific example of Gellhorn's 'competitiveness': visiting his Division, she claimed to have seen more war than he had.[164] Protesting to his mother-in-law, he lists the campaigns that the Division has participated in: the Normandy invasions, Paris, St Quentin, Le Cateau-Cambrésis (Hemingway calls it 'le Cateau'),[165] St Hubert, Houffalize (Hemingway calls it 'Hauffalege'),[166] Bastogne, entering Germany, the Siegfried Line, the Schnee Eifel, the Hürtgenwald and Luxembourg.[167] But crucially, Hemingway does not refer to these as having been accomplished by 'the Division'. Rather, he uses the first person plural: 'we'.

A casual reader of the letter might therefore be forgiven for assuming that Hemingway personally participated in all the campaigns he mentions. The reality was rather different. As a war correspondent, Hemingway was strictly a non-combatant and therefore not a member of any military unit (though he did closely attach himself to the Fourth Infantry Division and others).[168] His actual direct participation in combat consisted of leading some irregulars in the defence of Rambouillet on 19–20 August 1944 and defending a command post in the Hürtgenwald on 22 November 1944. As the Geneva Convention prevented correspondents from bearing arms, he faced interrogation by the Inspector General Third Army in respect of the former activity. But he watched the Normandy invasions from a transporter. He did not actually participate in capturing the French towns of St Quentin and Le Cateau-Cambrésis but went through them, when they had already been captured, en route to rejoining Colonel Buck Lanham and the 22nd Regiment at Pommereuil on 3 September 1944. He accompanied the regiment through the Belgian towns of St Hubert, Houffalize and Bastogne as an observing journalist. The first American tanks went into Germany on 12 September 1944: Hemingway watched. The 22nd Regiment attacked the Schnee Eifel, a wooded ridge in Germany, on 14 September 1944: Hemingway was in bed with a cold. After a period back at the Paris Ritz, he rejoined the 22nd as an observer on 15 November 1944 for an 18-day offensive to clear a path through the Hürtgenwald (thickly-forested hill country west of Düren, Germany). After another stay at the Ritz, he went back to the 22nd in the second week of December 1944 when the Germans launched an attack on the American First Army's defence line at Luxembourg: he arrived after the worst of the offensive had been contained.[169]

The technique used in the letter to convey the impression of direct participation is extremely simple: a subject pronoun. A similar sleight-of-hand occurs in a letter Hemingway wrote to his middle son, Patrick, on 15 September 1944:

> Dearest Mousie,
> It has been about 2 months since Papa came back to France after landing on D-Day on Omaha Beach.[170]

Hemingway did not, in fact, set foot on the invasion beaches: indeed, Bernice Kert puts the time he spent in the landing-craft, before being returned to the transport *Dorothea L. Dix*, as 'moments'.[171] But the simple elision of the word 'the' before 'landing' creates the impression that he did land: re-insertion of the 'the' would more accurately convey that the landing had been made by others. Then, there is the version given by Leicester Hemingway, who states that his brother 'went ashore under heavy fire in a 36-foot LCVP, through antitank obstacles on Fox Green beach' and recalls him saying 'afterward':

> Once we waded ashore, they [the Germans] began doing their stuff. I said [to a Lieutenant], 'let's get up the beach to where we can shoot back,' and I kicked him squarely in the butt as I got going forward [. . .] he followed with his men and we moved further in.[172]

This is a reported conversation subject to the vagaries of Leicester Hemingway's memory over nearly twenty years. None the less, in this instance, the language attributed to Hemingway stops being merely elliptical and begins to suggest that the 'fact' of the landing was becoming vital to his vision of himself. Even Gellhorn reported in an acerbic 'V-Mail' to her mother shortly after D-Day (14 June 1944): 'Bug had done a very fine long story; he was over in the first wave on D day, in naturally the most perilous circumstances.'[173] As Gellhorn did not see Hemingway from before D-Day until the liberation of Paris,[174] this is again hearsay evidence. In these instances, a myth is being formed (the mythopoeic process is discussed further in the next chapter). An inaccurate impression is left uncorrected so that the cumulative evidence says: Papa fought on D-Day. Clearly, combat experience – and superior combat experience, at that – is vital to Hemingway's self-assessment and assessment of the situation with Gellhorn.

Though it anticipates discussion in the next chapter on the writerly construction of the reporter, it is appropriate to look here at the textual expression of the rivalry between Gellhorn and Hemingway over D-Day, as evidenced in the *Collier's* edition of 22 July 1944.[175] The magazine's front cover sets the tone: 'Voyage to Victory / by / Ernest Hemingway'. Inside, in the column headed 'This Week – Articles', the leading item is: 'Ernest Hemingway, Voyage to Victory. Collier's correspondent rides in the war ferry to France.'[176] Third in the list (after 'The Great Zadma [. . .] How to Swallow a Sword') is another item: 'Martha Gellhorn, Over and Back. The invasion has become a commuter's war.'[177] A subtle hierarchy is already in place by page 4.[178]

Hemingway's piece occupies pages 11–13 and 56–7 of the edition; Gellhorn's is on a single page, 16. Page 11 carries a large photograph of Hemingway, bearded, uniformed, surrounded by young troops, very much the wise veteran, 'Papa'-incarnate (Figure 3). It is captioned, 'Ernest Hemingway, who gained his first fame as a war reporter in 1918, chats with G.I.s before leaving to cover biggest action yet':[179] the impression is that it is the reporter who is off to face the greatest danger. The headline reads (slightly more honestly): 'Collier's famed war correspondent watches, as our fighting men battle across the beaches into Normandy'.[180] Pages 12 and 13 carry photographs of D-Day by the *Collier's* photographer, Joe Dearing. One depicts a group of troops on board ship studying a chart, captioned, '*We* had studied the charts, the silhouettes, the data on the obstacles in the water and the defences all one morning'.[181] Another shows landing-craft being lowered from a transporter, the perspective that of a person on the transporter.[182] The photos on page 13 are of troops running on to the beach from the sea, with the photographer (and hence the reporter?) obviously already aground, and of troops standing beside a tank, looking ahead

Figure 3 Hemingway with GIs, *Collier's*, 22 July 1944

(Figure 4). The images (and their captions) therefore establish a veteran's perspective.

Page 16, which carries Gellhorn's piece, also has a photograph (Figure 5). This time, it is credited to the US Signal Corps: in other words, it is an official, pooled image, deemed, by some editorial choice, to be appropriate.[183] It shows a wounded GI, knees buckling, being supported by two other soldiers, one of whom is black (black soldiers made up the auxiliary corps). The caption reads: 'Back from the hell of Normandy beaches, this American paratroop officer is helped ashore by members of a medical corps unit, en route to hospital – and home.'[184] The headline to the article says, 'Already the invasion has become a commuters' war, as fighters shuttle between England's ports and Normandy's beaches'.[185] There is no photograph of Martha Gellhorn. The difference between the paratextual messages of the two articles could not, therefore, be more striking. Hemingway's experience of D-Day is news. Though published in the same edition, Gellhorn's piece is about an experience become familiar, even routine, 'commuter'-like.[186] The photographs reinforce the impression. The ones accompanying Hemingway's piece might be an illustration of his own (fictitious) victorious landing. The one with

Figure 4 D-Day from a veteran's perspective, *Collier's*, 22 July 1944

Gellhorn's piece is parapolemical: the wounded soldier, the auxiliary corpsmen.

These paratextual positionings were, of course, the choice of *Collier's* editors, who can perhaps be forgiven their enthusiasm for the big name author of *For Whom the Bell Tolls*.[187] But, it is important to note, within the texts themselves, the positioning continues. Hemingway opens his piece: 'No one remembers the date of the Battle of Shiloh. But the day we took Fox Green beach was the sixth of June, and the wind was blowing hard out of the northwest.'[188] 'We', of course, could legitimately refer to 'our troops' or 'Americans'. Yet the impression remains, uncorrected, irresistible and eventually even comical, that Hemingway was one of the ones who 'took Fox Green'. This impression persists to the end: 'If you want to know how it was in an LCV(P) on D-Day when we took Fox Green beach and Easy Red beach on the sixth of June, 1944, then this is as near as I can come to it.'[189] These closing words are then followed by a set of boxed italics:

While Mr. Hemingway was cabling this article, General Montgomery revealed in an interview that a German division was sent up to thicken the coastal defenses at the spot where Collier's correspondent landed. 'We hit it right on the nose,' Mr. Hemingway cabled.[190]

Figure 5 'Over and Back', *Collier's*, 22 July 1944

The effect would be to make the 'famed' correspondent's exploits all the more heroic, were it not for the vital point that Hemingway did not land. Gellhorn recalled of her own experiences of D-Day:

> The U.S. Army public relations officers, the bosses of the American press, were a doctrinaire bunch who objected to a woman being a correspondent with combat troops. I felt like a veteran of the Crimean War by then, and I had been sent to Europe to do my job, which was not to report the rear areas or the woman's angle. The P.R.O.s in London became definitely hostile when I stowed away on a hospital ship in order to see something of the invasion of Normandy. After that, I could only report the war on secondary fronts, in the company of admirable foreigners who were not fussy about official travel orders and accreditation.[191]

Having spent the morning of 6 June in 'a great guarded room in the Ministry of Information' in London,[192] Gellhorn immediately set off for the south coast ports (unidentified at this point, presumably for security reasons). In a D-Day 50th anniversary piece, she recounted:

> A military policeman stopped me and asked me my business. I said I was just going to interview the nurses, the women's angle for *Collier's*, the American magazine I was working for. Nobody gave a hoot about the women's angle, it served like a perfect forged passport. As soon as I got aboard [the hospital ship], I found a toilet and locked myself in.[193]

Here the fact of being a woman and covering 'the women's angle', serves almost to efface Gellhorn from the field, to render her invisible, even as, paradoxically, it gives her access (albeit to the parapolemical confines of a toilet on a hospital ship).[194] The piece continues: 'we waded the last strip of water on to a beach of big sliding pebbles'.[195] 'The Wounded Come Home', published in *Collier's* on 5 August 1944, describes her 'wad[ing] ashore, in water to our waists' to recover the wounded.[196] Gellhorn, unlike Hemingway, therefore did land on Omaha beach,[197] although there is some confusion as to exactly when. Her article, 'Over and Back' (*Collier's*, 22 June 1944), describes the port scene on 'D-plus-one'.[198] Yet 'The Wounded Come Home', the account of her stowing away on the hospital ship, states that the ship pulled 'out of harbour that night' and 'crossed by daylight' to France.[199] This could indicate that Gellhorn hid in the ship on the night of 6–7 June and crossed early in the morning of 7 June, so arriving on Omaha Red beach (and disembarking in order to help stretcher men back on to the ship) on D-Day+1, though it is also possible that 'that night' refers to 7 June, which would put her landing on D-Day+2. A line in a letter of 4 August 1944 to Hortense Flexner clinches it: 'Teechie dearest; I saw it allright. [. . .] I went over myself the night of the second day on a hospital ship [. . .] I went ashore looking for wounded too.'[200] Gellhorn's landing was thus 8 June 1944: D-Day+2.

The escapade had three consequences. The first was that Gellhorn was arrested and interned in a nurses' camp in England. She escaped and hitched a flight to Naples.[201] The second was that she therefore became 'unaccredited', unofficial, more than ever itinerant, facing more difficulty than ever in attaining the front: as she put it in an interview of 31 October 1980 with Bernice Kert, 'I had no papers, no travel orders, no PX rights, nothing. I was a gypsy in that war in order to report it'.[202] In a letter to her editor, Wallace Meyer, she recalled, she was forced to 'bum' her way around the European Theatre: 'it was always that: never could do anything right, because of being a woman'.[203] The third consequence, as Bernice Kert notes, was that Hemingway was 'so infuriated' that Gellhorn had landed on the invasion beaches 'that he convinced himself it never happened, explaining that Martha could not have made the landing because she did not have the proper credentials'.[204] This might explain Hemingway's reply to his brother, Leicester's, question, 'How did Marty make out?':

> 'She did everything possible to make the landing,' Ernest said, giving her full credit. 'Went over on a hospital ship. Got good human interest stuff. They refused to let her ashore because she didn't have accreditation to this area. A damned shame. She got good stuff though, and then came back here.'[205]

What makes this striking is that it is all *strictly* true. Gellhorn really did 'go over on a hospital ship'; she did indeed 'get good human interest stuff' (later written up in 'The Wounded Come Home'). The military authorities did 'refuse to let her ashore' – but it is at this point that the account becomes deceptive because Hemingway omits to tell the whole truth: despite the official 'refusal', he neglects to inform his brother, Gellhorn went ashore anyway. Jacqueline Orsagh notes simply, 'he never forgave her'.[206]

'It has always seemed to me that the war has been omitted as a field for the observation of the naturalist,' wrote Ernest Hemingway, adopting a tone of scientific fastidiousness in his short story 'A Natural History of the Dead' (1939).[207] This chapter has tried to characterise the war zone as a 'field of observation': a literal outdoor space but also an ideological and politico-military construction; ambiguous in outline; protean in shape; a locus where 'things are different'; most crucially, a gendered place. As Hemingway notes in 'A Natural History', 'regarding the sex of the dead it is a fact that one becomes so accustomed to the sight of all the dead being men that the sight of a dead woman is quite shocking'.[208]

The woman in the war zone does indeed provoke 'shock', underlining the figure's errant, contingent status. The Gellhorn–Hemingway rivalry over D-Day has been examined in some detail as it illustrates the practical issues facing women correspondents in general, and Gellhorn in particular, in the field. But these matters become increasingly issues of representation. Next to be considered is therefore another species of positioning: the war reporter in the text.

Notes

1 Gellhorn, 'Visit Italy', *Collier's* (6 May 1944) 62, 64–5: 65.
2 Rahv, Philip, 'The Cult of Experience in American Writing', *Partisan Review* 6 (1940) 412–24: 419.

3 Thucydides, *The Peloponnesian War*, trans. Warner, Rex (Harmondsworth: Penguin, 1954) 24.

4 Sheppard, Philippa, 'Tongues of War: Studies in the Military Rhetoric of Shakespeare's History Plays' (unpublished doctoral thesis, University of Oxford, 1994) 161.

5 I.i.23–4.

6 *I Henry IV*, I.iii.33, 36.

7 *I Henry IV*, I.iii.47–56.

8 I.iii.62.

9 The first chapter of Gellhorn's *Travels with Myself and Another* is entitled 'Credentials' and Gellhorn claims, 'after presenting my credentials [. . .] you will believe that I know whereof I speak' (*TMA* 12).

10 Palmer, Frederick, *With My Own Eyes: A Personal History of Battle Years* (London: Jarrolds, 1934) end-pages viii.

11 Simpson, John, *Strange Places, Questionable People* (London: Macmillan, 1998) back cover.

12 Quoted in Leaper, Glenn W., Löwstedt, Anthony and Madhoun, Husam, *Caught in the Crossfire. The Iraq War and the Media* (Vienna: The International Press Institute, 2003) 3.

13 Nelson, Emily and Rose, Matthew, 'Media Reassess Risks to Reporters in Iraq', *Wall Street Journal* (9 April 2003) B1, B10: B1.

14 Leaper, Löwstedt and Madhoun, *Caught in the Crossfire* 76.

15 Simpson, John, 'War Reporting: The New Vulnerability', The Reuters' Memorial Lecture 2003, given at St Catherine's College, Oxford, 27 June 2003.

16 Nelson and Rose, 'Media Reassess Risks', B10.

17 Hemingway, Ernest, *Selected Letters 1917–1961*, ed. Baker, Carlos (London: Granada, 1981) 105.

18 Ross, Lillian, 'How Do You Like It Now, Gentlemen?', *New Yorker* (13 May 1950) 36–8, 40–6, 49–56: 41. It is not known which writer is being referred to here. The reference to the *Bryn Mawr* hockey team might be a jibe at Gellhorn, who attended the women's college.

19 Hemingway, Ernest, ed., *Men at War: An Anthology* (London: Fontana, 1966) 8.

20 Hemingway, Ernest, *Across the River and into the Trees* (New York: Scribner, 1996) 128. Jacqueline Orsagh interprets Cantwell's line as a slur on Gellhorn, Hemingway's reasoning being that she wrote so well about war that she couldn't have been present at it (Orsagh, Jacqueline, 'A Critical Biography of Martha Gellhorn' (unpublished doctoral thesis, Michigan State University, 1977) 196). The suggestion is not unreasonable, although it seems unlikely that it was so narrowly targeted.

21 Kazin, Alfred, Review of Ernest Hemingway's *The Fifth Column and the First Forty-Nine Stories*, *New York Herald Tribune Books* (16 October 1938) 5; Wilson, Edmund, Review of Ernest Hemingway's *The Fifth Column and the First Forty-Nine Stories*, *Nation*, 147 (10 December 1938)

628, 30; Trilling, Lionel, Review of Ernest Hemingway's *The Fifth Column and the First Forty-Nine Stories*, *Partisan Review* 6 (Winter 1939) 52–60; MacDonald, Dwight, Review of Ernest Hemingway's *For Whom the Bell Tolls*, *Partisan Review*, 8 (January 1941) 24–8.

22 Baker, Carlos, *Ernest Hemingway, A Life Story* (Harmondsworth: Penguin, 1972) 541.

23 Trilling, Lionel, Review of Ernest Hemingway's *For Whom the Bell Tolls*, *Partisan Review*, 8 (January 1941) 63–7: 65.

24 Barea, Arturo, Review of Ernest Hemingway's *For Whom the Bell Tolls*, *Horizon*, 3 (May 1941) 350–61: 350, 361.

25 Quoted in Baker, *Ernest Hemingway*, 542.

26 Fussell, Paul, *Killing, in Verse and Prose and Other Essays* (London: Bellew Publishing, 1990) 39.

27 Clark, Ian, *Waging War: A Philosophical Introduction* (Oxford: Clarendon Press, 1988) 2.

28 Fussell, Paul, 'Introduction', *With the Old Breed at Peleliu and Okinawa* by Sledge, E. B. (New York and Oxford: Oxford University Press, 1990) xi–xx: xviii.

29 Keegan, John, *The Face of War* (London: Jonathan Cape, 1976) 15.

30 Burkeman, Oliver, 'Simpson of Kabul', *Guardian* (*G2*) (14 November 2001) 2–3: 3.

31 Delmer, Sefton, *Trail Sinister. An Autobiography. Volume One* (London: Secker & Warburg, 1961) 268, 275.

32 Carpenter, Iris, *No Woman's World* (Boston: Houghton Mifflin, 1946) 30.

33 Norris, Pippa, 'Introduction: Women, Media, and Politics', *Women, Media, and Politics*, ed. Norris, Pippa (Oxford and New York: Oxford University Press, 1997) 1–18: 2.

34 Leed, Eric J., *No Man's Land. Combat and Identity in World War I* (Cambridge: Cambridge University Press, 1979) 74.

35 Shay, Jonathan, *Achilles in Vietnam. Combat Trauma and the Undoing of Character* (New York and London: Simon & Schuster Touchstone, 1995) 189.

36 Hemingway, Ernest, *Across the River and into the Trees*, 129.

37 Simpson, 'War Reporting: The New Vulnerability'.

38 Tritle, Lawrence A., *From Melos to My Lai: War and Survival* (London, New York: Routledge, 2000) 107, 127.

39 Craig, David and Egan, Michael, *Extreme Situations. Literature and Crisis from the Great War to the Atom Bomb* (London and Basingstoke: Macmillan, 1979) 261–2.

40 Spender, Stephen, ' "Guernica" Picasso's "Guernica" at the New Burlington Gallery', *New Statesman* (15 October 1938) 567–8.

41 Dickens, Charles, *The Dent Uniform Edition of Dickens' Journalism. Sketches by Boz and Other Early Papers 1833–39*, ed. Slater, Michael (London: J. M. Dent, 1994): 199–210.

42 Limon, John, *Writing after War: American War Fiction from Realism to Post-Modernism* (New York and Oxford: Oxford University Press, 1994) 6.

43 Graves, Robert, 'The Garlands Wither', *Times Literary Supplement* (26 June 1930) 534.

44 Stendhal, *The Charterhouse of Parma*, trans. Shaw, Margaret R. B. (Harmondsworth: Penguin, 1958) 77, 88.

45 Crane, Stephen, *The University of Virginia Edition of the Works of Stephen Crane. Volume III. The Red Badge of Courage*, ed. Bowers, Fredson (Charlottesville: University of Virginia, 1975) 49.

46 Gellhorn, 'Cracking the Gothic Line', *Collier's* (28 October 1944) 24, 57–8: 57.

47 Hinz, Evelyn J., 'An Introduction to War and Literature: Ajax Versus Ulysses', *Mosaic* 23/3 (Summer 1990) v–xii: ix.

48 Felman, Shoshana and Laub, Dori, *Testimony. Crises of Witnessing in Literature, Psychoanalysis, and History* (New York and London: Routledge, 1992) 15.

49 II.5.a.

50 II.5.c.

51 As adumbrated by Terry Gifford in *Pastoral* (London and New York: Routledge, 1999) 24.

52 Empson, William, *Some Versions of Pastoral* (London: Chatto & Windus, 1935) 17.

53 Cooper, Helen, *Pastoral. Mediaeval into Renaissance* (Ipswich: D. S. Brewer, 1977) 2.

54 Entrikin, J. Nicholas, *The Betweenness of Place: Towards a Geography of Modernity* (Basingstoke and London: Macmillan, 1991) 6–7.

55 Borden, Mary, *The Forbidden Zone* (London: William Heinemann, 1929) preliminary pages, unpaginated.

56 James Clifford makes this point in relation to ethnographers arriving in the field (Clifford, James, 'On Ethnographic Allegory', *Writing Culture: The Poetics and Politics of Ethnography*, ed. Clifford, James and Marcus, George E. (Berkeley, Los Angeles and London: University of California, 1986) 98–121: 117).

57 See Marx, Leo, 'Pastoralism in America', *Ideology and Classic American Literature*, ed. Bercovitch, Sacvan and Jehlen, Myra (Cambridge: Cambridge University Press, 1986) 36–69: 43.

58 Spain, Daphne, *Gendered Spaces* (Chapel Hill: University of North Carolina, 1992) 3.

59 The sociologist Joshua S. Goldstein argues that the fact that war is, cross-culturally, 'masculinely gendered' is due only in small part to minor biological differences: for the most part, it is caused by the cultural moulding of tough, brave men, who feminise their enemies to encode domination (Goldstein, Joshua S., *War and Gender. How Gender Shapes the War System* (Cambridge: Cambridge University Press, 2001) 406).

60 Cooper, Helen, Munich, Adrienne and Squier, Susan, 'Introduction', *Arms and the Woman: War, Gender, and Literary Representation*, ed. Cooper, Helen M., Munich, Adrienne Auslander and Squier, Susan Merrill (Chapel

Hill and London: University of North Carolina, 1989) xiii–xx: xiii, and Cooper, Munich and Squier, 'Arms and the Woman: The Con(Tra)Ception of the War Text', *Arms and the Woman*, ed. Cooper, Munich and Squier, 9–24: 10.

61 See Adie, Kate, *Corsets to Camouflage: Women and War* (London: Hodder & Stoughton, in association with the Imperial War Museum, 2003) chapter 1.

62 Blanton, DeAnne and Cook, Lauren M., *They Fought Like Demons: Women Soldiers in the American Civil War* (Baton Rouge: Louisiana State University Press, 2002) 204.

63 Adie, *From Corsets to Camouflage*, 16.

64 Adie, *From Corsets to Camouflage*, 17.

65 Higonnet, Margaret and Higonnet, Patrice L.-R., 'The Double Helix', *Behind the Lines: Gender and the Two World Wars*, ed. Higonnet, Margaret, Jenson, Michel Sonya and Weitz, Margaret Collins (New Haven and London: Yale University Press, 1987) 31–47: 34.

66 Ogden, C. K. and Florence, Mary Sargant, 'Militarism Versus Feminism. An Enquiry and a Policy Demonstrating That Militarism Involves the Subjection of Women', *Militarism Versus Feminism. Writings on Women and War*, ed. Kamester, Margaret and Vellacott, Jo (London: Virago, 1987) 53–154: 57, 112.

67 Kamester, Margaret and Vellacott, Jo, 'Introduction', *Militarism Versus Feminism*, ed. Kamester and Vellacott (London: Virago, 1987) 1–34: 15.

68 Woolf, Virginia, 'Three Guineas', *A Room of One's Own / Three Guineas*, ed. Briggs, Julia (London: Penguin, 2000) 115–366: 241–2.

69 Adie, *From Corsets to Camouflage*, 60.

70 Adie, *From Corsets to Camouflage*, 63.

71 It is not being suggested that women took up these roles solely as a form of sight-seeing, but 'seeing action' was at least one motivation. Incidentally, Gellhorn's fiction presents a number of these roles: the overwhelming majority of her women at war are correspondents, but Dorothy Brock in *Point of No Return* is in the American Red Cross, Daphne Rutherford in *Love Goes to Press* is a troop entertainer and Jessica de Camberges in *His Own Man* works in a refugee centre. A number of her female characters also provide sexual gratification to soldiers.

72 Ruhl, *Arthur, Antwerp to Gallipoli. A Year of War on Many Fronts – and Behind Them* (New York: Scribner, 1916) 2.

73 Matthews, Caroline, *Experiences of a Woman Doctor in Serbia* (London: Mills and Boon, 1916) 1.

74 Matthews, *Experiences of a Woman Doctor*, 2–3.

75 Matthews, *Experiences of a Woman Doctor*, 69.

76 Gilbert, Sandra M., 'Literary Men, Literary Women, and the Great War', *Connecting Spheres. Women in the Western World, 1500 to the Present*, ed. Boxer, Marilyn J. and Quataert, Jean H. (Oxford and New York: Oxford University Press, 1987) 232–45: 233–4. This thesis is taken up in

Gilbert, Sandra M. and Gubar, Susan, *No Man's Land. The Place of the Woman Writer in the Twentieth Century. Volume 2. Sexchanges* (New Haven and London: Yale University Press, 1989).

77 Gilbert, 'Literary Men, Literary Women', 239.

78 Longenbach, James, 'The Women and Men of 1914', *Arms and the Woman: War, Gender, and Literary Representation*, ed. Cooper, Munich, and Squier, 97–123: 101.

79 In Peircean semiotics, the dead and wounded would signify battle in the same way that smoke signifies fire (Peirce, Charles S., From 'On the Algebra of Logic: A Contribution to the Philosophy of Notation', *The Essential Peirce: Selected Philosophical Writings. Volume 1 (1867–1893)*, ed. Hauser, Nathan and Kloesel, Christian (Bloomington and Indianapolis: Indiana University Press, 1992) 226–8).

80 E.g. 'Madrid to Morata', *New Yorker* (24 July 1937) 31, 34–5, 38–9; 'Visit to the Wounded', *Story Magazine* (October 1937) 58–61; 'Men Made Over', *Collier's* (20 May 1944) 32, 34–5; 'The Wounded Come Home', *Collier's* (5 August 1944) 14–15, 73–5; and 'You're on Your Way Home', *Collier's* (22 September 1945) 22, 39.

81 Whitman, Walt, *Prose Works 1892. Volume 1. Specimen Days*, ed. Stovall, Floyd (New York: New York University Press, 1963) 112–13. First published in the New York *Weekly Graphic* (no date given).

82 Bierce, Ambrose, *A Sole Survivor. Bits of Autobiography*, ed. Joskin, S. T. and Schultz, David E. (Knoxville: University of Tennessee, 1998) 19.

83 Higginson, T. W., 'Unmanly Manhood', *Women's Journal* XII (4 February 1882) 33.

84 Morris Jr, Roy, *The Better Angel: Walt Whitman in the Civil War* (Oxford: Oxford University Press, 2000) 113, 53.

85 Whitman, *Prose Works*, 88. First published in the *New York Times*, 6 March 1865, as 'A Few Words About Female Nurses for Soldiers'.

86 Freedom Forum European Centre, 'Freedom Forum Europe Pays Tribute to Martha Gellhorn' (London: Freedom Forum European Centre, 1996).

87 Gilbert, 'Literary Men, Literary Women', 245.

88 The argument is expanded on by Susan Gubar in Gilbert, Sandra M. and Gubar, Susan, *No Man's Land. The Place of the Woman Writer in the Twentieth Century. Volume 3. Letters from the Front* (New Haven and London: Yale University Press, 1994) chapter 5.

89 Rustad, Michael L., *Women in Khaki. The American Enlisted Woman* (New York: Praeger, 1982) 27.

90 Rustad, *Women in Khaki*, 28.

91 Campbell, D'Ann, *Women at War with America: Private Lives in a Patriotic Era* (Cambridge, Mass., and London: Harvard University Press, 1984) 20.

92 Campbell, *Women at War with America*, 20, 19.

93 Campbell, *Women at War with America*, 38.

94 Campbell, *Women at War with America*, 21.

95 Campbell, *Women at War with America*, 40.

96 Quoted in Campbell, *Women at War with America*, 43.

97 Campbell, *Women at War with America*, 43.

98 Campbell, *Women at War with America*, 53.

99 Campbell, *Women at War with America*, 51.

100 Campbell, *Women at War with America*, 54.

101 Sheldon, Sayre P., ed., *Her War Story: Twentieth-Century Women Write About War* (Carbondale and Edwardsville: University of Southern Illinois, 1999) 274.

102 Quoted in Lang, Caroline, *Keep Smiling Through: Women in the Second World War* (Cambridge: Cambridge University Press, 1989) 29.

103 Gellhorn, 'Postcards from Italy', *Collier's* (1 July 1944) 41, 56: 41. USO stands for United Service Organisations.

104 Gellhorn, 'Postcards from Italy', 1 July 1944, 41.

105 Carpenter, *No Woman's World*, 32.

106 This 'joke' – 'women as worse-than-the-enemy' – recurs in war representation. Kate Adie quotes some promotional Navy literature (unsourced): 'many a hard-bitten skipper has been shaken as no attack on the voyage has shaken him by the arrival of a trim Wren Boarding Officer' (Adie, *From Corsets to Camouflage*, 145).

107 Carpenter, *No Woman's World*, 32–3, 34.

108 'Fashion, cookery and domestic economy, furniture, the toilet, and (less exclusively) weddings and what is called society news', enumerated Arnold Bennett in *Journalism for Women. A Practical Guide* (London and New York: John Lane, The Bodley Head, 1898) 88.

109 Mills, Kay, 'What Difference Do Women Journalists Make?', *Women, Media, and Politics*, ed. Norris, Pippa (Oxford and New York: Oxford University Press, 1997) 41–55: 43. Mrs Roosevelt's briefings were attended by the *New York Herald Tribune* correspondent Ruth Gruber, who described them as 'a gentle poke in the stomach to her husband for his all-male conferences' (Gruber, Ruth, *Inside of Time. My Journey from Alaska to Israel* (New York: Carroll & Graf, 2003) 20).

110 Sorel, Nancy Caldwell, *The Women Who Wrote the War* (New York: Arcade Publishing, 1999) xiv.

111 Mills, 'What Difference Do Women Journalists Make?', 46; Edwards, Julia, *Women of the World: The Great Foreign Correspondents* (Boston: Houghton Mifflin, 1988) 5.

112 Freedom Forum European Centre, 3.

113 To give a *reductio ad absurdum*: Kay Mills recalls being told by one hiring editor that her usefulness was limited: ' "I need someone I can send anywhere [. . .] what would you do if someone you were covering ducked into the men's room?" ' (Mills, Kay, *A Place in the News. From the Women's Pages to the Front Page* (New York and Oxford: Columbia University Press, 1990) 1). It hardly needs pointing out that this assumes that newsworthy figures are exclusively male.

114 Carpenter, *No Woman's World*, 47.

115 Carpenter, *No Woman's World*, 47. Anne Sebba makes the point that men's 'clubbiness and booziness' enable them to get stories, while women must set forth alone to gather material, thereby incurring greater danger (Sebba, Anne, *Battling for News. The Rise of the Woman Reporter* (London, Sydney, Auckland: Hodder & Stoughton, 1994) 139).

116 Carpenter, *No Woman's World*, 47–8.

117 Carpenter, *No Woman's World*, 48.

118 Carpenter, *No Woman's World*, 48.

119 An article by Schultz, billed as 'a famous correspondent, with many years' experience in Germany' (Schultz, Sigrid, 'Invasion Lines', *Collier's* (25 March 1944) 11–12, 55, 57: 11) appeared in the same edition of *Collier's* as Gellhorn's 'Hatchet Day for the Dutch'.

120 Edwards, *Women of the World*, passim. <http://lcweb.loc.gov/exhibits/wcf/wcf005.html> provides a list of accredited American women correspondents during the Second World War: they were not, of course, accredited to the *front*.

121 De Certeau, Michel, *The Practice of Everyday Life* (Berkeley, Los Angeles and London: University of California, 1984) xix.

122 De Certeau, *The Practice of Everyday Life*, xix.

123 De Certeau, *The Practice of Everyday Life*, xx.

124 Gellhorn, letter of ? 1958 to Rosamond Lehmann: *SL* 269.

125 Bachelard, Gaston, *The Poetics of Space* (Boston: The Beacon Press, 1969) xxxi, 5.

126 E.g. 'To Be Treated As a Spy' in Davis, Richard Harding, *With the Allies* (London: Duckworth, 1915). Given the greater contingency of their status, as compared to men's, women in war are particularly vulnerable to accusations of espionage. There were many successful women spies in the Second World War (see Schofield, Mary Ann, 'Telling the Truth: Women Spy Narratives of the Second World War', *Visions of War. World War II Popular Literature and Culture*, ed. Holsinger, M. Paul and Schofield, Mary Ann (Bowling Green, Ohio: Bowling Green State University Popular Press, 1992) 56–66).

127 See Clifford, James, 'Introduction: Partial Truths', *Writing Culture*, ed. Clifford and Marcus, 1–26: 2, and Pratt, Mary Louise, 'Fieldwork in Common Place', *Writing Culture*, ed. Clifford and Marcus, 27–50.

128 Ruhl, *Antwerp to Gallipoli*, 232–3.

129 Ruhl, *Antwerp to Gallipoli*, 129, 53.

130 Simpson, John, 'War, Writing and Whisky with Martha', *Sunday Telegraph* (22 February 1998) 6.

131 *SL* 241.

132 *WMP* 148.

133 *HoA* 61.

134 *HP* 120.

135 *FoW* 12.

136 *FoW* 107.

137 Green, Henry, 'The Lull', *New Writing and Daylight* (Summer 1943) 11–21: 17, my emphasis. Commenting on Green's story, Rod Mengham notes that Michael Walsey's official account of the Wartime Fire Service contained a chapter entitled 'Waiting, Waiting, Waiting' (Mengham, Rod, 'Reading "The Lull" ', *Twentieth Century Literature* 29/4 (1983) 455–64: 456).

138 Green, Henry, *Caught* (London: The Hogarth Press, 1943).

139 Gellhorn, letter of 15 January 1972 to Betsy Drake: *SL* 378.

140 *LTT* 9.

141 *LTT* 55.

142 *LTT* 66.

143 *LTT* 67.

144 Gellhorn herself confessed that, in Mexico, she could not think rationally about Korea: 'so I have switched my mind about and tried to think of Sandy [her adopted son]' (Gellhorn, letter to Bernard Berenson, 18 July 1950, f. 1r).

145 Gellhorn, letter of June 1942 to Bill and Annie Davis: *SL* 126.

146 Gellhorn, letter of 1940, f. 1r.

147 Letter of 28 September 1940 to Charles Colebaugh, f. 1r.

148 F. 1r.

149 Gellhorn, letter of 11 June 1942, to Charles Colebaugh, f.1r,v.

150 Letter of 28 June 1942, to Charles Colebaugh, f. 1v. Paradoxically, femininity could also be a *way in* to the war zone: in a late letter to Betsy Drake, Gellhorn wrote that, 'my looks were a passport which somehow made tolerable the interruption of a furious woman' (*SL* 382).

151 *SL* 166–7.

152 F. 1r.

153 This cannot be quoted for copyright reasons.

154 Undated letter [June 1941], f. 1r.

155 Spanier, Sandra, 'Rivalry, Romance and War Reporters: Martha Gellhorn's *Love Goes to Press* and the *Collier's* Files', *Hemingway and Women*, ed. Broer, Lawrence R. and Holland, Gloria (Tuscaloosa and London: University of Alabama, 2002) 256–75: 274.

156 Where reference is made in this section to 'Gellhorn', it is to Martha Gellhorn, unless otherwise indicated.

157 The letter, unfortunately, can only be summarised as permission to quote directly from it has been withheld.

158 Kert, Bernice, *The Hemingway Women* (New York: Norton, 1983) 391.

159 Kert, *The Hemingway Women*, 392.

160 *PNR* 329.

161 Quoted in Reynolds, Michael, *Hemingway: The Final Years* (New York and London: Norton, 1999) 92.

162 Hemingway, 18 February 1945, f. 1v. As early as October 1941, Gellhorn resisted Hemingway's attempts to persuade her to publish *The Heart of*

Another under the name 'Martha Hemingway', although it was copy-righted by 'Martha Gellhorn Hemingway' (Kert, *The Hemingway Women*, 364; Reynolds, *Hemingway: The Final Years* 51). She told Charles Colebaugh in a letter of 16 July 1942 that her articles were always to be signed 'Martha Gellhorn': 'that is what I always was, and am and will be' (*SL* 131). On 17 May 1944, en route to her reunion with Hemingway in London, she wrote to Hortense Flexner: 'I want my own name back' (*SL* 164).

163 Hemingway, 18 February 1945, f. 4v.
164 Hemingway, 18 February 1945, f. 2v.
165 Hemingway, 18 February 1945, f. 3r.
166 Hemingway, 18 February 1945, f. 3r.
167 Hemingway, 18 February 1945, f. 3r.
168 Malcolm Cowley wrote in a *LIFE* profile: 'Officially Hemingway was a correspondent for *Collier's* attached to the Third Army, but he didn't enjoy being an observer and wrote only enough articles to keep from being sent home [. . .] he attached himself to the 4th Infantry Division of the First Army, where he found good friends and a satisfactory amount of fighting' (Cowley, Malcolm, 'A Portrait of Mister Papa', *LIFE* (10 January 1949) 86–90, 93–4, 96–8, 100–1: 87). See Chapter 5 for further discussion of the point.
169 Baker, *Ernest Hemingway*, 639–6.
170 Hemingway, Ernest, *Selected Letters*, 570.
171 Kert, *The Hemingway Women*, 405. Dorothea Dix (1802–87) was Superintendent of Women Nurses for the Union forces during the American Civil War (<http://www.civilwarhome.com/dixbio.htm>): a nice irony.
172 Hemingway, Leicester, *My Brother, Ernest Hemingway* (London: Weidenfeld and Nicolson, 1962) 242.
173 Gellhorn, 14 June 1944, f. 1r.
174 Moorehead, Caroline, *Martha Gellhorn: A Life* (London: Chatto & Windus, 2003) 265.
175 See also Spanier, 'Rivalry, Romance and War Reporters'.
176 'This Week', *Collier's* (22 July 1944) 4.
177 'This Week', 22 July 1944, 4.
178 It was ever thus: news of the couple's marriage was headlined in the *New York Times*, 'Hemingway Weds Magazine Writer' (22 November 1940) 25.
179 Hemingway, Ernest, 'Voyage to Victory', *Collier's* (22 July 1944) 11–13, 56–7: 11.
180 Hemingway, 'Voyage to Victory', 22 July 1944, 11.
181 Hemingway, 'Voyage to Victory', 22 July 1944, 12, added emphasis. The emphasis is added because the 'we' gives the impression that Hemingway is a member of the company.
182 Hemingway, 'Voyage to Victory' 12, 22 July 1944.

183 In a letter to Charles Colebaugh of 22 October 1938, Gellhorn commented, 'I have noticed that you always use better pictures for my articles than the ones I provide' (Gellhorn, 10 December 1938, f. 3r; the letter appears in *SL* 67–70 but this remark is omitted).

184 Gellhorn, 'Over and Back', *Collier's* (22 July 1944) 16.

185 Gellhorn, 'Over and Back', 22 July 1944, 16.

186 It was only on 5 August 1944 that her piece 'The Wounded Come Home' was published, revealing that she had travelled across the Channel on a hospital ship (see Chapter 4).

187 An article by Sandra Spanier on the *Collier's* archives reveals that an unknown hand scrawled across Hemingway's 'Voyage to Victory' cable, 'Lead All *Hemingway*' (Spanier, 'Rivalry, Romance and War Reporters' 270). Spanier goes on to show that Gellhorn's 'Hangdog Herrenvolk' was cabled to *Collier's* on 13 June 1944, the same day as 'Voyage to Victory', but twenty-five minutes earlier (9.55 pm as opposed to 10.20 pm). 'Over and Back' was in fact cabled on 14 June. Details that placed Gellhorn on the invasion beach were omitted in the published texts (Spanier, 'Rivalry, Romance and War Reporters', 270–2).

188 Hemingway, 'Voyage to Victory', 22 July 1944, 11.

189 Hemingway, 'Voyage to Victory', 22 July 1944, 57.

190 Hemingway, 'Voyage to Victory', 22 July 1944, 57.

191 *FoW* 108.

192 Gellhorn, 'Over and Back', 22 July 1944, 16.

193 Gellhorn, 'The Greatest Naval Jam in History', *Daily Telegraph* (3 June 1994) D4.

194 Gellhorn commented in 1996: 'A thing I've used wonderfully in my time – when I had no papers and I was stopped by the guard, I said, "Oh, I'm just doing a woman's angle, I just want to interview the nurses". The minute you say a woman's angle it just seems so innocuous, that you can get there' (Freedom Forum European Centre, 3).

195 Gellhorn, 'The Greatest Naval Jam in History', 3 June 1994.

196 Gellhorn, 'The Wounded Come Home', 5 August 1944, 74.

197 It must be acknowledged that there is only her word for this.

198 Gellhorn, 'Over and Back', 22 July 1944, 16.

199 Gellhorn, 'The Wounded Come Home', 5 August 1944, 14.

200 *SL* 167–8.

201 Orsagh, 'A Critical Biography', 175–6.

202 Kert, *The Hemingway Women*, 410.

203 Gellhorn, letter to Wallace Meyer, 1948, f. 2r.

204 Kert, *The Hemingway Women*, 406. Hemingway questions Gellhorn's war experience and motives at length in a letter to Bernard Berenson (Hemingway, 27 May 1953), which unfortunately cannot be quoted for copyright reasons.

205 Hemingway, Leicester, *My Brother, Ernest Hemingway* 243. Cf. Hemingway's letter to Maxwell Perkins of 14 January 1940 on 'Blood on

the Snow': 'Read Marty's piece this week in Colliers. It isn't so good militarily but boy she got out to that front when not a single correspondent had been there' (Hemingway, *The Only Thing That Counts*, 278).

206 Orsagh, 'A Critical Biography', 175. In later life, Gellhorn attempted a partial defence of her former husband's myth-making: Hemingway did become 'a shameful embarrassing apocryphiar about himself', 'but he was not like that in Spain' (Gellhorn, 'Guerre de Plume. Martha Gellhorn. On Apocryphism', *Paris Review*, 79 (1981) 280–301: 301).

207 Hemingway, Ernest, *The First Forty-Nine Stories* (London: Arrow Books, 1993) 417.

208 Hemingway, *The First Forty-Nine Stories*, 418.

4

Being there: the text

Though the two are distinct, the textual war reporter derives from the writer's positioning in the field. This chapter considers both the *figure* of the war reporter and his or her *orientation*. The former is a question of how the reporter is presented thematically: his or her role or persona.[1] The latter is a matter of how the figure is angled, 'spatially', emotionally and politically, with regard to the subject matter. The first section analyses in further detail how 'Ernest Hemingway, War Correspondent' was confected, now tracing the influence (and subversion) of the imperialist man-of-action persona, as exemplified by earlier American war reporter, Richard Harding Davis. Davis and Hemingway, themselves revealing the contradictions inherent in the figure of the war recorder, demonstrate the legacy with which Martha Gellhorn had to negotiate. Turning to these negotiations, the rest of the chapter analyses the textual production of 'Martha Gellhorn'.

Hyperreal Hemingway

'Ernest Hemingway, Man of War' was one of Ernest Hemingway's greatest fictional achievements. The creation can be termed 'Hyperreal Hemingway', given its ontology as a simulated concentrate of the actuality, more 'Hemingway-esque' than the man himself. This, then, is the 'Hemingway' of the lookalike competitions; of the Hemingway safaris and shoots; of the Hemingway-themed hotels; of the bars from Paris to Pamplona to Havana advertised as being those that Hemingway frequented;[2] of the 'Papa Doble'; of perpetuating fictions such as Michael Palin's *Hemingway's Chair* (1995). That the process was – and remains – one of artifice has been felt by various Hemingway commentators. 'Nobody would ever let papa just be human,' said his son Gregory.[3] 'To me,' said the poet John Pudney, who met him in the Second World War, 'he was a fellow obsessed with playing the part of Ernest Hemingway and "hamming" it to boot: a sentimental nineteenth-century actor called upon to act the part of a twentieth-century tough guy.'[4] 'He enjoyed playing the role of Papa, and found it a comfortable way to distance himself and deal with people who treated him as a great man,' said one biographer, Jeffrey Meyers.[5] 'Increasingly, [his] life was becoming his story, which he rehearsed and refined, embedding it with such vivid details that it would be difficult later to sort out his fictions,' said another, Michael Reynolds.[6]

The basic building-blocks were what Roland Barthes has termed 'biographemes'.[7] Like the mytheme, basic component of myth, the biographeme is the structural unit of biography, and, like mythopoeia, 'biopoeia' (or, in this case, 'autobiopoeia') is what Barthes elsewhere called 'a conjuring trick', the emptying out of history from reality.[8] The creation of 'Ernest Hemingway' can accordingly be seen as a palimpsestic process of fictionalisation: an assemblage of autobiographemes from which 'reality' has slowly been emptied out, leaving only image.

One Hemingway autobiographeme has already been seen in the previous chapter: the D-Day combat veteran. An earlier piece, 'The Saving of Madrid', in the British journal *FACT*, of 15 July 1938, shows a similar self-fashioning, though is more restrained. A number of pointers place the reporter at the physical centre of the conflict. The article is introduced as 'direct eye-witness reports of the Spanish war by Ernest Hemingway, the famous American author'.[9] It is written in the first person singular and contains liberal use of the phrase 'I saw'. The very act of writing is situated under fire: 'At the moment of writing this despatch back in my hotel a shell came down on the roof of a building just behind the hotel exploding with a great whoom.'[10] Of Brihuega, Hemingway remarks, 'you may not like it, and wish to believe it is propaganda, but I have seen the battlefield, the booty, the prisoners and the dead'.[11] A subtle positioning is taking place here, a gap being created and exploited between reporter and reader. This is unusual: the standard method in war correspondence is to use the second person to draw the reader in to the experience ('the ground under your bedroll would tremble and you could feel the awful breath of the blast push the tent walls and nudge your whole body ever so slightly [. . .]. Three weeks ago I was in Miami, eating fried chicken, sleeping in deep beds with white sheets,' Ernie Pyle told *his* readers, aligning himself as one of them).[12] But the experiential gap underlines the superior combat knowledge of the reporter – a strategy key to building the Hemingway reportorial persona.

It is not, though, the only strategy, and the complexity of this autobiographeme should not be underestimated. Two of Hemingway's 1944 articles, 'Battle for Paris' and 'How We Came to Paris' (published in *Collier's* on 30 September 1944 and 7 October 1944 respectively) furnish further evidence. In 'Battle for Paris', Hemingway carefully builds up a geographical positioning, inflected to reveal his personal, specialised knowledge of the area ('terrain,' he said elsewhere, 'is everything. If you don't have that, you have nothing'):[13]

> I knew the country and the roads around Epernon, Rambouillet, Trappes and Versailles well, as I had bicycled, walked and driven a car through this part of France for many years. It is by riding a bicycle that you learn the contours of a country best, since you have to sweat up the hills and can coast down them. Thus you remember them as they actually are.[14]

The claim here is that Hemingway has learnt the landscape bodily, a form of knowledge utterly dependent on presence and intellectually unassailable. The piece continues:

> After the U.S. Army reconnaissance units were withdrawn, the force defending Rambouillet was composed of mixed patrols of regulars and guerrillas [. . .]. I do not know if you understand what it means to have troops out ahead of you and then have them withdrawn and be left with [. . .] a large and beautiful town, completely undamaged and full of fine people, on your hands. There was nothing in the book issued to correspondents for their guidance through the intricacies of the military affairs which dealt with this situation; so it was decided to screen the town as well as possible and, if the Germans, observing the withdrawal of the American force advanced to make contact, to provide them with the necessary contact. This was done.[15]

This passage places official and unofficial troops on equal standing ('mixed patrols of regulars and guerrillas') and conveys the impression that the writer is personally responsible for the town's safety ('on your hands'). At the same time, the use of the passive serves to evade responsibility: 'it was decided', 'this was done'. In the piece, Hemingway explicitly acknowledges that 'war correspondents are forbidden to command troops',[16] and, indeed, in October 1944, he was summoned before the Inspector General Third Army to account for his activities in and around Rambouillet.[17] Within the text, therefore, he must balance his inclination to exhibit his superior military prowess ('I do not know if you understand what it means to have troops out ahead of you') and instinctive resourcefulness ('there was nothing in the book') against the legal requirement to remain an onlooker ('contact' obscures the fact of military engagement).

'Battle for Paris' ends mysteriously – 'it was necessary for me to leave on a patrol to St. Remy les Chevreuses'[18] (*necessary?*) – and the tale is taken up in 'How We Came to Paris', a piece replete with beautifully executed irony. It contains the following exchange:

By the time the contact was over, the column had two dead and five wounded, one tank burned up, and had knocked out two of the seven enemy tanks and silenced all of the 88s.

'*C'est un bel accrochage*,' the underground leader said to me jubilantly.

This means something like, 'We have grappled with them prettily' or 'We have tied into them beautifully,' searching in mind for the exact meaning of *accrochage*, which is what happens when two cars lock bumpers.

I shouted, 'Prettily! Prettily!'

At which a young French lieutenant, who did not have the air of having been mixed up in too many *accrochages* in his time but who, for all I know, may have participated in hundreds of them, said to me, 'Who the hell are you and what are you doing here in our column?'

'I am a war correspondent, monsieur,' I replied.

The lieutenant shouted: 'Do not let any war correspondents proceed until the column has passed. And especially do not let this one proceed.'

[. . .] I feared hostility might be creeping into his voice.[19]

This has various ingredients: the revelation of alien status ('what are you doing here in our column?'); self-identification ('I am a war correspondent' – though the thrust of the piece is that the reporter is entitled to priority); self-deprecation ('especially do not let this one proceed'). As this shows, while the Hemingway reportorial persona is undoubtedly self-promoting – glorifying, even – there is also a complicating self-mocking quality to it. The effect of the humour is actually to undermine the carefully built-up *machismo*, to reveal its very artificiality. This is Hemingway sending up 'Hemingway', a distancing of self from textual persona that was explicitly owned (though the textual persona, could, of course, be reconstructed in real life: for the *Daily Express* reporter, Alan Moorehead, in 1944, 'it was a little galling to find Ernest Hemingway sitting in the dining-room over a bottle of Heidsieck [. . .] he had liberated the Ritz just an hour before').[20] Charles Collingwood recalled that:

> After the war [Hemingway] asked me if I remembered a time in France when he had asked my opinion of a piece he had written for COLLIER'S and I said it sounded like a parody of Ernest Hemingway. 'You were right, of course,' he said.[21]

The last-quoted passage from 'How We Came To Paris' contains a further element, which emerges in the ironic cry 'Prettily! Prettily!'. It is notable that Hemingway's dispatches are flecked through with instances in which the reportorial figure quails before conflict. These are often expressed as humorous understatement: in the same article, for example, in the sentence 'it was much too beautiful for me, who had never been a great lover of contact anyway, and I hit the deck as an 88 shell burst alongside the road'.[22] This is not to criticise what is an entirely legitimate and understandable response but to flag another complexity in the 'Hyperreal Hemingway' reportorial persona.

The complexity has political aspects. Hemingway as man-of-action reprises the role played by an earlier American war correspondent: Richard Harding Davis (1864–1916). In Davis's case, the *macho* persona resonated with specific contemporary cultural discourses. The 1890s, culminating in the Spanish-American War, were a period of 'new' American imperialism. On 12 July 1893, in an address on 'The Significance of the Frontier in American History' at the World's Columbian Exposition in Chicago, Frederick Jackson Turner advanced the thesis that economic power, on which depended American individualism, nationalism, political institutions and democracy, was represented by free land. With the closing of the western frontier, new areas for expansion must be found if stagnation, institutional and individual, was to be avoided. This project, however, would comprise not a colonial territorial empire but proliferating commercial entanglements overseas.[23] For those in favour of such entanglements – Alfred Mahan, Charles Brooks Adams, Henry Cabot Lodge and Theodore Roosevelt were its leading advocates – the ultimate prizes were Latin America and Asia, not as sources of raw materials but as potential markets.[24] But, like the frontier spirit for which it was a substitute, the new mercantile imperialism also had mythological and psychosexual aspects. The avatars of the urge to expand were the original Puritan errand into the wilderness; 'Manifest Destiny'; Daniel Boone; James Fenimore Cooper's Hawkeye; cowboys and indians; the 'bonanza' mentality of the Gold Rush – all of which followed a process of regeneration through (male) violence.[25] In line with this, Amy Kaplan posits a 'libidinal map of U.S. geopolitics' during the shift from continental conquest to overseas commercial empire, linking nationhood and manhood in the imperialist dynamic.[26] As national power became 'disembodied', divorced from contiguous territorial expansion, masculine identity was reconceived as 'embodied', cultivated in the idealised robust muscular physique.[27] Theodore Roosevelt and his Rough Riders were obvious exemplars of the imperialistic 'strenuous life':[28] Richard Harding Davis was another.

Davis began his career on the Philadelphia *Record* and *Press*, later corresponding for the *New York Evening Sun*[29] and *Collier's Weekly* (making him Martha Gellhorn's predecessor). That he was, like her, eye-catching, is not in doubt. For Booth Tarkington, he was 'the beau ideal of jeunesse dorée'.[30] Winston Churchill recalled a 'peculiar thrill' on meeting him.[31] 'He was almost too good to be true,' wrote Gouverner Morris, 'he stood six feet and over, straight as a Sioux chief'.[32] His colleague John McCutcheon remarked that he was 'a conspicuous figure [. . .] wherever he went, he was pointed out [. . .] he was living a life of make-believe, wherein he was the hero of the story'.[33] These comments reveal a Davis of superhuman proportions, an 'eccentric' in the etymological sense (literally, too: he carried his bath-tub everywhere),[34] who lived his own myth (in a piece first published in *Collier's*, Finley Peter Dunne remarked that Davis's 'personality had a larger circulation than his literature').[35]

Like Hemingway, Davis achieved a significant degree of participation in warfare. In his memoir of the Spanish–American War, *The Rough Riders* (1899), Theodore Roosevelt recalled:

> It was Richard Harding Davis who gave us our first opportunity to shoot back with effect. He was behaving precisely like my officers, being on the extreme front of the line, and taking every opportunity to study with his glasses the ground where we thought the Spaniards were [. . .]. 'There they are, Colonel; look over there; I can see their hats near that glade.'[36]

Assimilated with the combatants (if still observing, rather than fighting), Davis here facilitates the course of conflict: he was even made a member of the regiment and given the same medal.[37] Resplendent in real life, 'Richard Harding Davis' is also a notable presence in his own texts. *With the Allies* (1915) contains that war reporter's calling-card, a reproduction of his passport,[38] and the dust-jacket of *With the French in France & Salonika* (1916) advertises the former work as follows:

> A first-hand account [. . .]. These descriptions are by a correspondent who has actually been in the thick of the fighting. Furthermore, they are by a writer with great experience in war matters, an intimate knowledge of military situations under modern conditions and a most vivid manner of telling. The book is well illustrated from photographs taken at the front.[39]

'The thick of the fighting' has advertising potency here. The 'overcoming of immense obstacles to being there' trope which is its necessary prelude features prominently in Davis's writing, also reinforcing certain values – bravery, persistence, reliability – which form an aura around the intrepid reporter. In *With the Allies*, for example, he recounts being captured as a spy[40] and lovingly describes how he accepted the surrender of a small Cuban town, afraid that if he did not take up the offer of the capitulating Spanish officer 'he would surrender to Paget or Jimmy'.[41] 'The Taking of Coamo' would make a fine story of reportorial initiative had not Davis also written a piece entitled 'How Stephen Crane Took Juana Dis':[42] one account of a reporter accepting a surrender may excite admiration but, when they all do it, a certain staginess creeps in. In one sense, the theatricality is its own justification: Davis was literally playing out an act of colonisation. But it also bespeaks a degree of headiness, as though, intoxicated by the role's possibilities (or already aware of its demise), Davis were hamming it up to the point of caricature.

It is a role which Davis explores again and again in his fiction, as though obsessed with reconciling its potentialities and problems. The fittingly titled story, 'The Reporter Who Made Himself King', concerns an aspiring young war correspondent, Albert Gordon,[43] who finds himself in the unlikely position of American Consul on the island of 'Opeki'. Crucially, the island has a cable, laid by the Yokahama Cable Company.[44] With slight creative exaggeration of an encounter between a German vessel and the Opekans, Albert provokes a full-scale international incident: requests for syndication arrive from all over world; the Secretary of State, the London *Times* and the British Embassy all make contact; and, as the story ends, warships mass off the coast.[45] This comic tale makes some serious points. Firstly, there is the 'snowballing' effect of journalistic language (a single cannon becomes 'the whole battery' and two huts 'the houses of the people').[46] Secondly, there is the extraordinary power of the cable – particularly when in exclusive hands. Thirdly, there is the expanding figure of the reporter himself. Adorned with medals reading 'Connecticut Agricultural State Fair. One Mile Bicycle Race. First Prize',[47] Albert metamorphoses into the King of Opeki: not only the sole source, guarantor and centre of the story but a force of colonisation and conquest.

In Davis – as in Albert – the role of war correspondent recuperated, if in diluted form, the now-defunct figure of the frontiersman. But there was another strand to his make-up: aristocratic elitism.[48] Davis was as much the verray parfit gentil knight as the testosterone-fuelled pioneer: indeed, John Seelye perceptively likens him to Edgar Rice Burroughs's Tarzan, Lord Greystoke (Hemingway called him 'a great snob').[49] As such, he embodied the 'dual errand' of the new imperialism: not only to carry US capitalism to 'under-developed' countries but to import 'civilised order' along with it.[50] This phenomenon is evident in 'The Reporter Who Made Himself King' (though surely ironised as Albert must slink away having wrought chaos), as the war-correspondent-cummonarch teaches his new subjects to play baseball.

Davis's masculine yet urbane image resulted in a theatrical 'star quality'. A generation later, Ernest Hemingway displayed similar staginess in his autobiographemic construction, in text and in life, of the macho war correspondent. The corollary, of course, was to preclude or complicate performance of the role by women: a challenge Martha Gellhorn had to meet. But in Davis's case, America's new, economic-imperial mission was in its hey-day and the war reporter figure embodied all its masculine vitality. By Hemingway's time, the 'new American imperial hero', like the frontiersman before him, was obsolescent, if not defunct. Where once the intrepid correspondent-combatant brought 'civilised' values as part of economic expansionism, now the same figure liberates the Paris Ritz. If Davis's tentative send-up of the figure had set the trend, Hemingway's full-blown version is replete with irony and self-sabotage, an atrophied version of a once more viable role.

'Martha Gellhorn' in the text

The woman reporter of the Second World War had, then, to position herself in relation to a male version of that figure which was well-entrenched if now politically moribund. Furthermore, if being there is predominantly a male experience, presence becomes, *prima facie*, a masculine textual quality. Requested to provide biographical information to prove she had 'been there' in order to validate *The Wine of Astonishment*, Gellhorn commented to her editor, Wallace Meyer:

> It is damn silly to beat your brains out for 14 months trying to write a book that is not a woman's book, and then have to explain how you came to be that way. [. . .] This is only useful to show that I had a good chance to look at a lot of men in combat [. . .] But something is always forgotten: the women of the countries where war was being fought – Italy and France and Holland and Belgium and Germany – simply stayed at home and saw combat: the war was fought all over them. And the women of England stayed home and learned about bombs. Anybody who was there knows; and my only advantage was that I was supposed to be writing about combat and combat troops, and I wore a uniform, and so I covered more mileage.[51]

Remarking the illogicality of conceptualising the front as an exclusively male preserve, Gellhorn here reflects the extent to which she, too, was assumed to act out an imperial, colonialist agenda. As for Hemingway, the role provided her with occasions for self-parody, but her sex complicated the situation still further. If masculinity had a well-defined place in the war-text, what place was there for femininity?

The rest of this chapter covers Gellhorn's attempts to grapple with this question, first in her journalism and then in her fiction. But, as a preliminary, getting a sense of how others represented her *qua* correspondent helps to gauge her own self-creations, in life and in her writings (the most notorious depiction of her, the portrayal of 'Dorothy Bridges' in Hemingway's play *The Fifth Column* (1938), is saved for comparison later with her own play, *Love Goes to Press*). To put this on a theoretical plane, anticipating the discussion in the next chapter, the gaze of others, in Sartre's words, 'confers spatiality upon me. To apprehend oneself as looked-at is to apprehend oneself as a spatializing-spatialized. But the Other's look is not only apprehended as spatializing; it is also *temporalizing*'.[52] In this sense, these representations of Gellhorn have a three-hundred-and-sixty-degree effect, contributing to her positioning in time and space.

Here, then, is Sefton Delmer, referring to the Spanish Civil War: 'When blond and beautiful writer Martha Gellhorn came with us[53] – she was to become Hemingway's third wife – he lectured her on how to observe things as a writer.'[54] Here is Josephine Herbst on the same period: 'Martha Gellhorn sailed in and out [of Madrid's Hotel Florida] in beautiful Saks Fifth Avenue pants, with a green chiffon scarf wound around her head.'[55] Here is Gustav Regler, also on the Spanish Civil War:

> the most devoted of all [was] Martha Gellhorn, witty and humane, of the best St. Louis stock [. . .] she saw our brigade in the making, strolled with Pacciardi in no-man's-land, provided the doctor with his first bandages, saw our amateurish weapons and wondered at the almost incredible modesty of our troops.[56]

Here is Mary Welsh Hemingway: 'I remember a cocktail party for Martha Gellhorn Hemingway months before, during which Miss G. had devoted her entire attention to a couple of Polish pilots.'[57] Here is Virginia Cowles: 'A tall, blonde girl with a brilliant gift for writing and a passionate concern for the underdog, she refused to take the woes of the world lightly.'[58] And here is Joyce Grenfell meeting Gellhorn at a party at the Duff Coopers:

> I thought her affected, surface bright and worthless. But after dinner, when we were girls together, she let down and the glimpses of reality were more encouraging. But there is a type of American new-intellectual who buzzes with know-all earnestness that I find rings hollow. She is obviously capable: I wonder how she writes.[59]

There are a number of elements (or biographemes) here: Gellhorn is at once attractive to men but inexperienced as a writer; the object of envy for other women; rude; intelligent; a passionate social reformer and a distinctively glamorous figure. Some of these correspond to aspects of Gellhorn's own multi-layered self-portraits, analysed next: all emphasise her conspicuousness, a quality about which she was to evince growing ambivalence.

The journalistic text

Paratextual detail surrounding Gellhorn's Second World War articles in *Collier's* magazine made its own contribution to her reportorial persona. She is billed so as to give the impression that she is a staff-writer, rather than an occasional freelance:[60] indeed, her name appears on the mast-head of editors. A positioning as 'roving emissary' is reinforced by the editorial language: 'into this tense and anxious country Collier's sent Martha Gellhorn'.[61] That the articles derive from the very centre of the conflict is reinforced by the legend 'Radioed from [X place]'. Further examples include: 'from the scene of Germany's triumph Martha Gellhorn sends you [. . .]';[62] 'history being made as you read';[63] 'from their front-row seats in Europe's war theater Collier's staff correspondents report to you weekly';[64] 'behind the front in gallant little Finland';[65] 'come behind the lines with Collier's staff correspondent';[66] 'under appalling difficulties, Martha Gellhorn made her way to the Canton fighting front'.[67] In 'The Week's Work' for 6 May 1944, Amy Porter wrote:

> Martha Gellhorn gives you a three-dimensional view of Cassino in her article, Visit Italy [. . .]. As a war correspondent for Collier's, Miss Gellhorn is one of the very few women reporters who actually get to the front. To gather material for this story, she jeeped along a road under constant enemy observation and spasmodic shellfire to the barracks on the outskirts of Cassino. [. . .] From the barracks she walked three quarters of a mile toward an antitank gun emplacement to a point where she could watch the brown smoke of German shellbursts in near-by buildings and the white-plumed bursts of American phosphorus shells.[68]

This account of intrepid resourcefulness is very much in the daredevil Davis mode (and explicitly distanced from the majority of women reporters, who do not 'actually get to the front' – the almost insuperable restrictions imposed on their access are unmentioned). But the accompanying photograph shows Gellhorn standing by a soldier, a snow-capped mountain in the background, gazing left to an unseen point, field glasses in hand (Figure 6). The image undermines the description by removing her from the fray and reinstating her as a chaperoned observer.

No other photographs of Gellhorn accompany her articles (except in 'These, Our Mountains', which bear the credit 'taken by Ernest Hemingway'[69] – somewhat oddly, since they also show him – and 'Her Day', which is a shot of Gellhorn, Hemingway and Madame Chiang-Kai Shek sitting round a table).[70] Their absence bespeaks reportorial efface-ment (as well as revealing that photographs, usually radioed back to

Figure 6 Gellhorn with binoculars, *Collier's*, 6 May 1944

Collier's by Joe Dearing, were not taken specifically to illustrate the text). But accompanying two of Gellhorn's articles are drawings. Those illustrating 'Blood on the Snow' (20 January 1940) are by Gregor Duncan. These show a glamorous 'girl correspondent', blonde and lipsticked, the only woman in the room, who is identified with Gellhorn by the use of direct, first person singular quotations from the text as captions (Figure 7).

The other article illustrated with drawings is 'Night Life in the Sky' (17 March 1945), an account of an extremely brave action on Gellhorn's part: taking a flight in the glass bulb in the rear of a Black Widow fighter plane. The girl reporter figure is this time even more closely identified with Gellhorn as captions of first person quotations from the text are reproduced as though in handwriting, giving them

Figure 7 Girl correspondent, *Collier's*, 20 January 1940

the look of diary entries. The editorial introduction makes explicit the danger: 'Collier's girl correspondent sat on a wobbly crate and flew over Germany looking for enemy planes at night. Her nose ran, her oxygen mask slipped off, her stomach got mad, she was scared and she froze.'[71] The drawings, however, completely subvert the effect of courage – albeit 'girl courage' – that has been built up since what they depict, bending before a lantern-jawed, pipe-smoking figure whose breadth of chest and inclined attitude embody solidity and protective-ness, is a rather simian-looking individual with a protruding jaw, unfeasibly long arms and an anatomically improbable left leg (Figure 8). Though this individual appears to be putting on her own stifling flying suit, the passive voice in the caption gives the impression of help-lessness. The overall idea of Gellhorn produced by the paratextual material in *Collier's* is therefore an intricate one: the magazine's 'own' envoy, placed at the centre of dangerous conflict, but tentatively and under protection, and depicted both as a glamour-figure and as ugly and masculine. The combination constitutes an anxious circling-round the Davis/Hemingway man-of-action persona, a feminisation of bravery involving contradictions that are returned to in the last two chapters.

y all have a right to shoot at us. I wouldn't advise it"

"I was zipped into flying pants, flying boots and a flying jacket, feeling more and more breathless at each layer"

Figure 8 'Night Life in the Sky', *Collier's*, 17 March 1945

If this complex is the *Collier's* version of Gellhorn-as-reporter, what message emerges from her own prose? The answer is similar ambiguity. In 'Night Life in the Sky', Gellhorn experiences a high degree of assimilation into the military: in effect, she is part of the crew of a fighter plane. The assimilation, though, is compromised, just as Gellhorn has nothing to contribute to the team (and even endangers them by her presence). After enduring agonies of anticipation – 'no one spoke in the jeep'[72] – she is inserted into the small glass bulb between the plane's tails (a space reminiscent of that occupied by Randall Jarrell's Ball Turret Gunner):[73]

> The radio operator was delegated to give me the necessary information. This was all so hopelessly mad that it could only be taken as a joke. He said in the dark, 'If anything happens, you turn this handle.'
>
> 'What handle? Where?' I said to myself nervously; I could not find the wretched thing.
>
> 'That will open the trap. Then turn this other handle on the right; it's wired but you won't have any trouble. That will drop the ladder out, and then all you have to do is fall out backward. You know where your ripcord is, don't you?'
>
> 'Yes,' I said sadly.
>
> 'If anything goes wrong with those two, you turn this handle on the cowling, and that whole piece of glass will fall out, and you can climb out through that; it's a little narrow with all those clothes on, but it will be all right, I guess. Well, that's about all,' said he. 'Have you got a cushion for her?' he asked the crew chief, and from nowhere a rather flat little sofa cushion appeared and was put on top of the wooden crate which was to be my seat. No one was intended to ride back here in the glass bulb between the twin tails, and there was no seat or safety belt.
>
> 'Oh, and here is your oxygen mask,' said the radio operator. 'It plugs in here and this is your earphone plug-in.'
>
> I had given up hope by now; it was all too complicated, and I thought gloomily that every one of these darned wires would come undone, I would fall out without meaning to or get hurled off my crate and mashed against the confused steel sides of my little glass case and I was already cold, and so I decided to try very hard to think of something else, like for instance a nice hot bath or next summer or going to the movies.[74]

This is a multi-layered set of positionings: hints are given so that the reader is left in no doubt as to the danger of the enterprise or to its de Certeauesque makeshift nature. That it is a gendered experience is also evident. Gellhorn is specifically placed in a space at the back where 'no one was intended' to be: a recapitulation in microcosm of the woman war correspondent's tenuous status. The lack of seat or safety belt, the escape hatch being too narrow, the suggestion that she may not even know how to operate her ripcord all underline her ignorance and conse-quent dependence on the crew. Giving her a cushion to sit on, however well-intentioned a gesture, suggests that she is associated with daintiness and fragility and also that she is tourist-like, being taken for a ride. The purpose of the bulb at the back of the fighter was to give the navi-gator or radar operator a clear rear view: Gellhorn's presence in it there-fore compromises the crew's safety (a point which looks forward to the 'fatal distraction' of the final chapter). At the same time, its glass sides reinforce her own visibility and her role of supervised observer rather than participant. The womb-like illusion of safety that the bulb confers masks her exposure to danger and separates her, at least to a degree, from the regular occupants of the aircraft. 'Night Life in the Sky' may be the closest that Gellhorn as reporter gets to the battle experience, but it confirms that that proximity is inescapably limited.

Gellhorn goes on to convey the sensation of absolute flight:

> We simply hurtled into the night and soared for the stars. I have never been part of such a take-off; and the actual feeling of flying became so intense that one felt free of the plane and as if one were moving nakedly and with no hindrance through a sky [. . .]. At hundreds of miles an hour we fled blindly through the night.[75]

The reporter is now one with the experience – the high point of assimilation – but the alignment shifts again:

> We climbed in a matter of seconds from 11,000 to 22,000 feet. That does not sound like much written out but it felt like nothing human. One's body turned to iron and was crushed down, feeling as if an enormous weight were pressing on something that would not yield. My oxygen mask was too large and had to be held on. As I held it with my right hand and held onto some kind of steel shelf with my left hand (so as not to fall backward off my darling little crate), I thought that (a) my stomach was going to be flattened against my backbone, and (b) that I was going to strangle. [. . .] I had now reached a stage of dull resignation and I only prayed that we would stop doing whatever we were doing, and do something else.[76]

In this passage, Gellhorn's inexperience and fear again distance her from the men in the front of the plane (who find the patrol 'boring'),[77] reflecting the physical distance between them. It is not, after all, an absolute 'fit', just as the equipment provided is the wrong size. The positioning is adjusted again by the use of '(a)' and '(b)' and the identification of the reporter's feelings as 'dull resignation': details which introduce a self-mocking quality. While similar tonal moments in Hemingway's reportage reveal moments when his courage wavers, their deployment here re-invests the reportorial figure with bravery by conveying her cool amusement at the situation. This, then, marks the legacy of the Richard Harding Davis daredevil persona in Gellhorn's war prose, even if the courage it evokes is more ironic *sang-froid* than swashbuckling bravado.

This impression is borne out in other dispatches. 'The Wounded Come Home' places the reportorial figure in a hospital ship serving the Normandy invasions (the experience described in Chapter 3). Gellhorn relates:

The endless varied ships in this invasion port were gray or camouflaged and they seemed to have the right idea. We, on the other hand, were all fixed up like a sitting pigeon. Our ship was snowy white [. . .] with many bright new red crosses painted on the hull and painted flat on the boat deck. [. . .] There was not so much as a pistol on board in the way of armament, and neither the English crew and ship's officers nor the American medical personnel had any notion of what happened to large, conspicuous white ships when they appeared at a war, though everyone knew the Geneva agreement concerning such ships, and everyone hoped the Germans would take the said agreement seriously.[78]

Using the first person plural subject pronoun rather than 'our ship', Gellhorn makes this deliberate visibility and consequent vulnerability to fire personal: 'We [. . .] were all fixed up like a sitting pigeon.' That no one has 'any notion' of what happens to 'large, conspicuous white ships' when they appear at a war echoes the suspect status of the attention-attracting female war correspondent (also theoretically entitled to safe passage under the Geneva Convention). Yet, even as the *faux-naïveté* of tone reveals the danger of the situation, it also, again, suggests a Davis-esque sanguinity. In the version of the piece collected in the 1959 edition of *The Face of War*, Gellhorn inserted the word 'wistfully' between 'everyone' and 'hoped' in the last clause,[79] an addition that reinforces the humour-driven impression of coolness under pressure. As it is presented here, then, the hospital ship reprises Gellhorn's own uneasy position in the war-zone: a cynosure that constitutes a potential safety-risk, albeit present with the best intentions.

Finally, 'Cracking the Gothic Line' continues this dialectic of problematic assimilation and self-satirising detachment. Labelled as 'radioed from Italy', the piece opens, typically, with a geographical siting: 'the Gothic Line, from where we stood, was a smashed village, an asphalt road and a pinkish brown hill'.[80] The third persons singular and plural are used – 'the infantry', 'they'[81] – but so, too, are the first persons singular and plural ('from where we stood'), the effect of which is to open a gap between observer and participant. This gap is rendered in explicit spatial terms: 'We watched the battle for the Gothic Line from a hill opposite, sitting in a batch of thistles and staring through binoculars. Our tanks looked like brown beetles.'[82] What here is an optical effect of great physical distance is reconfigured later as a psychological position:

Meanwhile you could sit in the sand with a book and a drink of sweet Italian rum and watch two British destroyers shelling Rimini just up the coast, see German shells landing on the front three kilometers away [. . .] hear a few German shells whistle overhead to land two hundred yards father down, and you were getting a fine sunburn, and life seemed an excellent invention.

> Historians will think about this campaign far better than we can who
> have seen it.[83]

Reading, drinking rum and getting 'a fine sunburn' while others are
shelled and a city destroyed expresses considerable emotional distance,
even while other indicators – shells landing only a few hundred yards
away, contemporaneity opposed to history – suggest proximity. This is a
characteristically complex and contradictory set of gradations of engagement and withdrawal on the part of the reportorial figure, the product
an irresolute textual standing.

Overall, then, from the dispatches, a distinct character emerges: a 'Martha
Gellhorn' who shares many of the attributes of the flesh-and-blood
Martha Gellhorn and who can be summed up as a fearless, feisty, independent individual with a nice line in understated humour.[84] It is a
character who shows a very high degree of self-awareness, knowing that
she is the object of attention as well as a professional onlooker. This
self-detachment is most commonly expressed in the touches of self-
deprecation which mark Gellhorn's journalistic writings – but the tone is
not exclusively self-deprecatory and the reader is left in no doubt about
the courage required to gather such material. In her fiction, to which this
chapter now turns, the war reporter continues to be a central presence in
the text, but the self-doubt is even stronger, reflecting Gellhorn's growing
disillusionment about her place in war.

The fictional text

The woman war reporter makes regular appearances in Martha
Gellhorn's fiction:[85] Mary Douglas in *A Stricken Field* (1940), Ann
Maynard in 'Portrait of a Lady' (1941), Elizabeth Dalton in 'Goodwill
to Men' (1941), Jane Mason and Annabelle Jones in *Love Goes to Press*
(1946); Lily Cameron in 'Week End at Grimsby' (1953), Mary Hallett in
'Till Death Us Do Part' (1958), Susanna in *The Lowest Trees Have Tops*
(1969), and the unnamed reporters in, 'Zoo in Madrid' (1941), 'A Sense
of Direction' (1941) and 'About Shorty' (1953). Of these, *The Lowest
Trees Have Tops* is discussed in Chapter 3, and *A Stricken Field*, 'Portrait
of a Lady', 'Goodwill to Men' and 'A Sense of Direction' are examined
in depth in the next chapters as they are more relevant to issues of participation. Affording Gellhorn greater distance from the correspondent
figure than is possible in relation to the persona in her dispatches, these
fictional texts are the venue for freer explorations of the contradictions
involved in representing war.

'Zoo in Madrid' and 'About Shorty' look back to the Spanish Civil War. In both, the unnamed narrator is a woman correspondent. The brief, dispatch-like 'Zoo in Madrid' pitches this figure, spatially and emotionally, both within and outside the conflict. Fighting is taking place 'far down the street'[86] as the narrator and her companion, during a minor lull, visit the park, with its 'old foolish statues of armoured heroes in fine attitudes',[87] and go to a bar. Showing ethical unease about the position of the safe observer, she reflects: 'We were sick of the war. We had no right to be since we were not the men in the trenches nor were we the blind American in the hospital at Salices nor the little Spaniard in the first-aid post near Jarama, who had no arm.'[88] This geographical and experiential distance is, however, confused by a sense that the two *do* feel like weary veterans and share a camaraderie which gives them some degree of 'ownership' of the conflict. This ambiguity is stated in visual terms when the pair enter the zoological gardens and Gellhorn conjures up a bewildering jumble of peace and war: 'We began to talk about how incredible it was to have everything mixed up together, the zoo and the gun positions behind the statue, and the café that grew up in one half of a shelled building.'[89] The first floor of the building is now a 'chaos': 'chairs hanging on a chandelier, an iron stove that was hurled down through the floor into the centre of a former cabaret, cracked mirrors'.[90] This has a mad, baroque theatricality about it (particularly the word 'cabaret'): the sheer topsi-turviness of the details reinforces the journalists' feeling that the war has put them, like the chairs hanging from the chandeliers, in a precarious, ill-defined position.

In 'About Shorty', published 12 years later, the woman journalist narrator is a veteran, like Gellhorn, of Poland, Finland, China and the Paris Peace Conference, as well as the Spanish Civil War:[91] a member of the 'voluntarily uprooted'.[92] But her sense of being a stake-holder is felt most strongly with regard to the Spanish conflict. 'That defeat was ours,' she reflects, 'we carried it with us in our minds, in our hearts';[93] 'we owned the country [. . .] in a small but devoted way'.[94] But if ownership is stated explicitly, there is also acknowledgement of the limitations of journalistic participation: 'we had done nothing but accomplish an act of presence'.[95] Lacking Davis-esque self-assurance, the narrators in 'Zoo in Madrid' and 'About Shorty' both negotiate apparently irreconcilable positions: they are deracinated ('uprooted') yet politically committed ('ours'), involved ('owned') yet helpless spectators.

'About Shorty' also features a variation on the theme of involvement discussed in detail in the next chapter. Shorty, a German girl, is married to Otto, a Jewish doctor working in the International Brigades, considered by the Republicans to be 'the finest man in Spain'.[96] When she becomes the mistress of a Russian journalist and later a Spanish Colonel, Juanito, a 'whore de combat',[97] the narrator's 'gentlemen war-correspondent friends' are 'surprisingly angry'.[98] Shorty, it is felt, is 'on Franco's side, distracting Juanito from his work and destroying Otto.'[99] This is a version of the woman at war encountered repeatedly in Gellhorn's work: sited parapolemically, she nevertheless interrupts and impedes the course of conflict, often with fatal results. In this story, the figure is 'redeemed': Shorty selflessly leaves her husband and baby in occupied Paris, knowing that, as a German anti-fascist, she would endanger them by her presence. The narrator herself finds her colleagues' 'free use of the Scarlet Letter tiresome and dishonest'.[100] 'About Shorty' is therefore a subtle collection of positionings: the narrating journalist is present (but 'only' present and feeling ambivalent towards her 'fine trade');[101] emotionally involved yet distanced through anonymity; sharing a bond with her male colleagues ('determined to do my job like a real newspaperman')[102] but not all their values; aware of the potentially lethal effect of female engagement in conflict yet none the less sympathetic towards Shorty ('probably Otto had a girl too').[103] The last element is most suggestive of the time lapse between the publication of this story and 'Zoo in Madrid', reflecting the disillusionment that was Martha Gellhorn's legacy from the Second World War.

Published in the same collection as 'About Shorty', 'Weekend at Grimsby' is another retrospective piece, nostalgic for the friendship and good times of the Second World War. The woman journalist narrator, Lily Cameron, finds the postwar period (the 'honeyed peace' of the collection's title) ghostly, unreal, desolate, unsatisfying – an 'endless duration':[104] 'You always think in terms of war, Lily told herself, the war is over. The war was so easy compared to this that they ought to reverse the words; this is much harder and longer than war ever was.'[105] Visiting the Poles she once knew as aristocratic officers and who now, bathetically, run a fish business in Grimsby, Lily feels like 'a ghost going to a reunion with fellow ghosts'.[106] What she finds instead is that the Poles have moved on: Sim is now with a very corporeal and un-ghostly local girl, with 'legs like tree-trunks', built on the 'scale of the Winged Victory'.[107] Defined by their absence, the war years therefore represent for the narrator a time when she was most alive: 'Witness the efficient way I advanced myself from Naples and Rome until I landed where I wished to be, in a line regiment of lovely goofy Poles, with sea bathing thrown in, at least in the summer.'[108] To be in a line regiment, and to share camaraderie as an equal as the narrator does is an 'engaged' position, reinforced by the military or topographical verbs of movement she applies to herself ('advance' and 'land') and facilitated by the fact that the 'lovely goofy Poles'' regiment was most likely part of the internationally constituted Eighth Army which fought its way up Italy, an army Gellhorn described affectionately after the war as a 'huge hodgepodge of humanity'.[109] In this mêlée, a woman correspondent would have encountered fewer official obstacles to blending in. Despite, or rather because of, this more informal status, the narrator of 'Weekend at Grimsby' can, unlike her colleagues in 'About Shorty' and 'Zoo in Madrid', therefore remember her place in war as well-defined and tenable. But her reminiscences again complicate her positioning as they simultaneously suggest a somewhat superficial experience of conflict (reminiscent of Gellhorn getting a 'fine sunburn' as shelling goes on down the coast):[110] a beach holiday in the company of attentive officers. Though the story is not as harshly self-critical as other examples of Gellhorn's fiction, this aspect of it reveals the basis of her negativity about women war correspondents: their frivolity, their seeking-out of attractive male combatants, their (illicit) enjoyment of the state of war.

Continuing the theme, the short story 'Till Death Us Do Part' features two recorders of war: a photographer, Tim Bara, based on Robert Capa, and a journalist, Mary Hallett ('Marushka'), based on Gellhorn. Gellhorn and Capa were friends – 'I loved [him] with my whole heart' she said, 'we counted on each other'[111] – and he took the photos after her wedding with Hemingway which appeared in *LIFE* on 6 January 1941.[112] In the story, Bara/Capa is capricious, mercurial, charismatic; 'the most famous war photographer in the world'; 'a conceited opera singer' whose very presence confers newsworthiness on a conflict and who, like his pictures, is 'always prominently displayed'.[113] His death is reported in the *New York Times* 'in a box on the front page with a picture'.[114]

Bara/Capa is, therefore, himself 'news'. In the story, his itinerant nature is emphasised. His passport (Capa was a Hungarian exile) is 'rather a long document. It appears to be handmade. [. . .] It's different bits of paper, in different languages, with stamps on it, stuck together with Sellotape.' The formality of his status, in other words, is entirely self-confected. Bara has no next of kin, consul or permanent home, but lives 'in the moment'.[115] He therefore takes on some of the qualities of his camera: the capacity to 'zoom' in and out (that is, to alter and exploit distance and perspective) and the detachment conferred by rootlessness. 'Marushka' shares these propensities: Bara notes that her attempt at postwar domesticity in London is like 'stabling a mule in a candy box'.[116] She has, he says, 'a pre-Soviet Russian soul, so fierce, so illogical, so elevated, so absurd'.[117]

This is a portrait of the war recorder as involved in conflict but none the less detached from it, circling round and within the subject. In this configuration, there are still further gradations. Lep, Bara's photographer friend, muses:

> A writer can have what emotions he wishes or cannot avoid, at the time of getting his material; later he can sit down for a while and bring order out of what he saw and remembers. But for the photographer there is no time; there is only that one instant; he cannot afford any emotions for himself.[118]

Being there, for the photographer, is the *sine qua non*: 'Bara was always there, where you had to be [. . .] always there, always seeing what had to be seen, always understanding what it meant, fast, fast, and with himself under control or forgotten, doing his work.'[119] Indeed, Bara is not only present at combat but, on occasion, seems actually to metamorphose into a combatant: he 'took pictures as if a camera was a gun [. . .] shot everything that moved'.[120] His pictures, which 'force everyone to see what there was to fight',[121] have a mobilising intent. Robert Capa's own 1947 autobiography, *Slightly Out of Focus*, is an extended account of evasions of bureaucracy, to the point where, instead of 'being there' forming the pre-condition of taking pictures, taking pictures becomes the only means (through the gaining of accredited status) of being there: the photographer jumps with the American paratroopers into Sicily to avoid being deported back to the United States.[122]

The story does not disguise the fact that Bara's photos are artifices: it is while choreographing two jeeps to seem like 'a fine big body of troops' – a tableau that is explicitly 'posed', 'fake'[123] – that he is killed by a sniper. 'Billings' of the fictional *Herald* comments (recalling the title of Capa's autobiography) that Bara's photos of D-Day 'were out of focus anyway'.[124] By coincidence, Robert Capa's own 'Instant of Death' image from the Spanish Civil War – a Loyalist soldier apparently thrown back in the air by the force of a shot – has formed the focus of debate about photographic authenticity in wartime. It was captioned in *LIFE* of 12 July 1937: 'Robert Capa's Camera Catches a Spanish Soldier the Instant He is Dropped by a Bullet Through the Head in front of Cordoba',[125] but whether the photograph really was an image of this referent has been questioned. Martha Gellhorn herself entered the debate on Capa's side, writing to Cornell Capa that the doubt, raised by Phillip Knightley, was 'disgusting rot'.[126] She prepared notes for a television defence of Capa, her most explicit demand for 'being there':

> To prove exactly how little Mr. Knightley understands real war and the work of correspondents and photographers, Knightley writes, 'How did Capa come to be alongside him (the militia man), camera aimed at him, lens

reasonably in focus, just as the man was shot dead?' Capa was there because that is where you had to be, where the action was – combat photographs are taken in combat or not at all.[127]

It can be inferred from this that Capa – whose maxim was 'if your pictures aren't good enough, you're not close enough'[128] – was risking death too: a case of the photograph conferring integrity on the photographer.

The taking of a photograph is in this sense also an expression of proximity. In the Second World War, the photographer reached the very centre of combat. Here is Capa on D-Day:

> Shooting from the sardine's angle, the foreground of my picture was filled with wet boots and green faces. Above the boots and faces, my picture frames were filled with shrapnel smoke; burnt tanks and sinking barges formed my background.[129]

Capa adds that when he tried to re-load his film, 'the empty camera trembled in my hands. It was a new kind of fear shaking my body from toe to hair, and twisting my face.'[130] His 106 shots, taken despite the odds, were later reduced to eight when an 'excited dark room assistant' (the young Larry Burrows who himself went on to become a distinguished war photographer in Vietnam) turned the heat up too high and melted the emulsions. 'The captions under the heat-blurred pictures read that Capa's hands were badly shaking,' Capa recorded in his autobiography:[131] an instance of the situation of the photographer being (erroneously) read out of a photo.

In these senses (the perspective and the emotional-physiological response recorded by the shot), a photograph is always of the photographer: from the photographic image it is possible to discern his or her position in relation to the photographed, in that the photographer is always where the picture is not (though, paradoxically, this also serves to put him or her 'in the picture'). If the advent of the long lens meant the photographer could get further away, at least the illusion of closeness was preserved. Translated into reportorial terms, this aspect of positioning is present in 'Till Death Us Do Part' as Marushka's response to the Nazi concentration camps. 'Bursting with angriness'[132] and 'frightening to see',[133] she displays an emotional engagement which corresponds to the photographer's shaking hand. It is a similar reaction to that noted by Cornell Capa when he wrote in the text accompanying the 1967 New York exhibition 'The Concerned Photographer' of his brother's 'intense empathy and involvement'.[134]

There are other, simpler, ways in which a photographer's intervention in conflict can be effected. 'I hated myself and my profession,' commented Capa, as he photographed soldiers being stretchered out of returning bombers, 'this sort of photography was only for undertakers, and I didn't like being one. If I was to share the funeral, I swore, I would have to share the procession.'[135] A photograph is also the record of the fact that the photographer did not stop to help the wounded, of a particular outcome to an ethical dilemma which has often been deeply felt. It is significant that sight of the concentration camps has rendered Marushka bedridden: the war recorder silenced, inactive, impotent. 'Till Death Us Do Part', then, exposing the potential and limitations of reportorial involvement, reflects, once again, Gellhorn's self-doubt.

The final texts for discussion in this chapter are Gellhorn and Cowles's play *Love Goes to Press* and *The Fifth Column*, Hemingway's Spanish Civil War play,[136] works in which concern surrounding the figure of the war reporter is expressed in particularly scathing terms. Hemingway's introduction to the latter again sites the act of composition not just close to the action but at its centre: it is literally 'written under fire'.[137] The play features Philip Rawlings, a secret agent engaged in counter-espionage against the rebel 'fifth column' in Madrid, and Dorothy Bridges, a journalist who writes pieces for *Cosmopolitan* magazine. Dorothy is described as a 'bored Vassar bitch'.[138] Her understanding of the conflict appears limited:

PRESTON: Do you understand anything that's happening here?
DOROTHY: No, darling, I understand a little bit about University City, but
            not too much. The Casa del Campo is a complete puzzle to
            me.[139]

Undercover as a newspaperman, Philip is constantly berated by Dorothy for his lack of action: 'you could do something serious and decent [. . .] you could do something *political* or something *military* and fine'.[140] This not only reveals Dorothy's relative ignorance – it is clear to the audience that Philip is involved in dangerous work – but also conveys the view (held even by a correspondent herself) that journalism, with its idle, cowardly and superficial practitioners, is an ideal cover for *real* action. The point is also made in the figure of Preston, another journalist, who 'never goes to the front [. . .] just writes about it'[141] and who reacts nervously to the bombardments. Philip, by contrast, is brave, tough, merciful, self-sacrificing and war-wearied: he is messy and drinks too much but the overall sense is that he is a messianic figure, the saviour of the Spanish people – a persona in the mould of the Davis-esque new imperialist, yet presented in this version with little apparent irony. Dorothy is shown as an interference to all this, with her demands to settle down with Philip to a self-indulgent, glamorous lifestyle. Philip responds to her yearnings with scorn which, on occasion, becomes aggression. 'Aren't you a lady war correspondent or something?' he demands. 'Get out of here and go and write an article. This is none of your business.'[142] At the end, he tells her, 'you're useless, really. You're uneducated, you're useless, you're a fool and you're lazy.'[143] 'Not useless,' she replies, implying that he can at least sleep with her, but Philip rejects even this 'commodity'.[144] Two other passages are worth quoting:

> PHILIP: Granted she's [Dorothy] lazy and spoiled, and rather stupid, and enormously on the make. Still she's very beautiful, very friendly, and very charming and rather innocent – and quite brave.[145]

> PHILIP: She [Dorothy] has the same background all American girls have that come to Europe with a certain amount of money. They're all the same. Camps, college, money in family [. . .] men, affairs, abortions, ambitions, and finally marry and settle down or don't marry and settle down. [. . .] This one writes. Quite well too, when she's not too lazy. Ask her about it all if you like. It's very dull though, I tell you.[146]

Jacqueline Orsagh comments:

> Many have pointed to the unmistakable resemblance between the heroine and Martha Gellhorn as further evidence of Hemingway's affections. While that may be so, an analysis of the emotional, mental, and spiritual qualities of the heroine prompts one to speculate on the cause of Hemingway's distortion. He took Gellhorn's work, her ability to make rooms homey, her accent, her beauty, and her silver fox cape and used these items to make his heroine ridiculous.[147]

It is not the intention here to contribute to the debate on the extent to which 'Dorothy Bridges' of *The Fifth Column* illuminates the Gellhorn–Hemingway personal relationship (or, indeed, the Hemingway–Pauline Pfeiffer personal relationship). What instead is to be noted is the exclusively negative portrait of the figure of the female war reporter: ignorant, lightweight, prone to prioritise domestic issues, lazy, privileged, boring, solely a source of sexual satisfaction (a satisfaction which, at that, does not compare to that of serving the *Causa*). Unexpectedly, it is a rendition of the role which is reprised in Gellhorn and Cowles's *Love Goes to Press*.[148]

The two women war reporters in this play are Jane Mason of the (fictional) *New York Bulletin* and Annabelle Jones of the (fictional) *San Francisco World*. In the 1995 edition of the work, Gellhorn revealed of their composition: 'The two female leads, Jane and Annabelle, were caricatures of Ginny [Cowles] and me. It is very long ago, but I believe that Ginny wrote most of Annabelle (me) and I wrote most of Jane

(Ginny).'[149] The play is, according to Gellhorn, 'a joke', a 'silly little tinsel play': it 'bears no resemblance whatever, of any kind at all, to war and war correspondents'.[150] Nevertheless, her introduction sketches a real-life Cowles who seems to maintain, in relation to war, a persona somewhere between cheerleader and society hostess. 'Ginny' 'breeze[s] in' to Italy, 'lark[s] about'; she is 'fearless', 'energetic', knows 'everyone in London'.[151] (In her own memoirs, Cowles describes herself as 'hurtling through the Czechoslovakian countryside' and 'motoring through the Midlands';[152] and she has a cameo role in Mary Welsh Hemingway's autobiography 'in a mink jacket' on the boat from occupied France to England.)[153] It seems apt therefore to treat 'Jane' and 'Annabelle' as car-icatures – that is, as exaggerations based on a grain of truth.

Without doubt, the two characters display on occasion the admirable characteristics of the 'Martha Gellhorn' of the *Collier's* articles. They are feisty, independent women, more resourceful and scrupulous than their male counterparts, dedicated to their profession and completely fearless. Sandra Spanier rightly calls them 'funny, daring, sexy, quick-witted'.[154] But these positive traits are constantly undermined by others. One of the first things the audience learns about Jane Mason, for instance (signifi-cantly revealed by one of her male colleagues), is that she 'wouldn't get out of bed [. . .] in Helsinki on the grounds that the climate was sub-human'.[155] This might seem to be the self-revelatory comment of a jealous competitor, but Jane's first remark to Annabelle reinforces the stereotype: 'I'll never forget when you turned up in Spain to battle for the under-dog in that black Schiaparelli number'.[156] Jane is not only lazy, afraid of the cold and obsessed with her appearance – 'Where *is* my lipstick?'[157] – but also falls for the plodding Philip (a choice of name suggesting a moment of revenge on the 'Philip' of *The Fifth Column*?),[158] whose idea of a suit-able womanly occupation is re-reading the works of Trollope while making cheese. (Jane is at least reprieved from this by sneaking off to report on the war in Burma instead of going to stay with Philip's mother in the English countryside.) The overall effect is confusing. While Jane is the embodied rejection of Dorothy Bridges's role, explicitly refusing the dull domesticity offered by Philip, she also displays (in abundance) the flighty, appearance-obsessed, 'feminine' qualities which render Dorothy lightweight. A contemporary review commented: 'If this is the way Martha Gellhorn and Virginia Cowles themselves behaved in the pursuit of their newspaper assignments, it would seem wise for the high command to banish all women journalists from the next war.'[159]

Love Goes to Press is, above all, a dramatisation of the gendering of access to war. The tension in the play between the male and female correspondents centres upon laying claim to information. Joe Rogers, divorced from Annabelle Jones, comments: 'I'm allergic to newspaper women. I married one once. They never stop trying to scoop you, and when you scoop them they divorce you.'[160] It emerges, however, that perhaps the reality was rather different: 'what would you think,' asks Annabelle, 'if your husband's first conscious act after the honeymoon was to steal your stories?'[161] The issue, which has estranged them once, does so again after an abortive reconciliation when Joe usurps Annabelle's trip to Poland. The irony in the play is that it is another female character who actually achieves the greatest scoop of the moment: due to being confused with Jane, Daphne Rutherford, the ENSA troop entertainer, witnesses the Americans' taking of Mount Sorello. The irony resides in the fact that Daphne is exclusively composed of the most flippant of feminine qualities, first appearing to Jane and Annabelle in a mink coat and concerned about her chipped nail varnish.[162] That these qualities prevail both in 'getting there' and 'being there' suggests an inversion of the 'double helix'. As is argued in the next two chapters, within the complex matrix of positionings which the woman war reporter may take up, Martha Gellhorn found this an ambiguous outcome.

The range of textual positionings occupied by 'Martha Gellhorn' and her fictional female reporters matches Martha Gellhorn's own extraordinary progress through the war zone. The woman war writer is at once itinerant, deracinated, fearless, needy, staunchly independent, patronised, glamorous, masculinised, flighty, pleased with her own daring, often low in self-esteem and coolly humorous. Above all, she is *noticed*: the cynosure of field and text. As such, she alters the course of war, if only by diverting attention. Her being there is more than a simple act of presence. By now, it should be clear that its extra qualities are by no means ones which Gellhorn found wholly positive. Her doubts emerge more strongly in her fiction than in her journalism, the product of her entire Second World War experience and her reflections on it. If nostalgia is the governing tone of these later fictions, it is a nostalgia marked with the clear awareness that the very foundation of these 'best of times' is deeply flawed.

The *Daily Express* writer Sefton Delmer opened the second volume of his autobiography, covering his years as a BBC broadcaster of 'black propaganda' to Germany during the Second World War, with a comment on his reportorial experiences in the Spanish Civil War and after:

> What I had seen during those weeks that had followed the German breakthrough, had made me fiercely determined to abandon my work as a

reporter and get myself a job more directly connected with the conduct of the war than writing articles about it.[163]

While this chapter has considered a complex set of textual positionings in relation to war, one aspect is still to be addressed. The next chapter moves from presence to participation, to consider the issue, deeply troubling to Martha Gellhorn, of the reporter's active engagement with war.

Notes

1 This might be likened to the Renaissance art theorist Leon Battista Alberti's concept of the figure who, from within a depicted scene, interprets the action for the viewer's response: 'in an *istoria* [a dramatic composition] I like to see someone who admonishes and points out to us what is happening there; or beckons with his hand to see [. . .] or invites us to weep or to laugh together with them' (Alberti, Leon Battista, *On Painting* (*Della Pittura*, 1435–36), trans. and with an introduction by Spencer, John R. (New Haven and London: Yale University Press, 1966) 78). John R. Spencer comments that 'not only is the perspective construction to form a spatial link between the painting and the observer, but the commentator is to establish the emotional link' (Spencer, John R., 'Introduction', *Leon Battista Alberti: On Painting* 11–38: 26).

2 A phenomenon so extensive as to invite parody, for example Patrick Caulfield's painting *Hemingway Never Ate Here* (1998–99).

3 Hemingway, Gregory H., *Papa: A Personal Memoir* (Boston: Houghton Mifflin, 1976) 90.

4 Baker, Carlos, *Ernest Hemingway: A Life Story* (Harmondsworth: Penguin, 1972) 597.

5 Meyers, Jeffrey, *Hemingway: A Biography* (London and Basingstoke: Macmillan, 1985) 392.

6 Reynolds, Michael, *Hemingway: The Final Years* (New York and London: Norton, 1999) 114.

7 Barthes, Roland, *Sade, Fourier, Loyola* (Paris: Éditions du Seuil, 1971) 15.

8 Barthes, Roland, *Mythologies* (London: Vintage, 1993) 142.

9 'Introduction', *FACT* (July 1938) 4–5: 4.

10 Hemingway, Ernest, 'The Saving of Madrid', *FACT* (July 1938) 7–33: 10.

11 Hemingway, 'The Saving of Madrid', 15 July 1938, 13.

12 Pyle, Ernie, *Ernie's War* (New York and Toronto: Random House, 1986) 175.

13 'The Hemingways in Sun Valley: The Novelist Takes a Wife', *LIFE* (6 January 1941) 49–57: 52.

14 Hemingway, Ernest, 'Battle for Paris', *Collier's* (30 September 1944) 11, 83–4, 86: 11.

15 Hemingway, 'Battle for Paris', 30 September 1944, 84.

16 Hemingway, 'Battle for Paris', 30 September 1944, 83.

17 Baker, *Ernest Hemingway*, 652.

18 Hemingway, Ernest, 'How We Came to Paris', *Collier's* (7 October 1944) 14, 65, 67: 86.

19 Hemingway, 'How We Came to Paris', 7 October 1944, 65, 67.

20 Moorehead, Alan, *Eclipse* (London: Granta, 2000) 159.

21 Quoted in Meyers, Jeffrey, *Hemingway: A Biography*, 404. The piece referred to, according to Meyers, is 'War in the Siegfried Line'. This is a somewhat odd attribution as the majority of the article is verbatim quotation of a Captain Howard Blazzard rather than Hemingway self-parody. At the end of Blazzard's story, Hemingway remarks, however, 'if you want to know [. . .] get someone who was there to tell you' (Hemingway, Ernest, 'War in the Siegfried Line', *Collier's* (18 November 1944) 18, 70–1, 73: 73). Though this justifies the extensive quotation from Blazzard, it also implies Hemingway's own authority to relate: 'If you wish, and I can still remember, I will be glad to tell you sometime what it was like in those woods for the next ten days,' he continues (Hemingway, 'War in the Siegfried Line', 18 November 1944, 73). By this time, Hemingway had been summoned for interrogation by the Inspector General Third Army to account for exceeding his correspondent's remit in his activities around Rambouillet from 18 to 25 August 1944 (Baker, *Ernest Hemingway*, 652). This may explain his uncharacteristic reticence in allowing Blazzard to tell the tale.

22 Hemingway, 'How We Came to Paris', 7 October 1944, 65.

23 LaFeber, Walter, *The New Empire: An Interpretation of American Expansion 1860–1898* (Ithaca: Cornell University Press, 1963) 66, 60–1.

24 LaFeber, *The New Empire*, 91.

25 Slotkin, Richard, *Gunfighter Nation: The Myth of the Frontier in Twentieth-Century America* (New York: Atheneum, 1992) 3, 14, 15, 18, 12.

26 Kaplan, Amy, 'Romancing the Empire: The Embodiment of American Masculinity in the Popular Historical Novel of the 1890s', *American Literary History* 2/4 (Winter 1990) 659–90: 661.

27 Kaplan, 'Romancing the Empire', 662.

28 Roosevelt's *The Strenuous Life* was published in 1899.

29 Bradley, Patricia, 'Richard Harding Davis', *A Sourcebook of American Literary Journalism*, ed. Connery, Thomas B. (New York and Westport, Conn.: Greenwood, 1992) 55–67: 58–9.

30 Tarkington, Booth, 'Richard Harding Davis', *The Novels and Stories of Richard Harding Davis. Volume 1 – Van Bibber Etc* (New York: Scribner, 1916) ix–xi: ix.

31 Churchill, Winston, 'Richard Harding Davis', *The Novels and Stories of Richard Harding Davis. Volume 9 – The Bar Sinister* (New York: Scribner, 1916) v–vi: v.

32 Morris, Gouverner, 'R.H.D.', *The Novels and Stories of Richard Harding Davis. Volume 11 – The Red Cross Girl* (New York: Scribner, 1916) vii–xx: vii, xiii.

33 McCutcheon, John, 'With Davis in Vera Cruz, Brussels, and Salonika', *The Novels and Stories of Richard Harding Davis. Volume 12 – The Lost Road* (New York: Scribner, 1916) vii–xxii: x, xii.

34 McCutcheon, 'With Davis in Vera Cruz', x.

35 Dunne, Finley Peter, 'Richard Harding Davis', *The Novels and Stories of Richard Harding Davis. Volume 8 – The Scarlet Car* (New York: Scribner, 1916) vii–xi: vii.

36 Roosevelt, Theodore, *The Rough Riders* (London: Kegan, Paul, Trench, Trübner, 1899) 90–1.

37 Roosevelt, Theodore, 'Davis and the Rough Riders', *The Novels and Stories of Richard Harding Davis. Volume 5 – Captain Macklin, His Memoirs* (New York: Scribner, 1916) vii–viii: vii.

38 Davis, Richard Harding, *With the Allies* (London: Duckworth, 1915) between 52 and 53.

39 Davis, Richard Harding, *With the French in France & Salonika* (London: Duckworth, 1916) dust-jacket.

40 Davis, *With the Allies* ch. 2; Wood, Leonard, 'Richard Harding Davis', *The Novels and Stories of Richard Harding Davis. Volume 10 – The Man Who Could Not Lose* (New York: Scribner, 1916) v–vi: v.

41 Davis, Richard Harding, *Notes of a War Correspondent* (New York: Scribner, 1911) 110.

42 Davis, Richard Harding, 'How Stephen Crane Took Juana Dis', *The War Dispatches of Stephen Crane*, ed. Stallman, R. W. and Hagemann, E. R. (London: Peter Owen, 1964) 196–9.

43 John Seelye points out the 'Anglophilia' of the name, suggesting that it derives from the Prince Consort and the hero of Khartoum (Seelye, John D., *War Games. Richard Harding Davis and the New Imperialism* (Boston: University of Massachusetts, 2003) 59).

44 Davis, Richard Harding, *The Novels and Stories of Richard Harding Davis. Volume 2 – The Exiles and Other Stories* (New York: Scribner, 1916) 272.

45 Davis, *The Novels and Stories of Richard Harding Davis. Volume 2*, 314, 316.

46 Davis, *The Novels and Stories of Richard Harding Davis. Volume 2*, 310.

47 Davis, *The Novels and Stories of Richard Harding Davis. Volume 2*, 271.

48 Seelye, *War Games* 21.

49 Hemingway, Ernest, *Selected Letters 1917–1961*, ed. Baker, Carlos (London: Granada, 1981) 775.

50 Seelye, *War Games*, 10.

51 Gellhorn, letter of 1948, ff. 1r-2r.

52 Sartre, Jean-Paul, *Being and Nothingness*, trans. Barnes, Hazel E., and with an introduction by Warnock, Mary (London: Routledge, 1969) 266, original emphasis.

53 That is, with Delmer, Hemingway and Herbert Matthews on their drives to various Spanish fronts.

54 Delmer, Sefton, *Trail Sinister. An Autobiography. Volume One* (London: Secker & Warburg, 1961) 329.

55 Herbst, Josephine, *The Starched Blue Sky of Spain and Other Memoirs* (New York: Harper Collins, 1991) 138. Herbst records Hemingway referring to Gellhorn as 'El Rubio' – 'The Blond' – somewhat oddly using the masculine article.

56 Regler, Gustav, *The Owl of Minerva*, trans. Denny, Norman (London: Rupert Hart-Davis, 1959) 283.

57 Hemingway, Mary Welsh, *How It Was* (London: Weidenfeld and Nicolson, 1977) 93. Could the 'two Polish pilots' have metamorphosed into the 'Three Poles' of Gellhorn's 18 March 1944 *Collier's* article or the two Polish pilots in her short story 'Le Voyage Forme la Jeunesse'?

58 Cowles, Virginia, *Looking for Trouble* (London: Hamish Hamilton, 1942) 133.

59 Grenfell, Joyce, *The Time of My Life: Entertaining the Troops. Her Wartime Journals*, ed. Roose-Evans, James (London: Hodder & Stoughton, 1989) 26. And here, after the fact, is William Boyd, in *Any Human Heart* (2002), through his protagonist Logan Mountstuart who is visiting the Spanish Civil War: 'Martha is a tall leggy blonde, not spectacularly pretty, but good fun and bracingly sure of herself, in that particularly American way. She and Hemingway must be lovers by now, though they are very discreet about it' (Boyd, William, *Any Human Heart* (London: Hamish Hamilton, 2002) 191).

60 'Miss Gellhorn' ('Next Week', *Collier's* (30 July 1938) 4), 'Collier's correspondent' (Gellhorn, 'Come Ahead, Adolf!', *Collier's* (6 August 1938) 12–13, 43–5: 13), 'Collier's Martha Gellhorn' (Gellhorn, 'Blood on the Snow', *Collier's* (20 January 1940) 9–11: 9), 'Martha Gellhorn, Collier's staff correspondent' ('Next Week', *Collier's* (27 January 1940) 4), 'a Collier's correspondent' (Gellhorn, 'Holland's Last Stand', *Collier's* (26 December 1942) 25, 28–9: 25), 'first girl correspondent to go on a combat mission' ('This Week', *Collier's* (17 March 1945) 4) and 'Collier's girl correspondent' ('This Week', *Collier's* (30 June 1945) 4). A *New York Times* article, 'Hemingways On Way Here' (23 November 1940 15), also described her as 'a staff member of Collier's'. By contrast, *Collier's* billed Hemingway as 'Collier's famed war correspondent' (Hemingway, Ernest, 'Voyage to Victory', *Collier's* (22 July 1944) 11–13, 56–7: 11).

61 'Next Week', *Colliers* (1 October 1938) 4.

62 'Next Week', *Colliers* (3 December 1938) 4.

63 'Next Week', *Colliers* (13 January 1940) 4.

64 Gellhorn, 'Bombs from a Low Sky', *Collier's* (27 January 1940) 12–13, 41: 12.

65 'Next Week', *Colliers* (3 February 1940) 4.

66 Gellhorn, 'Bombs from a Low Sky', (27 January 1940), 14.

67 Gellhorn, 'These, Our Mountains', *Collier's* (28 June 1941) 16–17, 38, 40–1, 44: 16. 'This Week' of 30 June 1945 confesses, in a spirit of de-mob

light-heartedness, 'Collier's girl correspondent never does get to cross the Elbe!'.

68 Porter, Amy, 'The Week's Work', *Collier's* (6 May 1944) 70.

69 Gellhorn, 'These, Our Mountains', 28 June 1941, 16.

70 Gellhorn, 'Her Day', *Collier's* (30 August 1941) 16, 53: 16. 'Her Day' is presumably a play on Eleanor Roosevelt's syndicated column, 'My Day', so linking the 'First Ladies' of China and America. There are also photos of Gellhorn accompanying Amy Porter's 'The Week's Work', *Collier's* (4 March 1944) 43 and 'The Week's Work', *Collier's* (3 February 1945) 73.

71 Gellhorn, 'Night Life in the Sky', *Collier's* (17 March 1945) 18–19, 31: 18.

72 Gellhorn, 'Night Life in the Sky', 17 March 1945, 19.

73 The gunner, on his violent death, is 'washed [. . .] out of the turret with a hose' (Jarrell, Randall, 'The Death of the Ball Turret Gunner', *The Oxford Book of War Poetry*, ed. Stallworthy, Jon (Oxford: Oxford University Press, 1984) 277), an image that has been read as a grotesque abortion (Gilbert, Sandra M. and Gubar, Susan, *No Man's Land. The Place of the Woman Writer in the Twentieth Century. Volume 3. Letters from the Front* (New Haven and London: Yale University Press, 1994) 238).

74 Gellhorn, 'Night Life in the Sky', 17 March 1945, 19.

75 Gellhorn, 'Night Life in the Sky', 17 March 1945, 19, 31.

76 Gellhorn, 'Night Life in the Sky', 17 March 1945, 31.

77 Gellhorn, 'Night Life in the Sky', 17 March 1945, 31.

78 Gellhorn, 'The Wounded Come Home', *Collier's* (5 August 1944) 14–15, 73–5: 14.

79 *FoW* 141. This is retained in later editions: see, for example, *FoW 1998* 119.

80 Gellhorn, 'Cracking the Gothic Line', *Collier's* (28 October 1944) 24, 57–8: 24.

81 Gellhorn, 'Cracking the Gothic Line', 28 October 1944, 24.

82 Gellhorn, 'Cracking the Gothic Line', 28 October 1944, 57. As mentioned, Amy Porter commented that Gellhorn's 'Visit Italy' was a 'three-dimensional view of Cassino' (Porter, Amy, 'The Week's Work', 6 May 1944, 70).

83 Gellhorn, 'Cracking the Gothic Line', 28 October 1944, 58.

84 Gellhorn's brother, Alfred, still speaks of his sister's 'glorious sense of humour and [. . .] joy in laughter' (email to the author, 1 December 2003).

85 Charis Day, in *What Mad Pursuit*, is a journalist, though strictly not a war reporter.

86 *HoA* 110.

87 *HoA* 109.

88 *HoA* 108.

89 *HoA* 111.

90 *HoA* 111.

91 *HP* 122, 120.

92 *HP* 117.

93 *HP* 120.

94 *HP* 117.

95 *HP* 117.

96 *HP* 114.

97 *HP* 116. Hemingway also used this term (Moorehead, Caroline, *Martha Gellhorn: A Life* (London: Chatto & Windus, 2003) 136). The pun on 'hors-de-combat' carries the suggestion of outsidership.

98 *HP* 115.

99 *HP* 119.

100 *HP* 115.

101 *HP* 120.

102 *HP* 116.

103 *HP* 115.

104 *HP* 79.

105 *HP* 77.

106 *HP* 54. Gellhorn wrote to Bernard Berenson that she felt like a 'ghost' in postwar Europe (*SL* 219).

107 *HP* 75.

108 *HP* 55–6.

109 *FoW* 170. The description is missing from the original dispatch in *Collier's*: Gellhorn, 'Cracking the Gothic Line', 28 October 1944.

110 Gellhorn, 'Cracking the Gothic Line', 28 October 1944, 58.

111 Gellhorn, letter of ? 1958 to Rosamond Lehmann: *SL* 268. See also letter of 4 January 1996 to Milton Wolff: *SL* 504–5.

112 'The Hemingways in Sun Valley: The Novelist Takes a Wife', 6 January 1941, 49–57. Gellhorn mentioned the experience in a letter of 8 November 1940 to Averell Harriman (*SL* 106). The magazine described the photos as 'intimate pictures of a great American at work and play' (49). A caption to a photo of Gellhorn with a rifle reads, 'Mrs. Hemingway's double-barreled Winchester shotgun is a birthday gift from her husband. Hemingway, an expert with firearms, taught her to shoot, is now proud of her marksmanship' (50). After these, there is a section headlined 'Life documents his new novel with war shots': photos taken by Capa during the Spanish Civil War are presented as illustrations of *For Whom the Bell Tolls* (52–7). An associate editor for this edition of *LIFE* was Carl Mydans, photographer for *Collier's*.

113 *Novellas* 273, 274, 278.

114 *Novellas* 277.

115 *Novellas* 271, 293.

116 *Novellas* 305.

117 *Novellas* 290.

118 *Novellas* 300.

119 *Novellas* 299, 300.

120 *Novellas* 295.

121 *Novellas*, 305.
122 Capa, Robert, *Slightly out of Focus* (New York: Henry Holt, 1947) 72–3.
123 *Novellas*, 274. Capa himself was killed 'in action' – that is, in the act of photographing war – by a landmine at Thai Binh, in 1954, during the French colonial war in Indo-China, trying to get closer for a picture. Gellhorn's story is set in the Indonesian uprising against the Dutch.
124 *Novellas*, 274.
125 'Death in Spain: The Civil War Has Taken 500,000 Lives in One Year', *LIFE* 3 No. 2 (12 July 1937) 19.
126 Gellhorn, letter of 12 November 1975, f. 1r. See also letter of 11 November 1975 to Alfred Gellhorn: *SL* 419–20.
127 Gellhorn, 'Notes for TV Interview in Defence of Robert Capa' (1975), f. 3r.
128 Lewinski, Jorge, *The Camera at War: War Photography from 1848 to the Present* (London: Octopus Books, 1986) 92.
129 Capa, *Slightly Out of Focus*, 148.
130 Capa, *Slightly Out of Focus*, 148.
131 Capa, *Slightly Out of Focus*, 151.
132 *Novellas*, 290.
133 *Novellas*, 298.
134 Capa, Cornell, *The Concerned Photographer 2* (London: Thames & Hudson, 1972) unpaginated.
135 Capa, *Slightly Out of Focus*, 25.
136 Hemingway's Jake Barnes in *The Sun Also Rises* (1927) is a newspaperman, but his professional activities receive only cursory mention. Jake notes that an important part of the business's ethics is that 'you should never seem to be working' (Hemingway, Ernest, *The Sun Also Rises / Fiesta* (London: Arrow Books, 1994) 9).
137 Hemingway, Ernest, *The Fifth Column* (Harmondsworth: Penguin, 1966) 6. Hemingway elsewhere questioned the worth of the play (Hemingway, letter to Bernard Berenson, 14 October 1952, f. 2r; exact words cannot be quoted for copyright reasons).
138 Hemingway, *The Fifth Column*, 9. Vassar College, now co-educational, is, like Gellhorn's *alma mater* Bryn Mawr, one of the 'Seven Sisters' women's liberal arts colleges founded between 1837 and 1889. The detail therefore identifies Dorothy closely with Gellhorn.
139 Hemingway, *The Fifth Column*, 9.
140 Hemingway, *The Fifth Column*, 26, 27.
141 Hemingway, *The Fifth Column*, 24.
142 Hemingway, *The Fifth Column*, 38.
143 Hemingway, *The Fifth Column*, 93.
144 Hemingway, *The Fifth Column*, 93–4.
145 Hemingway, *The Fifth Column*, 50.
146 Hemingway, *The Fifth Column*, 75.
147 Orsagh, Jacqueline, 'A Critical Biography of Martha Gellhorn' (unpublished doctoral thesis, Michigan State University, 1977) 88.

148 The play was originally titled *Men Must Weep* (Spanier, Sandra, 'Editor's Note', *Martha Gellhorn and Virginia Cowles, Love Goes to Press*, ed. Spanier, Sandra (Lincoln, Nebraska and London: University of Nebraska, 1995) xiii–xiv: xiii). It ran from 10 June 1946 for a week at the Devonshire Park, Eastbourne, transferred on 18 June to the Embassy Theatre, Swiss Cottage, London, moved to the Duchess Theatre in the West End for 40 performances from 22 July to 24 August 1946, then transferred unsuccessfully to the Biltmore Theater, Broadway, opening on 1 January 1947 and closing on 4 January (Spanier, Sandra, 'Afterword', *Martha Gellhorn and Virginia Cowles, Love Goes to Press*, 79–88: 79–80). Virginia Cowles (1910–1983), born in Boston, was a war correspondent for Hearst Newspapers, NANA and the London *Sunday Times*. She later became a historian and married a British MP.
149 *LGTP* ix.
150 *LGTP* vii; Gellhorn, letter to Charles Scribner, 31 December 1946, f. 2r; *LGTP* vii.
151 *LGTP* viii, ix.
152 Cowles, *Looking for Trouble*, 122, 130.
153 Hemingway, Mary Welsh, *How It Was*, 53.
154 Spanier, 'Afterword', 81.
155 *LGTP* 12.
156 *LGTP* 19. Gellhorn herself wore Schiaparelli for her FERA field trips (*VfG* 69).
157 *LGTP* 40.
158 Just as 'Jane Mason' might be an ironic allusion to Hemingway's affair with 'the beautiful Havana socialite' Jane Mason (Spanier, Sandra, 'Rivalry, Romance and War Reporters: Martha Gellhorn's *Love Goes to Press* and the *Collier's* Files', *Hemingway and Women*, ed. Broer, Lawrence R. and Holland, Gloria (Tuscaloosa and London: University of Alabama, 2002) 256–75: 266).
159 Gilder, Rosamond, 'Rainbow over Broadway', *Theater Arts* 31 (March 1947) 18.
160 *LGTP* 10.
161 *LGTP* 19.
162 *LGTP* 38–9.
163 Delmer, Sefton, *Black Boomerang: An Autobiography. Volume Two* (London: Secker & Warburg, 1962) 14.

5

From presence to participation

There often comes a time in the career of a war recorder when the need to put down the pen, camera or microphone and actually *do* something becomes, at last, overwhelming. 'I was kept busy interpreting, consoling and calming,' said Lee Miller of the American advance on St Mâlo, 'I forgot mostly to take pictures.'[1] 'I took no more pictures,' said Capa of D-Day, 'I was busy lifting stretchers.'[2] 'If you stand in front of a dying people, something more is required,' said the war photographer Don McCullin of Biafra, 'if you can't help, you shouldn't be there.'[3] Leaving Poland, where the first Nazi bombs were being dropped, for Britain, Sefton Delmer swore to himself 'that the observing and reporting stage of my wartime role was over, that by some means or other I would get into the fight myself'.[4] He went on to acquire a 'dual capacity as a War Correspondent and a Psychological Warrior', asked by Duff Cooper, Minister for Information, to do the BBC German broadcasts (he spoke German fluently) once or twice a week. In his autobiography, Delmer notes that his first task was therefore that of 'replying to Hitler himself': clearly an advance, in his eyes, on 'mere' journalism. Yet he also records a piece of Cooper's advice: ' "Don't drop your reporting for the *Daily Express* [. . .] that is valuable war work." '[5]

This chapter is about the far end of the continuum of involvement, which began with an aloofness assumed in the interests of objectivity and reached statements of presence in which simply 'being there' was coming to seem suspect. At what point – and this will be a matter of personal, as well as institutional, limits – does the war reporter go beyond empathetic engagement actually to participate in war? What, moreover, is the nature of the participation? The answer is, as Delmer's experiences illustrate, another set of possibilities, this time ranging from writing 'to make a difference', through intervention of various kinds in the course of combat, to unhelpful interference, even hindrance, in it. This chapter details the various versions of involvement, and their intellectual background, before turning to Martha Gellhorn: firstly her journalistic aims and methodology and then how she dramatises these matters in her fiction.

Writing 'to make a difference' (or 'perlocutionary writing') is the beginning of participation. Behind it lies the assumption that literature *can* bring about effects in the extra-textual world,[6] a belief that entails a certain conception not only of textuality but also of the role and nature of the author. Roland Barthes's 1968 essay, 'The Death of the Author', tends to be taken as a statement of the end of authorial involvement but, in fact, Barthes has this to say:

> As soon as a fact is *narrated* no longer with a view to acting directly on reality but intransitively, that is to say, finally outside of any function other than that of the very practice of the symbol itself, this disconnection occurs, the voice loses its origin, the author enters into his own death.[7]

What, then, is the situation if the fact *is* narrated with a view to acting directly on reality? What if writing is intended and taken to be *transitive*? The answer must be the resurrection of the author – a conception of the role which happens to fit the aesthetics of both the 1930s New Reportage and the Sartrean literature of commitment explored below.

For the former, as noted in Chapter 1, the 'presentation of fact' was a key means of educating and, crucially, mobilising public opinion. The objective of social amelioration had an equivalent effect in poetics: if the writer was 'there' in the field, he was also 'there' (albeit theoretically emotionless) in the text. As John Mander, in *The Writer and Commitment*, notes: 'In the novel the author is present in his creation only in veiled, indirect, immanent form; in "documentary" the author is a transcendent god who may visit and visibly interfere with his creation.'[8] 'A writer must be a man of action now,' said Martha Gellhorn at the Second Congress of American Writers in June 1937.[9] 'Action', in this context, requires unpacking. Gellhorn recalled of her early days at the Spanish Civil War:

> I did nothing except learn a little Spanish and a little about war, and visit the wounded, trying to amuse or distract them. It was a poor effort and one day, weeks after I had come to Madrid, a journalist friend observed that I ought to write: it was the only way I could serve the *Causa*.[10]

This is writing-as-activism in the New Reportage sense of revealing facts to inspire change. In this case and later during the Second World War itself, Gellhorn was writing for the eyes of Americans, trying to persuade them to help Spain and then other European states, through such means as material aid, volunteering and military action. Her intended audience was not only the *Collier's* readership but also her friends Franklin D. and Eleanor Roosevelt, whom she hoped to convince of the need to abandon the policy of non-interventionism. Her lecture tours and support for Joris Ivens's film *The Spanish Earth* were dedicated to the same end: to secure national participation. But the question remains: does this kind of 'action' go beyond disclosure to educate or mobilise? Is there any more to participation by the writer than the simple act of telling?[11]

In 1940, the issue was debated in *Horizon*. In his 'Comment' for the May issue, Cyril Connolly announced:

> The war is the enemy of creative activity, and writers and painters are wise and right to ignore it and to concentrate their talent on other subjects. Since they are politically impotent, they can use this time to develop at deeper emotional levels, or to improve their weapons by technical experiment.[12]

In the July issue, this was answered by a 'Letter from a Soldier'. Goronwy Rees disputed the idea that 'the war is the enemy of creative activity' (though he conceded that 'a mind numbed by soldiering is hardly capable of formulating an idea or phrasing a sentence').[13] Rees's proposition was not that 'the writer should lay down his pen and take up arms'[14] – a 'misconception of the artist's function'[15] – but rather that 'the soldier has the right to ask that those with perception of values comprehend, analyse, illuminate, commemorate his sacrifice and his suffering'.[16] In the same issue, Connolly gave his response, an admission that now 'we cannot afford the airy detachment of earlier numbers', that hitherto *Horizon* had 'failed to take the war sufficiently seriously'.[17] In October 1941, the journal carried a 'manifesto', 'Why Not War Writers?', signed by Arthur Calder-Marshall, Connolly, Bonamy Dobrée, Tom Harrisson, Arthur Koestler, Alun Lewis, George Orwell and Stephen Spender, which argued for making creative writing, like journalism, a reserved occupation:

> Creative writers [. . .] have a skill, imagination and human understanding which must be utilized as fully as the skill of journalists. They bring home with a depth and vividness impossible to the writer of a newspaper report or feature article, the significance of what is happening all about us.[18]

This is some distance from Connolly's original prescription that the writer should ignore the war. None the less it too falls short of recommending that the writer should put down his pen and take up arms. Gellhorn herself took the same line in a letter to her editor, Max Perkins of Scribner's, in the month of the 'manifesto' issue:

> It is as if all the time one were boiling inside with some kind of helpless ~~fury~~ indignation, enraged to see such a good-looking and possibly decent world always going to hell, and going to hell with such cruelty and waste [. . .].

I must say I was very disgusted to see that Dos,[19] at the P.E.N. Congress in London, said that writers should not write now. If a writer has any guts he should write all the time, and the lousier the world the harder a writer should work. For if he can do nothing positive, to make the world more livable [*sic*] or less cruel or stupid, he can at least record truly, and that is something no one else will do, and it is a job that must be done.[20]

The matter is given lengthy theoretical treatment in Jean-Paul Sartre's *What Is Literature?* (1948), the 'Bible of French Commitment',[21] and extended exposition of Sartre's concept of 'committed literature' ('*la littérature engagée*'). (Gellhorn read both Sartre and Camus.)[22] The date of first publication is significant. In her biography, *La force de l'âge*, Simone de Beauvoir confessed of her and Sartre's student days: 'Public affairs bored us; but we counted on events unfolding according to our wishes without us having to involve ourselves in them.'[23] The Second World War – the Nazi Occupation and the Resistance – changed all that: 'all at once we felt ourselves abruptly *situated*,' Sartre writes.[24] The war, then, demanded something different on the part of the writer – *engagement* or commitment – and, although *What Is Literature?* was published postwar, its thinking very much belonged to those years of conflict.

Commitment, Sartre makes plain in the first section, 'What Is Writing?', is the preserve of the prose-writer. Poets do not '*utilize*' words but render them into 'phrase-objects'; while as for art – 'that masterpiece, "The Massacre of Guernica", does anyone think that it won over a single heart to the Spanish cause?'[25] The prose-writer, by contrast, '*makes use*' of words: 'to speak is to act'; 'by speaking [. . .] I involve myself a little more in the world'.[26] Yet, in this first section, speaking has only limited perlocutionary effect: 'the prose-writer is a man who has chosen a certain method of secondary action which we may call action by disclosure'.[27] At this point, Sartrean commitment seems little different from New Reportage encyclopaedism: the position occupied by Raymond Aron's potentially oxymoronic 'committed observer' ('le spectateur engagé'):

> To be at one and the same time the observer of history as it was unfolding, to try to be as objective as possible regarding that history, and to be not totally detached from it – in other words, to be committed. I wanted to combine the dual role of actor and spectator.[28]

But Sartre pursues the question, 'why write?' (the title of his second section). In an important passage he states:

> The art of prose is bound up with the only régime in which prose has meaning, democracy. When one is threatened, the other is too. And it is not enough to defend them with the pen. A day comes when the pen is forced to stop, and the writer must then take up arms. Thus [. . .] literature throws

you into battle. Writing is a certain way of wanting freedom; once you have begun, you are committed, willy-nilly.[29]

This is a call to arms that goes beyond the textual tactics of the New Reportage. Yet, despite the line, 'a day comes when the pen is forced to stop', it is not – yet – a bid to end writing. Indeed, the pen once taken up, certain ethical consequences ensue: 'if a writer has chosen to remain silent on any aspect [. . .] of the world [. . .] one has the right to ask him, "why have you spoken of this rather than that?"'[30] Disclosure, therefore, must continue alongside extra-textual activism: 'We must transform his [the reader's] formal goodwill into a concrete and material will to change *this world* by specific means in order to help the coming of the concrete society of ends.'[31]

The consequence of this is to raise another question: 'for whom does one write?', the heading of Sartre's third section. (It is worth noting that Gellhorn asked the same questions at the outset of her journalistic career: 'how could I write about war, what did I know, and for whom would I write?')[32] Sartre's answer is 'contemporaries':

> People of the same period and community, who have lived through the same events, who have raised or avoided the same questions, have the same taste in their mouths; they have the same complicity, and there are the same corpses among them.[33]

Works of the mind, like bananas, should be 'eaten on the spot', 'freshly picked': each book 'proposes a concrete liberation on the basis of a particular alienation' only understood by the writer's own age and community.[34] A further aesthetic corollary attaches: Sartre remarks, in an echo of Lukács:[35]

> After [Saint-Exupéry], after Hemingway, how could we dream of describing? We must plunge things into action. Their density of being will be measured for the reader by the multiplicity of practical relations which they maintain with the characters [. . .]. Thus, the world and man reveal themselves by *undertakings*. And all the undertakings we might speak of reduce themselves to a single one, that of *making history*. So here we are, led by the hand to the moment when the literature of *exis* must be abandoned to inaugurate that of *praxis*.[36]

The Sartrean model is therefore of a 'situated' writer,[37] writing for his age (and within that age, for the proletariat, the last class that will rise up against alienation) a literature of disclosure ('exis') that is also one aimed at action ('praxis'): crucially, the writer will *also* be a man of action, this animating and validating his literary output. This last ingredient takes Sartrean aesthetics of commitment beyond those of the New Reportage.

But even this brand of writerly interventionism raises doubts. Theodor Adorno, writing on 'Commitment' in 1965, felt no wish 'to soften the saying that to write lyric poetry after Auschwitz is barbaric'.[38] Yet, he continued, 'when genocide becomes part of the cultural heritage in the themes of committed literature, it becomes easier to continue to play along with the culture which gave birth to murder'.[39] Instead, he called for 'autonomous' art to flourish:

> Committed works all too readily credit themselves with every noble value, and then manipulate them at their ease [. . .]. The notion of a 'message' in art, even when politically radical, already contains an accommodation to the world.[40]

Sartre himself arrived at a similar conclusion about words (in *Les Mots* (1964)), though from a different direction: 'For a long while I treated my pen as a sword: now I realise how helpless we are. [. . .] Culture saves nothing and nobody, nor does it justify.'[41]

To write in protest or to write without protest are therefore equally problematic: what, then, is left for the writer? Only silence. In his 1966 essay, 'Silence and the Poet', George Steiner identifies a 'powerful impulse' to silence in the twentieth century, which he dates, significantly, to 'c. 1914'.[42] The spectre haunting the literature of commitment, therefore, is the end of writing.

In war, this theoretical position is frequently matched by a practical humanitarian demand: if the pen is writing or the camera recording, then suffering is, by definition, continuing. Iris Carpenter describes a bombed school in England: 'we newspaper correspondents who were sent to cover the story brought out bits [of bodies] and sorted them into sacks'.[43] Gellhorn herself, on the hospital ship serving D-Day, helped feed the wounded, cut off their shoes, watch plasma bottles, light and hold cigarettes, pour coffee into bandaged mouths.[44] If this is participation which eases or perpetuates the course of conflict, further along the spectrum lies belligerence itself. But what scope does the war writer have for hostile engagement? When Richard Harding Davis was reporting from the Graeco-Turkish war, an early Geneva Convention, 'The Amelioration of the Condition of the Wounded on the Field of Battle (Red Cross Convention)' (1864),[45] was in force. This made provision for how 'the sick and wounded' were to be treated: no distinction was maintained between soldiers and civilians. Davis's memoirs could therefore contain a photograph of 'an American war correspondent [John Bass] directing the fire of the Greeks' at Velestino.[46] In the Second World War, a second Geneva Convention, 'The Convention Between the United States of

America and Other Powers, Relating to Prisoners of War' (1929), which concerned the treatment of prisoners of war, was also in force. Article 81 provided:

> Individuals who follow armed forces without directly belonging thereto, such as newspaper correspondents and reporters, sutlers, contractors, who fall into the enemy's hands and whom the latter think expedient to detain, shall be entitled to be treated as prisoners of war, provided they are in possession of a certificate from the military authorities of the armed forces which they were accompanying.[47]

The law of conflict therefore detached the correspondent from the armed forces ('without directly belonging thereto') while according them the same protection if taken prisoner. Ontologically, this is an ambiguous position:[48] legally, it is a clear one. Correspondents in 1944 could not act as combatants, and it was for this reason that, as already mentioned, Hemingway was summoned for interrogation by the Inspector General Third Army with regard to his activities at Rambouillet, charged with having 'persistently impeded the armies by trying to act like a character out of his own fiction'.[49]

If the legal situation was clear in the Second World War, the sartorial situation was muddier. As in the First World War, accredited male corre-spondents had to wear officer uniform less insignia, while women wore the same uniform with skirts or slacks and berets.[50] Martha Gellhorn herself had 'an identity war correspondent card with the simulated rank of captain and attendant privileges'.[51] Dress requirements contribute to the construction of the reporter figure, not least because the wearing or not of uniform (or quasi-uniform) reflects the degree to which the reporter is assimilated with the combatants. John Simpson, for example, feels 'not enthusiastic' about wearing military uniform when reporting,[52] an aspect of aiming for impartiality. At the other extreme, Don McCullin has created a persona as a combatant figure: the front cover of his *Unreasonable Behaviour. An Autobiography* (1992) carries a photo-graph of him in fatigues, a helmet, unshaven, obviously in the war zone.[53] The wearing of quasi-military dress interferes with the visual boundary between combatant and non-combatant, effectively bestowing on the reporter a degree of assimilation denied under international law.

The word 'impeded' in the Third Army's charge against Hemingway is significant. The far end of the participatory spectrum-within-a-spectrum goes beyond intervention in combat to interference, even hindrance. Philippa Sheppard notes that Shakespeare's military messengers 'inter-rupt' the course of battle:[54] war recorders may halt the flow of action or even alter it. Gender is central to this issue, and in the discussion of

Martha Gellhorn's journalism and fiction which follows in the next chapter, attention is paid to the effect of introducing females – glamorous females particularly – into the predominantly male arena of conflict.

Journalism and activism

Gellhorn's character as a participant has already been noted in her commitment to social reform. Her family history – particularly Edna Gellhorn's suffragism – was one of political activism. The magazine she corresponded for, *Collier's*, had a muck-raking tradition.[55] Her private views were the same. 'Do you think,' she asked Eleanor Roosevelt in 1938, 'any people have a right to a moral attitude which they will not back up with action?'[56] 'The only kick I have here', she told her mother in a 1944 V-Mail, 'is that women correspondents are treated too much like violets.'[57] Her urge to participate on equal terms, to change things for the better, was ingrained.

What action, then, could her Second World War dispatches hope to inspire? Who, moreover, could be expected to take this action? The answer seems to be an American readership a long distance – geographically, psychologically, politically – from the killing-fields. It was a long-standing long distance. In 1916, Theodore Roosevelt had battled against a Wilsonian anti-interventionism that, he claimed, 'would make Pontius Pilate quiver with envy'.[58] Roosevelt's friend Edith Wharton makes explicit reference to his policy of 'preparedness' (expounded in *America and the World War* (1915) and *America and Preparedness* (campaign speeches of 1916 collected in 1917)) in her novel *A Son at the Front* (1923). Her own campaign against pre-*Lusitania* isolationism took the form of conveying the geographical and moral merits of France to American readers in order to make them feel that they must be defended. She had, indeed, to negotiate two 'aporias' (the word is used here not in its usual sense of 'doubt' but in its strict etymological sense of something 'impervious to passage'):[59] the gap between (expatriate) civilian life in Paris and the front, and the gap between her American readership and the European war. To this end, she wrote essays on the French way of life (collected as *French Ways and Their Meaning* (1919)) with 'the idea of making France and things French more intelligible to the American soldier',[60] and sent dispatches from the trenches to *Scribner's Magazine* (collected as *Fighting France. From Dunkerque to Belfort* (1915)). After 14 months of war, Wharton reports in *Fighting France*, the attitude of the French people 'is one of exaltation, energy, the hot resolve to dominate the disaster'.[61] For some, the attempt to persuade by invoking America's own way of life and ideals succeeded: one contemporary review commented that Wharton 'illuminate[d] for her countrymen the figure of France at war'.[62] For others, it backfired: another reviewer spoke sharply about the contrast drawn between 'coarse pioneer faults' and faults 'contingent on an ancient civilisation': 'can it be possible that America will survive this apologist and France this defender?'[63]

A generation on, Gellhorn similarly despaired of the gulf in her American readers' experience – and used similar tactics in her attempts to bridge it. Of the Gothic Line, she wrote, 'it is impossible to describe the hardships of their life; it would take too long and the words would-n't mean anything';[64] of the Nazi torture rooms of Paris, 'you who are safe and will never be locked underground to die must force yourself to imagine this horror';[65] and, after a postwar tour of the United States:

> The reality of most of the world now is hunger and desolation, gutted houses and factories [. . .] the burned-out tank, the ration tickets, the devious anguish of the black markets, the hopelessly repaired clothes, the cracked shoes and the wretched allotment of coal. I do not see how anyone can make that reality clear to Americans, because they have not felt it and experience is not communicated through the mind.[66]

In fact, in the late 1930s, as Gellhorn began her career, the problem was even more complex: not just political isolationism-non-interventionism and public unawareness, but, as Nicholas John Cull puts it, an American public 'indignant at having been duped into World War One [and] still very suspicious of being propagandised'.[67] In *This Terrible Peace* (1939), the American journalist Helen Kirkpatrick offered a long, detailed list of reasons for this 'suspicion': Eden's resignation; Munich; the inadequacy of British defence preparations; Britain's failure to intervene in the Sino-Japanese War and over Abyssinia and German expansion; the 'Cliveden set's' 'peace at any percent'.[68] If American journalists at the beginning of the Second World War *were* to persuade – and the task of persuasion was to bring about US entry into a war which seemed very distant[69] – certain precautions had to be taken.

In politico-stylistic terms these resulted in a war reporting both subtle and self-reflexive: values are carefully encoded while the rhetorical tricks of suasion – or at least some of them – are deliberately exposed. The famous Second World War CBS broadcaster Ed Murrow, for example, was firmly in favour of American entry and early quoted to his listeners the *Daily Express* telling the United States, 'Don't be like we were at Munich.'[70] The following are a few more examples from Murrow's collected broadcasts, *This Is London* (1941). First, on 26 August 1940, after a night of bombing in London: 'Tonight they're [the British] magnificent. I've seen them, talked with them, and I know.'[71] On 3 September 1940, in a rare example of Murrow not addressing his listeners as 'you': 'One feels very small and humble. We can only continue to give Americans the news and the atmosphere in which it happens. They must reach their own conclusions.'[72] On 19 February 1941, after a factory visit: 'Since some of you in America are working in factories making similar things, perhaps you'd like to hear about it [. . .] all the machines were American.'[73] Murrow notices 'a shiny automatic machine made in Milwaukee' and quotes its British operator as saying, ' "such a lovely machine – it never makes a mistake" '.[74] In similar vein, the fabled war reporter Ernie Pyle told his American readers, 'at home you have all read about London's amazing ability to take it, and about the almost amazing calm of Englishmen in the face of Hitler's bombs [. . .] I just want to confirm that what you have read in this connection is true'. On seeing in a Tube station 'the bundled-up, patched-up people with lined faces that we have seen for years sitting dumbly in waiting lines at our own relief offices at home', Pyle feels, in his 'obviously American hat', 'a terrible feeling of guilt'.[75]

These examples are rhetorically highly complex, but it is possible to single out a few noteworthy strands: the pointed even-handedness ('you must reach your own conclusions'); the implication that the British are plucky (translatable as 'their efforts deserve our support'); the superiority of American technology ('they really need us'); and the innocence of the victims ('it behoves us to help the less fortunate'). The same encryptions appear in Martha Gellhorn's articles. Reviewing, in a series of pieces for *Collier's*, various countries' states of readiness at the outbreak of the Second World War, she emphasises a set of themes: democratic credentials (that is, conformity to traditional American ideals); preparedness, pluck and thrift; and the fact that, while it is too late for some nations, it is not for others.

Two of Gellhorn's *Collier's* articles in particular contain messages subtly designed to induce a desired reaction in American readers. The first is entitled 'The Lord Will Provide For England' and was published on 17 September 1938. Virginia Cowles, who accompanied Gellhorn on the fact-finding trip, provides the background:

> Martha had come to England to write an article for *Collier's* magazine. Her editor, three thousand miles away in New York, was alarmed; he saw a civil war raging in Spain, he saw the French Army manning three frontiers; the German Army elated after its absorption of Austria; and the Czech Army digging in its third line of defence only twelve miles from Prague. He saw the British Isles, once immune from attack, now transformed through the development of aircraft into one of the most vulnerable places in Europe. 'What is the reaction of the British public?' he cabled. 'Are the people alarmed? What do they think of Fascism, or Aggression, or the possibility of war?'[76]

Gellhorn, Cowles reports, 'was at her wits' end': ' "I can't cable back
'War! Who wants a war?' " she said indignantly.'[77] The article, none the
less, conveys as much. On the first page is a photograph which is a striking summation of its theme: it shows spectators at a bomb detonation
demonstration holding their hands over their ears – England is prepar-
ing, it implies, but not listening. The London press, Gellhorn notes,
'avoids scaring the readers'; radio 'is [. . .] discreetly advised not to
underline troublesome issues'; 'newsreels are trimmed, so that bombed
China and bombed Spain are avoided'.[78] More photos illustrate that
'decontamination squads will rush to wash the streets of deadly gas after
an air raid' but no one seems to realise the implications: 'it would be a
relief,' remarks Gellhorn, 'to see some other folk as worried as I'.[79] At a
lecture on air-raid warnings at a stately home, 'a white-haired lady with
small pearls in her ears' says 'somewhat crossly' to the lecturer: ' "I do
think ten minutes is an awfully small warning: it doesn't give you much
time to turn off the lights and close the windows and get everything ready
to go down into the shelter." ' Gellhorn reflects, 'the English are fortunate [. . .] they haven't any imagination at all'.[80] Her indignation, Cowles
recalls, 'knew no bounds'.[81] The article, criticising England's isolationism and complacency and failure to question what the rearmament might
be about, works in a slightly different way to the examples from Murrow
and Pyle already quoted. 'Do not be like this – act!' the message seems
to be, rather than, 'these people are like you – help them'.

As late as 1940, Gellhorn was sceptical of English motives. 'Those
English, *those* English, are using Finland for their own propaganda purposes in this country [America]', she wrote to Charles Colebaugh:

> I talked to Mrs. R.[oosevelt] on the phone. She only wants to know whether
> it was all real about Finland or was it being used to get us into war. The
> Finns, you know, being a small poor country, do not know the tricks. But
> those English.[82]

But by 1 April 1944, the publication date of the second article, 'English
Sunday', with Britain now five years into the war, things have changed.
Joe Dearing's photographs for *Collier's* are the mythemes of rural
England: a thatched and beamed village street, fishing in the Thames, a
country church – and a family at the fireside engaged in knitting (the
grandmother), reading (the children), contemplation (the grandfather
and the dog) (the missing generation, the parents, are presumably out on
war work, or worse) (Figure 9).[83]

In this England, everyone looks 'brushed and scrubbed and shabby' and
has 'polished but cracking shoes' (a complex image of effort, self-respect
and poverty which recalls Mrs Maddison in *The Trouble I've Seen*). The

Figure 9 'English Sunday', *Collier's*, 1 April 1944

lock keeper, 'who always won prizes for his flowers, would be spading the terraces where his begonias used to grow', while Spitfires drown out the vicar's closing blessing[84] – an image reminiscent of the ending of the 1942 propagandist film *Mrs Miniver*. Back in the idyllic village, there is further unassuming heroism (indeed, the degree of selflessness begins to come across as faintly comic). Mrs Thomas manages very well, Gellhorn notes, because:

> Her husband believed she ate a hot meal every noon while he was at the factory. Actually she ate some bread and tea and perhaps a bit of cheese, and that way she could save her rations for the week end when he would be home.[85]

The general attitude is summed up as 'we can't complain, can we?' It does not appear that political alertness is any greater in England than in 1938, but Gellhorn now recasts the atmosphere as a cheerful stoicism intended to reassure American readers. It is a matter no longer of drawing the United States into the war but of maintaining public support for it at home.

In these instances, certain values and images are invoked to prick and then salve the American conscience for political ends. These values and images correlate to the idea of 'England' described by Christopher Mulvey in his analyses of nineteenth-century Anglo-American travel literature. Mulvey's thesis is that American visitors (or, at least, those of them who were men of letters) looked for an 'England' that was 'part nature and part dream or haunting', a land of Shakespeare, ruins and gentle, cultivated landscapes, responding to what they found with a complex 'mythopoesis'.[86] The ghost of this 'England' haunts Gellhorn's 'English Sunday' and the 'British pluck' anecdotes of Murrow and Pyle: now, though, it assumes propagandist functions.

But appeals to a Jamesian idea(l) of literary England are no longer enough in the tough new world of the Second World War. Alongside these encoded messages are more overt stylistic attempts to maintain support for the war, to render what was happening in the European Theatre intelligible to home readers. These constitute another version of transatlantic mythopoesis, akin to what Paul Giles has termed the 'virtualisation' of America. Giles explains that a virtual image is 'an image [. . .] of virtual foci', 'refracted' or 'inverted' in a 'foreign mirror'.[87] Literature written from positions of 'estrangement' (for Frederick Douglass, being a slave; for Henry James, being across the Atlantic) from America illuminates the nation's 'unconscious assumptions, boundaries, proscribed areas' which 'national literature' tends to leave 'latent' or 'unexamined'.[88] For Giles, then, 'a virtual America would be a mythic America turned inside out'[89] (though it might be argued that virtualisation is itself another form of myth-making that creates its own assumptions, boundaries and proscriptions).

Applying this analysis to American war reporting from the European Theatre in fact produces some divergent results. One strategy dates from the early days of American international war journalism: trying to convey the strategic positions of the opposing Greek and Turkish armies at Velestino, Richard Harding Davis hit upon the idea of likening them to 'two football teams when they are lined up for a scrimmage'.[90] Davis's homebody comparisons grew sufficiently well known to be parodied by Charles Battell Loomis: 'The effect of the Greek fire [. . .] was to color the fog beautifully and make Richard Harding Davis think he was at a pyrotechnic display at Coney Island.'[91] The 'estrangement' brought about by crossing the Atlantic here seems to have resulted in, if anything, a *reinforcement* of traditional national mythography. What is happening is metaphor or translation (both of which have the etymological sense of 'carrying across'): unfamiliar scenes of war-torn Europe are being carried back across the ocean and reconfigured in familiar American reality. Gellhorn uses the same technique: land is 'as flat as Kansas',[92] a city 'seems like a combination of Times Square on New Year's eve, the subway at five-thirty in the afternoon, a three-alarm fire, a public auction and a country fair with the calliope playing'.[93] Yet this is not merely a one-way transaction. In another recurring trope, America is carried in the other direction across the Atlantic, in the sense that its full regional (though not necessarily ethnic) diversity is relocated in Europe:

> Men from Georgia and Oklahoma and Texas and California found one another and spoke a word [. . .] the knowledge that there were other men from their own piece of home seemed to comfort them in the midst of all this strangeness and uncertainty.[94]

'Bringing the war home' therefore covers a complex range of strategies that nevertheless have in common that they invoke myths (whether 'traditional' or 'virtual') about both England and America. This outcome is unsurprising because such myths assume greater potency in wartime, when they are – or are represented as being – under threat.

Carefully tailored hints to her American readership therefore reveal the perlocutionary intent of Gellhorn's dispatches. But, again, the questions must be asked. Can *tone* amount to activism? Are Gellhorn's attempts to mobilise her readers anything more than well-meant disclosure? Did she herself think that this was enough? The answer to this last question was, apparently, 'no'. As early as 1937, she remarked to Eleanor Roosevelt, 'you begin to doubt whether books or articles, or anything one does in any way explains and by explaining changes the way people look at facts'.[95] By the end of 1943, she hoped only that writing might create 'a little more receptivity in people who read it'.[96] After the war, she told Bernard Berenson, she felt as if she 'were stuffing cake while the world starved', seeing 'no solution except to babble and forget'.[97] In her 1959 Introduction to *The Face of War*, she described her disillusionment precisely:

> When I was young I believed in the perfectibility of man, and in progress, and thought of journalism as a guiding light. If people were told the truth, if dishonor and injustice were clearly shown to them, they would at once demand the saving action, punishment of wrong-doers, and care for the innocent. [. . .] A journalist's job was to bring news, to be eyes for their conscience. I think I must have imagined public opinion as a solid force, something like a tornado, always ready to blow on the side of the angels.

[. . .] It took nine years, and a great depression, and two wars ending in defeat, and one surrender without war, to break my faith in the benign power of the press. [. . .] The guiding light of journalism was no stronger than a glow-worm.[98]

Finland taught her that 'I could not fool myself that my war correspondent's work mattered a hoot'; Java that 'nothing anybody wrote was going to shorten this torment, nor save one victim, white or brown'.[99] The most the war reporter could hope to achieve was 'keeping the record straight'.[100] If there was a particular moment when Gellhorn lost faith, it was Dachau which, as discussed later in this chapter, was her personal 'watershed'.[101] In the ensuing strain of disillusionment she sporadically withdrew from war, her views on the reforming power of journalism characterised by growing wariness and scepticism. After the Second World War, she explored her doubts at length in her fiction, and it is to this that this chapter now turns.

Fiction and activism

Gellhorn's fiction falls into two types. The first, considered in the present section, can be characterised as dramatised attempts at benign intervention in conflict situations. The second, discussed in the next chapter, comprises cases where intervention becomes interference, involving specifically the effect of female presence – and its sexual consequences – in war.

Gellhorn visited Czechoslovakia in the spring and autumn of 1938, producing two articles for *Collier's*: 'Come Ahead, Adolf!' (6 August 1938) and 'Obituary of a Democracy' (10 December 1938).[102] She wrote *A Stricken Field* in Sun Valley, Idaho, in October 1939; it was published in March 1940.[103] The strategy of the articles feeds the preoccupations of the novel. 'Come Ahead, Adolf!' is hortatory and monitory. Gellhorn comments that, despite the country's willingness and readiness to defend itself, 'One wondered how long any armed peace can last, and just how long the people in a country can bear the strain of waiting and watching, and how long Europe can impoverish itself for guns.'[104] 'Obituary of a Democracy' was written after Munich.[105] Now anger is the overriding emotion. Gellhorn quotes a Corporal from the decommissioned Czech army who is walking home with his suitcase:

He began to talk, all by himself, as if he had to say it to somebody whether he was understood or not. 'You realize we were all alone,' he said. 'England and France will see for themselves when it is Alsace-Lorraine he wants, or the colonies. Even the Poles will see when he wants the Corridor.'[106]

Czechoslovakia, Gellhorn implies, has indeed been talking to itself, mis-understood: it has been needlessly, and dishonourably, abandoned. Even so, as the quotation suggests, it is not all over: there is still time, there is still danger. England, France, the United States must be persuaded, warned or frightened into action before more democracies fall. ('The Lord Will Provide for England', written between these two Czech pieces, is, as discussed, scathing about British complacency: 'Remember Czechoslovakia, the papers eagerly read and the speculation? We are on an island now, and the world is someplace else. This is England, and tomorrow there is probably a cricket match.')[107] *A Stricken Field* drama-tises and contributes to the efficacy of her attempts to convince.

Gellhorn commented in her Afterword to the 1986 edition of the novel, 'I found I could control and use the emotions of Spain [that is, the Spanish Civil War] in writing about Czechoslovakia'.[108] In her letters, she made the same connection: 'Czecho made me fighting mad and sick with rage: but Spain has really broken my heart.'[109] In fact, her theme – the necessity and limits of intervention on the part of governments and indi-viduals – matches both political situations. The Afterword quotes one of her letters sent after Munich: 'I am wild with anger.'[110] Another letter records, 'I'll maybe lose my mind with the fury and the helplessness'.[111] An American diplomat, George Kennan, in 1938 a junior in the Prague American Embassy, recalls a morning when 'an attractive young lady wearing a collegiate American fur coat and tossing, in her indignation, a most magnificent head of golden hair' burst into the office and 'pro-ceeded to burn us all up for our sleepy inactivity'.[112] The visitor – Gellhorn – spoke passionately about the Sudeten situation: 'It was time for us to bestir ourselves. "Why," she demanded to know, "don't you *do* something about it?" '[113] 'What in the world could we "do" about it?' asks Kennan, noting the legation's lack of resources and the fact that this was in 'the days before Food for Peace and foreign aid'. He and his col-leagues relegated Gellhorn 'to the category of ignorant, impractical do-gooders': 'we suspected that her fears were exaggerated'.[114]

'Why don't you *do* something about it?' might be *A Stricken Field*'s epigraph (its actual epigraph demands unflinching acknowledgement of uncomfortable situations: 'Close your eyes to nothing').[115] Written and published pre-Pearl Harbor (though the publication was some two years after Munich), this is a novel which dramatises issues of engagement in order to provoke engagement. As such, it resonated with politics of those like Winston Churchill, who advocated direct intervention in the Czech crisis. When the pro-appeasement British Prime Minister during Munich, Neville Chamberlain, famously referred to Czechoslovakia as 'a faraway country of whom we know nothing',[116] the Churchillian riposte was that 'to English ears, the name of Czechoslovakia sounds outlandish but still they are a virile people, they have their rights'.[117] Gellhorn, too, sought to bring the crisis nearer. The dust-jacket of the novel's first edition proclaims: '*A Stricken Field* cannot fail to stir, and stir deeply, any man or woman who values the right of man to live as a free and independent citizen under his own government.'[118] The *New York Times* review concurred: 'it is a book which should make all Americans conscious of living in a safe democracy.'[119] Having written for 'Collier's huge audience', Gellhorn herself recalled, 'gave me the brief illusion that I could affect how people thought by making them see what I have seen'.[120]

Yet the doubt that inheres in this last quotation (informed by the failure of 'Come Ahead, Adolf!' and 'Obituary of a Democracy' and Gellhorn's own practical efforts to stimulate intervention) permeates the novel. Arriving in Prague, the main protagonist, an American magazine journalist called Mary Douglas who has covered the Spanish Civil War,[121] finds the other (male) members of the press, sitting round a table, 'each in the pose that would some day become famous in a photograph on the cover of his own book of reminiscences (if not already famous)'.[122] 'Noting their well-fed, satisfied faces', she realises with disgust that they are 'thriving' on the catastrophe.[123] Already, there is a sense of journalism as narcissistic, potentially impotent, possibly even predatory. This is reportage aimed not at moving but at titillation. Mary rejects it: 'No propaganda they [her editors] would say. We want the inside story. Make it clear, make it colourful, make it lively. If I knew how, I would write a lament.'[124] To write to move public opinion, then, might be one form of action (as exemplified by the novel itself), but the work goes beyond this to consider what else might be done. Two of the three key instances nevertheless all involve some species of persuasion, rather than direct action, albeit persuasion aimed as individuals rather than at readerships-at-large. In the first instance, Mary attempts to drive out with a fellow correspondent, Tom Lambert, to the country residence of the Czech President, Edouard Beneš, hoping to get an interview with him and thus convey his point of view.[125] The trip is stalled when the car hits a 'little man' in Wenceslaus Square. Mary and Tom take the man into the car and try to persuade him to go to hospital, but at the word, 'his eyes were brilliant with fear and he said, no, no, and fumbled with the door of the car'.[126] Then, a police whistle blows and Mary watches the little man:

> He closed his eyes swiftly, as if the long pointed notes of the whistle hurt him. Then he slumped into the corner of the car, and his mouth sagged and trembled, and he could no longer keep back the despair that was blurring his face and bringing sharp tired tears to his eyes.[127]

There is real empathy in this description, but Mary and Tom have been thoughtless: in their attempt to save the Czech people, they have brought an individual Czech person – a Sudeten refugee – to the attention of the authorities. The little man is given 48 hours to leave Prague and Mary and Tom call off the trip to Beneš and instead go to the movies.[128] Intervention by the press has been worse than useless, Mary's effect on the situation positively deleterious.

The second instance which examines the limits of participation concerns another grand gesture. In her 1986 Afterword to the novel, Gellhorn noted that she 'had used two of my own small acts in that tragedy as part of the story'.[129] The first was her attempt to see Beneš, the other was delivering, on her second visit to Prague, a report on the displaced Sudetens to the League of Nations High Commissioner for Refugees, Sir Neill Malcolm. She also arranged a meeting between Malcolm, Sirovy, the Czech Prime Minister, and Faucher, former head of the French Military Mission,[130] aiming, at the very least, to get the 48-hour expulsion orders imposed on the refugees extended to a more reasonable fortnight. In *A Stricken Field*, Malcolm becomes 'Lord Balham' and General Faucher 'Labonne'. In front of the former, Mary Douglas has to find words that will persuade as never before:

> She talked very fast, to say it all before she was interrupted. [. . .] She spoke of the little man who had harmed nobody [. . .]. First, as she talked, she thought: this has to succeed, lay it on, lay on the charm, lay on the tears, anything, anything. But later, she forgot [. . .] who this English man was [. . .] what she remembered was the homeless people, and how little time was left for them.[131]

Moving from superficiality ('lay it on') to a real engagement with those on behalf of whom she speaks which makes her forget the tricks of self-presentation, Mary nevertheless feels when she stops talking that she has 'been shouting in a cave with echoes'.[132] The 48-hour expulsion orders are commuted to a mere 24 hours. Echoing Charis Day's explicit rejection of a female role combining heroism and self-sacrifice, she tells herself, 'I'm not Joan of Arc, I'm only a journalist'.[133] It is a rejection that configures her as inconspicuous and ineffective, the express opposite of an inspirational woman in war. Above all, it emphasises the failure of her rhetoric, in microcosm an indictment of her journalistic enterprise as a whole.

It is only in the third instance, the plot-strand concerning the communists remaining in Prague and their clandestine efforts on behalf of the victims of fascism, that Mary contemplates action other than attempts to persuade through speaking or writing. The action is no more than the miniscule gesture of offering cigarettes. Even this contribution is denied her:

> Mary took cigarettes from her bag and offered them to Rita, who refused. She did not know what to say, she feeling soft and alien, possessed of every safety and every guarantee, and doing nothing to save these others, and unable to do anything.[134]

The scene reinforces Mary's sense of powerlessness, a feeling which, along with the knowledge of her comparative security, is alienating. Unable to alleviate the situation even by a gesture, the journalist is here rendered actually speechless by the realisation of her limitations.

In January 1940 came an incident of intervention of a more personal kind. Returning to Cuba from Finland, where she had been reporting on the Russian offensive, Gellhorn stopped off in Paris. Gustav Regler, one-time communist, German novelist and member of the International Brigade in Spain, had (ironically given his anti-fascist convictions) been interned as an enemy alien in a French concentration camp at Vernet.[135] Gellhorn tried in vain to pull strings to get him released.[136] She later recalled:

> The only work I had to do in Paris was to try to rescue some friends who were imprisoned with the defeated Spanish army beside the Mediterranean, in holes dug on the beach at Argelès.[137] This project interested no one at all. As a successful politician said to me, while we both stuffed foie gras: My dear girl, a German and a former Communist, really, what do you expect? It was useless to point out that these men, forgotten behind barbed wire,[138] had been fighting Hitler long before anyone else thought of doing so, or had been forced to do so. I realized finally how unwise it was to be 'prematurely anti-Fascist'.[139]

In the short story, 'Goodwill to Men', written in the spring of 1940[140] and published in the collection *The Heart of Another* in 1946, an American journalist called Elizabeth Dalton attempts to get a German communist writer friend, Max Ohlau, who was badly wounded at Teruel, released from a French concentration camp. Elizabeth comments, hinting at the self-regarding though ineffective side of journalism: 'I enjoyed very much the kind of life I had; it gave me a great sense of importance to be always in a violent expensive hurry.'[141] In Paris, her efforts to persuade a French government minister; influential friends; various officials; Tom, an American journalist friend; and Karl Jensen, the head of the underground communists in the city to help Max all result in polite evasions. 'Forget your German Communist and eat a good lunch,' a French friend formerly known for her fearlessness tells her,[142] echoing Gellhorn's own experience of 'stuff[ing] foie gras' while others suffered. In the past, Tom has been enthusiastic about the power of the press – ' "if we all blow it ahead of time [. . .] we can make it harder for the sons of bitches anyhow" ' – but now he doesn't 'give a goddam what happens any more'.[143] Karl will do nothing to assist because Max is useful as a martyr in prison and could prove 'volatile', that is, critical of the Party, if released: he tells Elizabeth, ' "I [am] trying to correct a too limited and subjective view of this problem. I hope you will help all the political prisoners." '[144] The truth finally dawns: Elizabeth realises that Karl, whom she used to think of as an active force in Spain, 'was not in Madrid [. . .] he sent men into Germany, he organised it, but he did not come himself'.[145] Karl, that is, has not personally engaged in events. Elizabeth's last hope is therefore that he will be forced to experience war non-vicariously:

> I hope he [Karl] has to pay just once, he himself, with his fear and with the waiting nights [. . .] always knowing [. . .] that it could be you. I hope he gets caught [. . .] when the planes come over, I hope he lies at the edge of a road somewhere [. . .] with only his hands over the back of his head and his face on the ground, he trying to flatten himself into the dirt.[146]

Despite this flash of anger, the effect of all these refusals to help or get involved is to make Elizabeth question her own self-worth rather than to drive her to further activity. 'Who was I, this shrunken, almost invisible creature, to think I could help?' she asks herself.[147] The inability to persuade others feels personally diminishing, and it is significant that the word used for this sensation is 'invisible'. Unable here to exploit her conspicuousness, her failure to affect the situation renders the woman war reporter, at least in her own estimation, as good as hidden from view.

'Goodwill to Men', with its haunting line, 'it could be you', strips the issues of participation down to the individual's plight and the individual's response. Gustav Regler was released from Vernet because, he said, 'Hemingway, Lady Willert, Mrs. Eleanor Roosevelt and Martha Gellhorn had intervened on my behalf'.[148] None the less, by 1959, Gellhorn was writing in the Introduction to *The Face of War*: 'If a life could be saved from the first of the Gestapo in Prague, or another from behind the barbed wire on the sands at Argelès, that was a comfort but it was hardly journalism.'[149] The idea of 'peace on earth' is risible: war cannot be stopped; at most only individual lives can be pulled from the wreckage. This, Gellhorn acknowledges, is scarcely the result of a writer mobilising opinion but rather the result of the bargaining power of passports and currency. In 'Goodwill to Men' this sense of journalistic impotence is expressed as an inability to influence others. In the text discussed next, the issue is not so much the power of persuasion as the duty of an individual personally to intervene.

The last work to be considered in this chapter, *Point of No Return*, uses a specific issue – Jewishness – to explore the nature of possible participation. The matter has attracted critical and ethical debate. 'To write lyric poetry after Auschwitz is barbaric,' affirmed Adorno, but he also commended Enzensberger's retort: 'literature must resist this verdict [. . .] be such that its mere existence after Auschwitz is not a surrender to cynicism'.[150] For Raymond Aron, the issue was also one of genre and voice – the following quotation is reminiscent of Mary Douglas's findings in *A Stricken Field*: 'My writing style falters in the face of events of such magnitude [the Shoah]. One can write about these tragic events only by analyzing them.'[151] M. Adereth notes that, in engagé novels, the story often concerns private individuals, busily trying to solve their personal problems and initially unaware of the role of politics in shaping their destinies: *Point of No Return* conforms to this pattern.

Jewish blood was in Gellhorn's family: her father was a German Jewish atheist, her mother half-Jewish.[152] As a child, Gellhorn refused to attend a dance because a Jewish friend had not been invited.[153] In later life, between 1949 and 1971, she visited Israel seven times.[154] Israel was her 'commitment'.[155] Rosie Boycott calls it her 'blind spot',[156] on account of passages such as this from 'The Arabs of Palestine':

> A thousand-year Muslim Reich, the African continent ruled by Egypt, may be a mad dream, but we have experience of mad dreams and mad dreamers. We cannot be too careful. The echo of Hitler's voice is heard again in the land, now speaking Arabic.[157]

The turning-point was Gellhorn's visit to Dachau in May 1945. She likened it to 'walking off a cliff and being concussed for life'; it was 'the difference between the young and us'.[158] Her response was to feel 'guilt, which I will never lose' for the fact 'that I did not know, realise, find out, care, understand what was happening at the time – and I should have'.[159] The sentiment is Sartrean: 'one is always responsible for what one does not try to prevent'.[160]

Ignorance and apathy about Hitler's victims were widespread. On 22 April 1944, *Collier's* published an article by Frank Gervasi, 'The Jew as Soldier', which gives an idea of attitudes towards Jews current even in liberal publications. Gervasi describes a British Jew saving a drowning Nazi and provides examples of Jews fighting: 'despite this,' he notes, 'the myth persists that Jews are not a belligerent people, but rather a race of merchants and moneylenders'.[161] He goes on to reassure his readers that 'Palestinian Jews are more like Americans than Russians, down to appreciation of ice-cream sodas and Cellophane packaging'.[162] The Nazis' anti-semitism is 'a cold-bloodedly designed policy calculated to bolster nationalism internally and to create political and economic problems within the democratic countries to which refugees fled'.[163] The attitude expressed in the article is, though critical of anti-semitism, one in which the Jew is still firmly 'other', most evident in the surprising revelation that Jews might actually like ice-cream.

Point of No Return, set during in the latter stages of the American campaign in Europe (from the Hürtgenwald to Berlin), concerns awareness, engagement and action: the moral necessity of becoming a stake-holder in the war being waged against Nazism. Moving beyond the issue of the influential power of rhetoric, it considers practical, proactive versions of intervention. The two main protagonists are Lt Col John Dawson Smithers of the 20th Infantry Division and Jacob Levy, his jeep-driver. This job is significant. Like that of the journalist, it might be seen as adjectival in warfare, but, unlike that of the journalist, it is of obvious immediate practical use. Making Jacob Levy a driver allows Gellhorn to give him some detachment but also to afford him opportunities for action.

Jacob's ethnicity is noticed in the army (' "I haven't got a Jew in my battalion" ')[164] but not regarded as a serious issue by himself. He comes from a family which represses its ethnic identity: 'My old man don't belong to organizations or clubs and he don't see any other Jews but the Weinbergs and Isaacs because he says if you get in with a lot of Jews the first thing you know everybody's got trouble.'[165] Jacob has never been inside a synagogue; he has only considered the war so far as to think, 'what are the Americans doing here, and why didn't the Jews clear out of this stinking Europe long ago?'[166] He discards his Jewish identity without compunction: when he meets and falls in love with a Catholic, Luxembourgeoise girl, Kathe, and she asks him what he is called, he gives the impeccably White Anglo-Saxon Protestant name of his commanding officer, John Dawson Smithers, fearing that she will reject him if she realises he is Jewish. Jacob's love for Kathe is initially what gives him greater emotional investment in the war: worrying about her safety makes him realise 'this is the way men must feel when they [are] fighting at home'.[167]

But what finally engages Jacob Levy in the Second World War is his visit to the liberated Dachau. The visit is only a 'scheme' for getting away to spend time with Kathe, and Jacob nearly dispenses with it all together, before reflecting, 'I guess I ought to go'.[168] As he is shown round it, he therefore occupies much the same status as Gellhorn when she was taken through its horrors. What he sees leads him, on his departure, to drive his jeep into a group of laughing German civilians. Previously, he has borne no animosity towards the Germans, even hoping that he has not caused those he has fought against too much suffering: the crash, then, constitutes an example of immediate direct action, individual retribution swiftly dispensed. (Ronald Monson of *The Daily Telegraph* also drove his car into a group of Germans after witnessing Belsen.)[169] In the longer term, witnessing the death camp impels Jacob to insist on his Jewishness. Having once laid false claim to a WASP identity, in hospital after the crash he tells his lawyer his name 'ten times' and his letter to Kathe directing her to forget him prints his signature 'twice as large as the rest'.[170] But crucially, Jacob, having for the first time engaged in his ethnic community, receives confusing news: not all the Dachau inmates were actually Jews. Investment in the cause of the war, he quickly realises, must not just be on behalf of a particular group, but total: 'it was one case where men were the same. Now he was glad he had done it for the others, too. He was glad he had been able to stop the laughing, once, for everyone.'[171] Jacob can now understand and value his role as an American soldier fighting a faraway European war.

For Jacob, at least, there is the possibility of individual action bringing immediate results, plus the knowledge that he is part of the entire military effort. So much can be attributed to his job as a jeep-driver: he is not confined to the use of rhetoric in his wish to make a difference. The woman war reporter, as dramatised in Gellhorn's fiction examined so far, has less effect, fewer opportunities to contribute and a correspondingly lower profile: shrunken and invisible, Joan of Arc in negative. The next chapter moves on to consider Gellhorn's works of fiction which propose an even more pessimistic view of the participatory potential of the female non-combatant at war, a participation that becomes fatally distracting.

Notes

1 Quoted in Penrose, Antony, ed., *Lee Miller's War: Photographer and Correspondent with the Allies in Europe 1944–45* (London: Condé Nast, 1992) 36.
2 Capa, Robert, *Slightly out of Focus* (New York: Henry Holt, 1947) 147.
3 McCullin, Don, *Unreasonable Behaviour: An Autobiography* (London: Vintage, 1992) 124.
4 Delmer, Sefton, *Trail Sinister: An Autobiography. Volume One* (London: Secker & Warburg, 1961) 404.
5 Delmer, Sefton, *Black Boomerang: An Autobiography. Volume Two* (London: Secker & Warburg, 1962) 14–16, 20.

6 See Austin, J. L., *How to Do Things with Words* (Oxford: The Clarendon Press, 1962) 108.

7 Barthes, Roland, *Image, Music, Text* (London: Fontana, 1977) 142, original emphasis.

8 Mander, John, *The Writer and Commitment* (London: Martin Secker and Warburg, 1961) 106.

9 Gellhorn, 'Writers Fighting in Spain', *The Writer in a Changing World*, ed. Hart, Henry (London: Lawrence and Wishart, 1937) 63–8: 68.

10 *FoW* 12.

11 One writer who did 'do more' in the Spanish Civil War was George Orwell, who fought for the Trotskyist POUM. Even so, he was to write: 'the period seemed to have been one of the most futile of my whole life. I had joined the militia in order to fight against Fascism, and as yet I had scarcely fought at all, had merely existed as a sort of passive object [. . .]. I wish, indeed, that I could have served the Spanish Government a little more effectively' (Orwell, George, *Homage to Catalonia* (London: Penguin, 2000) 82).

12 Connolly, Cyril, 'Comment', *Horizon* (May 1940) 309–14: 314.

13 Rees, Goronwy, 'Letter from a Soldier', *Horizon* (July 1940) 467–71: 467.

14 Rees, 'Letter from a Soldier', 468.

15 Rees, 'Letter from a Soldier', 468.

16 Rees, 'Letter from a Soldier', 468.

17 Connolly, Cyril, 'Comment', *Horizon* (July 1940) 532–5: 533.

18 Calder-Marshall, Arthur *et al.*, 'Why Not War Writers? A Manifesto', *Horizon* (October 1941) 236, 238: 236.

19 John Dos Passos.

20 Gellhorn, letter of 17 October 1941 to Max Perkins: *SL* 118.

21 Adereth, M., *Commitment in Modern French Literature. A Brief Study of 'Littérature Engagée' in the Works of Péguy, Aragon and Sartre* (London: Victor Gollancz, 1967) 38.

22 Moorehead, Caroline, *Martha Gellhorn: A Life* (London: Chatto & Windus, 2003) 318.

23 De Beauvoir, Simone, *La force de l'âge* (Paris: Gallimard, 1960) 19. Similarly, Judith Narden in *What Mad Pursuit*: 'we didn't think about it all, really. We just were, don't you see' (*WMP* 134).

24 Sartre, Jean-Paul, *What Is Literature?*, trans. Frechtman, Bernard (London and New York: Routledge, 2001) 163.

25 Sartre, *What Is Literature?*, 5, 9, 4.

26 Sartre, *What Is Literature?*, 11, 13, 13–14.

27 Sartre, *What Is Literature?*, 14.

28 Aron, Raymond, *The Committed Observer. Interviews with Jean-Louis Missaka and Dominique Wolton* (Chicago: Regnery Gateway, 1983) 261.

29 Sartre, *What Is Literature?*, 48–9.

30 Sartre, *What Is Literature?*, 15. Adorno described this stance as ' "he who is not with me is against me" emptied of theology' (Adorno, Theodor,

'Commitment', *Aesthetics and Politics*, ed. Bloch, Ernest, Lukács, Georg, Brecht, Bertold, Benjamin, Walter and Adorno, Theodor (London: NLB, 1977) 177–95: 180).

31 Sartre, *What Is Literature?*, 212.

32 *FoW* 12.

33 Sartre, *What Is Literature?*, 51.

34 Sartre, *What Is Literature?*, 56, 248, 52.

35 Sartre comments, like Lukács, on nineteenth-century bourgeois writers that they understood the proletariat 'with their heads not hearts' (Sartre, *What Is Literature?*, 92). He also observes approvingly that 'the American writer has often practised manual occupations before writing his books [and] he goes back to them' (Sartre, *What Is Literature?*, 128).

36 Sartre, *What Is Literature?*, 183, original emphasis.

37 Sartre, *What Is Literature?*, 115.

38 Adorno, 'Commitment', 188. Though he used the word 'Gedicht' (poem) in his original formulation of this thought in his essay 'Kulturkritik und Gesellschaft' (1949), Adorno substituted 'Lyrik' (lyric poem) in his 1965 'Commitment' essay. This gives the sense that to write anything other than protest or committed literature after Auschwitz is barbaric (see Hofmann, Klaus, 'Poetry after Auschwitz – Adorno's Dictum', *German Life and Letters* 58/2 (April 2005) 182–94).

39 Adorno, 'Commitment', 189.

40 Adorno, 'Commitment', 193.

41 Sartre, Jean-Paul, *Words*, trans. Clephane, Irene (London: Penguin, 2000) 157.

42 Steiner, George, 'Silence and the Poet', *Language and Silence* (London: Faber, 1985) 55–74. In another essay, 'The Retreat from the Word' (1961), Steiner calls Hemingway's style 'a brilliant response to the diminution of linguistic possibility' (Steiner, *Language and Silence*, 49).

43 Carpenter, Iris, *No Woman's World* (Boston: Houghton Mifflin, 1946) ix.

44 Gellhorn, 'The Wounded Come Home', *Collier's* (5 August 1944) 14–15, 73–5: 15.

45 <http://www.yale.edu/lawweb/avalon/lawofwar/lawwar.htm>.

46 Davis, Richard Harding, *A Year from a Correspondent's Note-Book* (London and New York: Harper, 1898) 224–5.

47 <http://www.yale.edu/lawweb/avalon/lawofwar/lawwar.htm>.

48 The ambiguity is highlighted by subsequent legal reforms. The Geneva Conventions of 1949 extended all the protections due to combatants to war correspondents. They were not to be treated as spies and, even though their notebooks and film could be confiscated, they did not have to respond to interrogation. If they were sick or wounded, they were entitled to medical treatment and, if they were captured, they had to be treated humanely. This changed with the adoption of certain Protocols in 1977, which explicitly recognized journalists to be civilians and therefore due all the civilian (as opposed to military) protections. Now, journalists must not be deliberately

targeted, detained or otherwise mistreated any more than any other civilian. They therefore have an obligation to differentiate themselves from combatants by not wearing uniforms or openly carrying firearms. See <http://www.globalissuesgroup.com/geneva/history.html>.

49 Baker, Carlos, *Ernest Hemingway: A Life Story* (Harmondsworth: Penguin, 1972) 653.

50 Moeller, Susan D., *Shooting War: Photography and the American Experience of Combat* (New York: Basic Books, 1989) 183.

51 Kert, Bernice, *The Hemingway Women* (New York: Norton, 1983) 384.

52 Simpson, John, 'War Reporting: The New Vulnerability', The Reuters' Memorial Lecture 2003, given at St Catherine's College, Oxford, 27 June 2003.

53 McCullin, *Unreasonable Behaviour*, front cover.

54 Sheppard, Philippa, 'Tongues of War: Studies in the Military Rhetoric of Shakespeare's History Plays' (unpublished doctoral thesis, University of Oxford, 1994) 186.

55 Palmer, Frederick, *With My Own Eyes: A Personal History of Battle Years* (London: Jarrolds, 1934) 235.

56 Letter of December 1938, f. 1r.

57 Gellhorn, 14 June 1944, f. 1r.

58 Roosevelt, Theodore, *Americanism and Preparedness. Speeches of Theodore Roosevelt July to November, 1916* (New York: The Mail and Express Job Print, 1917) 142. Roosevelt was beaten for the 1916 Republican presidential nomination by Charles Evans Hughes, who went on to lose to Woodrow Wilson.

59 *OED*, 'aporetic': from the Greek *aporos*, impassable; *a*, privative, + *poros*, passage.

60 Wharton, Edith, *A Backward Glance* (New York and London: D. Appleton, 1934) 357.

61 Wharton, Edith, *Fighting France. From Dunkerque to Belfort* (London: Macmillan, 1915) 225.

62 Kelly, Florence Finch, 'Eye Witnesses of the War: Fighting France', *Bookman* 42 (December 1915) 462–3: 462 (quoted in Tuttleton, James W., Lauer, Kristin O., Murray, Margaret P., eds, *Edith Wharton: The Contemporary Reviews* (Cambridge: Cambridge University Press, 1992) 222).

63 *French Ways and Their Meaning* (review), *New Republic* 20 (25 September 1919) 241 (quoted in Tuttleton, Lauer and Murray, *Edith Wharton* 273).

64 Gellhorn, 'Cracking the Gothic Line', *Collier's* (28 October 1944) 24, 57–8: 24.

65 Gellhorn, 'The Wounds of Paris', *Collier's* (4 November 1944) 72–3: 73.

66 Gellhorn, 'An Odd, Restless, Beautiful Country', *New Republic* (4 August 1947) 26–8: 27.

67 Cull, Nicholas John, *Selling War: The British Propaganda Campaign against American 'Neutrality' in World War II* (New York and Oxford: Oxford University Press, 1995) 10, 29.

68 Kirkpatrick, Helen Paull, *This Terrible Peace* (London: Rich & Cowan, 1939) 15–41.
69 Gellhorn viewed American entry as a means to defeat fascism: there is no sense that, unlike some intellectuals, she had a political vision of the war as 'the [welcome] end of capitalism' (see Piette, Adam, *Imagination at War. British Fiction and Poetry 1939–1945* (London: Papermac, 1995) 40–1).
70 Murrow, Edward R., *This Is London* (London: Cassell, 1941) 143.
71 Murrow, *This Is London*, 165.
72 Murrow, *This Is London*, 168.
73 Murrow, *This Is London*, 252.
74 Murrow, *This Is London*, 253.
75 Pyle, Ernie, *Ernie's War* (New York and Toronto: Random House, 1986) 49, 53.
76 Cowles, Virginia, *Looking for Trouble* (London: Hamish Hamilton, 1942) 132.
77 Cowles, *Looking for Trouble*, 132.
78 Gellhorn, 'The Lord Will Provide for England', *Collier's* (17 September 1938) 15–17, 35–8: 15.
79 Gellhorn, 'The Lord Will Provide for England', 17 September 1938, 17.
80 Gellhorn, 'The Lord Will Provide for England', 17 September 1938, 36.
81 Cowles, *Looking for Trouble*, 136.
82 Gellhorn, 'Sunday', 1940, f. 3r.
83 Gellhorn, 'English Sunday', *Collier's* (1 April 1944) 60–2: 60, 61.
84 Gellhorn, 'English Sunday', 1 April 1944, 61, 61.
85 Gellhorn, 'English Sunday', 1 April 1944, 61.
86 Mulvey, Christopher, *Anglo-American Landscapes: A Study of Nineteenth-Century Anglo-American Travel Literature* (Cambridge: Cambridge University Press, 1983) 10, 257; Mulvey, Christopher, *Transatlantic Manners. Social Patterns in Nineteenth-Century Anglo-American Travel Literature* (Cambridge: Cambridge University Press, 1990) 7.
87 Giles, Paul, *Virtual Americas: Transnational Fictions and the Transatlantic Imaginary* (Durham, NC, and London: Duke University Press, 2002) 1–2.
88 Giles, *Virtual Americas*, 4.
89 Giles, *Virtual Americas*, 14.
90 Davis, *A Year from a Correspondent's Note-Book* 193.
91 Loomis, Charles Battell, 'ST-PH-N CR-N-', *The War Dispatches of Stephen Crane*, ed. Stallman, R. W. and Hagemann, E. R. (London: Peter Owen, 1964) 50–1: 51. Davis's colleague in the Spanish–American War and the Russo-Japanese War, John Fox Jr, said of him, 'out of any incident or situation he could pick the most details that would interest the most people and put them in a way that was pleasing to the most people' (Fox Jr, John, 'Richard Harding Davis', *The Novels and Stories of Richard Harding Davis. Volume 7 – The White Mice* (New York: Scribner, 1916) v–viii: vii).
92 Gellhorn, 'The Bomber Boys', *Collier's* (17 June 1944) 58, 60: 60.
93 Gellhorn, 'Time Bomb in Hong Kong', *Collier's* (7 June 1941) 13, 31–3: 13.

94 Gellhorn, 'Over and Back', *Collier's* (22 July 1944) 16.

95 Letter of 3–4 July 1937: *SL* 55.

96 Letter of 13 December 1943 to Ernest Hemingway: *SL* 158.

97 Gellhorn, 18 February 1959, f. 1v.

98 *FoW* 1–2.

99 *FoW* 2–3.

100 *FoW* 4.

101 Gellhorn, letter to Hortense Flexner, early 1970s, ff. 6r.

102 'The Lord Will Provide For England' is placed just before 'Obituary of a Democracy' in *VfG*, as though to emphasise Britain's lack of action in the matter.

103 Orsagh, Jacqueline, 'A Critical Biography of Martha Gellhorn' (unpublished doctoral thesis, Michigan State University, 1977) 92, 98, 108; Moorehead, *Martha Gellhorn* 176–8, 198.

104 Gellhorn, 'Come Ahead, Adolf!', *Collier's* (6 August 1938) 12–13, 43–5: 45. Winston Churchill commented on the situation: 'The Czechs had a million and half men armed behind the strongest fortress line in Europe, and equipped by a highly organised and powerful industrial machine' (Churchill, Winston, *The Second World War. Volume 1 – The Gathering Storm* (London: The Reprint Society, 1950) 258).

105 The Munich Pact of 29 September 1938, concluded between Britain, France, Germany and Italy, allowed Hitler to annex the Sudetenland, a German-speaking area of Czechoslovakia, despite the fact that the Czech army was ready to defend it. The Nazis in the Sudetenland were led by Konrad Henlein. Non-Henleinists, Social Democrats, communists, Jews and other minority groups were expelled from the area, becoming refugees.

106 Gellhorn, 'Obituary of a Democracy', *Collier's* (10 December 1938) 12–13, 28, 32–3, 36: 12. Virginia Cowles, in her 1942 memoirs, records a similar conversation with a Czech soldier: ' "When you get there [to France], you can tell them for us that one day they will look across that Maginot line of theirs and asks, 'Where are those two million Czechs?' And we won't exist. They will fight alone" ' (Cowles, *Looking for Trouble*, 187).

107 Gellhorn, 'The Lord Will Provide for England', 17 September 1938, 38. Similarly, Storm Jameson, in *Europe to Let* (1940), has the Czech General Jan Stehlík say about the English: 'it doesn't matter a damn about my little Heine and my Czech Bible, but your Shakespeare and your Bible, that's terrible. You don't care what happens to my soul, only about your own' (Jameson, Storm, *Europe to Let: The Memoirs of an Obscure Man* (London: Macmillan, 1940) 116).

108 *SF 1986* 309. In fact, Spain does break into the text: seeing the Sudeten refugee children, Mary Douglas is moved to think of the children in Spain (*SF* 82–3).

109 Gellhorn, letter of 8 June 1940 to Hortense Flexner and Wyncie King: *SL* 93.

110 *SF 1986* 307.

111 *SF 1986* 308.

112 Kennan, George, *Memoirs 1925–1950* (London: Hutchinson, 1968) 90.

113 Kennan, *Memoirs*, 91.

114 Kennan, *Memoirs*, 91. In fact, Gellhorn's assessment of the situation was correct: on 25 September 1939 Hitler said in Berlin that 'the Czechs must clear out of the Sudetenland by the 26th' (Churchill, *The Second World War*, 256). More than twenty thousand Jews living in the Sudetenland became refugees (Gilbert, Martin, *The Holocaust: The Jewish Tragedy* (London: Fontana, 1987) 66) and of course this did not include the non-Jewish Sudetens also expelled by the Nazis.

115 *SF* preliminary pages.

116 Broadcast of 27 September 1938, quoted in *Peace for Our Time? An up-to-Date Summary of the Gravest Crisis of Modern Times. Speeches of the Leaders* (Manchester and London: The Policy-Holder Journal Co., 1938) 22.

117 *Hansard* 14 March 1938, col. 96.

118 *SF* dust-jacket.

119 Clayton, Charles C., 'Grim Novel of Refugees under the Nazi Whip', *St Louis Globe-Democrat* (16 March 1940).

120 *SF 1986* 303.

121 'A transparent stand-in for Gellhorn', in Orsagh's view (Orsagh, 'A Critical Biography', 145).

122 *SF* 7. A line drawing of Gellhorn appears on the inside flap of the dust-jacket of the first edition of *FoW*.

123 *SF* 10.

124 *SF* 82. Gellhorn seems to have been musing on this point of genre in her letters on the subject: in her 8 June 1940 letter to Hortense Flexner and Wyncie King, she wrote of 'that land, those bald, always moving, forever hills, the claw sharp mountains, the green plains that go down to Aranjuez where they grow strawberries and asparagus. I don't know. Maybe that is not a book but a poem. A lament' (*SL* 93) – the letter again assimilates Czechoslovakia and Spain.

125 In her letter to Charles Colebaugh of 22 October 1938, Gellhorn explained her own motives for visiting Beneš: the Czech president 'for political reasons [. . .] could not talk or write' and was 'virtually a prisoner' in his country residence (*SL* 67, 68).

126 *SF* 33.

127 *SF* 33.

128 *SF* 45.

129 *SF 1986* 312.

130 Moorehead, *Martha Gellhorn*, 181–2.

131 *SF* 163.

132 *SF* 163.

133 *SF* 177. See *WMP* 80.

134 *SF* 55.

135 See Regler, Gustav, *The Owl of Minerva*, trans. Denny, Norman (London: Rupert Hart-Davis, 1959) ch. 16.

136 Orsagh, 'A Critical Biography', 112; Moorehead, *Martha Gellhorn*, 138, 196.

137 Argelès was a French concentration camp near Lourdes; Vernet is south of Toulouse.

138 In his memoirs, Regler specifically mentions the barbed wire (Regler, *The Owl of Minerva* 333).

139 *FoW* 74–5.

140 Moorehead, *Martha Gellhorn*, 201.

141 *HoA* 179.

142 *HoA* 170.

143 *HoA* 191.

144 *HoA* 222, 221. This is chillingly reminiscent of the reaction Regler recalls of John Collier, communist activist and director of Roosevelt's 'Indian [i.e. Native American] Ministry', whom Regler had asked for a lecturing job: ' "You have deserted us and that is treachery. No pity can be shown to traitors. Your idealism is dangerous [. . .]. Nobody stays long in the top rank with us particularly when they have rebellious quirks. You have never grasped that. If you go on fighting against us we shall liquidate you" ' (Regler, *The Owl of Minerva*, 365–6).

145 *HoA* 224.

146 *HoA* 225.

147 *HoA* 205.

148 Regler, *The Owl of Minerva*, 352.

149 *FoW* 2.

150 Adorno, 'Commitment', 188.

151 Aron, *The Committed Observer*, 90.

152 Moorehead, *Martha Gellhorn*, 15, 16, 18.

153 Moorehead, *Martha Gellhorn*, 19.

154 Moorehead, *Martha Gellhorn*, 326.

155 Gellhorn, letter to Hortense Flexner, early 1970s, f. 2r.

156 Boycott, Rosie, 'We Drank and Smoked, I Was One of Her Chaps', *The Times* (20 September 2003) 10–11: 10.

157 *VfG* 221.

158 Gellhorn, letter to Hortense Flexner, early 1970s, ff. 6r, 7r.

159 Gellhorn, letter to Hortense Flexner, early 1970s, f. 4r

160 Sartre, *What Is Literature?* 223.

161 Gervasi, Frank, 'The Jew as Soldier', *Collier's* (22 April 1944) 11, 28, 30, 32: 11.

162 Gervasi, 'The Jew as Soldier', 11, 28.

163 Gervasi, 'The Jew as Soldier', 29.

164 *WoA* 9. Aichinger describes anti-semitism in the American army in the European Theatre as 'endemic' (Aichinger, Peter, *The American Soldier in Fiction 1880–1963. A History of Attitudes toward Warfare and the*

Military Establishment (Ames, Iowa: Iowa State University Press, 1975) 56).

165 *WoA* 131.
166 *WoA* 135.
167 *WoA* 184.
168 *WoA* 267, 268.
169 Knightley, Phillip, *The First Casualty: The War Correspondent as Hero and Myth-Maker from the Crimea to Kosovo* (London: Prion Books, 2000) 346.
170 *WoA* 297, 300.
171 *WoA* 304.

6

Fatal distraction

Gellhorn's journalism was her own practical attempt to make a difference: to combat anti-interventionism, to help in individual cases and,
later, when published in collections, to protest against nuclear arms proliferation. From her fiction already considered, what emerges is her sense
of the limited efficacy of the attempt. In the fiction discussed in this
chapter – the short stories 'A Sense of Direction' and 'Portrait of a
Lady' – an even more negative view of 'involvement' emerges. Here,
intervening is not benign or even ineffective, but becomes distraction,
disruption, even fatal hindrance. Gellhorn's concerns centre on the figure
of the woman war correspondent who is (as she was) glamorous, and
who introduces sexual excitement and volatility into the male space that
is the war zone. To set the scene, this chapter begins by placing this phenomenon within a wartime cultural context of sartorial confusion: years
which saw both movie-star glamour and the imposition of latter-day
sumptuary laws. Glamour is investigated as a concept and as a presence
in civilian life and on the battle-field. The chapter concludes by advancing the theory of 'tokenism' as a possible explanation for Gellhorn's negative portraits of women in war.

Glamour

It is important to remember that Gellhorn grew up during the so-called
'first wave' of feminism, the era of the movement dedicated to achieving
equal rights for women, particularly the vote, rather than to problem-
atising the very nature of femininity (although Joan Riviere's
'Womanliness as Masquerade' essay, a landmark piece positing the contingency of gender, was published in *The International Journal of
Psychoanalysis* as early as 1929).[1] Edna Gellhorn was invited to become
the first president of the national Suffrage Association.[2] Martha's own
'sort of feminism', according to Caroline Moorehead, was that of seeing
no conflict 'between being a woman and achieving what you wanted'.[3]

Rosie Boycott comments, 'she took a dim view of any women who – as she saw it – needed to take shelter under the umbrella of the women's movement in order to prove the qualities that she had spent her whole life demonstrating'.[4] These remarks underline that to impose a standard feminist (or anti-feminist) agenda on Gellhorn runs the risk of being anachronistic. In her war reportorial career, she adopted (or exploited) a spectrum of guises, and 'guise' is here intended not in the post-feminist sense of gender-as-performance[5] but as practical and pragmatic.

What, then, were the guises that Gellhorn and others adopted? The answer seems to be a paradoxical – and enduring – complex of toughness and glamour.[6] Here is BBC war correspondent Kate Adie on the point:

> Wearing clothes that grab attention is wonderful on game shows and showbiz interviews, but if you insist on eye-catching garb, then you end up having your clothes discussed and your reports ignored. It'll happen anyway if you're a woman, with most viewers observing you lying on the deck of an operational aircraft carrier with jets streaking by and wondering why your shirt looks a bit crumpled. Better, I suppose, than being known as 'that one with the sparkly jewellery' or 'her with the frilly blouses'.[7]

As a popular British war song, sung to the tune of 'Funiculee, Funicular', had it:

> Some join the WAACs to get a bit of glamour,
> What a mistake, what a mistake!
> [. . .]
> We know they will soon be making brown beds
> And scrubbing floors.[8]

The two adjectives Iris Carpenter uses to describe Ruth Cowan are 'blonde' and 'dynamic'.[9] She invokes Lee Carson with reference to 'her lovely legs absorbed into their usual preposterous, shapeless, combat pants'.[10] Present at a visit by General Patton (a notorious opponent to women in the field) to the front, Carpenter recalls: 'All I could do was stick my chin well into the collar of the GI coat borrowed to hide my feminine gender, and hope that none of the blond curls so carefully pinned up under the tin hat would escape to give me away.'[11] The image of tin hat and blond curls encapsulates the image: a femininity which can be hidden under masculine accoutrements but which, nevertheless, threatens constantly to break through – glamour beneath a GI coat.[12]

What place has glamour in wartime, a set of circumstances in which necessity and sacrifice are to the fore? Glamour was certainly in the air in the late 1930s and early 1940s: Hollywood's hey-day. Titles published in the United States and Britain in the period – covering novels, plays and what today are known as 'self-help' books – include Juanita Savage's *Southern Glamour* (1936), Evadne Price's *Glamour Girl* (1937), Harold Shumate's *Glamour Boy* (1939), Barbara Stanton's *Give Me Glamour* (1940), Kathleen Lindsay's *Glamour Girl* (1942), Paul Rénin's *Glamour* (1942), Lorraine Blythe's *Glamour Parade* (1946), Beatrice Eleanor Kent's *The Glamour of Friendship: and Other Poems* (1938), Peggy Fernway's (a pseudonym for Wilbur Braun) *The Glamour Girl; A Farce in One Act for the Fair Sex* (1936), Florence Ryerson's *Glamour Preferred: A Comedy in Three Acts* (1941), Terry Hunt's *Design for Glamour* (1945), Sali Löbel's *Glamour and How to Achieve It* (1938) and Ern and Bud Westmore's *Beauty, Glamour and Personality* (1947). At the same time, the Second World War saw the introduction of price controls on clothing in America (and clothes rationing in Britain) and the entry of women into the auxiliary military services and factories, places where appearance was influenced more by utility than by fashion. Movie-star glamour therefore wafted tantalisingly above lives of hard work and mundane necessity.

Indeed, in contrast to the attention-grabbing film stars, American women in the services and the factories were effectively camouflaged for the duration. Uniforms for the WACs, the WAVES, the SPARs and the women marines were of a standard style: single-breasted, trimly-fitted jackets and slightly flared skirts to just below the knee, the colours forest-green, olive drab and blue and white.[13] In the factories, health and safety requirements meant that women workers had to swap dresses for Rosie-the-Riveter-style overalls, jumper-suits and slacks and cover their hair with snoods and kerchiefs to prevent it becoming entangled in the machinery (the film star Veronica Lake had her long hair cut short as part of a publicity campaign to persuade women to wear sensible hairstyles during the war[14] and in Britain the 'Liberty cut', 'like a man's haircut – just cut back like that so it was very easy to look after',[15] was popular).[16] The key was *covering*: these women's figures appeared bulkier, more masculine, their contours wrapped and thickened.

The American housewife, meanwhile, contended with the effect that price controls had on clothing. In the United States, governmental influence on consumer behaviour moved with the mobilisation process from early exhortation towards an 'elaborate mosaic' of agencies designed to control the wartime economy.[17] These included the War Production Board (WPB), which, in its hortatory phase, issued a number of standardisation orders for clothing. Asked to develop such an order for women's dresses, Stanley Marcus of the Dallas Neiman-Marcus department store decided to retain the styles current in the late 1930s and 1940s, with the rationale that, although they used considerable material, they were already in fashion and the introduction of wholly new styles would increase the demand for fabric.[18] The result was that the sartorial situation became static and conservative (even so, a skimpier two-piece bathing-suit was introduced to 'save material').[19] The WPB also had the power to order rationing, but responsibility for its administration lay with the Office of Price Administration (OPA).[20] At its peak, rationing in the United States during the Second World War covered slightly more than 20 per cent of the consumer price index at prewar prices,[21] a phenomenon that Rockoff attributes to the 'siege' mentality.[22] Yet, a few instances aside, the clothing industry, with its powerful cotton-producing friends in Congress, successfully resisted rationing in the sector. Imposed instead were a series of price control measures,[23] an effective latter-day sumptuary-law regime. Ruling L-58, issued in 1942, limited dimensions and designs on civilian garments: women's dresses were reduced in yardage by 15 per cent and 'extravagant' items such as turnover cuffs, patch pockets, balloon sleeves, matching sashes, double yokes, attached hoods and shawls were forbidden.[24] Maternity dresses were exempt from these strictures and their sales increased as women took the opportunity to buy larger, decorated garments.[25] Swathed in dresses intended for pregnancy, women's contours were again concealed. In January 1943, Maximum Price Regulation 302 established price ceilings at the wholesale and manufacturing levels for most garments and specified their construction in great detail – even down to the diameter of the buttons. The Maximum Average Price Regulation issued on 19 April 1945 then divided clothing into about four hundred different categories, requiring that the average price of the items in that category should not exceed the (weighted) average of a specified base period.[26] This created artificial shortages as manufacturers exceeded their averages and were not allowed to deliver clothes to the public.[27] But American consumers faced real shortages of all forms of clothing during the war years in that they could not buy what they wanted at OPA price ceilings.[28] Though the situation was never as extreme as in Britain, a 1945 survey showed that only 53 per cent of the demand for house dresses was being met.[29]

How, then, did women outside the military services and the factories generally appear? Shirley Miles O'Donnol writes of 'a rather curious combination of masculine and tailored efficiency topped by very feminine coiffures'.[30] The silhouette was peculiarly broad-shouldered: almost every garment had generous shoulder-pads.[31] Skirts were flared and shorter than in the 1930s, worn to just below the knee.[32] The *Ladies Home Journal* advised: 'if you are a trouser type – slim enough, straight enough and, above all, not bulgy at the hipline – you can have a whole trouser wardrobe.'[33] Bras were designed 'to mould and lift':[34] the Alene Bra advert claimed it to be 'a revolutionary new bra wired for witchery. At last [. . .] a bra that speaks glamour's own language.'[35] Nylon was channelled into parachute production, so women put make-up on their legs to suggest the effect of stockings.[36] Mouths were also brightly made-up[37] (during the war, beauticians' wages rose by 28 per cent).[38] The overall impression is indeed 'curious'. A squareness of shoulder, serious tailoring and figure-disguising maternity-wear resulted in an unfeminine effect and inconspicuousness, but this was contradicted by lifted breasts, waved or curled shoulder-length hair and reddened lips. Like the movies which punctuated everyday existence, glamorous details glimmered here and there in wartime appearance.

Those who promoted such glamour – the fashion and movie industries – often interpreted and justified it for consumption in the war period by, paradoxically, noting its utilitarian qualities. The *Collier's* edition that carried Gellhorn's 'Children Are Soldiers Too'[39] also contained an article by the war correspondent Ruth Carson on black lingerie. Demand, Carson reported, was biggest 'around the camps and war plants', the best-selling items being 'gossamer-sheer, lace-rich night-gowns', followed by panties 'from $1.95 to $35 for a wisp of lace'.[40] But what could account for the popularity?

> Ask the boys who buy it, and they say they like black lingerie because it's feminine, alluring, and more than a little bit wicked.
> Ask the clerks who sell it and they'll say 'The war, new money, desire for extravagance and allure.'
> [. . .] Ask the girls who buy it, and they'll give you the same reasons as the men – plus another: It's practical. It's good for travelling.[41]

In its 6 May 1945 issue, *Collier's* carried an advert for 'Sani-Flush' that explicitly linked practical hygiene with glamour: 'I used to be a glamour girl. Well, go right on being all that's lovely. Don't do that offensive task by hand. Sani-Flush makes toilet bowls sparkling white the quick, easy, sanitary way.' Publications devoted to fashion sent out a mixed message of attractiveness and utility. An edition of British *Vogue* carrying Gellhorn's photo contained an article titled 'According to Your Cloth' which warned, 'the coupons you have saved for spring must give you full measure of value in your suit or dress',[42] and American *Vogue* told its readers how to create ten different looks with 'one short black dinner sheath' so that its purchase would pay off 'all spring and summer'.[43] The self-help books in particular (like their modern counterparts) had a hor-tatory, verging on didactic, tone. Sali Löbel's entrancing *Glamour and*

How to Achieve It is sub-titled 'The Art of Living for Everywoman and Everyman'. The first chapter sets out the 'essential ingredients of glamour':

(a) Perfect Health.
(b) The ability to succeed and yet to dream.
(c) The power in the mind to winnow from life those things to remember and those to forget.
(d) Work.
(e) Laughter and Love.[44]

As Löbel notes, she has said 'nothing about personal or physical beauty':[45] glamour here is a mixture of cleanliness, exercise, industry and a cheerful outlook – all useful qualities, from the point of view of the authorities, to encourage in a population during war. Löbel's other tips are also mindful of wartime economy: 'shampoo the hair each week if a blonde and every ten days if a red-head or a brunette'; 'better a heavy cloth coat [. . .] than a cheap dyed fur'.[46] In this version of glamour, the emphasis is on thrift and resourcefulness: to achieve it, the woman consumer must (like the woman reporter accessing the war zone) resort to de Certeauesque tactics of ingenuity and cunning (indeed, Cohen suggests that consumer behaviour defines women's impact on the war effort).[47] As the 'Consumer's Pledge Song' (sung to the tune of the 'Battle Hymn of the Republic') had it:

> Take the best care of your wearables, and mend them when they tear,
> You can swap the children's outgrown things for things that they can wear.[48]

But if this was its sensible, utilitarian side, glamour, of course, had other qualities: indeed, arguably, the very essence of glamour is effortlessness rather than ingenuity. In contrast to the make-do-and-mend styles, Hollywood make-up artists Ern and Bud Westmores' *Beauty, Glamour and Personality* claimed to be 'the first to lay down fundamental principles governing the application of make-up as a means of dramatizing the personality and enhancing a woman's charm'.[49] This is a much less dutiful version of glamour, now become a form of escapism from dull, albeit dangerous, wartime conditions. Containing photographs of Hollywood 'stars'[50] such as Lana Turner, Sonja Henie, Rosemary Lane and Hedy Lamarr, *Beauty, Glamour and Personality* features examples of what today are called 'makeovers': instances of the transformatory, protean, magical nature of glamour, 'the thing you so often see portrayed on the screen'.[51] Glamour', sharing its etymology with 'grammar', has a sense of 'magic, enchantment, spell':[52] here its bewitching associations (the Alene Bra's 'witchery') are to the fore. *Daily Express* reader Mrs Nichols thinks her changed appearance 'greatly improved' by Ern and Bud's arts of maquillage but wipes all the make-up off before going home to her husband, worried about his reaction: 'still, Mr. Nichols thought the permanent wave looked very nice'.[53] Ern and Bud remark:

> Glamour [. . .] can both reflect and excite thoughts – the kind of thoughts which, in appropriate circumstances and surroundings may intoxicate the holder and beholder alike, and find swift and exciting expression without words – if you know what I mean![54]

The illusory qualities of this version of glamour therefore constituted an antidote to the inconspicuousness which many women during the Second World War experienced, underlining a sharper-than-usual contrast with the habiliments of movie stars and certain female war correspondents. This is glamour as allure: transformative; sexually inviting and also sexually powerful; that specious 'special something' which makes a woman stand apart; dramatic and beguiling.[55] It is a version of the phenomenon familiar today as post-feminism, explained here by Camille Paglia, writing on Madonna: 'Women's sexual glamour has bewitched and destroyed men since Delilah and Helen of Troy. Madonna [. . .] has cured the ills of feminism by reasserting women's command of the sexual realm.'[56]

How, then, does glamour such as this function in the war zone? War correspondents, whether men or women, inevitably have the propensity to seem 'different', which is, of course, the beginnings of glamour. 'I create an immediate sensation,' Walt Whitman told a friend, 'everybody here is so like everybody else – and I am Walt Whitman.'[57] In the hospitals of the American Civil War, his charismatic presence formed a cynosure: 'it is delicious to be the object of so much love and reliance,' he wrote.[58] In 'My Preparations for Visits', he related:

> In my visits to the hospitals I found it was in the simple matter of personal presence, and emanating ordinary cheer and magnetism, that I succeeded and help'd more than by medical nursing, or delicacies, or gifts of money, or anything else. During the war I possess'd the perfection of physical health.[59]

An image emerges of a larger-than-life Whitman walking the wards, upright where the soldiers are bed-ridden, in perfect health where they are wounded, 'magnetic' and cheerful where they are dying. It is the figure of the 'master' from an early poem, 'Pictures' (1825):

> Here Athens itself, – it is a clear forenoon,
> Young men, pupils, collect in the gardens of a favorite master, waiting for him,
> [. . .]

Till, beyond, the master appears advancing – his form shows above the
  crowd, a head taller than they,
His gait is erect, calm and dignified – his features are colossal.[60]

To some degree, the journalist in conflict is always solitary, peripatetic,
ambiguously sited between subject and reader: this is Whitman's
'glamour'. But the Hollywood-style glamour that female reporters
tended to espouse rendered them particularly egregious (in the etymological sense) in the field of the Second World War. The point made in
Chapter 3 is worth reiterating here: the standardisation of military
uniform in the nineteenth century made women (who did not wear it)
'stand out' (an irony as uniform itself is aimed at making a section of the
community noticeably different).[61] It is a representation which is evident
in the many titles of reviews and articles relating to Martha Gellhorn
predicated on the figure of the woman reporter as lone individual, the
literal 'eccentric' in the belligerent context: 'A Woman at the Wars',[62] 'A
World of Men',[63] 'A Woman at War with the World'.[64] If not too fanci-
ful, the comparison can then be drawn between the attractive female
reporter in the male space of war, the movie as a break from factory or
house work (films were screened during the night to accommodate shift
work)[65] and the lipsticked mouth as noticeable detail in an otherwise
drab appearance: all three are *glamorous* as they are conspicuous;
suggest the possibility of magical transformation or escape from prevailing conditions; and are strictly superfluous. This last quality, in particular, results, for the woman war correspondent, in anxious questioning of
self-worth.

When such glamorous figures, with their heightened visibility, enter the
space of war, the effect is considerable. As Higonnet and Higonnet point
out, war politicises human reproduction, and hence the sexual act, for
the simple reason that for warring nations maintaining the population
level (and creating the next generation of warriors) is at a premium.[66]
This politico-symbolic emphasis on women as reproducers increases the
sexual tension that would be introduced in any event when women pene-
trate the predominantly male arena of the front.[67] Dame Helen Gwynne-
Vaughan, Controller of the Queen Mary's Army Auxiliary Corps and the
Auxiliary Territorial Service, wrote:

> No doubt the association of war and love is one of the oldest in our make-
> up and goes back to the roots of the subconscious and the earliest combats
> of two males for the female. Possibly the unconscious desire to leave off-
> spring when life is to be risked is also a factor. At any rate, it is clear that,
> in war, the man is more ardent, the women more vulnerable.[68]

There are three key consequences. The first is that the effect is used to justify restricting women's access even further. Virginia Cowles recalled that during the Russo-Finnish war a Swedish woman journalist reported that a Finnish Press Officer had made advances to her: 'the authorities, exasperated [. . .] promptly slapped down the rule that no more women could visit the front'.[69] The second, and related, consequence is a de-sexualisation on the part of women. Mary Borden reflected on her First World War hospital experiences:

> There are no men here, so why should I be a woman? There are heads and knees and mangled testicles. There are chests with holes as big as your fist, and pulpy thighs, shapeless; and stumps where legs once were fastened [. . .]. How could I be a woman and not die of it?[70]

The third consequence is that the war experience for women becomes primarily one of attracting notice and surprise – 'beauty,' writes Elaine Scarry, 'causes us to gape and suspend all thought'[71] – the opposite of Elizabeth Dalton's sense of being 'shrunken and invisible' in 'Goodwill to Men'.[72] On her trips to the front during the First World War, Edith Wharton met with the 'speechless astonishment of officers and men at the sight of a wandering woman',[73] while war photographer and correspondent for *Vogue*, Lee Miller, attracted 'wide-eyed double-take[s]'[74] from the soldiers she encountered in the Second World War.

The phenomenon reached the pages of British *Vogue* in its March 1944 edition. This contained a feature, 'News Makers and News Breakers', with photographs of Colonel Oveta Culp Hobby (director of the American WAACs);[75] Miss Florence Horsburgh, MP, Parliamentary Secretary to the Ministry of Health; Miss Barbara Ward, Foreign Editor of *The Economist*; Virginia Cowles and Martha Gellhorn (Gellhorn's photo is by Lee Miller). It explained:

> These are women in the news. Two of them – the chief of a women's army, and a Parliamentary Secretary – help to make it. The others record it: but with so sensational a success that in breaking the news, they have become News themselves.[76]

In actually constituting, as opposed to reporting, 'News', Gellhorn, like other glamorous women, became the object of attention. Unsurprisingly, on her visits to the war zone, the soldiers (all of them men), deprived in the field of sexual activity, turned to look at her. The nature and effect of the 'male gaze' has been debated since the term was coined by Laura Mulvey in her 1975 essay 'Visual Pleasure and Narrative Cinema'. In patriarchal, scopophilic culture, Mulvey argued, men are 'bearers of the look', while women connote 'to-be-looked-at-ness'.[77] The controlling male gaze is both voyeuristic and fetishistic, the latter producing such phenomena as the cult of the female movie star.[78] Indeed, the visual presence of women in film works to freeze the flow of action in moments of erotic contemplation offered to the male spectator:[79] to use a rhetorical term, this break in the diegesis is a *tmesis* or cut. Mulvey's thesis has been challenged by those who query whether the only spectator is the male spectator,[80] an important qualification in relation to film. But in the Second World War zone, the 'audience' *was* exclusively male. In this narrative, the appearance (in both senses) of Martha Gellhorn and women like her was tmetic. Action froze.

Jean-Paul Sartre, writing thirty years before Mulvey, takes the thesis a stage further. In *L'Être et le néant* (*Being and Nothingness*) (1943), he noted that being looked at entails 'an irruption of self'.[81] Indeed, another's look removes the possibility of perceiving the world because 'to perceive is to *look at*, and to apprehend a look [. . .] is to be conscious of *being looked at*'.[82] The result is a literal self-consciousness as the original viewing subject suddenly sees himself or herself as a contemplated object, or, in other words, perceives himself or herself from the outside. To translate Sartre's concept of 'le régard' ('the Look') from its specifically ontological context,[83] the woman war journalist's professional task of observing and reporting battle is compromised as she herself, by virtue of being 'news breaker', becomes 'news maker'. High visibility is translated into low efficacy.

Martha Gellhorn was extremely conscious of her appearance and was frequently acknowledged to be glamorous.[84] The *St Louis Globe-Democrat*, in a 'will-she-won't-she' piece on marriage plans to Hemingway, noted that 'Miss Gellhorn spent a number of years in Paris, where she was correspondent for Vogue, a fashion magazine'.[85] She recalled during these days writing about 'fashion', 'face-lifting' and 'corset advertising'.[86] In 1934, the *St Louis Post-Dispatch* reported that she was 'a familiar in all the great dress-making salons.'[87] *Time's* review of *A Stricken Field* was headed 'Glamor Girl'.[88] In a 1936 *Post-Dispatch* review of *The Troubles I've Seen*, Marguerite Martyn found it appropriate to note:

> Tall, slim, blonde, with a gracefully poised head set off with the smartest of haircuts, it was the delight of Paris dressmakers to dress her up in their newest models and have her parade them, not as the usual mannequin at the race tracks, but as a personality among personages. She wore the first halter neck backless gown at the World Economic Congress in London [. . .] it became a hit that swept the fashion world.[89]

Gellhorn herself, in a letter of 15 December 1936, recalled of these experiences: 'I was in Paris for a while last summer [. . .]. There is terrible trouble in the world [. . .] but somehow it still matters whether Madam Zilch wore sequins or a fine gown made exclusively of cellophane and feather boas.'[90] To her interview with Harry Hopkins for the job of 'social worker in Federal employment', Gellhorn wore 'a Schiaparelli suit in nubby brown tweed fastened up to its Chinese collar with large brown leather clips, and Schiap's version of an Anzac hat in brown crochet work adorned by a spike of cock pheasant feathers', her face 'painted [. . .] like Parisian ladies, lots of eyeshadow, mascara and lipstick'.[91] According to Richard Collier, she 'walked with a movie star's sway'.[92] 'She was Lauren Bacall,' said Bill Buford, 'but smarter and sexier'.[93] A *Collier's* editorial remarked:

> She stands out among gal correspondents not only for her writing but for her good looks. Blond, tall, dashing, and with a manner – she comes pretty close to living up to Hollywood's idea of what a big-league woman reporter should be.[94]

Finally, in a 2003 work, *Seductress: Women Who Ravished the World and Their Lost Art of Love*, Betsy Prioleau lists Gellhorn (alongside Ninon de Lenclos, Lou Andreas-Salomé and Madame de Staël) as a 'Scholar-Siren'. Gellhorn, according to Prioleau, had 'burn-your-boats bravado', 'a killer siren who wowed men [and] notched up the choice honeys on her garter belt'.[95] Her nine-year romance with Hemingway 'was one long erotic arm wrestle' but she 'suffered no shit'.[96]

Yet, impressive as this seems, it was not the whole story. Photographs of Gellhorn in the Second World War frequently show her in the company of soldiers: there is Martha in Finland in December 1939, Martha on a base in the UK in 1943, Martha with the Carpathian Lancers (Figure 10). In each case, Gellhorn is the only woman in the group – yet what is striking is how assimilated she seems. Where the UK pilots wear boiler suits, Gellhorn is in casual shirt and slacks. In Finland she wears a long coat like the others. With the Carpathian Lancers, she is actually sitting in their jeep, holding a rifle. This, then, is a glamorous woman who is also very much 'one of the boys'. Significantly, Graham Greene, reviewing *The Trouble I've Seen*, called Gellhorn's writing 'amazingly unfeminine'.[97] Gellhorn herself, questioning why she tended to write about men, told Eleanor Roosevelt:

> Perhaps it's because I've never lived in a proper woman's world, nor had a proper woman's life, and so – feeling myself personally to be floating uncertainly somewhere between the sexes – I opt for what seems to me the more interesting of the two. [. . .] Or is that right? Women are just as interesting as men, often more so: but their lives seem to me either too hard, with an unendurable daily drab hardness, or too soft and whipped cream.[98]

Figure 10 Gellhorn with the Carpathian Lancers, June 1944

In the same letter, she recorded her pleasure that Max Perkins had said of *The Wine of Astonishment*, 'I wouldn't have thought a woman had written it'.[99] Elsewhere, she explained, 'I wrote a war novel, only men really; and as if I were a man, being a man all the time in my mind'.[100] It is not that the glamour-factor and the 'one-of-the-boys'-factor are anti-feminist. Rather, they signify the anxiegenic complex of tensions surrounding female presence at war. It is this which is now discussed in relation to two key works of Gellhorn's fiction.

Fiction and lethal interference

Gellhorn wrote 'A Sense of Direction' at the end of the Spanish Civil War[101] and it was published in *The Heart of Another*. The story concerns an unnamed woman war reporter who is invited to go out to the Loyalist front and have dinner with Giorgio, an Italian commandante in the International Brigades who has obviously 'been saying successful things to women all his life'.[102] The reporter agrees to go 'because there had been nothing to write about for weeks since no one was interested in another shelling of Madrid':[103] her instincts, therefore, are purely professional. That the Commandante's instincts are not purely professional is hinted at when the woman's chauffeur and soldier chaperone leave him with her and go off laughing.[104] After visiting the trenches, the Commandante takes the reporter for a nocturnal ramble: known for his poor sense of direction, he refuses to be accompanied. The woman thinks, 'three is a nice number at a war where there is an outstanding scarcity of women.'[105] There is a tense atmosphere, ostensibly created by the fact that the pair might wander into enemy territory at any time but less overtly based on the threat of sexual predation on the part of the Commandante. He is taking the woman where she does not want to go: 'how bored or how lonely is he, how serious can this get? [. . .] Where are we anyhow?'[106]

Yet 'A Sense of Direction' is more nuanced than a simple account of male predation. It is notable that the presence of the woman reporter is inescapably one of *difference*: she is too tall for the trenches, the soldiers regard her as talismanic.[107] When the Commandante lies down next to her, she asks him, ' "haven't you a wife?" ',[108] but quickly reflects: 'I thought rapidly all the old sentimental things: he might be killed tomorrow, that kind of thing. Only here, wherever we were, it was not so sentimental. He might be killed tomorrow at that.'[109] As the object of the Commandante's contemplation, the woman journalist has ceased to be the observing or reporting subject in relation to war. In Sartre's terms 'looked at', she now feels 'ashamed'.[110] (Sartre writes: 'shame [. . .] is shame of *self*; it is the *recognition* of the fact that I am indeed that object which the Other is looking at and judging'.)[111] What 'A Sense of Direction' evokes, therefore, is precisely a lack of a sense of direction: the path a woman committed to the cause should take in such transformed circumstances.

'Portrait of a Lady', written in the spring of 1940 at the same time as 'Goodwill to Men' and published in *The Heart of Another*,[112] takes the issue even further, investigating the possibility that female presence does not just 'interrupt' the course of conflict but actually, through the sexual consequences, causes harm. Iris Carpenter commented:

Always they [the Army's Public Relations' Division] came back to the conclusion that, no matter how good or necessary the [women's] reportage, it would still never make up for the embarrassment of having women in the front lines. They might get hurt. And nobody wanted that in his command. Apart from getting hurt, there was still what the British War Office persisted with nice reticence in referring to as 'the cloakroom question' and the Americans bluntly described as 'the latrine business'.[113]

Carpenter relates that Dixie Tighe of the International News Service asked for 'a little girl's room and a sentry'. Then, with a 'dazzling smile' at the Colonel, she said, ' "Guess you'd do" '. Another anecdote mentions a woman correspondent leaping out of a car in the desert 'to give a soldier, fundamentally occupied with unaffectedness common to men secure in the belief that they are habitating [*sic*] a purely masculine world, a bigger shock than he ever got from the enemy'.[114] This, then, is distraction, potentially even hindrance. In 'Portrait of a Lady', it becomes lethal.

The story features another American woman war reporter, Ann Maynard, sent, like Gellhorn and Cowles, to report on the Russo-Finnish War. Her initial engagement in the conflict is professional, the seeking of facts or (the word is important, given its sexual connotations) *knowledge*. Early in the story, Mrs Maynard is waiting in the forest with the Finnish soldiers, anticipating an attack: 'I am here, she thought. I am here where no one has been. I know them, I have seen it and heard it and I am the only one.'[115] The 'knowledge' in which she here exults is the scoop of the investigative journalist. Yet meeting Lahti, an ace Finnish pilot,[116] stirs other feelings in Mrs Maynard. He, she continually senses, regards her as a non-participant, an outsider: 'as a woman and a foreigner besides, she would have no right to speak of the war.'[117] This sense, and her growing attraction to Lahti, affect Mrs Maynard's perception of journalistic usefulness and hence her own participatory potential. Telling him defensively, 'it makes good propaganda, you know, the writing, and that helps your country', she broods to herself, 'I've [. . .] helped them [. . .] I put the blame squarely on the Russians [. . .] my God, they couldn't buy such propaganda.'[118] Even so, fearing that this is inadequate, she resolves to be of service 'not just with the writing' but in going to London, Paris and Washington, to 'speak to the right people' in order to get the Finns more planes. But that, too, seems insufficient, so she will 'stand for six hours on the roofs [. . .] to watch for planes and sound the air-raid signals'.[119]

Question-marks, therefore, hover over Mrs Maynard's presence and usefulness. 'It is not safe for a woman,' one of the Finns remarks; another tells her, 'it is ridiculous for you to be here at all'.[120] Lahti thinks 'furiously': 'she came, almost naked [. . .] to disturb them, to make their work harder'.[121] Mrs Maynard constantly complains of the cold[122] yet wears a silk shirt for dinner, she takes scarce servants away from their duties to build a fire for her, she always wants to sleep and fails to realise that, if she does not hurry out of the way of the bombs, she is endangering others' lives too.[123] Above all, she is glamorous: 'She was used to looking beautiful and she liked it and needed it: and she hated looking this way [red with cold] [. . .] even if only that fool of a Benno and that

nice ox Carl were there to see her.'[124] Dressing for dinner with the officers, she ponders, 'would it be better to leave off the mascara and go
down with my eyes looking shiny and crinkled up?'; looking at her
clothes, she thinks almost comically, 'how can I combine?', eventually
deciding on a silk shirt with her ski-pants, 'feminine to the waist' (a significant androgyny reminiscent of Iris Carpenter's tin hat and curls and
Lee Carson's 'lovely legs' in combat pants).[125] Her perception of the
Russo-Finnish conflict is: 'I'll never get over this trip; my skin is practi-
cally ruined.'[126] This focus on the individual body part – the eyes, the
legs, the skin – is reminiscent of the cinematic close-up which, in Laura
Mulvey's words, 'destroys the Renaissance space [of a film], the illusion
of depth demanded by the narrative; [. . .] gives flatness, the quality of a
cut-out or icon'.[127] In a similar way, Mrs Maynard no longer, as reporter,
produces the psychophysiological space of war, but rather appears
pasted on to a two-dimensional plane.

Mrs Maynard's is the seductive, predatory face of glamour. It is not
lost on Lahti, who hates her 'for the way she entered a room, demanding everyone's attention, forcing herself and her body on them all'. The
crucial point is the deleterious effect it will have on the men: her being
there 'will make it harder for his pilots, to make them want what they
can't have'.[128] The men sitting in the same mess watch, listen to and smell
her. At the front, they 'sit up straight and stare'.[129] Here glamour confers
egregiousness, the quality of standing out, which in turn disrupts and dis-
tracts from the smooth operation of war. This is tmesis. A literal break
in the action, it casts doubt on ability of women reporters to act, and to
act to good effect. In Lahti's view, Mrs Maynard is 'a spoiled mean lap-
dog' – 'this war is not run for visiting women'[130] – and the reader is
inclined to agree. When he finally kisses her, she is 'sick-ashamed that he
should have seen what she wanted and given it to her so casually':[131]
another instance of Satrean shame.

Intercourse with Lahti represents Mrs Maynard's fullest 'engagement'
in the Russo-Finnish conflict, an engagement from which she withdraws
the following morning on receiving news of his air-crash. Far from fur-
thering his cause, she has actually helped to kill him by depriving him of
the sleep he needed before the morning's mission; moreover, she has set
back the Finns' cause by removing their leading pilot. Seductive, glamorous female sexuality has indeed proved fatal. The participation she
sought has finally, ironically, assailed her: 'You write about it. It is terrible. But it is not someone of yours [. . .] [but] it could happen to you.
The torn-up rags on the street could be you too, now. The torn-up rags
could have a name.'[132] In her shock, she disengages, 'do not be a part of
it, do not belong in it, do not understand it'.[133]

What, then, is the significance of these spoiled women at war, who interfere with, impede, even endanger armies, and who, as they do so, call
attention to 'feminine' qualities such as flightiness, vanity and precious-
ness? Why do such figures feature so predominantly in Gellhorn's fiction?
Was she, in essence, criticising herself? On this point, a comment in a
letter to Charles Colebaugh is illuminating:

> You thought I was joking about how those prima donna women corre-
> spondents have spoiled the racket for us obscure girls. I wasn't though.
> Everybody I've ever heard from makes the most glowing accounts of the
> nuisance value of the ladies, who – being so important – naturally attract
> much attention the whiles they are getting in all comers' hair.[134]

The implication is that Gellhorn did not include herself in the 'prima
donna' category. Describing herself as 'obscure' suggests some lack of
self-awareness, but her remarks must be judged in the context of an
extremely frustrating correspondence over the non-accreditation of
women correspondents to US task forces.[135] It is clear that Gellhorn on
occasion regarded her place and efficacy in the field with despair, but this
does not seem adequately to account for the vicious nature of her depictions of women correspondents. Can feminist theory explain the por-
trayals? A Kristevan point could be made: the woman writer as a rogue
element in the male space of war, the semiotic as opposed to the symbolic, the phenotext in the genotext.[136] Undoubtedly Gellhorn was
'unruly': disobedient and iconoclastic. Or the phenomenon could be cast
as post-feminist: an exploitation of a range of guises available to women
that embraces both *machismo* and a fondness for lipstick. Or perhaps it
is just plain peer competitiveness (the same emotion which made her
politely detached from the Russian women soldiers crossing the Elbe)[137]
or even anti-feminism.[138] In a letter of Spring 1943 to Nelson Algren,
Gellhorn suggested something of this in her claim that the story was 'an
exercise for myself: trying to write about a creature I despised'.[139]

These theories, though, smack of the artificial imposition of hindsight.
However they appear today, it is unlikely that Gellhorn was setting up
her characters either as feminist targets or as post-feminist role models.
The most plausible explanation for these unflattering depictions both
proceeds from and contributes to the very scarcity of such women. In
Women in Khaki: The American Enlisted Woman, the sociologist
Michael L. Rustad suggests that the reasons the United States Army has
accepted a few 'token' women include an anxiety to create the impression of being an equal opportunities employer. But 'tokenism' brings its
own problems: social isolation, loss of individuality, mistaken identity,
aloneness, and, in particular, pressure to adopt stereotyped roles.[140]

Rustad is specifically discussing women serving in the military, but his conclusions also illuminate the situation of the minority of war reporters who happen to be women. The stereotypical (indeed 'mythical') roles which the token woman soldier assumes, in Rustad's analysis, fall into two categories: the 'Hyper-Female' and the 'Super-Soldier'. Each of these comprises further sub-categories, all personae adopted in order to ease life within the dominant male culture. The 'Hyper-Female' includes 'Daddy's Little Girl', a persona apt to incite acts of paternalistic assistance from men soldiers anxious 'not to feel outdone';[141] the 'Sex-Pot', who exploits her sexuality in order to be accepted; and 'Mama', who functions as a comforting mother-figure for the men. The 'Super-Soldier' includes the woman who acts as 'One of the Guys' and 'the Lone Ranger of Women's Liberation'.[142] There is no reason why, in order to survive in the male zone of war, a woman might not shift between all these roles: if Daphne Rutherford is the classic 'Daddy's Little Girl', Jane Mason, Annabelle Jones and Ann Maynard are, at various junctures, both 'Hyper-Females' *and* 'Super-Soldiers'. Their flightiness and feistiness can therefore be seen as symptom of their basic status – women outnumbered in their profession – and, in turn, as its cause. In the negative elements of her women war journalists, Gellhorn is expressing the troubled tenure of the 'outstanding' few.

In Gellhorn's work, movement beyond 'mere' presence produces at best frustration and at worst disaster. If the range of alignments she proposes were plotted on a graph, the line that joined them would now begin to turn downwards, towards a self-protective withdrawal. 'The first thing to do is not to go on talking,' Gellhorn wrote of occupied France.[143] As George Steiner noted, the parabola ends in silence.[144]

Notes

1 See Phoca, Sophia, *Introducing Postfeminism* (Cambridge: Icon Books, 1999) 30.
2 Moorehead, Caroline, *Martha Gellhorn: A Life* (London: Chatto & Windus, 2003) 21–2. She refused, but was active in local suffrage associations.
3 Moorehead, *Martha Gellhorn*, 477.
4 Boycott, Rosie, 'We Drank and Smoked, I Was One of Her Chaps', *The Times* (20 September 2003) 10–11: 10.
5 See Butler, Judith, *Gender Trouble. Feminism and the Subversion of Identity* (New York and London: Routledge, 1990) 136.
6 Hermione Lee, noting that Gellhorn 'trekk[ed] alone across the Pyrenees while writing fashion articles for American magazines,' comments that

'that sort of bold contrast was typical of her life' (Lee, Hermione, 'One of the Chaps', *Guardian (Review)* (1 November 2003) 13).

7 Adie, Kate, *The Kindness of Strangers* (London: Headline, 2003) 263.

8 Quoted in Burke, Carole, ' "If You're Nervous in the Service": Training Songs of Female Soldiers in the '40s', *Visions of War. World War II Popular Literature and Culture*, ed. Holsinger, M. Paul and Schofield, Mary Ann (Bowling Green, Ohio: Bowling Green State University Popular Press, 1992) 127–37: 128.

9 Carpenter, Iris, *No Woman's World* (Boston: Houghton Mifflin, 1946) 48.

10 Carpenter, *No Woman's World*, 208.

11 Carpenter, *No Woman's World*, 175.

12 Or, as another popular song ran: 'We don't tote guns or bayonets, / Our powder comes in compact sets. / We're petticoat soldiers, / Wacky WAACs!' (quoted in Burke, 'If You're Nervous', 132). Kate Muir notes that 'soldier girls are sexual icons' (Muir, Kate, *Arms and the Woman* (London: Coronet, 1993) 217).

13 O'Donnol, Shirley Miles, *American Costume, 1915–1970. A Source Book for the Stage Costumer* (Bloomington: Indiana University Press, 1982) 129.

14 Campbell, D'Ann, *Women at War with America: Private Lives in a Patriotic Era* (Cambridge, Mass., and London: Harvard University Press, 1984) 123.

15 Quoted in Wood, Maggie, *'We Wore What We'd Got': Women's Clothes in World War II* (Exeter: Warwickshire Books, 1989) 63.

16 Campbell, *Women at War with America*, 124; O'Donnol, *American Costume*, 114.

17 Rockoff, Hugh, *Drastic Measures. A History of Wage and Price Controls in the United States* (Cambridge: Cambridge University Press, 1984) 85. This account of clothes rationing in America derives largely from Rockoff.

18 Rockoff, *Drastic Measures*, 117–18; Marcus, Stanley, *Minding the Store* (Boston: Little, Brown, 1974) 115.

19 Rockoff, *Drastic Measures* 118, Marcus; *Minding the Store*, 115.

20 Rockoff, *Drastic Measures*, 89, 115.

21 Rockoff, *Drastic Measures*, 127.

22 Rockoff, *Drastic Measures*, 127.

23 Rockoff, *Drastic Measures*, 135, 150.

24 O'Donnol, *American Costume*, 114.

25 Campbell, *Women at War with America*, 177.

26 Rockoff, *Drastic Measures*, 153.

27 Rockoff, *Drastic Measures*, 154.

28 Rockoff, *Drastic Measures*, 135.

29 Rockoff, *Drastic Measures*, 152.

30 O'Donnol, *American Costume*, 124.

31 O'Donnol, *American Costume*, 115, 123–4.

32 O'Donnol, *American Costume*, 114, 126.
33 Packard, Ruth Mary, 'Trousers Are So Practical', *Ladies Home Journal* (February 1942) 95, quoted in O'Donnol, *American Costume*, 127.
34 O'Donnol, *American Costume*, 125.
35 Alene Bra advertisement, *McCall's* (November 1946) 169, quoted in O'Donnol, *American Costume*, 125.
36 O'Donnol, *American Costume*, 124.
37 O'Donnol, *American Costume*, 124.
38 Campbell, *Women at War with America*, 104.
39 Gellhorn, 'Children Are Soldiers Too', *Collier's* (4 March 1944) 21, 27.
40 Carson, Ruth, 'Black Market', *Collier's* (4 March 1944) 18–19: 19.
41 Carson, 'Black Market', 19.
42 'According to Your Cloth', *Vogue* (London) (March 1944) 46–9: 46.
43 'One Dress into Ten', *Vogue* (New York) (1 April 1943) 71.
44 Löbel, Sali, *Glamour and How to Achieve It* (London: Hutchinson, 1938) 11–12.
45 Löbel, *Glamour and How to Achieve It*, 12.
46 Löbel, *Glamour and How to Achieve It*, 61, 98.
47 Cohen, Lizabeth, *A Consumer's Republic: The Politics of Mass Consumption in Postwar America* (New York: Vintage, 2003) 75.
48 Quoted in Cohen, *A Consumer's Republic*, 68.
49 Westmore, Ern and Bud, *Beauty, Glamour and Personality* (London: George Harrap, 1947) v.
50 The book also has a little double twinkle-star motif on each page.
51 Westmore, *Beauty, Glamour and Personality*, vi.
52 *OED* 1.
53 Westmore, *Beauty, Glamour and Personality*, 10.
54 Westmore, *Beauty, Glamour and Personality*, 18.
55 Carole Angier makes the acute point, in relation to Gellhorn's glamour, that 'Martha was a natural self-publicist, who always got herself noticed' (Angier, Carole, 'She Wore a Yellow Nightie', *Literary Review* (October 2003) 6).
56 Paglia, Camille, *Sex, Art, and American Culture. Essays* (London: Viking, 1992) 10–11.
57 Quoted in Zweig, Paul, *Walt Whitman: The Making of the Poet* (Harmondsworth and New York: Viking, 1985) 15, but otherwise unsourced.
58 Quoted in Zweig, *Walt Whitman* 20, but otherwise unsourced.
59 Whitman, Walt, *Prose Works 1892. Volume 1. Specimen Days*, ed. Stovall, Floyd (New York: New York University Press, 1963) 51–2. First published in *Memoranda During the War*. Whitman's health did, in fact, deteriorate in the infectious atmosphere of the hospitals and he also sustained a deep cut to the hand when handing instruments to a surgeon during an operation (Morris Jr, Roy, *The Better Angel: Walt Whitman in the Civil War* (Oxford: Oxford University Press, 2000) 119–20).

60 Whitman, Walt, *Leaves of Grass: Reader's Edition*, ed. Blodgett, Harold W. and Bradley, Sculley (London: London University Press, 1965) 644–5.

61 Ewing, Elizabeth, *Women in Uniform through the Centuries* (London and Sydney: Batsford, 1975) 11.

62 Nicolson, Nigel, 'A Woman at the Wars', *New Statesman* LVIII 1492 (17 October 1959) 517–18.

63 Caute, David, 'A World of Men', *Times Literary Supplement* (7 November 2003) 4–5: 4.

64 Hughes, Kathryn, 'A Woman at War with the World', *Mail on Sunday* (30 November 2003) 64. In this vein, Kate Adie compares women in war with the American 'female pioneer' (Adie, Kate, *Corsets to Camouflage: Women and War* (London: Hodder & Stoughton, in association with the Imperial War Museum, 2003) 94).

65 Campbell, *Women at War with America*, 123.

66 Higonnet, Margaret and Higonnet, Patrice L.-R., 'The Double Helix', *Behind the Lines: Gender and the Two World Wars*, ed. Higonnet, Margaret, Jenson, Michel Sonya and Weitz, Margaret Collins (New Haven and London: Yale University Press, 1987) 31–47: 37.

67 Linda Mizejewski notes, in relation to the Second World War, that 'wartime sociological shifts result in male sexual anxieties that [. . .] are experienced more acutely than class conflict or other kinds of differences during the war years' (Mizejewski, Linda, *Divine Decadence. Fascism, Female Spectacle, and the Makings of Sally Bowles* (Princeton: Princeton University Press, 1992) 34).

68 Gwynne-Vaughan, Helen, *Service with the Army* (London: Hutchinson, 1942) 49.

69 Cowles, Virginia, *Looking for Trouble* (London: Hamish Hamilton, 1942) 301.

70 Borden, Mary, *The Forbidden Zone* (London: William Heinemann, 1929) 60.

71 Scarry, Elaine, *On Beauty and Being Just* (London: Duckworths, 2002) 29.

72 *HoA* 205. Jean Gallagher notes the distinction between the woman war recorder as 'ground of perception' and as 'object of contemplation' (Gallagher, Jean, *The World Wars Through the Female Gaze* (Carbondale and Edwardsville: Southern Illinois University Press, 1998) 17).

73 Wharton, Edith, *A Backward Glance* (New York and London: D. Appleton, 1934) 351.

74 Scherman, David E. 'Foreword', *Lee Miller's War*, ed. Penrose, Antony (London: Condé Nast Books, 1992) 7–13: 7.

75 See Campbell, *Women at War with America*, 25.

76 'News Makers and News Breakers', *Vogue* (London) (March 1944) 42–3: 42.

77 Mulvey, Laura, 'Visual Pleasure and Narrative Cinema', *Visual and Other Pleasures* (Basingstoke: Macmillan, 1989) 14–26: 20, 19.

78 Mulvey, 'Visual Pleasure and Narrative Cinema', 21.

79 Mulvey, 'Visual Pleasure and Narrative Cinema', 19.

80 E.g. Kaplan, E. Ann, *Women and Film: Both Sides of the Camera* (New York: Methuen, 1983); Silverman, Kaja, 'Masochism and Subjectivity', *Framework* 12 (1980) 2–9; Stacey, Jackie, 'Desperately Seeking Audience', *The Sexual Subject: A 'Screen' Reader in Sexuality*, ed. Caughie, John, Kuhn, Annette and Merck, Mandy (London: Routledge, 1992) 244–57; see also Daniel Chandler, <http://www.aber.ac.uk/media/Documents/gaze/ gaze09.html>.

81 Sartre, Jean-Paul, *Being and Nothingness*, trans. Barnes, Hazel E., and with an introduction by Warnock, Mary (London: Routledge, 1969) 260.

82 Sartre, *Being and Nothingness*, 258.

83 'Being-for-Others': Sartre, *Being and Nothingness*, 252–302.

84 Carole Angier's review of Moorehead's biography is titled 'She Wore a Yellow Nightie' and features a photo captioned 'Glamorous Gellhorn'. 'Not only did Martha work hard at keeping herself glamorous,' writes Angier, 'everyone around her (it seems) had to be as well' (Angier, 'She Wore a Yellow Nightie', 6). Hemingway, on hearing that Clare Boothe Luce was going to Burma as well as Gellhorn, named the phenomenon 'the race of glamour girls to the war' (Gellhorn, letter to Averell Harriman, 'Saturday' ?1941, f. 3r).

85 'Martha Gellhorn Denies Plan to Wed Hemingway at Once', *St Louis Globe-Democrat* (6 November 1940) 13A.

86 Gellhorn, letter of 23 August 1940 to Charles Scribner: *SL* 97.

87 Martyn, Marguerite, 'St. Louis Girl Turns Author', *St Louis Post-Dispatch* (1934).

88 'Glamor Girl', *Time* (18 March 1940) 92.

89 'St. Louis' Young Woman Novelist', *St Louis Post-Dispatch* (3 October 1936) 2C.

90 Gellhorn, letter to Gladys Tilden, 15 December 1936, f. 1r.

91 *VfG* 69. This outfit apparently owed more to having to dress in *soldes* (bargain off-casts) than a predilection for designer labels. According to Vicki Woods, Elsa Schiaparelli, inventor of shocking-pink, is remembered as 'a snazzy name with faint celebrity echoes' (Woods, Vicki, 'Chic Value', *Sunday Telegraph Magazine* (19 October 2003) 28–31: 29). In another story, Gellhorn refers to 'the smart new war-models of Molyneux and Schiaparelli which made everyone look so trim and military' (*HoA* 171). It is worth noting that Charis Day, in *What Mad Pursuit*, refuses to buy a dress on the grounds that 'a striker's family could live for two months on the price of that rag' (*WMP* 79).

92 Collier, Richard, *The Warcos: The War Correspondents of World War Two* (London: Weidenfeld and Nicolson, 1989) 16.

93 Ferrari, Michelle, compiler, *Reporting America at War. An Oral History*, commentary by Tobin, James (New York: Hyperion, 2003) 35.

94 Porter, Amy, 'The Week's Work', *Collier's* (4 March 1944) 43. In the same piece, some two-handed remarks from Hemingway somewhat undermine the effect: 'She hates cold and it really hurts her. But she was the first

journalist, man or woman, to get to the front in the Finnish War and she wrote fine dispatches from there, with the cold never above twenty below zero. She gets to the place, gets the story, writes it and comes home. That last is the best part' (Porter, 'The Week's Work', 4 March 1944, 43).

95 Prioleau, Betsy, *Seductress: Women Who Ravished the World and Their Lost Art of Love* (New York: Viking, 2003) 141.

96 Prioleau, *Seductress* 141, 142.

97 Greene, Graham, 'Short Stories', *Spectator* (22 May 1937) 950.

98 Gellhorn, letter of 16 May 1948, f. 2r.

99 Gellhorn, letter of 16 May 1948, f. 2r.

100 *SL* 244.

101 Moorehead, *Martha Gellhorn*, 163.

102 *HoA* 121. Caroline Moorehead identifies 'Giorgio' as Randolfo Pacciardi, first commander of the Garibaldi Battalion in Spain, who tried to get Gellhorn to put her hand on the front of his trousers during a car trip (Moorehead, *Martha Gellhorn* 163). Jacqueline Orsagh suggests he is one General Modesto, who made three passes at Gellhorn in front of Hemingway (Orsagh, Jacqueline, 'A Critical Biography of Martha Gellhorn' (unpublished doctoral thesis, Michigan State University, 1977) 85).

103 *HoA* 122.

104 *HoA* 126.

105 *HoA* 126.

106 *HoA* 137.

107 *HoA* 129, 130.

108 *HoA* 138.

109 *HoA* 138–9.

110 *HoA* 138.

111 Sartre, *Being and Nothingness*, 261.

112 Moorehead, *Martha Gellhorn*, 201.

113 Carpenter, *No Woman's World*, 34. Gellhorn mentions the point in a letter to Hortense Flexner and Wyncie King of 17 May 1940 (*SL* 91).

114 Carpenter, *No Woman's World*, 35.

115 *HoA* 65.

116 Apparently based on an aviator Gellhorn herself met in Finland (see letter of 17 May 1940 to Hortense Flexner and Wyncie King: *SL* 91).

117 *HoA* 70.

118 *HoA* 61, 74.

119 *HoA* 74.

120 *HoA* 52, 65.

121 *HoA* 81.

122 Gellhorn herself wrote of Finland, 'snow is very pretty if you like it but I do not like it, and I feel one hundred years old and frozen into my marrow and dead with weariness and almost sick to get back' (Gellhorn, letter to Hortense Flexner, 20 December 1940, f. 1r).

123 *HoA* 78.

124 *HoA* 51.

125 *HoA* 78.

126 *HoA* 73–4.

127 Mulvey, 'Visual Pleasure and Narrative Cinema', 20.

128 *HoA* 81.

129 *HoA* 62.

130 *HoA* 72.

131 *HoA* 62.

132 *HoA* 104. 'It could be you' is also the refrain of 'Goodwill to Men' (see Chapter 5).

133 *HoA* 106.

134 Gellhorn, letter of 21 May 1942, f. 1r.

135 See Gellhorn's letters to Charles Colebaugh of 3 February 1942 (*SL* 123–4), 21 May 1942, 23 May 1942, 11 June 1942 and 28 June 1942 and his to her of 26 January 1942 and 19 June 1942.

136 Kristeva, Julia, 'The System and the Speaking Subject', *The Kristeva Reader*, ed. Moi, Toril (Oxford: Blackwell, 1986) 28.

137 Gellhorn, 'The Russians' Invisible Wall', *Collier's* (30 June 1945) 24, 54.

138 'There is esprit de corps, as the[y] say, even among women; and far be it from me to write about a sister employee,' Gellhorn somewhat disingenuously commented in a letter of 23 May 1942 to Charles Colebaugh (f. 1r).

139 *SL* 140.

140 Rustad, Michael L., *Women in Khaki: The American Enlisted Woman* (New York: Praeger, 1982) 57, 140.

141 Rustad, *Women in Khaki*, 159.

142 Rustad, *Women in Khaki*, 158–69.

143 Gellhorn, 'The Love Albert L. Guérard Spurns', *New Republic* (10 August 1942) 173–5: 175.

144 Steiner, George, *Language and Silence* (London: Faber, 1985) 69.

Conclusion

'My *NO* is this book,' Martha Gellhorn wrote in her 1959 Introduction to *The Face of War*.[1] She had reached a limit with regard to nuclear arms proliferation and would no longer stay silent: the collection was a 'stand'.[2] Gellhorn used another term for such a moment as the original title for her novel about another personal 'watershed',[3] Dachau. 'The point of no return' is, as she defined it, 'a specific time limit, stated in hours and minutes. When reached, the pilot must head the plane back or it would have insufficient fuel to stay airborne and land.'[4] The instant is therefore definitive in several respects. It plots the way of the narrative: continue or turn? It forms a milestone in psychological development: Jacob Levy cannot go back to being the young man he was before. It constitutes the *ich kann nicht anders* of personal morality: beyond this, is unacceptable.

Standpoints have been both subject and methodology of this book. The aim has been to illuminate an aspect of war recording that is always inherent in descriptions of it but rarely acknowledged. Stance (physical involvement, emotional engagement, political inclination) affects standing (knowledge and hence authenticity and authoritativeness) – as such, they are, and have always been, essential to the poesis of conflict, and as the political and economic crises of the twentieth century mounted, they became increasingly articulated in thought about representing them. That these standpoints are gendered is too important to overlook, but it is equally important to remember that there are other factors in play.

To 'stand' has the nautical meaning of 'to hold a specified course': to stand in relation to war is as much about mobile trajectories as it is about entrenched positions. How the reporter moves to, in, around and out of the battle-ground, physically and textually, is another key aspect of polemical aesthetics. Reporters have to stand their ground, and it is arguable whether they should stand out. Status, in conflict, affects how the recorder can represent war, and also how involvement in war is written about: not only a matter of poetics, then, but also of historiography. Women's role in battle has been polarised: either regarded as so ancillary as to be invisible, or so exceptional – what might be called the 'Joan-of-Arc-syndrome' – as to be inimitable.

There at every turn is the huge premium placed on presence as a guarantee for war representation. The right to write about war must be earned, it is widely felt, and is in direct proportion to the degree of proximity to the action. No other field of human existence seems to impose such an exacting requirement, not even death or childbirth, and the result is that purely imaginative depictions of war attract ethical, as well as aesthetic, scrutiny. There are implications for literary criticism as well, not least that the critic without combat experience must examine his or her own position with care. As an account of a particular war recorder, then, this book functions a case-study. As such, it offers a methodology transferable to any investigation, whether literary or historical, of the representation of war: the suggestion that awareness of positioning – the critic's or historian's of the recorder's and the critic's or historian's of his or her own – is an essential element of the project.

Gellhorn's own experiences took their toll. In a letter of 3 April 1940 to Charles Colebaugh, she reflected:

> As a writer, I am pretty much getting branded as a disaster-girl. This has certainly not been my fault, because nobody lurking around Europe these last years could have arrived at any very happy conclusions [. . .]. But if you see only disaster, and write only disaster, there is the danger of being regarded as one who is blind to everything else, or even an inventor of catastrophe [. . .]. And finally, from being an accurate reporter of actual tragedy (through there being too many tragedies) one can just slip into the class of a sob-sister, and before people read you, they know what you are going to say.[5]

Disillusionment set in fast. As the war progressed, Gellhorn spoke less of wanting to write 'happily about happy people'.[6] Dachau made the point irrefutable. Her profession, journalism, was 'a Federation of Cassandras':[7] doomed to prophesy and not be listened to.

Did Gellhorn, then, continue to 'stand'? Not at first. Declaring 'a separate private peace',[8] she sat out the Korean War in Mexico, '[giving] up reading newspapers as a matter of principle, [listening] to music instead of news bulletins'.[9] But, in the 1960s, she did report on the Six Day War and on Vietnam. Of the latter, she said, as ever alert to the 'voice' of war representation: 'all the war reports I could find sounded inhuman, like describing a deadly football game between a team of heroes and a team of devils and chalking up the score by "body counts" and "kill ratio".'[10] Despite her reluctance, she went to Vietnam 'because I had to learn for myself, since I could not learn from anyone else, what was happening to the voiceless Vietnamese people':[11] her six articles led the South Vietnamese government to refuse her a visa to return. In the 1980s, nearly 80 herself, she reported on Reagan's 'interventions' in El Salvador, Nicaragua and Panama, her voice retaining the characteristic outrage of her earliest days in Spain. She particularly admired stands such as those taken at Greenham Common and the demonstration protesting against the Kent State murders: this latter was a 'Beautiful Day of Dissent'.[12]

So, though it was easy to keep silent or withdraw completely in disillusionment, Gellhorn retained the belief that 'if you can do nothing else you must scream':

> If you can't change it you must at least record it, so that it cannot just be ignored or forgotten. It is some place on the record and it seemed to me personally that it was my job to get things on the record in the hopes that at some point or other, somebody couldn't absolutely lie about it.[13]

Gellhorn's course in and around war was dazzling: hitching rides, stowing away, travelling on dynamite-laden ships through mined waters, flying in ancient planes and deadly fighter jets, driving from battle-field to battle-field, mucking in, standing out. Her trajectory within her prose is equally versatile: impassive recorder, human presence, concerned witness, advocate and polemicist. Her itineraries might be called virtuosic were they not so indispensable. War is too huge and important an issue to 'get wrong', however much its very massiveness and complexity resist easy communication. How it is represented matters vitally to all of us. Gellhorn went where she did to get it right.

Notes

1 *FoW* 5.
2 Gellhorn, letter to Bernard Berenson, 17 August 1958, f. 1r.
3 Gellhorn, letter to Hortense Flexner, early 1970s, ff. 6r, 7r.
4 *PNR* 327.
5 F. 1r.
6 *SL* 88.
7 *FoW* 2.
8 *FoW 1998* 246.
9 *FoW 1998* 246.
10 *FoW 1998* 248.
11 *FoW 1998* 248.
12 *VfG* 301–9.

13 Freedom Forum European Centre, 'Freedom Forum Europe Pays Tribute to
    Martha Gellhorn' (London: Freedom Forum European Centre, 1996) 7. 'If
    there is nothing else to do one must scream' alludes to Nadezhda
    Mandelstam's *Hope Against Hope* (1970) (see Gellhorn, letter of 2 February
    ?1980 to Mary Blume: *SL* 440).

Bibliography

Contents

Primary sources – Martha Gellhorn

Unpublished letters from Martha Gellhorn

Letters are arranged in alphabetical order of recipient, and then in chronological order. Gellhorn did not date all her letters but as much information about dates as possible is given.

Berenson, Bernard (all held at the Bernard Berenson Archive, Villa I Tatti, Fiesole, Italy)
1 undated
10 March 195?

8 August 195?
13 May 1950
18 July 1950
25 April 1953
17 July 1953
10 August 1953
11 September 1953
27 December 1953
15 March 1954
30 March 1954
14 April 1954
14 December 1955
14 March 1956
23 March 1956
6 September 1956
4 October 1957
17 August 1958
8 January 1959
18 February 1959
17 August 1959
14 November ?1959
12 December ?1959

Capa, Cornell
12 November 1975 (collection of Caroline Moorehead)

Chenery, William L.
Undated [June 1941], (Crowell-Collier Publishing Company Records, Manuscripts and Archives Division, The New York Public Library: Astor, Lenox and Tilden Foundations: *ZZ-32493, box 349)

Colebaugh, Charles (all held in the Crowell-Collier Publishing Company Records: *ZZ-32493)
22 October 1938 (box 316)
'Sunday' (no month given), 1940 (box 316)
31 March 1940 (box 316)
28 September 1940 (box 316)
17 July 1941 (box 316)
3 February 1942 (box 349)
21 May 1942 (box 349)
23 May 1942 (box 349)
11 June 1942 (box 349)
28 June 1942 (box 349)

Flexner, Hortense (all but the last held in the Howard Gotlieb Archival Center, Boston University)
'Saturday' (no month or year given)
1940
20 December 1940
Early 1970s (Hortense Flexner Collection, Special Collections, The Ekstrom Library, University of Louisville, Kentucky)

Gellhorn, Edna
'V-Mail', 14 June 1944 (collection of Caroline Moorehead)

Gellhorn, Sandy
13 November 1969 (Howard Gotlieb Archival Center)

Grover, Allen
14 July 1943 (collection of Caroline Moorehead)
12 March 1945 (collection of Caroline Moorehead)

Harriman, Averell
'Saturday', ?1941 (Library of Congress)

Lindley, Denver (all held in the Crowell-Collier Publishing Company Records: *ZZ-32493)
7 July 1938 (box 316)
Telegraph, 25 August 1938 (box 316)
3 February 1939 (box 316)

Meyer, Wallace
1948 (Rare Books and Special Collections, Princeton University)

Paoloczi-Horvath, George
30 October 1969 (Howard Gotlieb Archival Centre)

Roosevelt, Eleanor
2 December 1936 (collection of Caroline Moorehead)
16 January 1937 (Folder: Fr-Gi; Papers of Eleanor Roosevelt; Franklin D. Roosevelt Library, Hyde Park, New York)
24/25 April 1938 (Howard Gotlieb Archival Center)
19 October 1938 (Folder: Fr-Gi; Papers of Eleanor Roosevelt; Franklin D. Roosevelt Library)
December 1938 (Howard Gotlieb Archival Center)
3 December 1938 (Howard Gotlieb Archival Center)
1/2 November 1941 (collection of Caroline Moorehead)
16 May 1948 (Folder: Fr-Gi; Papers of Eleanor Roosevelt; Franklin D. Roosevelt Library)

Scribner, Charles
31 December 1946 (Rare Books and Special Collections, Princeton University)

Tilden, Gladys
15 December 1936 (BANC MSS 89/229 box 5:11 Gladys Tilden Papers, The Bancroft Library, University of California, Berkeley)

Unpublished writings and drafts
'Diary' (typewritten ms., unfoliated), kept in Spain 1937 (collection of Caroline Moorehead)
'Night Life in the Sky' (draft cable), 8.30 pm 24 January 1945 (Crowell-Collier Publishing Company Records: *ZZ-32493, box 610)
'Notes for TV Interview in Defence of Robert Capa' (typewritten ms.), 1975 (Howard Gotlieb Archival Center)
'Saturday at Creve Coeur' (typewritten ms.), undated (collection of Caroline Moorehead)

Contract
22 March 1938, between Martha Gellhorn and *Collier's Weekly* (Crowell-Collier Publishing Company Records: *ZZ-32493, box 316)

Book-length works
What Mad Pursuit (New York: Frederick A. Stokes, 1934)
A Stricken Field (New York: Duell, Sloan and Pearce, 1940)
The Heart of Another (London: Home & Van Thal, 1946)
The Wine of Astonishment (New York: Scribner, 1948)
The Honeyed Peace (London: Andre Deutsch, 1954)
The Face of War (New York: Simon and Schuster, 1959)
His Own Man (New York: Macfadden, 1962)
The Lowest Trees Have Tops (New York: Dodd, Mead, 1969)
Travels with Myself and Another (London: Allen Lane, 1979)
A Stricken Field (London: Virago, 1986)
Liana (Harmondsworth and London: Penguin / Virago, 1987)
The View from the Ground (New York: The Atlantic Monthly Press, 1988)
The Novellas of Martha Gellhorn (New York: Alfred A. Knopf, 1993)
Point of No Return (Lincoln, Nebraska: Bison Books, 1995)
With Virginia Cowles, *Love Goes to Press* (Lincoln, Nebraska, and London: University of Nebraska, 1995)
The Face of War (Cambridge: Granta, 1998)
The Letters of Martha Gellhorn, selected and ed. Moorehead, Caroline (London: Chatto & Windus, 2006)

Articles
'Rudy Vallée: God's Gift to Us Girls', *New Republic* LIX 766 (7 August 1929), pp. 310–11
'Toronto Express', *New Republic* LXII 804 (30 April 1930), pp. 297–8
'The Federal Theatre', *Spectator* (10 July 1936), pp. 51–2
'Justice at Night', *Spectator* (21 August 1936), pp. 304–5

'Writers Fighting in Spain', *The Writer in a Changing World*, ed. Hart, Henry (London: Lawrence and Wishart, 1937), pp. 63–8

'Returning Prosperity', *Survey Graphic* (26 February 1937)

'Only the Shells Whine', *Collier's* (17 July 1937), pp. 12–13, 64–5

'Madrid to Morata', *New Yorker* (24 July 1937), pp. 31, 34–5, 38–9

'Visit to the Wounded', *Story Magazine* (October 1937), pp. 58–61

'Men without Medals', *Collier's* (15 January 1938), pp. 9–10, 49

'City at War', *Collier's* (2 April 1938), pp. 18–19, 59–60

'Come Ahead, Adolf!', *Collier's* (6 August 1938), pp. 12–13, 43–5

'The Lord Will Provide for England', *Collier's* (17 September 1938), pp. 15–17, 35–8

'Guns against France', *Collier's* (8 October 1938), pp. 14–15, 34, 36–7

'Obituary of a Democracy', *Collier's* (10 December 1938), pp. 12–13, 28, 32–3, 36

'Slow Boat to War', *Collier's* (6 January 1940), pp. 10–12, 45

'Blood on the Snow', *Collier's* (20 January 1940), pp. 9–11

'Bombs from a Low Sky', *Collier's* (27 January 1940), pp. 12–13, 41

'Fear Comes to Sweden', *Collier's* (3 February 1940), pp. 20–2

'Death in the Present Tense', *Collier's* (10 February 1940), pp. 14–15, 46

'Flight into Peril', *Collier's* (31 May 1941), pp. 21, 85–7

'Time Bomb in Hong Kong', *Collier's* (7 June 1941), pp. 13, 31–3

'These, Our Mountains', *Collier's* (28 June 1941), pp. 16–17, 38, 40–1, 44

'Fire Guards the Indies', *Collier's* (2 August 1941), pp. 20–1, 50–1

'Singapore Scenario', *Collier's* (9 August 1941), pp. 20–1, 43–4

Advertisement for Hans Habe's *A Thousand Shall Fall*, *New York Times* (27 August 1941), p. 17

'Her Day', *Collier's* (30 August 1941), pp. 16, 53

'The Love Albert L. Guérard Spurns', *New Republic* (10 August 1942), pp. 173–5

'A Little Worse Than Peace', *Collier's* (14 November 1942), pp. 18–19, 84–6

'Holland's Last Stand', *Collier's* (26 December 1942), pp. 25, 28–9

'Children Are Soldiers Too', *Collier's* (4 March 1944), pp. 21, 27

'Three Poles', *Collier's* (18 March 1944), pp. 16–17

'Hatchet Day for the Dutch', *Collier's* (25 March 1944), pp. 27, 59

'English Sunday', *Collier's* (1 April 1944), pp. 60–2

'Visit Italy', *Collier's* (6 May 1944), pp. 62, 64–5

'Men Made Over', *Collier's* (20 May 1944), pp. 32, 34–5

'The Bomber Boys', *Collier's* (17 June 1944), pp. 58, 60

'Postcards from Italy', *Collier's* (1 July 1944), pp. 41, 56

'Over and Back', *Collier's* (22 July 1944), p. 16

'Hangdog Herrenvolk', *Collier's* (29 July 1944), pp. 24, 40

'The Wounded Come Home', *Collier's* (5 August 1944), pp. 14–15, 73–5

'Treasure City', *Collier's* (30 September 1944), pp. 22, 30, 32

'Cracking the Gothic Line', *Collier's* (28 October 1944), pp. 24, 57–8

'The Wounds of Paris', *Collier's* (4 November 1944), pp. 72–3

'Rough and Tumble', *Collier's* (2 December 1944), pp. 12, 70
'Death of a Dutch Town', *Collier's* (23 December 1944), pp. 21, 58–9
'The Undefeated', *Collier's* (3 March 1945), pp. 42, 44
'Night Life in the Sky', *Collier's* (17 March 1945), pp. 18–19, 31
'We Were Never Nazis', *Collier's* (26 May 1945), pp. 13, 36
'Dachau: Experimental Murder', *Collier's* (23 June 1945), pp. 16, 28, 30
'The Russians' Invisible Wall', *Collier's* (30 June 1945), pp. 24, 54
'You're on Your Way Home', *Collier's* (22 September 1945), pp. 22, 39
'The Paths of Glory', *Collier's* (9 November 1946), pp. 21, 74–6
'They Talked of Peace', *Collier's* (14 December 1946), pp. 19, 83–5
'An Odd, Restless, Beautiful Country', *New Republic* (4 August 1947), pp. 26–8
'Guerre De Plume. Martha Gellhorn. On Apocryphism', *Paris Review* 79 (1981), pp. 280–301
'Introduction', *Eleanor Roosevelt's 'My Day'. Her Acclaimed Columns 1936–1945* (New York: Pharos Books, 1989), pp. ix–xiii
'The Greatest Naval Jam in History', *Daily Telegraph* (3 June 1994), p. D4

Short story
'The Smell of Lilies', *Atlantic Monthly* (August 1956), pp. 41–54

Primary sources – others

Unpublished letters
Chenery, William L., to Martha Gellhorn, 18 June 1941 (Crowell-Collier Publishing Company Records: *ZZ-32493, box 349)
Colebaugh, Charles, to Martha Gellhorn, 12 April 1940 (Crowell-Collier Publishing Company Records: *ZZ-32493, box 316)
——, to Martha Gellhorn, 5 September 1941 (Crowell-Collier Publishing Company Records: *ZZ-32493, box 349)
——, to Martha Gellhorn, 26 January 1942 (Crowell-Collier Publishing Company Records: *ZZ-32493, box 349)
——, to Martha Gellhorn, 19 June 1942 (Crowell-Collier Publishing Company Records: *ZZ-32493, box 349)
Gellhorn, George, to Martha Gellhorn, Summer 1935 (collection of Caroline Moorehead)
Hemingway, Ernest, to William L. Chenery, 18 June 1941 [dated 1942] (Crowell-Collier Publishing Company Records: *ZZ-32493, box 349)
——, to Edna Gellhorn, 18 February 1945 (Bodley MS. Eng. c. 6174 (formerly MS. Res. c. 597), Bodleian Library, University of Oxford)
——, to Bernard Berenson, 14 October 1952 (Bernard Berenson Archive)
——, to Bernard Berenson, 27 May 1953 (Bernard Berenson Archive)
——, to Bernard Berenson, 9 July 1955, containing a cutting of Gellhorn's article, 'The Smell of Lilies', *The Atlantic* (August 1956) pp. 41–54, annotated by Hemingway (Bernard Berenson Archive)

Lindley, Denver, to Martha Gellhorn, 20 January 1938 (Crowell-Collier Publishing Company Records: *ZZ-32493, box 316)
——, 27 January 1938 (Crowell-Collier Publishing Company Records: *ZZ-32493, box 316)
Lindley, Denver, to Martha Gellhorn, 6 or 8 February 1939 (Crowell-Collier Publishing Company Records: *ZZ-32493, box 316)
Roosevelt, Eleanor, to Martha Gellhorn, 16 January 1937 (Folder: Fr-Gi; Papers of Eleanor Roosevelt; Franklin D. Roosevelt Library, Hyde Park, New York)

Books and articles
Anonymous items are given first (in chronological order).

'Real War Pictures and the Other Kind', *Collier's* (26 January 1918), pp. 12–13
'*French Ways and Their Meaning*' (review), *New Republic* 20 (25 September 1919), p. 241
'The New Novels – American Tragedies', *Times Literary Supplement* (6 June 1936), p. 477
'Girl Investigator Writes of Experiences in FERA', *New York World Telegram* (19 September 1936)
Authors Take Sides on the Spanish War (London: The Left Review, 1937)
'Next Week', *Collier's* (10 July 1937), p. 4
'Death in Spain: The Civil War Has Taken 500,000 Lives in One Year', *LIFE* 3 No. 2 (12 July 1937), p. 19
'Women Lecturers Found Unpopular', *New York Times* (28 November 1937), pp. 1–2
Peace for Our Time? An Up-to-Date Summary of the Gravest Crisis of Modern Times. Speeches of the Leaders (Manchester and London: The Policy-Holder Journal Co., 1938)
'Martha Gellhorn Sees Spain as Breeding Place for World War', *St Louis Daily Globe-Democrat* (28 January 1938), p. 2C
'Introduction', *FACT* 16 (15 July 1938), pp. 4–5
'Next Week', *Collier's* (30 July 1938), p. 4
'Next Week', *Collier's* (10 September 1938), p. 4
'Next Week', *Collier's* (1 October 1938), p. 4
'Next Week', *Collier's* (3 December 1938), p. 4
'Next Week', *Collier's* (13 January 1940), p. 4
'Next Week', *Collier's* (27 January 1940), p. 4
'Next Week', *Collier's* (3 February 1940), p. 4
'Glamor Girl', *Time* (18 March 1940), p. 92
'Martha Gellhorn Denies Plan to Wed Hemingway at Once', *St Louis Globe-Democrat* (6 November 1940), p. 13A
'Hemingway Weds Magazine Writer', *New York Times* (22 November 1940), p. 25
'Hemingways On Way Here', *New York Times* (23 November 1940), p. 15
'The Hemingways in Sun Valley: The Novelist Takes a Wife', *LIFE* (6 January 1941), pp. 49–57
Du Pont No. 7 Car Polish advertisement, *Collier's* (23 June 1941), p. 38

Fortune Shoes for Men advertisement, *Collier's* (14 November 1942), p. 85

Long's Hats advertisement, *Collier's* (14 November 1942), p. 86

Johnnie Walker whisky advertisement, *Collier's* (26 December 1942), p. 29

'One Dress into Ten', *Vogue* (New York) (1 April 1943), p. 71

'According to Your Cloth', *Vogue* (London) (March 1944), pp. 46–9

'News Makers and News Breakers', *Vogue* (London) (March 1944), pp. 42–3

Jockey underwear advertisement, *Collier's* (1 April 1944), p. 62

Sani-Flush advertisement, *Collier's* (6 May 1944), p. 65

Jones' Haps advertisement, *Collier's* (6 May 1944), p. 65

Gem Razors and Blades advertisement, *Collier's* (20 May 1944), p. 34

Yello-Bole pipe tobacco advertisement, *Collier's* (20 May 1944), p. 86

'This Week', *Collier's* (22 July 1944), p. 4

Mojud hosiery advertisement, *Collier's* (18 November 1944), p. 70

Woolfoam advertisement, *Collier's* (18 November 1944), p. 70

Dromedary Gingerbread Mix advertisement, *Collier's* (18 November 1944), p. 73

Seaforth Grooming Aids for Men advertisement, *Collier's* (23 December 1944), p. 59

'This Week', *Collier's* (17 March 1945), p. 4

'Dachau Captured by Americans Who Kill Guards, Liberate 32,000', *New York Times* (1 May 1945), pp. 1, 5

'Camp Horror Films Are Exhibited Here', *New York Times* (2 May 1945), p. 3

'Abraham & Straus: Everlasting Lure of Black', *New York Times* (6 May 1945), p. 16

'B. Altman & Co. Summer Black', *New York Times* (6 May 1945), p. 9

'Editors Condemn Nazis' Brutality', *New York Times* (6 May 1945), p. 8

'Russel's: Your Coat in Black Persian', *New York Times* (6 May 1945), p. 6

'Story of Dachau', *New York Times* (6 May 1945), p. E2

'Wedding Rings of Buchenwald Victims', *New York Times* (11 May 1945), p. 6

'Nazi Horrors Told by Saltonstall', *New York Times* (14 May 1945), p. 3

Sol Hepatica laxative advertisement, *Collier's* (23 June 1945), p. 28

Uncle Ned's Home Repair Hints advertisement, *Collier's* (23 June 1945), p. 30

'This Week', *Collier's* (30 June 1945), p. 4

Alene Bra advertisement, *McCall's* (November 1946), p. 169

'Dame Edna of Saint Louis', *Greater St Louis Magazine* (November 1968), pp. 21–2

Adie, Kate, *The Kindness of Strangers* (London: Headline, 2003)

Adorno, Theodor, 'Commitment', *Aesthetics and Politics*, ed. Bloch, Ernest, Lukács, Georg, Brecht, Bertold, Benjamin, Walter and Adorno, Theodor (London: NLB, 1977), pp. 177–95

Agee, James and Evans, Walker, *Let Us Now Praise Famous Men* (Boston: Houghton Mifflin, 1960)

Alberti, Leon Battista, *On Painting* (*Della Pittura*, 1435–36), trans. and with an introduction by Spencer, John R. (New Haven and London: Yale UP, 1966)

Aristotle, 'The Art of Rhetoric', trans. Freese, John Henry (Loeb Classical Library) (London and Cambridge, Mass.: William Heinemann, 1957)

Arvin, Newton, 'The Democratic Tradition in American Letters', *The Writer in a Changing World*, ed. Hart, Henry (London: Lawrence and Wishart, 1937), pp. 34–43

Barea, Arturo, Review of Ernest Hemingway's *For Whom the Bell Tolls, Horizon* 3 (May 1941), pp. 350–61

Barthes, Roland, *Sade, Fourier, Loyola* (Paris: Éditions du Seuil, 1971)

——, *Image, Music, Text* (London: Fontana, 1977)

——, 'The Reality Effect', *French Literary Theory Today*, ed. Todorov, Tzvetan, trans. Carter, R. (New York: Cambridge UP, 1982), pp. 11–17

——, *Mythologies* (London: Vintage, 1993)

Bennett, Arnold, *Journalism for Women: A Practical Guide* (London and New York: John Lane, The Bodley Head, 1898)

Bierce, Ambrose, *A Sole Survivor: Bits of Autobiography*, ed. Joskin, S. T. and Schultz, David E. (Knoxville: University of Tennessee, 1998)

Borden, Mary, *The Forbidden Zone* (London: William Heinemann, 1929)

Boyd, William, *Any Human Heart* (London: Hamish Hamilton, 2002)

Browder, Earl, 'The Writer and Politics', *The Writer in a Changing World*, ed. Hart, Henry (London: Lawrence and Wishart, 1937), pp. 48–55

Burger, Knox, ed., *Collier's Best: A Selection of Short Stories from the Magazine* (New York: Harper & Brothers, 1951)

Calder-Marshall, Arthur *et al.*, 'Fiction', *FACT* 4 (1937), pp. 38–44

——, *et al.*, 'Why Not War Writers? A Manifesto', *Horizon* (October 1941), pp. 236, 238

Capa, Cornell, *The Concerned Photographer 2* (London: Thames & Hudson, 1972)

Capa, Robert, *Slightly Out of Focus* (New York: Henry Holt, 1947)

Carpenter, Iris, *No Woman's World* (Boston: Houghton Mifflin, 1946)

Carson, Ruth, 'Black Market', *Collier's* (4 March 1944), pp. 18–19

Cather, Willa, *One of Ours* (London: Virago, 1986)

Churchill, Awnsham and Churchill, John, eds, *A Collection of Voyages and Travels...* (London: 1704)

Churchill, Winston, 'Richard Harding Davis', *The Novels and Stories of Richard Harding Davis. Volume 9 – The Bar Sinister* (New York: Scribner's, 1916), pp. v–vi

——, *The Second World War. Volume 1 – The Gathering Storm* (London: The Reprint Society, 1950)

Clark, Olga, 'Martha Gellhorn's Book Translated for Paris Readers', *St Louis Globe-Democrat* (2 February 1939), p. 1C

Clausewitz, Carl von, *On War*, trans. Howard, Michael and Paret, Peter (Princeton, New Jersey: Princeton University Press, 1976)

Clayton, Charles C., 'Grim Novel of Refugees under the Nazi Whip', *St Louis Globe-Democrat* (16 March 1940)

Cohen, Lester, 'Bloody Ground', *Harlan Miners Speak*, ed. Dreiser, Theodore (New York: Scribner, 1970), pp. 17–19

Connolly, Cyril, 'Comment', *Horizon* (May 1940), pp. 309–14

——, 'Comment', *Horizon* (July 1940), pp. 532–5

Cowles, Virginia, *Looking for Trouble* (London: Hamish Hamilton, 1942)

Cowley, Malcolm, 'The Seven Years of Crisis', *The Writer in a Changing World*, ed. Hart, Henry (London: Lawrence and Wishart, 1937), pp. 44–7

Cowley, Malcolm, 'A Portrait of Mister Papa', *LIFE* (10 January 1949), pp. 86–90, 93–4, 96–8, 100–1

Crane, Stephen, *The University of Virginia Edition of the Works of Stephen Crane. Volume III. The Red Badge of Courage*, ed. Bowers, Fredson (Charlottesville: University of Virginia, 1975)

Crawford, Bruce, 'Harlan County and the Press', *Harlan Miners Speak*, ed. Dreiser, Theodore (New York: Scribner, 1970), pp. 75–80

Davis, Richard Harding, *A Year from a Correspondent's Note-Book* (London and New York: Harper, 1898)

——, *Notes of a War Correspondent* (New York: Scribner, 1911)

——, *With the Allies* (London: Duckworth, 1915)

——, *The Novels and Stories of Richard Harding Davis. Volume 2 – The Exiles and Other Stories* (New York: Scribner, 1916)

——, *With the French in France & Salonika* (London: Duckworth, 1916)

——, 'How Stephen Crane Took Juana Dis', *The War Dispatches of Stephen Crane*, ed. Stallman, R. W. and Hagemann, E. R. (London: Peter Owen, 1964), pp. 196–9

de Beauvoir, Simone, *La force de l'âge* (Paris: Gallimard, 1960)

de Certeau, Michel, *The Practice of Everyday Life* (Berkeley, Los Angeles and London: University of California, 1984)

Delmer, Sefton, *Trail Sinister: An Autobiography. Volume One* (London: Secker & Warburg, 1961)

——, *Black Boomerang: An Autobiography. Volume Two* (London: Secker & Warburg, 1962)

Dickens, Charles, *The Dent Uniform Edition of Dickens' Journalism. Sketches by Boz and Other Early Papers 1833–39*, ed. Slater, Michael (London: J. M. Dent, 1994)

Dos Passos, John, *U.S.A.* (Harmondsworth: Penguin, 1978)

Dreiser, Theodore, *The Carnegie Works at Pittsburgh* (Chelsea, New York: Private Printing, 1927)

——, 'Introduction', *Harlan Miners Speak*, ed. Dreiser, Theodore (New York: Da Capo Press, 1970), pp. 3–16

——, *et al.*, ed., *Harlan Miners Speak* (New York: Da Capo Press, 1970)

Dunne, Finley Peter, 'Richard Harding Davis', *The Novels and Stories of Richard Harding Davis. Volume 8 – The Scarlet Car* (New York: Scribner, 1916), pp. vii–xi

Eliot, George, *Essays of George Eliot*, ed. Pinney, Thomas (New York: Columbia UP, 1963)

Foucault, Michel, 'What Is an Author?', *Modern Criticism and Theory: A Reader*, ed. Lodge, David and Wood, Nigel (Essex and New York: Longman, 2000), pp. 174–87

Frank, Waldo, 'Foreword', *American Writers' Congress*, ed. Hart, Henry (London: Martin Lawrence, 1936), p. 5

Freeman, Joseph, 'Towards the Forties', *The Writer in a Changing World*, ed. Hart, Henry (London: Lawrence and Wishart, 1937), pp. 9–33

Gellhorn, George, *Non-Operative Treatment in Gynecology* (New York and London: D. Appleton, 1923)

Gervasi, Frank, 'The Jew as Soldier', *Collier's* (22 April 1944), pp. 11, 28, 30, 32

Gilder, Rosamond, 'Rainbow over Broadway', *Theater Arts,* 31 (March 1947), p. 18

Gordimer, Nadine, *Writing and Being* (Cambridge, Mass., and London: Harvard UP, 1995)

Graves, Robert, 'The Garlands Wither', *Times Literary Supplement* (26 June 1930), p. 534

Green, Henry, 'The Lull', *New Writing and Daylight* (Summer 1943), pp. 11–21

——, *Caught* (London: The Hogarth Press, 1943)

Greene, Graham, 'Short Stories', *Spectator* (22 May 1937), p. 950

Grenfell, Joyce, *The Time of My Life: Entertaining the Troops. Her Wartime Journals*, ed. Roose-Evans, James (London: Hodder and Stoughton, 1989)

Grierson, John, 'The First Principles of Documentary', *Grierson on Documentary*, ed. Hardy, Forsyth (London: Collins, 1946), pp. 78–89

Gruber, Ruth, *Inside of Time. My Journey from Alaska to Israel* (New York: Carroll & Graf, 2003)

Gwynne-Vaughan, Helen, *Service with the Army* (London: Hutchinson, 1942)

Habe, Hans, *A Thousand Shall Fall* (London: George Harrap, 1942)

Haraway, Donna, 'A Manifesto for Cyborgs: Science, Technology, and Socialist Feminism in the 1980s', *The Haraway Reader* (New York and London: Routledge, 2004), pp. 7–45

Hardy, Forsyth, ed., *Grierson on Documentary* (London: Collins, 1946)

Hart, Henry, 'Introduction', *American Writers' Congress*, ed. Hart, Henry (London: Martin Lawrence, 1936), pp. 9–17

——, ed., *The Writer in a Changing World* (London: Lawrence and Wishart, 1937)

Hemingway, Ernest, *In Our Time* (London: Jonathan Cape, 1926)

——, 'The War in Spain Makes a Movie with Captions by Ernest Hemingway', *LIFE* 3/2 (12 July 1937), pp. 20–25

——, 'The Writer and War', *The Writer in a Changing World*, ed. Hart, Henry (London: Lawrence and Wishart, 1937), pp. 69–73

——, 'The Saving of Madrid', *FACT* (July 1938), pp. 7–33

——, *For Whom the Bell Tolls* (New York: Scribner, 1941)

——, 'Voyage to Victory', *Collier's* (22 July 1944), pp. 11–13, 56–7

——, 'Battle for Paris', *Collier's* (30 September 1944), pp. 11, 83–4, 86

——, 'How We Came to Paris', *Collier's* (7 October 1944), pp. 14, 65, 67

——, 'The G.I. And the General', *Collier's* (4 November 1944), pp. 11, 46–7

——, 'War in the Siegfried Line', *Collier's* (18 November 1944), pp. 18, 70–1, 73

——, *The Fifth Column* (Harmondsworth: Penguin, 1966)

——, ed., *Men at War. An Anthology* (London: Fontana, 1966)

——, *Ernest Hemingway, Cub Reporter*, ed. Bruccoli, Matthew J. (Pittsburgh: University of Pittsburgh, 1970)

Hemingway, Ernest, *Selected Letters 1917–1961*, ed. Baker, Carlos (London: Granada, 1981)

——, *Dateline: Toronto. The Complete 'Toronto Star' Dispatches, 1920–1924*, ed. White, William (New York: Scribner, 1985)

——, *The First Forty-Nine Stories* (London: Arrow Books, 1993)

——, *The Sun Also Rises / Fiesta* (London: Arrow Books, 1994)

——, *Across the River and into the Trees* (New York: Scribner, 1996)

——, *The Only Thing That Counts. The Ernest Hemingway – Maxwell Perkins Correspondence*, ed. Bruccoli, Matthew J. (New York: Scribner, 1996)

——, *By-Line: Ernest Hemingway*, ed. White, William (New York: Simon & Schuster, 1998)

——, *A Farewell to Arms* (London: Vintage, 1999)

Hemingway, Gregory H., *Papa. A Personal Memoir* (Boston: Houghton Mifflin, 1976)

Hemingway, Leicester, *My Brother, Ernest Hemingway* (London: Weidenfeld and Nicolson, 1962)

Hemingway, Mary Welsh, *How It Was* (London: Weidenfeld and Nicolson, 1977)

Herbst, Josephine, *The Starched Blue Sky of Spain and Other Memoirs* (New York: Harper Collins, 1991)

Hicks, Granville, 'The American Writer Faces the Future', *The Writer in a Changing World*, ed. Hart, Henry (London: Lawrence and Wishart, 1937), pp. 180–94

Higginson, T. W., 'Unmanly Manhood', *Women's Journal* XII (4 February 1882), p. 33

Holmes, Eugene, 'A Writer's Social Obligations', *The Writer in a Changing World*, ed. Hart, Henry (London: Lawrence and Wishart, 1937), pp. 172–9

Homer, *The Odyssey*, trans. Rieu, E. V. (Harmondsworth: Penguin, 1946)

Howells, William Dean, *Literature and Life* (New York: Harper, 1902)

Isherwood, Christopher, *The Berlin Novels* (London: Vintage, 1999)

Israel, Boris, 'Representing the Press', *Harlan Miners Speak*, ed. Dreiser, Theodore (New York: Scribner, 1970), pp. 80–2

Ivens, Joris, *The Camera and I* (Berlin: Seven Seas Books, 1969)

James, Henry, *The Art of Fiction and Other Essays* (New York: Oxford University Press, 1948)

——, *The Bostonians* (London: The Bodley Head, 1967)

Jameson, Storm, 'Socialists Born and Made', *FACT* (May 1937), p. 87

——, 'Documents', *FACT* (July 1937), pp. 9–18

——, *Europe to Let. The Memoirs of an Obscure Man* (London: Macmillan, 1940)

——, 'Foreword', *The Diary of Anne Frank* (London: Pan Books, 1954), pp. 5–11

Jarrell, Randall, 'The Death of the Ball Turret Gunner', *The Oxford Book of War Poetry*, ed. Stallworthy, Jon (Oxford: Oxford University Press, 1984), p. 277

Josephson, Matthew, 'The Role of the Writer in the Soviet Union', *American Writers' Congress*, ed. Hart, Henry (London: Martin Lawrence, 1936), pp. 38–45

Kazin, Alfred, Review of Ernest Hemingway's *The Fifth Column and the First Forty-Nine Stories*, *New York Herald Tribune Books* (16 October 1938), p. 5

Kelly, Florence Finch, 'Eye Witnesses of the War: *Fighting France*', *Bookman*, 42 (December 1915), pp. 462–3

Kennan, George, *Memoirs 1925–1950* (London: Hutchinson, 1968)

Kirkpatrick, Helen Paull, *This Terrible Peace* (London: Rich & Cowan, 1939)

Kristeva, Julia, *Pouvoirs de l'horreur. Essais sur l'abjection* (Paris: Éditions du Seuil, 1980)

——, 'The System and the Speaking Subject', *The Kristeva Reader*, ed. Moi, Toril (Oxford: Blackwell, 1986)

Kurtz, Russell H., 'Relief and the American Temperament', *Survey Graphic* (May 1935)

Lacan, Jacques, *The Four Fundamental Concepts of Psycho-Analysis*, ed. Miller, Jacques-Alain, trans. Sheridan, Alan (New York and London: W. W. Norton, 1978)

Levy, Melvin P., 'Class War in Kentucky', *Harlan Miners Speak*, ed. Dreiser, Theodore (New York: Scribner, 1970), pp. 20–37

Löbel, Sali, *Glamour and How to Achieve It* (London: Hutchinson, 1938)

Loomis, Charles Battell, 'ST-PH-N CR-N-', *The War Dispatches of Stephen Crane*, ed. Stallman, R. W. and Hagemann, E. R. (London: Peter Owen, 1964), pp. 50–1

Lukács, Georg, 'Narrate or Describe?', *Writer and Critic and Other Essays*, ed. Kahn, Arthur (London: Merlin Press, 1970), pp. 110–48

——, 'Reportage or Portrayal?', *Essays on Realism*, ed. Livingstone, Rodney (London: Lawrence and Wishart, 1980), pp. 45–75

McCullin, Don, *Unreasonable Behaviour: An Autobiography* (London: Vintage, 1992)

McCutcheon, John, 'With Davis in Vera Cruz, Brussels, and Salonika', *The Novels and Stories of Richard Harding Davis. Volume 12 – The Lost Road* (New York: Scribner, 1916), pp. vii–xxii

MacDonald, Dwight, Review of Ernest Hemingway's *For Whom the Bell Tolls*, *Partisan Review*, 8 (January 1941), pp. 24–8

Marcus, Stanley, *Minding the Store* (Boston: Little, Brown, 1974)

Martyn, Marguerite, 'St. Louis Girl Turns Author', *St Louis Post-Dispatch* (1934)

——, 'St. Louis' Young Woman Novelist', *St Louis Post-Dispatch* (3 October 1936), p. 2C

Matthews, Caroline, *Experiences of a Woman Doctor in Serbia* (London: Mills and Boon, 1916)

Matthews, Herbert, *Eyewitness in Abyssinia. With Marshal Badoglio's Forces to Addis Ababa* (London: Martin Secker & Warburg, 1937)

Matthews, T. S., *O My America! Notes on a Trip* (New York: Simon & Schuster, 1962)

Moorehead, Alan, *Eclipse* (London: Granta, 2000)

Morris, Gouverner, 'R.H.D.', *The Novels and Stories of Richard Harding Davis. Volume 11 – The Red Cross Girl* (New York: Scribner, 1916), pp. vii–xx

Murrow, Edward R., *This Is London* (London: Cassell, 1941)

Mydans, Carl, *More Than Meets the Eye* (London: Hutchinson, 1961)

Nicolson, Nigel, 'A Woman at the Wars', *New Statesman* LVIII 1492 (17 October 1959), pp. 517–8

North, Joseph, 'Reportage', *American Writers' Congress*, ed. Hart, Henry (London: Martin Lawrence, 1936), pp. 120–3

Nourse, E. G., 'Hard Times for Farmers', *New Republic* LXII 804 (30 April 1930), pp. 288–91

Ogden, C. K. and Florence, Mary Sargant, 'Militarism Versus Feminism. An Enquiry and a Policy Demonstrating That Militarism Involves the Subjection of Women', *Militarism Versus Feminism: Writings on Women and War*, ed. Kamester, Margaret and Vellacott, Jo (London: Virago, 1987), pp. 53–154

Orwell, George, *Homage to Catalonia* (London: Penguin, 2000)

'Ourselves', 'Editorial', *FACT* (April 1937), pp. 6–8

Packard, Ruth Mary, 'Trousers Are So Practical', *Ladies Home Journal* (February 1942), p. 95

Palin, Michael, *Hemingway's Chair* (London, New York, Sydney, Toronto: BCA, 1995)

Palmer, Frederick, *With My Own Eyes. A Personal History of Battle Years* (London: Jarrolds, 1934)

Peirce, Charles S., From 'On the Algebra of Logic: A Contribution to the Philosophy of Notation', *The Essential Peirce. Selected Philosophical Writings. Volume 1 (1867–1893)*, ed. Hauser, Nathan and Kloesel, Christian (Bloomington and Indianapolis: Indiana University Press, 1992), pp. 226–8

Plato, *The Republic*, trans. Lee, Desmond (Harmondsworth: Penguin, 1985)

Porter, Amy, 'The Week's Work', *Collier's* (4 March 1944), p. 43

——, 'The Week's Work', *Collier's* (6 May 1944), p. 70

——, 'The Week's Work', *Collier's* (3 February 1945), p 73

Pound, Ezra, *Abc of Reading* (London: Routledge, 1934)

Pyle, Ernie, *Ernie's War* (New York and Toronto: Random House, 1986)

Rahv, Philip, 'The Cult of Experience in American Writing', *Partisan Review*, 6 (1940), pp. 412–424

Reed, John, *Ten Days That Shook the World* (London: Lawrence & Wishart, 1961)

Rees, Goronwy, 'Letter from a Soldier', *Horizon*, 1 (July 1940), pp. 467–71

Regler, Gustav, *The Owl of Minerva*, trans. Denny, Norman (London: Rupert Hart-Davis, 1959)

Roosevelt, Eleanor, *Eleanor Roosevelt's 'My Day'. Her Acclaimed Columns 1936–1945* (New York: Pharos Books, 1989)

Roosevelt, Theodore, *The Rough Riders* (London: Kegan, Paul, Trench, Trübner, 1899)

——, *America and the World War* (London: John Murray, 1915)

Roosevelt, Theodore, 'Davis and the Rough Riders', *The Novels and Stories of Richard Harding Davis. Volume 5 – Captain Macklin, His Memoirs* (New York: Scribner, 1916), pp. vii–viii

——, *Americanism and Preparedness. Speeches of Theodore Roosevelt July to November, 1916* (New York: The Mail and Express Job Print, 1917)

——, *The Strenuous Life. Volume 13 of the Works of Theodore Roosevelt* (New York: Scribner, 1926)

Ross, Lillian, 'How Do You Like It Now, Gentlemen?', *New Yorker* (13 May 1950), pp. 36–8, 40–6, 49–56

Ruhl, Arthur, *Antwerp to Gallipoli. A Year of War on Many Fronts – and Behind Them* (New York: Scribner, 1916)

Sartre, Jean-Paul, *Being and Nothingness*, trans. Barnes, Hazel E., and with an introduction by Warnock, Mary (London: Routledge, 1969)

——, *Words*, trans. Clephane, Irene (London: Penguin, 2000)

——, *What is Literature?*, trans. Frechtman, Bernard (London and New York: Routledge, 2001)

Schultz, Sigrid, 'Invasion Lines', *Collier's* (25 March 1944), pp. 11–12, 55, 57

Sebald, W. G., *On the Natural History of Destruction*, trans. Bell, Anthea (London: Hamish Hamilton, 2003)

Shakespeare, William, *Henry IV Part I, The Complete Works*, ed. Alexander, Peter, (London and Glasgow: Collins, 1951, 1992)

——, *Henry IV Part II, The Complete Works*, ed. Alexander, Peter, (London and Glasgow: Collins, 1951, 1992)

Shklovsky, Viktor, 'Art as Technique', *Modern Literary Theory. A Reader*, ed. Rice, Philip and Waugh, Patricia (London and New York: Hodder Headline, 1996), pp. 17–21

Simpson, John, *Strange Places, Questionable People* (London: Macmillan, 1998)

Sledge, E. B., *With the Old Breed at Peleliu and Okinawa* (New York and Oxford: Oxford University Press, 1990)

Smalley, George Washburn, *Anglo-American Memories* (London: Duckworth, 1911)

Spender, Stephen, '"Guernica." Picasso's "Guernica" at the New Burlington Gallery', *New Statesman* (15 October 1938), pp. 567–8

Stendhal, *The Charterhouse of Parma*, trans. Shaw, Margaret R. B. (Harmondsworth: Penguin, 1958)

Sulzberger, C. L., 'Oswiecim Killings Placed at 4,000,000', *New York Times* (8 May 1945), p. 12

Tarkington, Booth, 'Richard Harding Davis', *The Novels and Stories of Richard Harding Davis. Volume 1 – Van Bibber Etc* (New York: Scribner, 1916), pp. ix–xi

Thucydides, *The Peloponnesian War*, trans. Warner, Rex (Harmondsworth: Penguin, 1954)

Trilling, Lionel, Review of Ernest Hemingway's *The Fifth Column and the First Forty-Nine Stories*, *Partisan Review*, 6 (Winter 1939), pp. 52–60

Trilling, Lionel, Review of Ernest Hemingway's *For Whom the Bell Tolls*, *Partisan Review*, 8 (January 1941), pp. 63–7

Waugh, Evelyn, *Scoop. A Novel About Journalists* (London: Chapman and Hall, 1948)

Westmore, Ern and Bud, *Beauty, Glamour and Personality* (London: George Harrap, 1947)

Wharton, Edith, *Fighting France. From Dunkerque to Belfort* (London: Macmillan, 1915)

——, *A Backward Glance* (New York and London: D. Appleton, 1934)

White, William S., 'War Crimes Report Horrifies Capital', *New York Times* (16 May 1945), p. 10

Whitman, Walt, *Prose Works 1892. Volume 1. Specimen Days*, ed. Stovall, Floyd (New York: New York University Press, 1963)

——, *Leaves of Grass. Reader's Edition*, ed. Blodgett, Harold W. and Bradley, Sculley (London: London University Press, 1965)

Wilson, Edmund, Review of Ernest Hemingway's *The Fifth Column and the First Forty-Nine Stories*, *Nation* 147 (10 December 1938), pp. 628, 30

——, 'Ernest Hemingway: Gauge of Morale', *Atlantic*, 164 (July 1939), pp 36–46

Wolfe, Tom, *The New Journalism* (New York: Harper and Row, 1973)

Woolf, Virginia, 'Three Guineas', *A Room of One's Own / Three Guineas*, ed. Briggs, Julia (London: Penguin, 2000), pp. 115–366

Government publications

Official Report (Parliamentary Debates) (Hansard) 5th Series 1937–38. Vol. 333. March 14 to April 1. (London: HMSO, 1938)

Official Report (Parliamentary Debates) (Hansard) 5th Series 1940–41. Vol. 370. March 18 to April 10. (London: HMSO, 1941)

Secondary Sources

Books, articles and theses

Anonymous item is given first.

'Obituaries – Martha Gellhorn. War Reporter Who Stowed Away to Reach the D-Day Beaches and Married Hemingway', *Daily Telegraph* (17 February 1998), p. 23

Aaron, Daniel, *The Unwritten War: American Writers and the Civil War* (New York: Alfred A. Knopf, 1973)

——, *Writers on the Left* (Oxford and New York: Oxford University Press, 1977)

Adereth, M., *Commitment in Modern French Literature. A Brief Study of 'Littérature Engagée' in the Works of Péguy, Aragon and Sartre* (London: Victor Gollancz, 1967)

Adie, Kate, *Corsets to Camouflage. Women and War* (London: Hodder & Stoughton, in association with the Imperial War Museum, 2003)

Aichinger, Peter, *The American Soldier in Fiction 1880–1963. A History of Attitudes toward Warfare and the Military Establishment* (Ames, Iowa: Iowa State University Press, 1975)

Angier, Carole, 'She Wore a Yellow Nightie', *Literary Review* (October 2003), pp. 6–7

Aron, Raymond, *The Committed Observer. Interviews with Jean-Louis Missaka and Dominique Wolton* (Chicago: Regnery Gateway, 1983)

Austin, J. L., *How to Do Things with Words* (Oxford: The Clarendon Press, 1962)

Ayer, N. W., *Directory of Newspapers and Periodicals* (Philadelphia: N. W. Ayer and Sons, 1936)

Bachelard, Gaston, *The Poetics of Space* (Boston: The Beacon Press, 1969)

Baker, Carlos, *Ernest Hemingway. A Life Story* (Harmondsworth: Penguin, 1972)

Benson, Frederick R., *Writers in Arms. The Literary Impact of the Spanish Civil War* (London: University of London, 1968)

Berger, John, *Ways of Seeing* (London and Harmondsworth: BBC and Penguin, 1972)

Blanton, DeAnne and Cook, Lauren M., *They Fought Like Demons: Women Soldiers in the American Civil War* (Baton Rouge: Louisiana State University Press, 2002)

Boorstin, Daniel J., *The Image* (London: Weidenfeld and Nicolson, 1961)

Boycott, Rosie, 'We Drank and Smoked, I Was One of Her Chaps', *The Times* (20 September 2003), pp. 10–11

Bradley, Patricia, 'Richard Harding Davis', *A Sourcebook of American Literary Journalism*, ed. Connery, Thomas B. (New York and Westport, Conn.: Greenwood, 1992), pp. 55–67

Bryson, Norman, 'The Gaze in the Extended Field', *Vision and Visuality (Dia Art Foundation Discussions in Contemporary Culture 2)*, ed. Foster, Hal (Seattle: Bay Press, 1988), pp. 87–108

Burke, Carole, "If You're Nervous in the Service': Training Songs of Female Soldiers in the '40s', *Visions of War. World War II Popular Literature and Culture*, ed. Holsinger, M. Paul and Schofield, Mary Ann (Bowling Green, Ohio: Bowling Green State University Popular Press, 1992), pp. 127–37

Burkeman, Oliver, 'Simpson of Kabul', *Guardian (G2)* (14 November 2001), pp. 2–3

Butler, Judith, *Gender Trouble. Feminism and the Subversion of Identity* (New York and London: Routledge, 1990)

Campbell, D'Ann, *Women at War with America. Private Lives in a Patriotic Era* (Cambridge, Mass., and London: Harvard University Press, 1984)

Carey, James W., *Communication as Culture. Essays on Media and Society* (Winchester, Mass., and London: Unwin Hyman, 1989)
Carey, John, ed., *The Faber Book of Reportage* (London and Boston: Faber and Faber, 1987)
Caute, David, 'A World of Men', *Times Literary Supplement* (7 November 2003), pp. 4–5
Clark, Ian, *Waging War. A Philosophical Introduction* (Oxford: The Clarendon Press, 1988)
Clifford, James, 'Introduction: Partial Truths', *Writing Culture: The Poetics and Politics of Ethnography*, ed. Clifford, James and Marcus, George E. (Berkeley, Los Angeles and London: University of California, 1986), pp. 1–26
——, 'On Ethnographic Allegory', *Writing Culture: The Poetics and Politics of Ethnography*, ed. Clifford, James and Marcus, George E. (Berkeley, Los Angeles and London: University of California, 1986), pp. 98–121
Cohen, Lizabeth, *A Consumer's Republic. The Politics of Mass Consumption in Postwar America* (New York: Vintage, 2003)
Collier, Richard, *The Warcos. The War Correspondents of World War Two* (London: Weidenfeld and Nicolson, 1989)
Colvert, James B., 'Introduction', *The University of Virginia Edition of the Works of Stephen Crane. Volume IX. Reports of War. War Dispatches. Great Battles of the World*, ed. Bowers, Fredson (Charlottesville: University Press of Virginia, 1971), pp. xix–xxix
Cooper, Helen, *Pastoral. Mediaeval into Renaissance* (Ipswich: D. S. Brewer, 1977)
Cooper, Helen, Munich, Adrienne and Squier, Susan, 'Arms and the Woman: The Con(Tra)Ception of the War Text', *Arms and the Woman: War, Gender, and Literary Representation*, ed. Cooper, Helen M., Munich, Adrienne Auslander and Squier, Susan Merrill (Chapel Hill and London: University of North Carolina, 1989), pp. 9–24
——, 'Introduction', *Arms and the Woman: War, Gender, and Literary Representation*, ed. Cooper, Helen M., Munich, Adrienne Auslander and Squier, Susan Merrill (Chapel Hill and London: University of North Carolina, 1989), pp. xiii–xx
Corbett, Katharine T., *In Her Place. A Guide to St. Louis Women's History* (St Louis, Missouri: Missouri Historical Society Press, undated)
Craig, David and Egan, Michael, *Extreme Situations. Literature and Crisis from the Great War to the Atom Bomb* (London and Basingstoke: Macmillan, 1979)
Crapanzano, Vincent, 'Hermes' Dilemma: The Making of Subversion in Ethnographic Description', *Writing Culture. The Poetics and Politics of Ethnography*, ed. Clifford, James and Marcus, George E. (Berkeley, Los Angeles and London: University of California, 1986)
Crary, Jonathan, *Techniques of the Observer* (Cambridge, Mass., and London: MIT Press, 1990)
Cull, Nicholas John, *Selling War. The British Propaganda Campaign against*

American 'Neutrality' in World War II (New York and Oxford: Oxford University Press, 1995)

Cunningham, Valentine, ed., *The Penguin Book of Spanish Civil War Verse* (Harmondsworth: Penguin, 1980)

——, 'Introduction', *Spanish Front. Writers on the Civil War*, ed. Cunningham, Valentine (Oxford and New York: Oxford University Press, 1986), pp. xix–xxxiii

——, *British Writers of the Thirties* (Oxford and New York: Oxford University Press, 1988)

Davis, Lennard J., *Factual Fictions: The Origins of the English Novel* (New York: Columbia University Press, 1983)

Doherty, Thomas, *Projections of War: Hollywood, American Culture, and World War II* (New York: Columbia University Press, 1993)

Downs, Robert B. and Downs, Jane B., *Journalists of the United States* (Jefferson, North Carolina, and London: McFarland, 1991)

Edwards, Julia, *Women of the World. The Great Foreign Correspondents* (Boston: Houghton Mifflin, 1988)

Empson, William, *Some Versions of Pastoral* (London: Chatto & Windus, 1935)

Entrikin, J. Nicholas, *The Betweenness of Place: Towards a Geography of Modernity* (Basingstoke and London: Macmillan, 1991)

Ewing, Elizabeth, *Women in Uniform through the Centuries* (London and Sydney: Batsford, 1975)

Felman, Shoshana, and Laub, Dori, *Testimony. Crises of Witnessing in Literature, Psychoanalysis, and History* (New York and London: Routledge, 1992)

Fenton, Charles, *The Apprenticeship of Ernest Hemingway* (New Haven: Yale University Press, 1954)

Ferrari, Michelle, compiler, *Reporting America at War. An Oral History*, commentary by Tobin, James (New York: Hyperion, 2003)

Fox Jr, John, 'Richard Harding Davis', *The Novels and Stories of Richard Harding Davis. Volume 7 – The White Mice* (New York: Scribner, 1916), pp. v–viii

Freedom Forum European Centre, 'Freedom Forum Europe Pays Tribute to Martha Gellhorn' (London: Freedom Forum European Centre, 1996)

Frus, Phyllis, *The Politics and Poetics of Journalistic Narrative* (Cambridge: Cambridge University Press, 1994)

Fussell, Paul, *Wartime. Understanding and Behaviour in the Second World War* (Oxford: Oxford University Press, 1989)

——, 'Introduction', *With the Old Breed at Peleliu and Okinawa* by Sledge, E. B. (New York and Oxford: Oxford University Press, 1990), pp. xi–xx

——, *Killing, in Verse and Prose and Other Essays* (London: Bellew Publishing, 1990)

Gallagher, Jean, *The World Wars Through the Female Gaze* (Carbondale and Edwardsville: Southern Illinois University Press, 1998)

Geertz, Clifford, *The Interpretation of Cultures* (London: Fontana, 1993)

Gifford, Terry, *Pastoral* (London and New York: Routledge, 1999)

Gilbert, Martin, *The Holocaust. The Jewish Tragedy* (London: Fontana, 1987)

Gilbert, Sandra M., 'Literary Men, Literary Women, and the Great War', *Connecting Spheres. Women in the Western World, 1500 to the Present*, ed. Boxer, Marilyn J. and Quataert, Jean H. (Oxford and New York: Oxford University Press, 1987), pp. 232–45

—— and Gubar, Susan, *No Man's Land. The Place of the Woman Writer in the Twentieth Century. Volume 2. Sexchanges* (New Haven and London: Yale University Press, 1989)

——, *No Man's Land: The Place of the Woman Writer in the Twentieth Century. Volume 3. Letters from the Front* (New Haven and London: Yale University Press, 1994)

Giles, Paul, *Virtual Americas. Transnational Fictions and the Transatlantic Imaginary* (Durham, NC, and London: Duke University Press, 2002)

Goldstein, Joshua S., *War and Gender. How Gender Shapes the War System* (Cambridge: Cambridge University Press, 2001)

Gombrich, E. H., 'Standards of Truth: The Arrested Image and the Moving Eye', *The Language of Images*, ed. Mitchell, W. T. J. (Chicago and London: University of Chicago, 1980), pp. 181–217

Hall, David F., Loftus, Elizabeth F. and Tousignant, James P., 'Postevent Information and Changes in Recollection for a Natural Event', *Eyewitness Testimony: Psychological Perspectives*, ed. Wells, Gary L. and Loftus, Elizabeth F. (Cambridge: Cambridge University Press, 1984), pp. 124–41

Hall, Stuart, 'A World at One with Itself', *The Manufacture of News. Social Problems, Deviance and the Mass Media*, ed. Cohen, Stanley and Young, Jock (London: Constable, 1973), pp. 85–94

Hevener, John W., *Which Side Are You On? The Harlan County Coal Miners, 1931–39* (Urbana, Chicago, London: University of Illinois, 1978)

Higonnet, Margaret and Higonnet, Patrice L.-R., 'The Double Helix', *Behind the Lines: Gender and the Two World Wars*, ed. Higonnet, Margaret, Jenson, Michel Sonya and Weitz, Margaret Collins (New Haven and London: Yale University Press, 1987), pp. 31–47

Hinz, Evelyn J., 'An Introduction to War and Literature: Ajax Versus Ulysses', *Mosaic*, 23/3 (Summer 1990), pp. v–xii

Hofmann, Klaus, 'Poetry after Auschwitz – Adorno's Dictum', *German Life and Letters*, 58/2 (April 2005), pp. 182–94

Hohenberg, John, *Foreign Correspondence. The Great Reporters and Their Times* (New York and London: Columbia University Press, 1967)

Hollowell, John, *Fact & Fiction. The New Journalism and the Nonfiction Novel* (Chapel Hill: University of North Carolina, 1977)

Homberger, Eric, 'The American War Novel and the Defeated Liberal', *The Second World War in Literature: Eight Essays*, ed. Higgins, Ian (Edinburgh and London: Scottish Academic Press, 1986), pp. 32–44

Hughes, Kathryn, 'A Woman at War with the World', *Mail on Sunday* (30 November 2003), p. 64

Hughes, Linda K. and Lund, Michael, *The Victorian Serial* (Charlottesville and London: University of Virginia, 1991)

Hughes, Robert, 'The Unflinching Eye', *Guardian* (4 October 2003), pp. 4–6

Hume, Mick, *Whose War Is It Anyway? The Dangers of the Journalism of Attachment* (London: InformInc, 1997)

Inglis, Fred, *People's Witness. The Journalist in Modern Politics* (New Haven and London: Yale University Press, 2002)

Jaffe, Audrey, *Scenes of Sympathy: Identity and Representation in Victorian Fiction* (Ithaca and London: Cornell University Press, 2000)

Kamester, Margaret and Vellacott, Jo, 'Introduction', *Militarism Versus Feminism: Writings on Women and War*, ed. Kamester, Margaret and Vellacott, Jo (London: Virago, 1987), pp. 1–34

Kaplan, Amy, 'Romancing the Empire: The Embodiment of American Masculinity in the Popular Historical Novel of the 1890s', *American Literary History*, 2/4 (Winter 1990): pp. 659–90

Kaplan, E. Ann, *Women and Film: Both Sides of the Camera* (New York: Methuen, 1983)

Keane, Adrian, *The Modern Law of Evidence* 2nd edition (London: Butterworths, 1989)

Keegan, John, *The Face of War* (London: Jonathan Cape, 1976)

Kert, Bernice, *The Hemingway Women* (New York: Norton, 1983)

Knightley, Phillip, *The First Casualty. The War Correspondent as Hero and Myth-Maker from the Crimea to Kosovo* (London: Prion Books, 2000)

——, 'Introduction', *Eclipse* by Moorehead, Alan (London: Granta, 2000), pp. xiii–xvii

Kutulas, Judy, *The Long War: The Intellectual People's Front and Anti-Stalinism* (Durham and London: Duke University Press, 1995)

LaFeber, Walter, *The New Empire. An Interpretation of American Expansion 1860–1898* (Ithaca: Cornell University Press, 1963)

Lang, Caroline, *Keep Smiling Through. Women in the Second World War* (Cambridge: Cambridge University Press, 1989)

Lassner, Phyllis, "Camp Follower of Catastrophe': Martha Gellhorn's World War II Challenge to the Modernist War', *Modern Fiction Studies*, 44/3 (Fall 1998), pp. 792–812

Leaper, Glenn W., Löwstedt, Anthony and Madhoun, Husam, *Caught in the Crossfire: The Iraq War and the Media* (Vienna: The International Press Institute, 2003)

Lee, Hermione, 'One of the Chaps', *Guardian (Review)* (1 November 2003), p. 13

Leed, Eric J., *No Man's Land: Combat and Identity in World War I* (Cambridge: Cambridge University Press, 1979)

Lefebvre, Henri, *The Production of Space* (Oxford and Cambridge, Mass.: Blackwell, 1991)

Levine, Lawrence W., *Highbrow / Lowbrow: The Emergence of Cultural Hierarchy in America* (Cambridge, Mass., and London: Harvard University Press, 1988)

Lewinski, Jorge, *The Camera at War: War Photography from 1848 to the Present* (London: Octopus Books, 1986)

Limon, John, *Writing after War: American War Fiction from Realism to Post-Modernism* (New York and Oxford: Oxford University Press, 1994)

Longenbach, James, 'The Women and Men of 1914', *Arms and the Woman: War, Gender, and Literary Representation*, ed. Cooper, Helen M., Munich, Adrienne Auslander and Squier, Susan Merrill (Chapel Hill and London: University of North Carolina, 1989), pp. 97–123

Lyman, Rick, 'Obituary', *New York Times* (17 February 1998), p. B11

McKeon, Michael, *The Origins of the English Novel 1600–1740* (London: Radius, 1988)

McNair, Brian, *News and Journalism in the UK* (London: Routledge, 1999)

Mander, John, *The Writer and Commitment* (London: Martin Secker and Warburg, 1961)

Marshall, David, *The Surprising Effects of Sympathy. Marivaux, Diderot, Rousseau, and Mary Shelley* (Chicago and London: University of Chicago, 1988)

Marx, Leo, 'Pastoralism in America', *Ideology and Classic American Literature*, ed. Bercovitch, Sacvan and Jehlen, Myra (Cambridge: Cambridge University Press, 1986), pp. 36–69

Mengham, Rod, 'Reading "The Lull" ', *Twentieth Century Literature*, 29/4 (1983), pp. 455–64

Meyers, Jeffrey, *Hemingway: A Biography* (London and Basingstoke: Macmillan, 1985)

Mills, Kay, *A Place in the News: From the Women's Pages to the Front Page* (New York and Oxford: Columbia University Press, 1990)

——, 'What Difference Do Women Journalists Make?' *Women, Media, and Politics*, ed. Norris, Pippa (Oxford and New York: Oxford University Press, 1997), pp. 41–55

Mills, Nicolaus, ed., *The New Journalism: A Historical Anthology* (New York: McGraw-Hill, 1974)

Mitchell, W. T. J., *Picture Theory: Essays on Verbal and Visual Representation* (Chicago: University of Chicago, 1994)

Mizejewski, Linda, *Divine Decadence: Fascism, Female Spectacle, and the Makings of Sally Bowles* (Princeton: Princeton University Press, 1992)

Moeller, Susan D., *Shooting War: Photography and the American Experience of Combat* (New York: Basic Books, 1989)

Monteath, Peter, *Writing the Good Fight: Political Commitment in the International Literature of the Spanish Civil War* (Westport, Conn., and London: Greenwood Press, 1994)

Moorehead, Caroline, *Martha Gellhorn: A Life* (London: Chatto & Windus, 2003)

Morris Jr, Roy, *The Better Angel: Walt Whitman in the Civil War* (Oxford: Oxford University Press, 2000)

Muir, Kate, *Arms and the Woman* (London: Coronet, 1993)

Mulvey, Christopher, *Anglo-American Landscapes: A Study of Nineteenth-*

Century Anglo-American Travel Literature (Cambridge: Cambridge University Press, 1983)

——, *Transatlantic Manners: Social Patterns in Nineteenth-Century Anglo-American Travel Literature* (Cambridge: Cambridge University Press, 1990)

Mulvey, Laura, 'Visual Pleasure and Narrative Cinema', *Visual and Other Pleasures* (Basingstoke: Macmillan, 1989), pp. 14–26

Nelson, Emily and Rose, Matthew, 'Media Reassess Risks to Reporters in Iraq', *Wall Street Journal* (9 April 2003), pp. B1, B10

Norris, Pippa, 'Introduction: Women, Media, and Politics', *Women, Media, and Politics*, ed. Norris, Pippa (Oxford and New York: Oxford University Press, 1997), pp. 1–18

O'Donnol, Shirley Miles, *American Costume, 1915–1970: A Source Book for the Stage Costumer* (Bloomington: Indiana University Press, 1982)

Orsagh, Jacqueline, 'A Critical Biography of Martha Gellhorn' (unpublished doctoral thesis, Michigan State University, 1977)

Paglia, Camille, *Sex, Art, and American Culture. Essays* (London: Viking, 1992)

Panofsky, Erwin, *Perspective as Symbolic Form* (New York: Zone Books, 1991)

Penrose, Antony, ed., *Lee Miller's War: Photographer and Correspondent with the Allies in Europe 1944–45* (London: Condé Nast, 1992)

Phoca, Sophia, *Introducing Postfeminism* (Cambridge: Icon Books, 1999)

Piette, Adam, *Imagination at War: British Fiction and Poetry 1939–1945* (London: Papermac, 1995)

Piper, Don, 'Soviet Union', *The Second World War in Fiction*, ed. Klein, Holger Michael (London and Basingstoke: Macmillan, 1984), pp. 131–72

Pratt, Mary Louise, 'Fieldwork in Common Place', *Writing Culture: The Poetics and Politics of Ethnography*, ed. Clifford, James and Marcus, George E. (Berkeley, Los Angeles and London: University of California Press, 1986), pp. 27–50

Prioleau, Betsy, *Seductress: Women Who Ravished the World and Their Lost Art of Love* (New York: Viking, 2003)

Rawlinson, Mark, *British Writing of the Second World War* (Oxford: The Clarendon Press, 2000)

Reynolds, Michael, *Hemingway: The Final Years* (New York and London: Norton, 1999)

Robertson, Michael, *Stephen Crane, Journalism, and the Making of Modern American Literature* (New York and Chichester: Columbia University Press, 1997)

Rockoff, Hugh, *Drastic Measures. A History of Wage and Price Controls in the United States* (Cambridge: Cambridge University Press, 1984)

Rustad, Michael L., *Women in Khaki: The American Enlisted Woman* (New York: Praeger, 1982)

Scarry, Elaine, *On Beauty and Being Just* (London: Duckworths, 2002)

Scherman, David E. 'Foreword', *Lee Miller's War*, ed. Penrose, Antony (London: Condé Nast Books, 1992), pp. 7–13

Schofield, Mary Ann, 'Telling the Truth: Women Spy Narratives of the Second World War', *Visions of War: World War II Popular Literature and Culture*, ed. Holsinger, M. Paul and Schofield, Mary Ann (Bowling Green, Ohio: Bowling Green State University Popular Press, 1992), pp. 56–66

Schudson, Michael, *Discovering the News: A Social History of American Newspapers* (New York: Basic Books, 1978)

Sebba, Anne, *Battling for News. The Rise of the Woman Reporter* (London, Sydney, Auckland: Hodder & Stoughton, 1994)

Seelye, John D., *War Games: Richard Harding Davis and the New Imperialism* (Boston: University of Massachusetts, 2003)

Sennett, Richard, *Respect: The Formation of Character in a World of Inequality* (London: Allen Lane, 2003)

Shay, Jonathan, *Achilles in Vietnam: Combat Trauma and the Undoing of Character* (New York and London: Simon & Schuster Touchstone, 1995)

Sheldon, Sayre P., ed., *Her War Story. Twentieth-Century Women Write About War* (Carbondale and Edwardsville: University of Southern Illinois, 1999)

Sheppard, Philippa, 'Tongues of War: Studies in the Military Rhetoric of Shakespeare's History Plays' (unpublished doctoral thesis, University of Oxford, 1994)

Silverman, Kaja, 'Masochism and Subjectivity', *Framework*, 12 (1980), pp. 2–9

Simpson, John, 'War, Writing and Whisky with Martha', *Sunday Telegraph* (22 February 1998), p. 6

Slotkin, Richard, *Gunfighter Nation. The Myth of the Frontier in Twentieth-Century America* (New York: Atheneum, 1992)

Smith, Anthony, 'The Long Road to Objectivity and Back Again: The Kinds of Truth We Get in Journalism', *Newspaper History from the Seventeenth Century to the Present Day*, ed. Bryce, George, Curran, James and Wright, Pauline (London: Constable, 1978), pp. 153–71

Sontag, Susan, *On Photography* (Harmondsworth: Penguin, 1979)

Sorel, Nancy Caldwell, *The Women Who Wrote the War* (New York: Arcade Publishing, 1999)

Spain, Daphne, *Gendered Spaces* (Chapel Hill: University of North Carolina, 1992)

Spanier, Sandra, 'Afterword', *Martha Gellhorn and Virginia Cowles, Love Goes to Press*, ed. Spanier, Sandra (Lincoln, Nebraska and London: University of Nebraska, 1995), pp. 79–88

——, 'Editor's Note', *Martha Gellhorn and Virginia Cowles, Love Goes to Press*, ed. Spanier, Sandra (Lincoln, Nebraska and London: University of Nebraska, 1995), pp. xiii–xiv

——, 'Rivalry, Romance and War Reporters: Martha Gellhorn's *Love Goes to Press* and the *Collier's* Files', *Hemingway and Women*, ed. Broer, Lawrence R. and Holland, Gloria (Tuscaloosa and London: University of Alabama, 2002), pp. 256–75

Spencer, John R. 'Introduction', *Leon Battista Alberti: On Painting*, trans. and with an introduction by Spencer, John R. (New Haven and London: Yale University Press, 1966), pp. 11–38

Stacey, Jackie, 'Desperately Seeking Audience', *The Sexual Subject: A 'Screen' Reader in Sexuality*, ed. Caughie, John, Kuhn, Annette and Merck, Mandy (London: Routledge, 1992), pp. 244–57

Steiner, George, *Language and Silence* (London: Faber, 1985)

Stephens, Mitchell, *A History of News* (Fort Worth: Harcourt Brace, 1997)

Stott, William, *Documentary Expression and Thirties America* (London, Oxford, New York: Oxford University Press, 1973)

Tagg, John, 'The Currency of the Photograph', *Thinking Photography*, ed. Burgin, Victor (Basingstoke: Macmillan, 1982), pp. 110–41

Tritle, Lawrence A., *From Melos to My Lai: War and Survival* (London, New York: Routledge, 2000)

Tuchman, Gaye, 'Objectivity as Strategic Ritual: An Examination of Newsmen's Notions of Objectivity', *American Journal of Sociology*, 77/4 (1972), pp. 660–79

Tuttleton, James W., Lauer, Kristin O., Murray, Margaret P., eds, *Edith Wharton. The Contemporary Reviews* (Cambridge: Cambridge University Press, 1992)

Weber, Ronald, *Hemingway's Art of Non-Fiction* (Basingstoke: Macmillan, 1990)

Weintraub, Stanley, *The Last Great Cause: The Intellectuals and the Spanish Civil War* (London: W. H. Allen, 1968)

Wells, Gary L. and Murray, Donna M., 'Eyewitness Confidence', *Eyewitness Testimony: Psychological Perspectives*, ed. Wells, Gary L. and Loftus, Elizabeth F. (Cambridge: Cambridge University Press, 1984): pp. 155–70

Williams, Keith, 'The Will to Objectivity: Egon Erwin Kisch's "Der Rasende Reporter"', *Modern Language Review* 85 (1990), pp. 92–106

——, 'Reportage in the Thirties' (unpublished doctoral thesis, University of Oxford, 1991)

——, '"History as I Saw It": Inter-War New Reportage', *Literature & History* (Autumn 1992), pp. 39–54

——, 'Post/Modern Documentary: Orwell, Agee and the New Reportage', *Rewriting the Thirties: Modernism and After*, ed. Williams, Keith and Matthews, Steven (London and New York: Longman, 1997), pp. 163–81

Winfield, Betty Houchin, *FDR and the News Media* (New York: Columbia University Press, 1994)

Wood, Leonard, 'Richard Harding Davis', *The Novels and Stories of Richard Harding Davis. Volume 10 – The Man Who Could Not Lose* (New York: Scribner, 1916), pp. v–vi

Wood, Maggie, *'We Wore What We'd Got'. Women's Clothes in World War II* (Exeter: Warwickshire Books, 1989)

Woods, Vicki, 'Chic Value', *Sunday Telegraph Magazine* (19 October 2003), pp. 28–31

Zweig, Paul, *Walt Whitman: The Making of the Poet* (Harmondsworth and New York: Viking, 1985)

Electronic Resources
<http://lcweb.loc.gov/exhibits/wcf/wcf005.html>
<http://newdeal.feri.org/texts>
<http://newdeal.feri.org/texts/hop01.htm>
<http://newdeal.feri.org/texts/hop08.htm>
<http://newdeal.feri.org/texts.hop22.htm>
<http://www.aber.ac.uk/media/Documents/gaze/gaze09.html>
<http://www.civilwarhome.com/dixbio.htm>
<http://www.globalissuesgroup.com/geneva/history.html>
<http://www.yale.edu/lawweb/avalon/lawofwar/lawwar.htm>
<http://xroads.virginia.edu/~1930s>

Interview
Caroline Moorehead, 4 December 2003 (Oxford)

Broadcasts
Pilger, John (dir. and interviewer), 'The Outsiders', Carlton, 1983
Shakespeare, Nicholas (dir. and interviewer), 'Omnibus', BBC1, 1991

Lecture
Simpson, John, 'War Reporting: The New Vulnerability', The Reuters' Memorial
   Lecture 2003, given at St Catherine's College, Oxford, 27 June 2003

Other media
Caulfield, Patrick, *Hemingway Never Ate Here*, 1998–99, acrylic on canvas,
   190.5 by 182.9 cm, Tate Britain, London
Women and War, exhibition at the Imperial War Museum, London (13 October
   2003 to 18 April 2004)

Other sources
Gellhorn, Alfred, emails to the author, 1 December and 4 December 2003

Index

Cabot Lodge, Henry, 142
Calder-Marshall, Arthur, 28, 174
Caldwell, Erskine, 27
Campbell, D'Ann, 107
Campbell, Doon, 99
Camus, Albert, 175
Capa, Cornell, 158–9
Capa, Robert, 157–60, 172
Carpenter, Iris, 67, 77, 99, 110–11,
    118, 177, 204, 215–17
Carson, Lee, 111, 204, 217
Carson, Ruth, 207
Cather, Willa, 97
censorship, 12, 63, 96
Chamberlain, Neville, 187
Cheever, John, 70
Chekhov, Anton, 70
Chenery, William L., 7, 67, 117
Chiang-Kai-Shek, Madame, 147
Churchill, Winston, 142, 187–8
Clark, Ian, 98–9
Clausewitz, Carl von, 1
Cobbett, William, 27
Cockburn, Claud, 70
Coeur d'Alene, 37
Cohen, Lester, 41–2
Cohen, Lizabeth A., 208
Colebaugh, Charles, 7, 9, 115, 182,
    218, 227
Colette, 70
Collier, Richard, 213
Collier, Robert, 7
Collier's magazine, 7, 59, 67, 110–11,
    118–25, 142–3, 147–50, 162,
    179, 182, 192, 207
  Gellhorn's writing for, 6–13, 42–3,
    46, 66–9, 75–6, 181, 186, 188
Collingwood, Charles, 141
Comintern, the, 25, 98
Communist Party USA (CPUSA), 25,
    39
Compton-Burnett, Ivy, 69–70
Connolly, Cyril, 174
Conrad, Joseph, 12
Cooks, Cordelia, 109
Cooper, Duff, 146, 172
Cooper, Helen, 102

Cooper, Helen M., 103
Cooper, James Fenimore, 142
Cowan, Ruth, 111, 204
Cowles, Virginia, 6, 111, 146, 160–2,
    181–2, 211, 216
Cowley, Malcolm, 39
Crane, Stephen, 12, 27, 101
Crary, Jonathan, 3
Crawford, Bruce, 41–2
Crichton, Kyle, 7
Crouch, Arthur, 7
Cull, Nicholas John, 180
Cunard, Nancy, 40
Cunningham, Valentine, 40, 47
Czechoslovakia, 187–9

Dachau, 65–8, 73–6, 80–1, 186,
    192–4, 226–7
Dahl, Roald, 118
Daily Courant, 60–1
Daily Express, 70, 180
Davenport, Walter, 7
Davis, Richard Harding, 12–13, 27,
    96, 138, 142–5, 152, 177, 184
D-Day landings (June 1944), 113–14,
    117–26, 152, 159
de Certeau, Michel, 83, 112, 151, 208
Dearing, Joe, 121, 147–8, 182
death camps, 64–8, 73–6, 80–1, 186,
    192–4, 226–7
Delmer, Sefton, 42, 99, 146, 163–4,
    172
Dickens, Charles, 100–1
Diderot, Denis, 26
Dobrée, Bonamy, 174
Dos Passos, John, 26, 41, 175
Dostoevsky, Fyodor, 69
Douglass, Frederick, 184
Dreiser, Theodore, 41, 47, 69
dress, 178, 205–10, 213
Duncan, Gregor, 148
Dunne, Finley Peter, 143
Duras, Marguerite, 99

Ehrenberg, Ilya, 42
Eighth Army, 157
Eisenhower, Dwight D., 67, 116